Care Work

Care Work | Gender, Class, and the Welfare State

Edited by | Madonna Harrington Meyer

Routledge
New York   London
2000

Published in 2000 by

Routledge
29 West 35th Street
New York, NY 10001

Published in Great Britain by

Routledge
11 New Fetter Lane
London EC4P 4EE

Library of Congress Cataloging-in-Publication Data
Care work : gender, class, and the welfare state /
Madonna Harrington Meyer, editor.
    p. cm.
  Includes bibliographical references and index.
  ISBN 0-415-92541-X (HC) — ISBN 0-415-92542-8 (PB)
  1. Public welfare—United States.   2. Social service—United States.
  3. Sex role—United States.   4. United States—Social Policy.
  I. Meyer, Madonna, Harrington, 1959–
HV91.C357   2000
361.973—dc21   99-048313

dedicated to
care workers

Contents

Acknowledgments

*T*he work represented in this volume began with the development of an international conference on care work. The conference, held at the University of Illinois in November 1997, was organized by Professors Sonya Michel, Francesca Cancian, Demie Kurz, and me. As a group, we are indebted to many. Funding for the conference was granted by the American Sociological Association Fund for the Advancement of the Discipline, the University of Illinois International Programs and Studies, the University of Illinois Women's Studies program, the University of California at Irvine, the University of Pennsylvania, and Syracuse University. In addition, many people at the University of Illinois worked tirelessly to pull the three-day conference together. We especially appreciate the efforts of Jacque Kahn, Anne Berggren, Tara McCauley, and Sari Schnitzlein.

Over the past year, a team at Syracuse University has worked to transform the series of conference papers into this edited volume. We are thankful to Pam Herd, Research Assistant Extraordinaire, for reading and making editorial comments on every paper in the volume, for assisting with introductory remarks, and for overseeing much of the communication between editors and authors. We are thankful to the entire staff at Center for Policy Research for their assistance in copy editing, word processing, and administrating the project, including Peggy Austin, Martha Bonney, and Esther Gray. We are particularly thankful to staff members Ann Wicks and Denise Paul for working so hard on the final drafts of the articles and, in Ann's case, for her good humor in enforcing our time line.

We also want to thank the editors at Routledge, particularly Ilene Kalish, for their timely and knowledgeable assistance.

Ultimately, our thanks go to each participant at the conference and every contributor to this volume. Collectively, we are indebted to the care workers, nearly all of whom are women, who not only perform care work on a daily basis but also were willing to share their struggles with researchers hoping to affect public policies. This book has been a synergistic process for us — linking scholarly work across the globe, across the life course, and across various academic disciplines. At times it has been a personal process as well. Much of what is reported here hits close to home; scholars by day, many of us devote the remainder of our time to the care of small children, disabled adults, or frail older relatives.

It is to the care worker in each of us that this volume is dedicated.

Madonna Harrington Meyer, editor   *January 2000*

Introduction

The Right to—or Not to—Care

*E*ach of us has moments of dependency, moments when we rely on the kindness or generosity of others to provide for our most basic needs. Most often, our needs are met by our family members—the mother who tends to her child's cut knee, the husband who massages his wife's back during childbirth, the daughter who delivers lunch to her mother as she recovers from a hip replacement. For those with sufficient resources, many moments of dependency are handled via market-based services—the day-care provider who tends to a child's cut knee, the midwife who massages the back of a laboring mother, the home care provider who delivers lunch to the client recovering from a hip replacement. But many citizens, particularly children, poor disabled adults, and a significant proportion of the frail elderly, lack the resources to draw on market-based services. They rely instead on their families. Sometimes, however, the dependency is simply too great for family members, who must also juggle paid work, care of other family members, and their own physical and mental health. Where do we, in our respective societies, want to locate the burden of this dependency?

Historically, most societies have placed the burden of dependency squarely on the shoulders of families—and most notably the women within those families. Architects of welfare states that aim to locate the burden of dependency on individual families develop very few welfare programs that would spread that burden across society more generally. In the United States in particular, families were, and continue to be, seen as the primary source of care, regardless of the consequences for either the care provider or care receiver. By contrast, Scandinavian countries have long adhered to a philosophy that a key role of the state is to socialize the burden of dependency by creating welfare state programs that provide a wide array of options for those who need assistance at various stages of life. Taken together, the papers in this volume explore this question of how best to locate the burden of dependency. What are the complexities, strengths, and weaknesses of emphasizing families, market-based solutions, or welfare state programs? How might we best create a mixture of options that balances the burden across all three spheres?

The scholarly and public policy literature on the complexities of care work is extensive, but much of it takes for granted the reigning emphasis on family-based rather than market- or welfare state-based solutions. Even the frequently used term *caregiver* takes for granted that families, particularly women within families, willingly provide care, regardless of the personal consequences. As best we can tell, the term *caregiver* was coined in the gerontological literature in an attempt to distinguish care providers from care receivers. But the term has taken on a political and economic meaning with problematic consequences. *Caregiver* implies that the care is given freely, either at no cost or at a cost that the giver is willing and able to shoulder. Implicit in the term is the notion of choice. But as we take stock of several decades of literature on care work, it is clear that individual choices regarding care work are highly restricted by a persistent ideology about the gendered nature of care work, conflicting demands and expectations regarding paid and unpaid labor, the paucity of affordable market-based options, and the instability of social supports implemented via welfare states.

In an attempt to set the stage for serious reform of care work policies and practices across the globe, the papers in this volume steer clear of conventional assumptions that care work is inherently women's work, or that care work is cost-free if the fees are not enumerated in public-spending spreadsheets. We focus instead on an integrated analytical framework that encompasses the paid as well as unpaid care work of individuals, families, communities, and social service agency employees. We also emphasize the complexities of care work across the globe and across the life course. Ultimately, we assess the range of family, market, and welfare state supports that are — or could be — available to care workers.

It is our belief that the range of supports must create an environment in which families, most notably women, have the right and ability to perform care work — as well as the right or ability to be free of care work. This principle emerged as the central theme at the conference on "Gender, Citizenship, and the Work of Caring" held in November 1997 at the University of Illinois at Urbana-Champaign under the aegis of the Women's Studies Program. Twenty-five scholars from across North America and Northern Europe gathered to discuss the nature of care work and the impact of social policy on the quality of care and on the recognition and compensation care workers receive. The consensus among the authors is that care work must become a recognized component of citizenship, for both women and men. The current state of affairs is that many who wish to provide care for loved ones are either unable to do so or are compelled to do so under untenable conditions. Alternately, many who are unable or unwilling to provide care find precious few alternatives to which they can turn.

Central to the analyses included in this volume are issues of gender, race, ethnicity, and class. We explore and challenge historical assumptions, prevalent in both private and public arenas, that the provision of care work is more naturally suited to women or best performed by unpaid family members rather than trained professionals. We also assess the gender, race, ethnic, and class implications of dynamic and unstable welfare state supports in the United States and abroad. We document how failed attempts to implement universal child care, long term care, or other forms of family supports have proved particularly problematic for families who are poor, minority, or immigrant. And we applaud the successes of a foster care program that placed many poor, black, and Latino children into permanent family and educational arrangements where their chances of flourishing are maximized.

The authors contributing to this volume come from various disciplines and perspectives, including women's studies, sociology, political science, economics, history, and public policy. Our effort to develop a multidisciplinary perspective opens the way for comparative analyses of the systems and networks of care that have emerged in North America, Western Europe, and Scandinavia. Recognition of international variation in the degree of support for care work provides common intellectual ground for chapters focusing on subspecialties such as elder care, child care, and care for the chronically ill and disabled. On the one hand, the volume addresses the failure of care workers in both public and private spheres to reap adequate rewards for their work. Care workers pay a financial, physical, and emotional price that frequently remains unaccounted for and unnoticed. On the other hand, the volume addresses the inability of certain groups of women to give priority to care work because of economic and other structural barriers. Simply, they do not have the option to care. As a collective, the chapters suggest movement in a direction that permits families, mainly women, the capacity to provide care when they choose to do so—as well as the right to sidestep unpaid care work when they choose instead to emphasize paid labor.

Opponents of welfare programs that would promote and stabilize care work argue that providing the needed supports to care workers would be too expensive. As the articles in this volume contend, however, it is too expensive not to provide this support. The costs of unacknowledged and uncompensated care work are enormous, particularly for women, the poor, and persons of color. Socializing the costs of dependency through welfare state programs represents a great opportunity to ameliorate inequalities. By contrast, locating dependency within individual families serves as yet another method that sustains, and even magnifies, socioeconomic inequalities.

The lack of support for care work adversely affects care providers and care recipients alike. Bureaucratization and stinting on resources deprives recipients of good care—jeopardizing the ability of our most vulnerable constituents to receive even the most basic of social rights. Moreover, inadequate recognition of, and compensation for, care work bars providers from participating as full citizens with full opportunities in political, social, and economic institutions. Given that the vast majority of us will either require care work or be compelled to provide care work at some time in our lives, it is in the best interest of the care worker in each of us to actively pursue stable supports for care work.

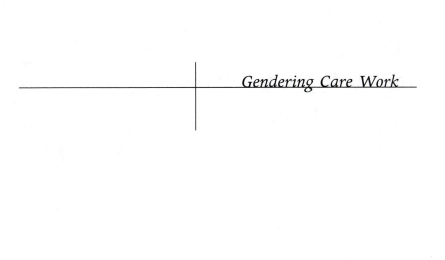

Gendering Care Work

Gendering Care Work

*C*are work is an act that, for the most part, women do; it is a gendered activity. The articles in Part I challenge the gendered construction of care by viewing care and its connection with women as a socially constructed phenomenon. The myth that women have a *natural* capacity and desire to care has proved to further reinforce gender inequalities by disproportionately burdening women with unpaid or low-paid care work (Abel 1990; Hooyman and Gonyea 1995). But what are the processes that led to, and continue to reinforce, the construction of care work around women? The authors in this section attempt to answer this question by looking to history, and particularly to motherhood and fatherhood.

In examining women's care for sick and disabled family members and friends in the United States between 1850 and 1940, historian Emily Abel shows how not only gender, but class and race differences as well, shape the construction of care work. Specifically, while middle-class white women were often forced to perform care work, poor women and women of color were often not allowed to care for the people they loved. Historically, white middle-class women in the late eighteenth and early nineteenth centuries participated in the medicalization of care work, helping to debase the nurturing aspects of care work and construct poor, immigrant, and black women who focused on the emotional or spiritual dimensions of caring as irrational.

The nurturing aspects of care work, most often associated with women and rarely associated with men, are often debased. The question is, why? In an historical piece

6

that parallels Abel's, sociologists Scott Coltrane and Justin Galt trace the historical development of fatherhood, revealing how men increasingly moved away from, and women became largely accountable for, primary parenting responsibilities. Their essay argues that men can and should perform the nurturing aspects of care work. Just as caring for children may play a pivotal role in defining motherhood, and women more broadly, they argue that caring for children may play a pivotal role in defining fatherhood, and men more generally.

Subsequent chapters present more contemporary tensions that shape and reshape lines between motherhood and care work. They look to the ways mothers organize in the public sphere, and how that affects the intertwining threads of motherhood, caring, gender, and class. Traditional notions of motherhood can reinforce class inequalities among women, historian Sonya Michel argues, when middle- and upper-class stay-at-home mothers fail to advocate for subsidized day-care policies that would allow poor women similar choices. These notions also can guide changing gender identities for women who choose to move toward work outside of the home. In sociologist Ann Herda-Rapp's analysis of stay-at-home mothers who became politically active, she found that many mothers justified their participation in the toxic waste movement, and their decision to downsize unpaid domestic responsibilities, by stating they were working to make a safer and healthier world for their children. In both of these pieces, women's roles as mothers and/or care workers shape the types of activities they do and do not do. In turn, these activities serve to reshape their roles as mothers and/or care workers.

In the end, it appears that care work is defined and redefined across history and across continents as women's work, and particularly low-income women's work, at least in part because this arrangement is perceived of as maximally beneficial to those with substantial resources. Isolated from the day-to-day rigors of care work, many middle- and upper-class men and women rarely devote their time or economic or political clout toward developing a more realistic or humane care work system. Overwhelmed by the day-to-day rigors of providing care, care workers rarely have the time, or economic or political clout, to pursue policies that would ease their burdens.

A Historical Perspective on Care

*D*uring the past few years I have been studying the history of women caregivers for sick and disabled family members and friends in the United States, specifically in the period between 1850 and 1940. My original intention was to challenge how researchers and policy analysts use the past. Highlighting the growth of the frail elderly population, some argue that the demands for informal care are greater today than ever before. Nadine F. Marks (1996:27), for example, recently wrote that "demographic changes have now increased the relative risk of becoming a caregiver at some time — or even multiple times — during a lifetime." Clinging to a romantic vision of a vanished world, others argue that the nineteenth century was the golden age, because women delivered care selflessly and sensitively. The implication is that we should return to nineteenth-century methods of care.

As expected, although nineteenth-century women had relatively few eldercare responsibilities, obligations for birthing women and sick, disabled, and dying people of all ages were constant and unremitting. Some women complained bitterly that caregiving confined them to the home, caused serious physical and emotional health problems, and added to domestic labor, which was grueling even in the best of times (see Abel in press).

Historical inquiry has highlighted both the social forces *compelling* women to provide care for intimates and the social conditions *preventing* women from doing the same. Most of the feminists writing about care have been white and middle-class women; many belong to the generation brought up to be wives and mothers rather than full-time workers. Therefore, it is perhaps not surprising that a major theme in our writing has been the oppressive ideological and material forces compelling women to deliver care. In a study of present-day adult daughters caring for frail elderly parents, I noted that the absence of universal long term care services in the United States means that many women lack the power to determine when they will begin to care for elderly relatives, to control the intrusions of caregiving in their lives, and to relinquish responsibilities that have become overwhelming (Abel 1991).

It is equally important to point out that poor women, especially women of color, historically have had to struggle to be able to care for intimates. Although a host of illnesses ravaged slave quarters in the antebellum South (see Savitt 1978:49–82), enslaved women could eke out time to care for their families only when they returned at night, exhausted from work in the fields or big house. Fannie Moore, a former slave, told interviewers that when her younger brother was dying, "Granny she doctah him as bes' she could, evah time she git away from de white folks' kitchen. My mammy nevah git chance to see him, 'cept when she git home in de evenin'." When the mother learned one night that her son had died, she knelt "by the bed and cry her heart out." Shortly afterward, the boy's uncle buried him. The mother "just plow and watch 'em put George in de ground" (Rawick 1972:130–31). Slaves also were vulnerable to loss of children through sale.

Waged work prevented many poor women from delivering care during the late nineteenth and early twentieth centuries. Some women with caregiving responsibilities found remunerative work they could do at home, such as taking in laundry, boarders, and piecework, but such work consumed time and energy needed for care. The mother of a severely disabled seven-year-old boy, in a letter to Eleanor Roosevelt in 1938, complained that when she added sewing for pay to her normal housework, she lacked "time to give him the attention & care that he needed" (C.R.S. 1938). Women working outside the home sometimes left sick or disabled family members alone. In 1907, a dressmaker asked a physician to send her two young tubercular sons to a sanatorium where they previously had resided. Although the boys "were well for some time after coming home," she now found them "as bad as ever." "Having no mother during the day," they ran "wild" and returned each night with wet feet (C.E. 1907). A physician employed in the New York City Department of Health noted in 1916 that some working mothers locked children with whooping cough in the home (Dickson 1916: 19–20). By the turn of the century, caregiving increasingly included transporting family members to medical appointments and visiting hospitalized patients. But those tasks, too, were impossible for many women in the labor force: Most offices and clinics were open only during regular working hours. In 1903, the mother of a blind 15-year-old boy in New York City rejected a clinic appointment for him because she worked full time, and he could not go alone (Community Service Society 1888–1918). Hospital visiting hours also conflicted with laborers' working day (Peter Brent Brigham Hospital 1931).

The difficulty of caring for sick and disabled family members was especially great for domestic servants. Between the mid-nineteenth century and 1930, more women entered domestic service than any other occupation (Glenn 1986:99). Excluded from many forms of paid employment, African-American, Mexican-American, and Japanese-American women were especially likely to work as servants (Glenn 1992). As Phyllis Palmer (1989:87) notes, "Domestics were envisioned as single women, young or old, cut off from any attachments except those to the employer's family." Servants who lived in had virtually no opportunity to provide care. An African-American southern woman stated, "I see my own children only when they happen to see me on the street when I am out with the [employer's] children or when my children come to the 'yard' to see me" (quoted in Hunter 1997:106). Day laborers, too, complained about their long hours. One wrote to the National Association for the Protection of Colored People in 1931, "I leave home quarter of 7 every morning. I finish 9:30 P.M. When I get home it is 10 o'clock. The people treat me as one of their family and I suppose I should not kick. But I certainly would like to know more about Domestic rules and laws if there be any" (quoted in Palmer 1989:87). Essays by Pierrette Hondagneu-Sotelo and Stacey Oliker in this volume remind us that the problems of reconciling paid employment and caregiving responsibilities remain formidable for poor women, immigrant women, and women of color.

Historical research also helped to illuminate another theme that dominates feminist analyses of care—the paltriness of the rewards caregivers receive. Although the social fabric relies on our collective ability to sustain life, nurture the weak, and respond to the needs of intimates, we routinely disparage those services. Caregiving shares the low status accorded all of women's domestic labor. By disregarding the care on which we depend, we create the illusion of independence.

Another explanation may be that the cultural value of the three major components of caregiving (instrumental, spiritual, and emotional) declined between 1850 and 1940. Instrumental services in the nineteenth century encompassed not just cooking, cleaning, and assisting sick people with feeding and mobility, but also delivering skilled medical care. Women dispensed herbal remedies, dressed wounds, bound broken bones, sewed severed fingers, cleaned bedsores, and removed bullets (see Abel in press).

The display of unusual healing abilities conferred honor and prestige on women in diverse social locations. Because knowledge acquired through practical education was considered as important as that gleaned in the laboratory and taught in schools, some women could translate caregiving skills into paid employment. As Susan M. Reverby (1987:15–16) writes, "Marriage to a very poor man, divorce or abandonment, or widowhood were often preconditions for nursing. Widowhood, in particular, appears to have been an important, if cruel, pathway into nursing. With no need for formal credentials, a woman could offer her experience of caring for a dying husband as her qualifications to nurse." Women also converted healing abilities into employment as midwives. A 1916 study of childbirth in a rural Wisconsin county wrote that "it frequently happens that one of the neighbor women who are called upon to help in emergencies develops special skill in such work and soon finds herself more and more drafted into service" (quoted in Borst 1995:54). Although African-American midwives in the South viewed their work as a spiritual calling, they also based the claim to expertise on informal caregiving experience (Fraser 1998).

Struggling to establish themselves as professionals, nineteenth-century doctors denigrated women's healing knowledge and tried to restrict the information available to the public. But many doctors were well aware of their own educational deficiencies. Most nineteenth-century medical schools were poorly funded commercial enterprises, taught by part-time instructors; some lacked laboratories and libraries (see Rothstein 1985:288–89; Starr 1982:118–19). A few doctors later acknowledged their debts to older women caregivers. Dr. Charles Beneulyn Johnson (1926:95), for example, wrote that he "got through" his first delivery "with the help (and truth compels me to acknowledge), advice and instruction of some good women who knew much more of the practical side of obstetrics than I did."

Because sickness and death were religious as well as medical events, caregiving had an important spiritual dimension. Enslaved healers in the antebellum South sought to address both the metaphysical and natural causes of disease and to connect patients to their ancestors. Although fewer whites associated healing with spirituality, white women routinely reported reading the Bible to care recipients, praying with them, and urging them to accept death openly and peacefully. In 1863, Eliza Webber, her sister Emma, and her brother Alpha left their home in Glover, Vermont, to sell children's books door to door in upstate New York. The project ended abruptly when Alpha contracted typhoid fever. In a letter notifying their parents of the disaster, Eliza noted that she and Emma in addition to sitting with Alpha at night and rubbing his body with alcohol throughout the day, "read in the Bible everyday to him." The sisters summoned both a doctor and two ministers who came "a number of times and . . . prayed with him." Perhaps as a result, Eliza was able to reassure her parents that her brother was "perfectly prepared to die" (Webber 1863).

A major concern of many wives was to persuade sick and dying husbands to embrace a religion they did not want. In the early 1860s, Sam Curd, a young Missouri woman, discussed salvation with her dying husband, read the Bible to him, and encouraged him to go to church. In doing so, she sought not only to prepare him for death but also to confront her own impending loss. She wanted to accept rather than shield herself from her husband's growing frailty, but she had to struggle against the despair that threatened to engulf her. She looked to the religion she offered her husband for the strength to engage in that struggle (Arpad 1984).

The emotional component of caregiving included bestowing special attention on sick relatives and friends. When her beloved mother was ill in 1874, Louisa May Alcott wrote to a friend, "I had the great pleasure of supplying all her needs and fancies" (Cheney 1892:300). In addition, many women identified closely with the distress of others. Although women's writings often omitted the physical details of sickness, they dwelt on suffering and anguish. Intimate bonds tied many women to the recipients of care. The afflictions women witnessed often elicted tremendous sympathy from them. Some female attendants who watched birthing women bleed to death were pregnant themselves. Women caring for seriously ill infants in the community often had children the same ages at home.

Nineteenth-century medicine dignified the emotional dimension of care. Most doctors agreed that attention, sympathy, and reassurance alleviated emotional stress and promoted healing. Prevailing medical beliefs also encouraged doctors to value personal relationships as a source of knowledge. Assuming that disease arose from the interaction of individuals with their environments, doctors sought to gain particularistic knowledge about patients and the context of their lives (Rosenberg 1985).

Popular literature further affirmed the emotional work of care, encouraging women to find meaning in their closeness to the suffering of others. The extensive "consolation literature" that arose midcentury suggested that women could transcend suffering by reaching out to others. Several writers portrayed female characters who drew closer to other women. According to the biographer Joan D. Hedrick (1994:281), Harriet Beecher Stowe's novels depicted "an informal 'priesthood' of women who have suffered." Stowe based that priesthood on her own experiences. As she wrote, only people who had known "great affliction" were qualified to "guide those who are struggling in it" (quoted in Hedrick 1994:282).

The broad cultural support for these three components of caregiving eroded during the late nineteenth and early twentieth centuries. Caregivers' knowledge was increasingly regarded as superstition, acceptance of God's will disparaged as resignation, and solicitude condemned as indulgence. Discovery of the bacteriological causes of specific diseases made it more acceptable for physicians to maintain distance from patients and treat them as fungible. Biological reductionism rendered irrelevant the patient's emotional and moral state, interaction with providers, and physical surroundings (see Rosenberg 1987). The balance of power shifted from family caregivers to physicians. Such fearsome diseases as cholera, typhus fever, and smallpox, which had attained epidemic proportions decades earlier, were virtually eliminated, and other common killers, including rickets, syphilis, and dysentery, lost much of their menace. Although historians now debate the extent to which medical advances contributed to the decline in infectious disease, many contemporaries credited medical science alone (see Starr

1982:134–40). Physicians who still could offer few effective treatments acquired enormous prestige by allying with those advances. As the reputation of doctors rose, they could more persuasively portray family caregivers as ignorant and their healing knowledge as superstition.

Scientific optimism also undermined the spiritual component of care. Rather than looking to religion for the strength to accept the worst, caregivers were expected to mobilize all available medical resources in the fight for recovery. Doctors helped to foster the illusion that the body no longer was subject to uncontrolled forces. Until death was imminent, prominent doctors continually promised cure to family members. Spiritual preparation had no place in medical regimes. Far from being an important achievement, acceptance of God's will was now portrayed as a sign of passivity, inadequate willpower, and failure to appreciate the benefits of modern medicine.

Simultaneously, the emotional dimension of care was devalued. The ideal was now the purely rational being freed from any disturbing passions or selfish interests. Both doctors and nurses prided themselves on the self-control that shielded them from the pain and suffering they witnessed. New therapeutic approaches emphasized the importance of monitoring patients' behavior, not responding to their wishes. Rather than producing important knowledge about disease, intense personal connection was believed to distort understanding of patient needs and lead to dangerous indulgence. A late-nineteenth-century hospital administrator intoned, "It can be put down as one of the advantages of a hospital that the relatives and friends do not take care of the patient. It is much better for patients not to be under the care of anyone who is over-concerned for them" (quoted in Rosner 1982:78).

The shift in cultural values had the most serious consequences for the least privileged women. Although the new confidence in medical science created a pretext for physicians to lavish attention on the education of all mothers, poor women were especially likely to be perceived as needing instruction (see Meckel 1990). The Social Service Department of Massachusetts General Hospital (1918) wrote, "Underlying [children's] acute or chronic illness is usually ignorance on the part of their parents, ignorance of the essentials of health, hygiene, and child training." Poor women also were extremely likely to be condemned as being discouraged and resigned. S. Josephine Baker (1939:58), the chief of New York's Bureau of Child Hygiene, later recalled that immigrant mothers "were just horribly fatalistic about [infant death]. Babies always died in the summer and there was no point in trying to do anything about it. . . . I might as well have been trying to tell them to keep it from raining." A public health nurse described a Hispanic Arizona woman this way:

Gregoria was twenty-two years old and she had two babies. Five babies had been born to her in the seven years of her married life, but the good God had taken three of them. They had lived a few miserable months, and had then died. Gregoria sat huddled over their door-step and thought that nothing was of any use. The baby was always sick and some day the good God would take him as He had the others. (Erion 1921)

And poor women were considered especially likely to be swayed by excessive emotion and thus to indulge offspring. A report of the Out-Patient Department of the New York Society for the Relief of the Ruptured and Crippled (1918) criticized the mother of George, a "boy of 11 years [who] had been coming to clinic for some time with a tuberculous hip. As he was not improving, was referred for home investigation. The worker found boy to be an only child, very much spoiled by over-kindness."

As charity workers, public health nurses, and occasionally government officials, white, middle-class women helped to construct the portrait of poor women, immigrant women, and women of color as superstitious, fatalistic, and irrational. Such a depiction not only skewed the services provided to those groups but also contributed to the denigration of an activity with which all women were associated.

The History of Men's Caring

Evaluating Precedents for Fathers' Family Involvement

N ational opinion polls report that modern American men value their families over their jobs, and television commercials now use images of "new" fathers cuddling babies to sell everything from life insurance to razor blades. At the same time, cultural images of "broken" families, single mothers, deadbeat dads, and delinquent children compete for our attention. As we enter the new millennium, politicians continue to talk nostalgically about reclaiming lost family values and researchers continue to define fatherhood in terms of physical presence, breadwinning, and moral leadership. And even though women continue to enter the paid labor force in record numbers, men remain helpers in the domestic realm and seem to be able to avoid responsibility for the routine care work it takes to raise children and maintain families.

In this chapter, we explore these paradoxes and investigate the historical conditions under which men assume or avoid responsibility for care work in families. We pay particular attention to past and present ideologies of gender difference that portray men as emotionally distant breadwinners, incompetent parents and housekeepers, and deserving of women's domestic services. In so doing, we explore cultural contradictions and ambivalence associated with the development of separate spheres, show how men's care work in families has historical precedents, and discuss how men's avoidance of care work contributes to the maintenance of male dominance. Throughout the chapter, we use historical examples to show how fathering and the performance of care work by men are socially constructed and variable. Like other social practices, men's care work and perceptions of it are influenced by larger economic, political, and cultural forces.

We are especially concerned with countering recent arguments that men should be encouraged to adopt the so-called traditional practices of fatherhood rather than assuming direct responsibility for housework and the nurturing of children. To the contrary, we suggest that men's ability to stay aloof from routine family work has enabled them to dominate women and enjoy special masculine privileges. Only by examining historical contexts for gendered divisions of family work can we explore how male dominance and care work are mutually forged and reciprocally reproduced. Although caring is typically associated with women, including men in our theories and empirical studies of caring can help us understand the complex social, economic, and psychological processes that make care work gendered. By documenting the shifting historical and cultural conditions shaping family work for both men and women, we can better understand how the social organization of care work supports gender inequality, and perhaps better predict how changes in economic and social conditions might produce more equal gender relations in the future.

Gender and Care Work

Care is the activity of attending to others and responding to their emotions and needs. We say that someone *cares* for another when he or she is sensitive to that person's desires and helps meet the physical and social needs of everyday life. We think of children, the sick, and the frail as especially in need of care, but everyone needs to be cared for in essential ways. The mental and physical labor entailed in caring for others can seem invisible to those who are its regular recipients, but care work is essential to "social reproduction" (Laslett and Brenner 1989). Human existence depends on the routine activities that feed, clothe, shelter, and care for both children and adults. Recent estimates suggest that the total amount of time spent in direct family care work (including child care, housework, and other household labor) is about equal to the time spent in paid labor (Robinson and Godbey 1997). In addition, the type of care we give and receive as individuals and family members tends to define the quality of our lives. Not surprisingly, most researchers report that care is a central component of love, though love is often defined as including other psychological and behavioral dimensions (Abel and Nelson 1990; Cancian 1987; Cancian and Oliker 1999; Finch and Groves 1983; Thompson 1993). Caring is normatively linked to gender, insofar as women have felt socially obligated to provide it, and men have felt entitled to receive it.

Despite some recent changes, studies show that family work continues to be allocated according to gender, with women spending at least twice as much time on these tasks as men, typically taking responsibility for monitoring and supervising the work, even when they pay for domestic services or delegate tasks to other family members. Studies also show that women perform a greater share of the domestic work when they are married and when they have children (Coltrane 2000; Shelton 1992). Despite the enormous importance of care work and its theoretical role in the maintenance of society, little systematic attention has been paid to documenting cultural expectations for men's caring and the social, political, and historical conditions that might promote it.

Research on Men as Family Care Providers

Following assumptions about separate work and family spheres for men and women, most social science research on parental care in the twentieth century has focused on mothers, documenting how the right combination of maternal warmth, encouragement, and control can lead to positive child outcomes. Claims about the importance of fathers have tended to be more theoretical, with most research focusing on the potential problems associated with father absence and few studies directly measuring men's parenting or care work. Social theories from the 1950s and 1960s considered the hypothetical significance of fathers, especially in terms of breadwinning, discipline, and modeling masculinity, but few studies paid attention to what fathers actually did around the house or for children. In the 1970s, that pattern began to change. Not only did a putatively "new" fatherhood ideal surface in popular culture, but family studies began to report that fathers were indeed capable of participating in the routine aspects of family work, even if they did less than their wives and remained in a helper role (Fein 1978; LaRossa and LaRossa 1981; Lamb 1976; Parke 1981). A few studies conducted in the 1970s and 1980s focused on nurturing fathers who shared in virtually all aspects of parenting (e.g., Coltrane 1989; Ehrensaft 1987; Pruett 1987; Russell 1983), though the absolute time the average American man devoted to family work rose only slightly (Pleck 1983). As women worked more hours on the job and cut back on their housework hours, and as men's domestic labor inched up, national time use surveys in the late 1980s began to document a significant shift toward more relative sharing of family work (Coltrane 2000).

In the 1990s, as mothers and fathers of young children struggled to balance the competing demands of jobs and family and as women's childbearing became less dependent on the presence of a man, public debates about the future of marriage and the proper role of fathers gained renewed attention (e.g., Blankenhorn 1995; Glenn 1997; Popenoe 1996; Stacey 1996). Most commentators decried men's lack of support for their children and championed some form of increased father involvement, but ideal images of the involved father ranged from a sensitive egalitarian partner who changed diapers and cooked meals to a stern but kindly patriarch who exercised family leadership according to biblical teachings or biological imperatives (Coltrane and Adams in press). As described below, family scholars and practitioners began to promote competing visions of what constitutes good fathering, basing their views on academic, religious, political, and emotional criteria. In this chapter, we investigate and evaluate rhetorical attempts to justify these fatherhood ideals by invoking putative historical precedents. In so doing, we decry the disingenuous deployment of nostalgia in the service of masculine hegemony and demonstrate the value of a balanced historical approach to understanding fatherhood.

Renewed Visions of Gender-Segregated Fathering

A growing number of family scholars in the 1990s re-emphasized the theoretical importance of family structure (father presence vs. father absence) and promoted more "traditional" measures of paternal involvement, including economic provision, maternal support, and moral leadership. The new emphasis on "responsible" fathering includes an explicit focus on the importance of marriage to men's assumption of responsibility for children (e.g., Blankenhorn 1995; Doherty, Kouneski, and Erickson 1998; Nock 1998; Popenoe 1996). This research is part of a larger ideological campaign to shore up the (supposedly declining) institution of marriage and thereby restore faith in the image of harmonious male-headed heterosexual families (Smith 1993; Stacey 1996). David Blankenhorn (1995:1), founder and president of the Institute for American Values, rhetorically asserts, "Fatherlessness is the most harmful demographic trend of this generation. It is the leading cause of declining child well-being in our society. It is also the engine driving our most urgent social problems, from crime to adolescent pregnancy to child sexual abuse to domestic violence against women." In their quest to better society, Blankenhorn and his colleagues at the Institute for American Values's Council on Families (e.g., Glenn 1997; Popenoe 1996) have fixed upon the singular need to reinstate the father as head of the family: "The most urgent domestic challenge facing the United States at the close of the twentieth century is the re-creation of fatherhood as a vital social role for men. At stake is nothing less than the success of the American experiment" (Blankenhorn 1995:222).

These conservative defenders of traditional fatherhood present a clear picture of men's limited capacity for direct care, and not incidentally, their inherent suitability for leadership: "Historically, the good father protects his family, provides for its material needs, devotes himself to the education of his children, and represents his family's interest in the larger world. This work is necessarily rooted in a repertoire of inherited male values: . . . These values are not limited to toughness, competition, instrumentalism, and aggression, but they certainly include them" (Blankenhorn 1995:122). Similarly, Popenoe (1996:183) selectively reviews anthropological evidence to posit a finite set of universal features of fatherhood: "In every premodern society, fathers have played the roles of protector, provider, and culture transmitter. And fathers have virtually everywhere been authority figures, although more so following the rise of civilization. These, then are the earliest evolutionary roles of fathers and the primary roles around which men have organized their lives over the course of history. These are also, presumably, the roles for which men are biologically best adapted." Popenoe, Blankenhorn, and others thus argue that since distinct parenting styles and personality traits are biologically built in, men and women should not be called on to do the same sorts of things around the house or with children. What's more, they suggest that the functional dictates of child socialization require mothers and fathers to act differently, and necessitate the presence of fathers: "Ultimately, the division of parental labor is the consequence of our biological embodiment as sexual beings and of the inherent requirements of effective parenthood" (Blankenhorn 1995:122).

Belief in gender-segregated parenting continues to find support among some social scientists and family professionals. For example, measures of mother-child interaction are rejected as inappropriate instruments for studying father-child interaction (Day and Mackey 1986; LaRossa 1988), and research comparing men's care work to women's is labeled a "deficit model" (Doherty 1991) or the "role inadequacy perspective" (Hawkins and Dollahite 1997). Human service professionals also promote gender-segregated parenting by invoking historical precedents and asserting that mothers and fathers are fundamentally and inalterably different. For example, in discussing parent and family life education programs, Palm (1997:172−73) notes that the "generic or androgynous parent is represented by a predominately [*sic*] female model for 'good parenting.'" In contrast, he suggests that "the male style of interaction must be understood as a distinct style that has some real benefits for the child" (Palm 1997:175). Similarly, a lead article in *Families in Society: The Journal of Contemporary Human Services* promoted the idea that gender-segregated parenting was natural and inevitable: "Fathers are not mothers; they respond to their children differently from the way mothers do" (Coolsen 1993:3). Even some proponents of greater father involvement, like Kyle Pruett of the Yale Child Study Center (and author of *The Nurturing Father*, 1987), warn men against trying to act too much like mothers: "Obviously, fathers are not mothers—they never will be and shouldn't try. . . . The mother-mimic tactic soon falters. It feels wrong at all levels, because it is. The child doesn't expect it, and the father can't do it. This lesson is his first on the journey to complete himself as a man-now-father: Fathering is not mothering any more than mothering is ever fathering" (Pruett 1993:46).

Images of gender-neutral parenting and the idea that men should provide nurturing care tend to evoke very strong emotions from these conservative fatherhood proponents: "Fathers are not merely would-be mothers. The two sexes are different to the core. . . . [I]t is resolutely silly to think of embarking on a mass reeducation campaign just so that men can do halfheartedly what women can do better" (Popenoe 1996:197, 213). In contrast to such pronouncements, feminist scholars remind us that patriarchy (literally "rule by fathers") is based on men's genetic ties, an ideology of gender difference, and the denigration of nurturance (Rothman 1989). Taking a critical perspective, we can see the renewed emphasis on traditional fatherhood as part of a cultural backlash against women's independence, exemplified by Dan Quayle's attack on the television character Murphy Brown for having a baby without having a husband (Stacey 1996; Whitehead 1993). The separate-spheres ideology inherent in the call for a return to "traditional" marriage and fatherhood thus includes a direct message about women's dependence on men: a woman's true calling is not only to raise children and maintain a home, but also to serve a husband. Proponents advocating a "return" to "traditional" family values invoke the supposedly overwhelming weight of evidence from biology and history to support the naturalness of this arrangement. Our reading of history tells a very different story. According to Stephanie Coontz (1992:9), the "traditional family" promoted by the conservative defenders of fatherhood is a nostalgic myth: "It is an historical amalgam of structures, values, and behaviors that never co-existed in the same time and place."

In Search of a History of Fatherhood: A Critique of Theory

Almost two decades ago, the historian John Demos noted that the history of fatherhood was yet to be written (Demos 1982). The claim that fatherhood has been ignored seems paradoxical, since historians have produced volumes about men's lives and their achievements since the beginning of written records. Nevertheless, it is men's public lives—their work, political exploits, literary accomplishments, scientific discoveries, and heroic battles—that have been chronicled, leaving their private lives as fathers, husbands, and care workers largely unexplored (Mintz 1998).

The paucity of detailed historical information has not prevented researchers from proposing a variety of stage theories and functionalist models of long term fatherhood trends. Unfortunately, most early stage models have been limited by their tendency to either romanticize or demonize men's familial roles of the past, thus using historical research to argue contemporary issues (Mintz 1998). Depending on the point being made in contemporary debates, historical fathers have been seen as either intensely and actively involved in childrearing or as domestic patriarchs who dominated their children and tyrannized their wives (Mintz 1998:4). Both extremes have historical precedents and thus could be considered to contain an element of "truth," but using either to construct simple models about the evolution of fatherhood is more misleading than helpful.

Thanks to recent scholarship by social historians and social scientists, we are beginning to gain a more differentiated and complex portrait of the behavior and emotions of everyday family life in the past. The primary benefit has been increased understanding about motherhood and childhood, but an important by-product has also been more historical knowledge about men's emotional lives and family practices. Though studies are still few in number and results remain contradictory, we are moving toward a more nuanced and multifaceted view of the ways that fathers have cared and provided for their families (Griswold 1993; Kimmel 1996; LaRossa 1996; Marsh 1988; Parke and Stearns 1993; Rotundo 1993). Before we begin our own brief historical review of men as care providers, we offer a few observations about the limitations of research and theory in this area.

Among the major shortcomings of early historical studies of fatherhood are the assumptions that most fathers act the same way, and that changes from one era to the next have been linear and progressive (Coltrane and Parke 1998). For example, early family history emphasized that peasant families were extended, and therefore contained powerful patriarchs who dominated women and children, whereas market societies produced companionate marriages and nuclear families with more loving and cooperative husbands and fathers. In fact, historical patterns of fathering, like historical patterns of mothering, have responded to a complex array of social and economic forces, varying considerably across regions and time periods. Although it is useful to identify the general ways that men's (and women's) relationship to work and production have shaped their public and private status (as we do below), actual relations have been quite varied, and fatherhood ideals have followed different trajectories in different regions of the same country (Griswold 1993; Mintz 1998). For example, as most of the United States was undergoing industrialization, large pockets remained relatively untouched by it. Griswold (1993:17) shows how the experience of white planters in the antebellum South was both similar to and unlike that of men in the commercial and industrial North. Though both became increasingly child-centered during the late eighteenth century, the experience of those in the North was strongly influenced by industrialization and a changing domestic ideology, whereas the white Southern gentry were more likely to hold to "a vision of patriarchy predicated upon veneration of forefathers and to child rearing practices that used shame and humiliation to inculcate a sense of hierarchy and honor" (Griswold 1993:19). A second major drawback of early historical studies of fatherhood is the tendency to overgeneralize for the entire society based on the experiences of those who are white and middle-class (Coltrane and Parke 1998). As we learn more about fatherhood in the past, we ought to guard against the tendency to artificially homogenize men's experience across class, ethnic, or geographical lines. For example, not only were there major differences between the fathering of men in the South and the North, but slave fathers and freedmen in the South had much different experiences than either group of white men (Griswold 1993; McDaniel 1994). Only by including men of color, paying attention to work status, and studying different regional economies can we generalize to larger groups of men and understand how social, political, and economic forces shape fatherhood.

As noted above, early attempts to understand the history of fatherhood painted a simple before-and-after picture: before the industrial revolution, families were rural and extended, and patriarchal fathers were stern moralists; after the industrial revolution, families were urban and nuclear, and wage-earning fathers became companionate husbands, distant breadwinners, and occasional playmates to their children. This picture captures something important about general shifts in work and family life, but its simple assumption of unidirectional linear change can be misleading (Coontz 1992; Hareven 1991; Skolnick 1991). A binary conceptualization contrasting "patriarchal" roles in the past with "egalitarian" roles in the present introduces almost as many problems as assuming that "traditional" families are timeless and biologically determined.

Historical Images of Men's Care Work in Families

Studies by anthropologists and sociologists show that in every society at least a few tasks are defined as the province of men, whereas some others are defined as the province of women (Coltrane 1998). Nevertheless, divisions of labor in most nonindustrial societies have been more flexible and cooperative than popular stereotypes imply. Except for breastfeeding and the earliest care of infants, there appear to be no cross-cultural universals in the tasks that women do and men do (Rosaldo 1980; Tiffany 1982; Johnson 1988). In some societies, the worlds of men and women were so separated that they had little contact with one another and rarely performed the same tasks (Herdt 1981; Spain 1992). In other societies, however, women routinely shared tasks like hunting, and men routinely shared tasks like caring for babies (Coltrane 1988; 1992). In fact, in most societies, the majority of tasks could be performed by either men or women, and a great many tasks were performed jointly or cooperatively between them (Sanday 1981; Whyte 1978). This does not mean that these societies thought men and women were interchangeable in all matters, for most considered the sexes to be different from one another in at least a few important ways. But the cross-cultural historical record is very clear in revealing that the tasks men and women are supposedly suited for varies enormously among societies and across time periods (Mead 1949).

Divisions of labor between men and women in modern societies have been strongly influenced by subsistence and market economies. The colonial economy of seventeenth- and eighteenth-century America was based on agriculture and the family household. For the many families who owned farms or small artisan shops, one's place of work was also one's home. Slaves, indentured servants, and others were expected to work on family estates in return for food, a place to live, and sometimes other rewards. In this pattern of household- or family-based production, men, women, and children worked side by side, along with hired hands, servants, apprentices, and sometimes slaves. Regional variations could be quite large, and fathers and mothers often did somewhat different types of work, but many tasks required for subsistence and family survival were interchangeable, and both mothers and fathers took responsibility for child care and training.

Because the sentimental individualism of the modern era had not yet blossomed, emotional involvement with children in the Western world during the seventeenth and early eighteenth centuries is generally regarded as having been more limited than it is today (Ariès 1962; Shorter 1975; Synnott 1983). In addition, prevailing images of children were different from our modern ideas about the innocence and purity of children. Religious teachings, particularly those of the American Puritans, stressed the "corrupt nature" and "evil dispositions" of children, and fathers were admonished to demand strict obedience and use swift physical punishment to cleanse children of their sinful ways (Muir and Brett 1980). Puritan fathers justified their extensive involvement in children's lives with reference to the unfitness of women to be disciplinarians and moral or intellectual teachers. Griswold (1997) points out, however, that stern unaffectionate fathering, though not confined just to Puritans, was not representative of all segments of the population. In fact, the majority of American fathers attempted to shape and guide their children's characters, not break them or "beat the devil out of them" (Straus 1994). As eighteenth-century fathers gained enough affluence to have some leisure time, many were affectionate with their children and delighted in playing with them (Griswold 1997).

Parts of the Puritan fatherhood ideal are incorporated into modern claims about fathers' unique ability to discipline children, provide moral instruction, and promote civic duty. By the time of the American Revolution, however, those tasks were already being shared with most American wives and mothers. According to Griswold (1997), the American Revolution provided women with the patriotic and political role of ensuring that children developed proper character, thereby securing America's place as a free country. From the late eighteenth century to the end of the nineteenth century, historical documents also show that men sometimes shared in the physical and emotional aspects of child care that we tend to think of as "women's work." Linda Pollock provides examples, such as an 1802 letter from a father who sat up for two nights with his gravely ill daughter, administering her medicine every hour (1987:118), and an 1887 letter describing how a father fed his two-year-old son breakfast and lunch, then played with him in the afternoon (1987:80). As early as 1832, Tocqueville (1969), the French observer of early American culture, similarly noted that relations between American fathers and their children were gentle and intimate. Other historical documents show how husbands began attending childbirth in the 1830s and continued the practice until the early twentieth century, when hospital births became the norm (Suitor 1981). In short, historical records show that American men in previous centuries sometimes performed routine family care work and many took on domestic tasks that we now label "women's work."

The Ascendance of the Ideal of Separate Spheres

As America made the transition from an agrarian economy to a market economy, the general pattern of overlapping roles embedded in household production was slowly transformed into a cultural ideal demarcating relatively distinct and separate spheres for men and women. The simple story is that as commercial markets grew and industrialization spread, men were drawn out of the home into work for wages, leaving women to manage the home and care for the children. Tocqueville was among the first to note, and criticize, the American separation of spheres: "In America, more than anywhere else in the world, care has been taken to constantly trace clearly the distinct spheres of action of the two sexes and both are required to keep in step, but along paths that are never the same" (Tocqueville [1832] 1969:601).

The movement toward separate work and home spheres accelerated dramatically between 1870 and 1900, when centralized industrial production in the United States increased fivefold. As late as 1871, two-thirds of the American population was still self-employed, but by the early 1900s a majority of Americans depended on wage labor to support their families. The ideal of separate spheres that emerged during this time drew sharp contrasts between home and work and between women and men. Kimmel (1996:52) notes, "It is significant that the doctrine of separate spheres was a 'male creation,' first promoted by male writers of advice books and said to 'serve men's needs.' Only later was it picked up, embraced, and elaborated by women writers celebrating domesticity." The middle-class home eventually came to symbolize a haven from the harsh competitive world of industry, and women's "nature" changed to conform. For example, middle- and upper-class women wore tight corsets that epitomized women's incapacity and made it virtually impossible to perform hard labor. Well-to-do families kept the parts of the house devoted to productive work—like cooking, laundry, and bathing—isolated and out of sight. The areas of relaxation—like the parlor and dining room—were more public and visible, creating the illusion that the home was not a place of work (Coltrane 1998; Davidoff and Hall 1987; Reskin and Padavic 1994).

The development of separate spheres for men and women also carried prescriptions for the proper behavior of fathers and mothers in terms of caring for their families. In the rural agricultural era, American fathers were supposed to serve as moral overseers, as well as masters, of their families. According to the leading middle-class ideals of the time, men performed their civic duty and developed themselves by emphasizing their home-based family roles. Even though mothers provided most of the direct caretaking of infants and young children, men were very active in training and tutoring children, especially as they got older. Before the nineteenth century, most parental advice was addressed to fathers rather than mothers. Because they were moral teachers and family heads, fathers were thought to have far greater responsibility for, and influence on, their children than mothers. Not only were middle-class fathers involved in the direct moral and practical instruction of older children, but they were also generally held responsible for how the children acted outside of the home (Degler 1980; Pleck 1987; Rotundo 1993).

Many scholars have emphasized that before the modern era, men were a visible presence in children's lives, because their work—whether farming, artisanship, or trade—occurred in the household context. Furthermore, most work in the household economy of the agricultural era was directed by the father. Men introduced sons to farming or craft work, oversaw the work of others, and were responsible for maintaining harmonious relations in the household. The home was thus a system of control as well as a center of production, and both functions tended to reinforce the father's authority (Degler 1980; Griswold 1993; Pleck 1987). As noted above, the diaries and letters of some agrarian fathers show more sentimentality and devotion to children than stereotypes of stern patriarchs imply, giving rise to scholarly debates about possible distinctions between European and American styles of fathering and about the extent to which the landed gentry demonstrated affection toward their children (Demos 1986; Parke and Stearns 1993; Pollock 1983).

According to most historical readings, after the wage labor economy developed in the nineteenth century, an ideology of separate gender spheres grew in importance, diminishing men's symbolic role in the home. This does not mean, however, that men stopped participating in family activities or became disengaged from their children. In fact, according to Griswold (1993) this is the era of the first "new" fatherhood movement. Middle-class fathers in the nineteenth century helped their wives through childbirth, romped with their offspring, worried about their sons' vocations and education, and forged close emotional bonds with their daughters: "Although many men still conceptualized the father-child relationship in contractual terms, . . . a growing number of men highlighted the expressive, affective dimension to the relationship and underscored fatherly self-sacrifice for the well-being of their progeny" (Griswold 1997:78). At the same time, men's occupational achievements outside the family took on moral overtones. Men came to be seen as partially fulfilling their family and civic duty not by teaching and interacting with their children, but by being good providers. Men's moral obligations began to shift from direct family activities to wage earning, and a father's family duty began to be conceptualized as one of financial support. The home, previously the normal site of production, consumption, and virtually everything else in life, was slowly being transformed (at least symbolically) into a nurturant child-centered haven set apart from the impersonal world of work, politics, and other public pursuits. The middle-class home became the mother's domain (Coontz 1992; Lasch 1977; Ryan 1981).

Although we are concerned here with historical images of fathers, one cannot understand such imagery without recognizing the cultural shift from housewifery to housework and the accompanying symbolic identities available to women. Practiced predominantly prior to the early nineteenth century, housewifery consisted of many more tasks than mere housework, including the production of marketable commodities (such as butter, cheese, beer, candles, and wool) for both exchange and household use (Jackson 1992). Women played an integral role in such production, and many plied their trade and craft on the open market, though husbands typically benefited from their wives' housewifery skills. As industrial capitalism spread, items formerly produced at home became available for purchase and men took over traditional female trades and crafts. Men blocked women from work in factories and mines through exclusionary trade union practices and demands for a "family wage," resulting in more families becoming dependent on men's wages for subsistence (Jackson 1992:158). As the household and paid workplace became more segregated, women were left with responsibility for routine housework and child care, which took on heightened moral significance.

According to the separate spheres ideology that resulted, middle-class women were supposed to realize their "true" nature by marrying, giving birth, and most important, tending children. Motherhood was elevated to a revered status, and wives' homemaking came to be seen as a moral calling and worthy profession. The True Woman was supposed to be inherently unselfish, and her moral purity, nurturant character, and gentle temperament were seen as uniquely qualifying her to rear young children (Coontz 1992; Skolnick 1991). Women had been involved in the everyday aspects of child care to begin with, but as the middle-class home was separated from work and morally elevated, women came to be seen as the ones most capable of training children and instilling proper values in them (Coltrane 1996). As women became more responsible for children's overall well-being, they were also charged with preparing them to become proper adults. In line with prevailing ideas about gender, mothers encouraged girls to develop domestic sensitivities and encouraged boys to be competitive and industrious (Ryan 1981; Davidoff and Hall 1987; Ferree 1990).

As images of the ideal middle-class woman became more fragile and caring, images of the ideal middle-class man shifted toward rugged individualism. Since men's and women's underlying physical and emotional capacities changed only slightly during this time period, we must look elsewhere to understand why the contrast between men and women was drawn so sharply. Many scholars suggest that men's and women's ideal "natures" diverged because of changes in the labor market and increased competition between them for jobs. The nineteenth century was marked by a huge influx of men into waged labor of all types, but because of the expansion of the economy near the turn of the century, unprecedented numbers of unmarried women also entered the wage labor force. Many joined the ranks of formerly all-male occupations such as clerks, typists, bookkeepers, cashiers, and sales personnel. This influx of women into what were previously men's jobs contributed to a masculinist backlash and promoted a rigid Victorian-era belief in separate spheres for men and women (Kimmel 1996; Degler 1980).

Paradoxes of the Separate Spheres Ideal

The ideal that paid work was only for men and that only women were suited to care for others remained an unattainable myth rather than an everyday reality for most families. Many working-class fathers were not able to earn the "family wage" assumed by the separate spheres ideal, and a majority of African-American, Latino, Asian-American, and immigrant men could not fulfill the good provider role that the cultural ideal implied. Women in these families either had to work for wages, participate in production at home, or figure other ways to pool resources and make ends meet. Although the romantic ideal held that women should be sensitive and pure keepers of the home on a full-time basis, the reality was that women in less advantaged households had no choice but to be workers and mothers at the same time. In fact, many working-class and ethnic minority women had to leave their own homes and children to take care of other peoples' children and houses (Dill 1994; Glenn 1992; Rollins 1985; Romero 1992). Even during the heyday of separate spheres in the early part of the twentieth century, minority women, young single women, widows, and married women whose husbands could not support them worked for wages. Married immigrant women and former slaves were the most likely to be employed, because staying out of the labor force would have meant starvation (Reskin and Padavic 1994).

The ideal of separate spheres carried other inherent paradoxes. Michael Kimmel (1996) documents how, at the end of the nineteenth century, more husbands and wives spent their days in separate worlds than ever before; he away all day at work and she tending the children and keeping house. Both domains were becoming increasingly mechanized and industrialized —"his, by the assembly line, mass production, and growth of white-collar clerical positions, and hers, by innovations in household technology that made the home look like a little factory. . . . At the moment of perhaps their greatest separation, husbands and wives were told they should establish what critics called companionate marriage. Husband and wife should be more devoted, more emotionally connected, than ever before" (Kimmel 1996:158–59). At the same time, according to Kimmel and other historical researchers, the movement for involved fatherhood garnered renewed enthusiasm. Catharine Beecher and her sister Harriet Beecher Stowe wrote in *The American Woman's Home* (1869), "It is far more needful for children that a father should attend to the formation of their character and habits, and end in developing their social, intellectual, and moral nature, than it is that he should earn money to furnish them with handsome clothes and a variety of tempting food" (cited in Kimmel 1996:159). Just as feminists like Charlotte Perkins Gilman were championing the belief that women should seek out a sense of individual achievement and identity that had been chiefly men's domain, some women advice writers began promoting egalitarian marriages and "masculine domesticity" (Marsh 1988). In 1905, the editors of *American Homes and Gardens* announced, "The responsibility of the home is not the wife's alone, but equally the husbands, there is no reason at all why men should not sweep and dust, make beds, clean windows, fix the fire, clean the grate, arrange the furniture, and cook" (Kimmel 1996:159). Masculine domesticity, according to Marsh (1988), entailed men taking more responsibility for day-to-day child-care tasks, as well as spending more time teaching children and playing with them. Middle-class men's increasing job security, leisure time, and more spacious suburban living arrangements encouraged a new emphasis on companionate marriage. Male advice givers increasingly urged men to be emotionally closer to their wives and children and to spend more time with the family in popular turn-of-the-century recreational activities such as croquet, roller skating, and bicycling. Thus, while economic conditions promoted separate work spheres and a belief in inherent gender differences, the same structural contexts simultaneously encouraged a symbolic merging of parental duties and family activities for men and women.

This analysis calls into question simple models of natural family precedents or linear historical change and alerts us to the fact that behaviors and ideals often conflict. Griswold (1997:82) notes that "traditional sources of male identity in work, religion, and community had slowly declined during the second half of the nineteenth century; meanwhile, the emergence of the new woman and feminism posed basic challenges to assumptions about men's and women's place in society." In response, the ideal conception of fathering shifted at the turn of the century, from emphasis on economic provision, discipline, and moral instruction, to a more nurturing and friendly relationship between father and offspring—especially sons: "Family experts—drawn from social work, sociology, psychology, home economics, and psychiatry—articulated a new vision of fathering that emphasized father-child companionship and men's contributions to the development of their children's personality and sex role identity" (Griswold 1997:72). The emergence of an idealized fatherhood movement in the early part of the twentieth century was, in part, a response to the increasingly distinct work spheres of men and women at the time. New visions of involved fathers are also seen by some as an attempt by men to reclaim authority in the home and promote manliness in their sons (Kimmel 1996).

Throughout the twentieth century, repeated calls for greater paternal involvement coexisted with the physical presence, but relative emotional and functional absence, of fathers (LaRossa 1996). Nevertheless, many fathers reported that they remained involved in their children's lives. By the 1930s, three of four American fathers said they regularly read magazine articles about child care, and nearly as many men as women were members of the PTA (Kimmel 1996:201), but mothers bore most of the responsibility for care of homes and families. Increases in women's labor force participation during the 1940s, with accompanying "Rosie the Riveter" imagery, briefly challenged the ideal of separate spheres, but the postwar era, with its high rates of marriage, marked a new high point in the resurgence of separate gender spheres. The ideal father in the 1950s was seen as a "good provider," who "set a good table, provided a decent home, paid the mortgage, bought the shoes, and kept his children warmly clothed" (Bernard 1981:3–4). As they had during the earlier Victorian era, middle-class women were expected to be consumed and fulfilled by their "natural" wifely and motherly duties. With Ozzie and Harriet–style families as the 1950s model, women surprised demographers by marrying earlier and having more children than any group of American women before them. Rapid expansion of the American economy fueled a phenomenal growth of suburbs, and the consumer culture that developed out of that era idealized domestic life on radio and television. Isolated in suburban houses, many mothers now had almost sole responsibility for raising children, aided by occasional reference to expert guides from pediatricians and child psychologists.

Fathers of the 1950s were also told to get involved with child care — but not too involved: " 'Of course I don't mean that the father has to give just as many bottles, or change just as many diapers as the mother,' Dr. Benjamin Spock wrote in an early edition of his best-selling *Baby and Child Care*. 'But it's fine for him to do these things occasionally. He might make the formula on Sunday' " (Kimmel 1996:246). The separate spheres of men and women were thus maintained, though experts deemed them permeable enough for men to participate regularly as a helper to the mother. *Life* magazine declared 1954 "the year of the domestication of American men," even though the baby boom was in full swing and men were contributing little to direct child care or housework (Kimmel 1996:245). Suburban domesticity, replete with isolated mother-intensive parenting, was certainly not trouble-free for many women, as reflected in high depression levels among stay-at-home housewives in the 1950s and 1960s (Rubin 1976; Warren 1987). Nevertheless, a majority of working-class American women aspired to full-time homemaker status during the baby boom era.

Men's Care Work in an Era of Employed Mothers

In 1950, families with breadwinner fathers and stay-at-home mothers were twice as numerous in the United States as any other family type. Today, there are twice as many two-earner families as families where only the man works. The rapid increase in the number of mothers holding jobs is arguably the most important social trend of the past half-century. Today, three of four mothers with school-age children and two of three mothers with preschool children are in the paid labor force, most working full time. In a dramatic departure from the 1950s, most mothers return to work before their first child turns one year old (U.S. Bureau of the Census 1999).

Since midcentury, with more mothers likely to be employed, under the influence of an ideal of "companionate marriage," and in response to the second wave of the women's movement, many observers expected men to assume responsibility for a larger share of family care work. Several decades of research, however, have shown that most women still perform the bulk of the domestic work, remain the child-care experts, and continue to serve as the emotional managers for their families. Research also shows that family divisions of labor usually become more gender-segregated upon having children: men tend to work more hours at paid jobs, but sometimes also increase their contributions to child care. New mothers, in contrast, tend to work fewer hours on the job and begin to put in significantly more hours of housework and child care (Cowan and Cowan 1992; Johnson and Huston 1998; MacDermid, Huston, and McHale 1990; Sanchez and Thomson 1997; Shelton 1992). Although both men and women do more care work after children arrive, since women increase their domestic labor hours more than men, they end up doing a larger proportionate share of family work, especially as the number of children increases (Greenstein 1996; Hersch and Stratton 1994; Presser 1994; Shelton and John 1996). Since we typically assume that women should be responsible for managing both housework and child care, it is not surprising that employed wives enjoy less leisure and experience more stress than employed husbands, especially when they have little control over setting schedules for the work (Barnett and Shen 1997; Bird and Ross 1993; Hochschild and Machung 1989; Robinson and Godbey 1997; Schor 1991).

Gendered divisions of family care work thus remain the norm, despite the fact that men have been doing more at home. Mothers are still more likely than fathers to take time off from their jobs to provide continuous child care, spending significantly more time than fathers feeding, dressing, cleaning, and watching young children. Studies find that mothers spent double the time of fathers in these activities, even though many men did increase the time they spend with preschool and school-age children during the 1980s and 1990s, especially in conventional gender-typed activities like physical play, but also in direct child care (Coltrane and Adams in press; Levine and Pittinsky 1997; O'Connell 1994; Parke 1996; Pleck 1997). The child-care gap between mothers and fathers is narrowest in two-earner families and continues to shrink, at least when measured as time spent interacting with children. For example, Levine and Pittinsky (1997:25–26) found that between 1977 and 1997, employed fathers increased their time interacting with children (in both care and play) by one half-hour per workday, from 1.8 to 2.3 hours, compared to about three hours per workday for employed mothers during both time periods.

Some recent attempts to measure men's involvement in family work include more careful consideration of the specific types of father-child contact involved, especially distinguishing between routine child-care activities and involvement in play or leisure (McBride 1990; Parke 1995; Radin 1994). As Pleck (1997) notes, these newer forms of measuring father involvement move beyond simple accounting of time spent with a child to focus on specific activities that are likely to promote positive child development. When compared to mothers, fathers are likely to spend a much greater proportion of their interaction time with children in play or leisure; such activities have been found to make unique contributions to children's emotional self-regulation and social competence (Parke 1996).

Several researchers have also stressed the importance of the responsibility dimension of father involvement, which includes the more hidden managerial aspects of child care. Managerial functions refer to the ways in which parents organize and arrange the child's environment, thereby regulating the child's access and opportunities for social contacts (Parke 1999). In infancy, management includes setting boundaries for play, taking the child to the doctor, arranging day care, or setting up opportunities for interacting with others. In middle childhood, managerial responsibility includes regulating meals, baths, clean-up, and continuing to monitor or arrange for play with other children. Parke (1999) suggests that the managerial role that parents play may be just as important for child development as time spent in face-to-face interaction, since the amount of time children spend in social environments far exceeds their time interacting directly with parents. As Pleck (1997) notes, mothers remain child-care managers in the vast majority of households, but evidence from some studies indicates that at least some fathers are taking a more active role in this domain (Coltrane 1996; Risman and Johnson-Sumerford 1998).

The gender gap in housework has also narrowed in the past several decades, albeit more slowly than for child care. According to several large-scale surveys, the five most time-consuming of the major household tasks associated with family care are (1) meal preparation or cooking; (2) housecleaning; (3) shopping for groceries and household goods; (4) washing dishes or cleaning up after meals; and (5) laundry (including washing, drying, folding, ironing, and mending clothes) (Blair and Lichter 1991; Robinson and Godbey 1997). These routine household tasks are not only the most time-consuming, they are also less optional and less able to be postponed than other tasks (e.g., yard care, gardening, household repairs). Studies consistently show that the routine housework remains gender segregated, with married women reporting that they spend about three times as much time on these tasks as their husbands (Coltrane 2000; Demo and Acock 1993; Presser 1994; Shelton 1992).

Over the past few decades, however, women have reduced, and men have increased, their hourly contributions to these important housework tasks. For example, Robinson and Godbey (1997), using an intensive time-diary data collection technique, report that American women's time spent on housework declined substantially between 1965 and 1985, with employed women shifting considerable housework to the weekends and doing one-third less than other women. At the same time, men's hourly contributions doubled. As a consequence, men's proportionate contribution to housework more than doubled between 1965 and 1985: from 15 to 33 percent. Broadly similar results have been reported using national survey data such as the National Survey of Families and Households, the National Survey of Children, the National Longitudinal Surveys of Young Women, and the Panel Study of Income Dynamics (Coltrane 2000). Most studies also show that when wives have more equal levels of employment and earnings, and when both spouses hold more liberal attitudes toward women's rights, they tend to share more (but not most) of the housework. More balanced divisions of housework, in turn, are associated with wives perceiving more fairness, experiencing less depression, and enjoying higher marital satisfaction (Coltrane 2000).

In summary, we have witnessed a noticeable (i.e., statistically significant) change in the gender distribution of family work in the United States, but since wives still do at least twice as much of the work as their husbands, we can also conclude that divisions of household labor continue to be shaped strongly by gender. In order to explore how and why this might change in the future, it is useful to ask what we consider reasonable to expect from men as fathers and husbands. One way to investigate this topic is to evaluate what family researchers and policy makers have been advocating as ways to measure father involvement.

Gender-Segregated versus Activity-Based Models of Care Work

Following a fatherhood summit called by then vice president Al Gore, a recent Federal Interagency Forum report on fathers proposed a gender-segregated model of fatherhood highlighting men's roles in shaping their children's life chances (Federal Interagency Forum on Child and Family Statistics 1998). In a chapter on "conceptualizing male parenting," the report's authors proposed that paternal involvement should be defined theoretically as containing four major dimensions: (1) nurturing and providing care; (2) moral and ethical guidance; (3) economic provisioning or breadwinning; and (4) support of female partners. In contrast to much of the recent research on father-child interaction as noted above, these authors claimed that fathers' direct nurturing and care is the least important of the ways that fathers can contribute to their children's development. Echoing the theme of natural gender differences as discussed in the early part of this chapter, the authors suggested that men's economic support was the most important contribution men could make to their children, followed by physical and emotional support of wives, and by moral and ethical leadership. Finally, labeling direct care work by fathers as "secondary," they implied that we should be measuring and encouraging more "traditional" styles of fatherhood: "While most observers view fathers' nurturance as a desirable form of fathering, there continues to be widespread disagreement about the importance of this dimension relative to other aspects of fathering. Even though (or perhaps because) this dimension approximates 'mothering' in many respects, it is almost universally viewed as secondary — less important than mothering by mothers, and less important than the other dimensions of fatherhood" (Federal Interagency Forum on Child and Family Statistics 1998:109–10).

Like some other researchers (e.g., Doherty 1997; Hawkins and Dollahite 1997; Palkovitz 1997), these researchers claim that the moral and ethical aspects of fatherhood should be given more research attention and granted a larger role in academic discourse about families. According to this view, moral and ethical guidance is achieved through direct instruction by fathers (and mothers), but also through children's identification with and imitation of their fathers (Federal Interagency Forum on Child and Family Statistics 1998:110). While the economic provisioning dimension of fatherhood is mentioned as important in most studies, breadwinning is rarely compared to other variables to ascertain its relative influence on child development. The fourth aspect of paternal involvement, according to the Federal Interagency Forum Report (1998:110)—fathers' emotional, practical, and psychosocial support of female partners — is another neglected aspect of men's family involvement that is more important than interaction with and care for children.

Embracing a gender-segregated (read "separate spheres") view of parenting, some researchers are thus calling for treating breadwinning as *the* central dimension of paternal involvement (e.g., Blankenhorn 1995; Popenoe 1996). Apparently ignorant of historical research showing how the "good-provider role" was short-lived and dependent on a unique set of historical economic conditions (e.g., Bernard 1981; Hood 1986), some researchers also seem to ignore the emerging literature, noted above, that shows how men have performed a wide variety of family care work in the past. We suggest that the recent call for a return to gender-segregated models of fatherhood research reflects a reactionary backlash against women's increasing autonomy, much as the initial development of separate spheres ideology reflected men's increasing insecurity about the erosion of patriarchal privilege at the turn of the century (Kimmel 1996).

The brief historical review presented above suggests a different approach from that proposed by the defenders of so-called traditional fatherhood (e.g., Blankenhorn 1995). Although we acknowledge that fathers' breadwinning, modeling, and support of mothers have been important historically, we emphatically note that men's direct participation in childrearing also has a long history and substantial potential to influence family dynamics. Rather than assuming that the direct care work fathers do is least important, we suggest that it is likely to be the most important. We agree with Hawkins and Dollahite (1997:20-21) that "fatherhood" describes cultural or normative expectations, whereas "fatherwork"— including activities like housework and child care that involve men in sustained effort — describes the actual conduct of generative fathering. While acknowledging that the more positional or structural aspects of fatherhood can influence children and families, we are more concerned with direct and indirect fatherwork — those father-child interactions and child maintenance activities that are recognized as having substantial direct influence on child development, marital satisfaction, and family well-being.

We therefore adopt what we call an activity-based approach to men's provision of care, rather than the gender-segregated approach described earlier. An activity-based approach focuses on the activities that men (or women) perform. In particular, it focuses on those interactions that foster positive child development (such as nurturing and direct instruction), those management activities that help structure children's learning environments (such as anticipating children's needs and regulating social contacts), and those maintenance activities that sustain family members (such as routine dressing, cooking, and cleaning). Rather than assuming that men are far less capable than women of performing the emotional and physical tasks that support children, an activity-based approach assumes that both men and women can be important nurturers. This approach reflects our understanding of both contemporary and historical patterns of family work. It is important to note that such activities are just as "traditional" as breadwinning, which only became associated with fatherhood after the relatively recent historical development of market economies and waged labor. The activity-based approach that we advocate shifts the focus from what we assume men and women can do to what they actually do. Significantly, it allows researchers to focus on the ways that men and women express a full range of human capacities. According to recent research on child and adult development, an activity-based approach to care work also carries the greatest potential for meeting the future needs of women, men, and children (Coltrane 1998; Coltrane and Parke 1998).

Raising Expectations for Fathers

Women still perform most of the routine cooking and cleaning chores necessary to maintain households, put in most of the hours spent on direct child care, and take responsibility for the majority of the home management and emotional labor that sustains children and families. Nevertheless, compared to the 1950s, 1960s, or 1970s, fewer American husbands are ignoring the routine needs of children or confining their efforts to the occasional outside chore. As noted above, when men do more of the routine family work, women say the division of labor is more fair, are less depressed, and enjoy higher levels of marital satisfaction. Care work by husbands and fathers is not trivial.

As our historical analysis suggests, care work is socially constructed. It represents a complex set of material and symbolic practices that cannot be separated from cultural beliefs, structural constraints, and the rituals of everyday life. The task before us is to specify in more detail how the performance of care work in different families is embedded in various social and economic reproductive processes and how its distribution will affect families in the future. The conditions promoting the sharing of care work between women and men — including more equal earnings, more similar employment schedules, and gender egalitarian ideologies — are all more likely than they were just a decade ago. In addition, men's contributions to direct child care and housework appear to be rising. Since men's care work has been found to promote positive outcomes for both children and fathers, and because men's partial assumption of responsibility for housework and child care reduces wives' stress, why do we not ask men to do more?

According to our review of the history of fathering practices in this country, men have always had at least a minimal role in direct child care, and their involvement has ranged from very little to significant responsibility. Many fathers have focused on the more fun and playful activities, and our analysis shows how such activities can co-exist with, or even sustain, patriarchal family practices. Our primary concern has been to emphasize the historical precedents for men to do more of the mundane and routine child and home maintenance tasks and emotional labor that we label care work. In this, we part ways with some of the recent advocates of "responsible" fatherhood. They claim that academics have focused too much on how men interact with children and put too much emphasis on the things that men do not do. In place of this "deficit model," they promote what they take to be an older vision of fatherhood, one that focuses on the breadwinning and moral leadership that males are supposedly biologically equipped to provide. We suggest that the historical record tells a much more complicated and variable story about the kinds of paternal care that are possible or desirable. Instead of invoking a history of fatherhood that helps men feel better about their limited contributions to care work, we think that a more complete understanding of history can also encourage us to raise our expectations for fathers' involvement in care work.

Using a partial, selective, and nostalgic history of fatherhood to promote a categorical distinction between mothering and fathering carries some profound intellectual and political risks. Most mothers and fathers do act differently, and many are happy with that arrangement. But even apparently benign assumptions about inherent parenting differences resonate with claims made by those who advocate a return to patriarchal family arrangements (Coltrane and Allan 1994; Coltrane and Hickman 1992). Critical theories show that an emphasis on essential gender difference helps men maintain power over women and other, less privileged men (Connell 1987; Lorber 1994). Men's domestic incompetence and emotional inexpressiveness (both feigned and real) also act as resources which men use to protect their privileged status (Goode 1992; Sattel 1998). Accepting gender differences in caring as natural thus serves to maintain hierarchical structures both inside families and in the larger society. Whether absent or physically present and doing little, the ability of fathers to stay aloof from day-to-day family life is fundamentally linked to the reproduction of systemic male dominance (e.g., Coltrane 1996; Hochschild 1989; Thompson and Walker 1989).

Because categorical beliefs in parenting and gender differences mask relations of power and inequality, asking fathers to do more family work is both discomforting and necessary. It may be unrealistic to assume that men will do half the parenting and housework as long as the labor market favors men, but we should not automatically set significantly lower standards for fathers than for mothers. We need to stop assuming that men are not fully capable of nurturing children, or that asking them to fold laundry or clean toilets is somehow beneath them. If we are to break down the patriarchal assumptions of separate spheres ideology, we should make direct comparisons between fathers' and mothers' care work. This will likely produce discomfort and marital conflict, but these direct comparisons can also open productive dialogues about women's stereotypical family gatekeeping and men's stereotypical inattentiveness to home and children (Coltrane and Adams in press). Instead of seeing an increase in men's discomfort as justification for lowering expectations and returning to patriarchal definitions of fatherhood, we ought to view men's and women's struggles to share more family work as an opportunity for promoting gender equity in families and in society at large. History tells us that such struggles are rarely completely successful, but we can take comfort in knowing that our future actions are neither fixed by biology nor determined by a simple gender-segregated model of care passed down through the generations.

Claiming the Right to Care

*T*hroughout Western societies, motherhood has long been seen as women's "natural" function and even duty, yet the *right* to mother is not firmly established in the law, nor do social arrangements guarantee women the wherewithal to fulfill their socially and culturally ordained obligations. These conflicting values are nowhere more evident than in contemporary America, where motherhood continues to be extolled but where individual women must claim the right to actually *be* mothers.

The conditions under which such claims are made, however — and their ultimate success — differ according to women's race, class, and marital status. The *defense* of motherhood has divided along these lines because the assault on motherhood has been similarly divided. While poor mothers have been targeted by public policy, working- and middle-class mothers are subject to more subtle cues from family, community, and the wider culture. Married women in income brackets ranging from working-class to upper-middle-class feel that they must defend their choice to be "stay-at-home moms" against expectations that they participate in the paid labor force. For poor and low-income mothers, especially single women of color, the situation is very different. Not having the benefit of a husband's financial support, they are forced to seek public assistance. While this course was never easy, under the terms of the Personal Responsibility and Work Opportunity Act of 1996, it is no longer a viable option. By requiring nearly all applicants to seek paid employment, the new law denies low-income women the right to care for their own children or other family members (Mink 1998:133).

In the debate surrounding passage of this legislation, poor women's claims that they were already performing valuable work as caretakers went largely unheard. Legislators on both sides of the issue, determined to "end welfare as we know it," restricted the definition of "work" to wage-earning activities outside the home, and no amount of lobbying on the part of either welfare recipients or their advocates could alter the discourse.[1] Congressional refusal to acknowledge the value of caregiving was deeply rooted in long-standing assumptions about which groups of women "deserved" to be supported as full-time mothers at home, and which ones should be compelled to work (Goodwin 1997).

Women on public assistance began mobilizing to claim their right to mother as early as 1966, when, in the face of the first federal efforts to replace welfare with workfare, they formed the National Welfare Rights Organization (U.S. Congress 1968:77–79; Tillmon 1972). Married working- and middle-class women did not perceive the need to defend at-home motherhood until the women's movement got under way in the 1970s. As motherhood advocate Arlene Rossen Cardozo complained in 1976, "The woman who elects to stay at home to raise her family has received little social support for her decision during the past decade" (Cardozo 1976:ix). She went on:

> Feminism has helped to free the single woman, the childless married woman, and the working mother for jobs outside home without sex bias and for pursuit of their choices without stigma. But feminist spokespersons, in their zeal to create an alternative view, have established — intentionally or unintentionally — a position antithetical to a woman's staying at home to raise her family. (Ibid.)

According to Cardozo, motherhood suffered from the growing expectation that *all* women would work outside the home, whether or not they had children, and from the simultaneous devaluation of the work mothers did in the home.

While Cardozo regarded hostility to motherhood as an unintended consequence of the women's movement, later advocates came to blame feminists for the plight of at-home motherhood. In their view, feminism has so permeated the political culture that "our point of view is often ignored when policy is discussed" (Myers 1997:1). After attending a conference of women leaders at Harvard University in 1997, Catherine M. Myers, a representative of Mothers at Home (MAH), a national organization founded in 1984, observed, "All of the participants I met were polite, but some seemed puzzled, or even threatened, by my presence" (ibid.).

Comparing Mothers' Organizations

The current wave of organizations by and for mothers are the latest in a history of American mothers' clubs and movements that traces back to the mid-nineteenth century (Ladd-Taylor 1994).[2] The initial purpose of these first organizations was to help women become better mothers; soon, however, women began to seek ways to apply the values they attached to motherhood (nurturance, sensitivity, morality, etc.) to society as a whole, deploying a politics of reform that historians have labeled "maternalist" (Koven and Michel 1993:Introduction). The majority of these early mother-activists came from the middle or upper class, but, following the racial politics of the period, their organizations were strictly segregated (Gordon 1991; Boris 1993).

It is instructive to compare the contemporary mothers' movement with the earlier one. Today's expressions of mothers' vocation differ subtly from those of the late nineteenth and early twentieth centuries. Because feminism succeeded in "denaturalizing" motherhood as women's destiny, mothers now present themselves as making a self-conscious choice to stay at home with children. Moreover, because full-time motherhood is no longer (in their view) a social expectation, they feel the need to justify and defend their choice.[3] Finally, though today's organizations are not formally segregated, they often divide along racial as well as class lines. Unlike maternalist clubwomen of the late nineteenth and early twentieth centuries, however, contemporary motherhood advocates tend to be more self-serving; that is, they seek to address their own needs and those of women like themselves, rather than presenting those needs as symbolic of larger social issues requiring broad political solutions.

As a survey of their literature and Web sites reveals, current organizations of stay-at-home mothers vary widely in size and range across the political, religious, and cultural spectrums. At the conservative end, one can find a number of small, religiously oriented, independent groups and individuals. Hearts at Home, founded in 1994, in Normal, Illinois, presents itself as a "non-denominational, Christ-centered, professional organization for mothers at home or those who want to be." Its members "desire to exalt God while educating and encouraging children in their personal and family lives. . . . We want moms to understand their God-given value and the important role they play in society" (Hearts at Home n.d.). Similarly, Connie Fourré Zimney, author of *In Praise of Homemaking: Affirming the Choice to be a Mother-at-Home*, calls for a theology of homemaking (1984:14) and asserts, "If we want to pass our faith on to our children, it is essential that we make life with God *concrete* for them" (ibid.:124). Zimney conducts workshops on "Christian Homemaking" from her home in Hamel, Minnesota. In contrast to these localized efforts, the Family Research Council (FRC), a conservative think tank based in Washington, D.C., operates prominently on the national stage, funding research, tracking legislation, and publishing a bimonthly journal, *Family Policy*. Its president, Gary Bauer, appears frequently on the talk show circuit and lobbies vocally on behalf of conservative family policy (Family Research Council n.d.).[4]

Mothers at Home (MAH) is one of several national organizations located at midspectrum. Founded in 1984, its mission includes "affirming the choice to be home throughout the many stages of motherhood; . . . correcting society's misconceptions and refuting stereotypes about parents and children; . . . [and] encouraging and enabling mothers to preserve and improve the opportunity for all women to choose home" (Mothers at Home, "Missions and Values" n.d.:1). While explicitly secular, its values nonetheless mesh well with those of groups like the FRC. (Indeed, representatives of both groups appeared at a 1998 symposium on the needs of children hosted by conservative senator Daniel Coats [R-IN], chair of the Senate Subcommittee on Children and Families [Connole 1998].) But in certain respects MAH is also more flexible than the conservative organizations. Under the rubric of "at-home mothers," for example, MAH includes those "who choose to work from home or in various part-time or flex-time capacities" (Mothers at Home, "Mission and Values" n.d.:1).

More flexible still is FEMALE (Formerly Employed Mothers At the Leading Edge), "an international not-for-profit organization supporting sequencing mothers — women who have altered their career paths in order to care for their children at home" (FEMALE n.d.:1). FEMALE

> advocates for public and employment policies that accommodate sequencing — the combination of work and family in a number of creative ways that begin to meet the financial and personal needs of women and their families. We recognize that some mothers will continue to work full-time, for financial or personal reasons, and that some mothers will contribute to society as full-time caregivers until their children leave home. (Ibid.:2)

Both FEMALE and MAH operate at several levels simultaneously, offering support through community groups, conducting research, and disseminating their views through a variety of public fora, including speaking, publishing, and lobbying. FEMALE, in addition, works closely with both working women and employers, advocating adaptable work arrangements such as short- and long term leaves, and encouraging "best practices" by presenting "annual Family Friendly Business Awards to exceptional employers who recognize and accommodate their employees' family needs" (ibid.:5).

Another moderate large-scale organization, the national association of At-Home Mothers, presents itself primarily as a commercial enterprise. In addition to moral support, it offers dues-paying members a number of benefits, including *At-Home Mother Magazine*, free "Info Guides," and the opportunity to apply for a $500 cash grant to start a home business. "Our mission is simple," says the At-Home Mothers Web page: "to support the at-home motherhood lifestyle. We are not an advocacy group, nor do we have a religious or political agenda. We simply offer practical information, inspiration, services, support and encouragement for mothers at home and those who would like to be."

In a similar vein, Ellen Parlapiano and Patricia Cobe (1996:5) publish a guide urging women to become "mompreneurs"—running small businesses out of their own homes—in order to gain family flexibility and control of their lives and to offer their children positive role models. According to the two writer-mothers, thousands of women are making this choice after discovering that the "mommy track" will not take them "up the corporate ladder" and "through the glass ceiling." Unlike most advocates for at-home motherhood, who argue that their mothering *is* work, Parlapiano and Cole make a distinction between work-at-home moms and non-earning mothers or homemakers.

Other Web sites grapple with the difficulties facing mothers in specific occupations. For example, more than 150 women in the music industry have connected to "Mother Rock Star . . . a Network," a Web site that offers crucial services ranging from retail promotion and publicity to child-care referrals. It also promotes an annual Women in Music Symposium. Founder Annie Melvin describes herself thus:

> Ten years after the enchantment of rock 'n' roll has worn off, but still too stubborn to give up the freedom and great folks I am surrounded by, I find myself HERE. Not playing anymore, but trying to mesh motherhood with music industry. Mother Rock Star was inspired by my discovery that I am certainly not alone in this mama/music reality. (Mother Rock Star)

Mother Rock Star leads us to the radical end of the cultural spectrum and the Web site of Feminist Mothers at Home (n.d.). Here one can find links to the "Webpage of a Mad Housewife," which laments, over the photo of a newborn, "The Mad Housewife is too busy being one to play one on the Web," and to "hipMama," which, among other things, answers the crucial question, "Will nipple piercing interfere with breastfeeding?" (hipMama n.d.)

As numerous women's historians have discovered, advice to mothers is not new (Margolis 1984; see also bibliography in Apple and Golden 1997:565–66). Even in periods when motherhood was vaunted as woman's supreme duty and the highest fulfillment of her nature, mothers felt the need to turn to expert guides and form early versions of "support groups."[5] Few contemporary advocates present motherhood as natural, but rather something that must be learned, encouraged, and continually supported. Yet while seeking to help mothers who have chosen to stay at home, contemporary advice books and Web pages may actually be aggravating modern mothers' dilemma by creating the expectation of what sociologist Sharon Hays (1996) calls "intensive mothering." The "cultural contradictions of motherhood," according to Hays, "put mothers in a double bind between achieving or maintaining middle-class status (or higher) through paid employment and fulfilling the dictates of this new form of parenting." She believes that no matter which option women choose, they will feel conflicted (chap. 1; see also Villani and Ryan 1997).

Emotional Economics

As the authors of the MAH guide *What's a Smart Woman Like You Doing at Home?* observe, for both groups of mothers, "guilt takes many forms" (Burton, Dittmer, and Loveless 1992:30). Wage-earning mothers feel guilty "when [they] have to accept less than the best childcare arrangements; . . . when [they] miss schools events or . . . don't have time to volunteer as often as [they] think [they] should; . . . when [they] end up using [their] 'quality time' hours . . . to do routine household chores and errands; . . . when the house isn't spotless . . . and the cookies aren't homemade" (p. 31). The litany of stay-at-home mothers also reveals the strain of their decisions. They feel guilty for "leaving the entire responsibility to meet the family's financial obligations to [their] husbands; . . . not using [their] education; . . . not contributing something 'important' to society; . . . [and] letting down the women's movement" (pp. 31–35).

While conceding that wage-earning mothers may indeed have legitimate concerns, MAH, of course, focuses on those who stay at home. The organization's monthly journal, *Welcome Home*, features a regular "Problems and Solutions" column, and those deemed particularly significant are reprinted on the MAH Web site. In the July 1996 issue, for example, readers responded to the mother whose husband refused to support her decision to stay at home. One attributed his attitude to "a lack of knowledge and respect for what you do all day," and described how her husband's attitude had been reversed when she left him to care for their six-month-old for two days while she went off to take a course. Another suggested that the troubled mother acknowledge that her decision "adds to his level of stress. . . . . Encourage him to tell you what is worrying him. Share with him what you hope to achieve by being at home." A third was simply practical: "Get the housework and errands done while he's at work, have a hot meal ready when he comes home" (Mothers at Home, "Problems and Solutions," 1996:1–2).

To convince husbands that staying at home makes sense, several of the MAH respondents echoed a line of advice frequently found elsewhere, namely presenting mothers' work in financial terms. They offered two different tactics: either calculating the net income from mother's paid employment, or totaling up the annual cost of the services routinely provided by at-home mothers. As one woman pointed out, "Even if I found a job on the high end of the pay scale, by subtracting day care and transportation I would be left with a mere $80 a week" (ibid.). Another calculated that the market value of all the tasks she performed (child care, transportation, running errands, cleaning, laundry, planning and preparing meals, etc.) was nearly $36,000 per year. While this woman estimated most of the tasks at minimum wage, she put a higher value on child care on the assumption that "maternal care is generally considered priceless" (Sefton 1998:1–2). As one MAH mother put it, "I feel that nobody can love, understand, and care for my children like I can. If we owned the Hope Diamond, would we pay someone

$3 an hour to clean, polish and protect it?" (Mothers at Home, "Problems and So-
lutions," 1996:2).

While these women willingly cast motherhood as a form of work or even a
profession, others are reluctant to present it in those terms. This is particularly
true for religiously motivated advocates. Connie Zimney (1984), for example,
likes to think of her homemaking as a form of artistry and urges women to create
their homes as spiritual spaces for themselves and their families. Though she
does not eschew the term *work* for what she does, she rejects the idea that it
should be paid. "The homemaker can discover her worth . . . by a look at the
value of the work for other people, by its role in personal development, and by
drawing on the church's theology of work" (Zimney 1984:86). Similarly, Donna
Otto (1991) refers to "the ministry of being a mom" (chap. 3).

Secular women also emphasize the nonmonetary rewards of staying at home;
for Arlene Cardozo (1976:148), "forming close human relationships is the first
priority"—something she contends cannot be done in the workplace. Indeed, to
be carried out fully, Cardozo recommended that the decision to put relationships
first should involve the entire family. She praised a physician who gave up his
downtown office so he could practice general medicine out of his home and thus
integrate his work with his family life.[6]

While some at-home mothers lament their lost incomes, others wear their reduced lifestyles like a badge of honor, implicitly criticizing the materialism of
high-income households that require dual incomes.[7] "We eliminated going out to
dinner," one woman told *Ladies' Home Journal*. "And our furniture is getting tat-
tered. But whenever I think how nice it would be to have a new sofa, I think of
all the benefits of not working and I realize I don't want those material posses-
sions that badly" (Wagner and Grant 1984:89). As former professionals explained
their decision to stay at home, a tone of self-righteousness inevitably seemed to
creep into their accounts, with the implication that the higher the status and income of the jobs they have given up, the greater their sacrifice and thus the more
significant their performance as mothers (ibid. 1984).

Policy Implications

Most advocates of nonmaterialistic at-home motherhood would reject the message of the "mompreneurs," who tell women they can have it all: flexible hours
and workplaces, time with their children, *and* substantial incomes. Few, however, are entirely oblivious to the financial implications of their choice—implications that are, according to critics, only exacerbated by contemporary public
policy. Conservatives oppose the current federal emphasis on funding child
care, since such services do not benefit families with mothers at home. "Such a
narrowly targeted, but well-funded benefit . . . discriminates against low-to-
middle-income American families who are struggling to keep one parent at

home with their children," complains FRC representative Charmaine Crouse Yoest (1998:3—4).

While the more centrist MAH endorses "family-friendly employment practices" that make it easier for mothers to work part-time or put in flexible hours, the organization also calls for more policy supports for families with full-time at-home mothers. These might include a lower tax burden, a higher personal exemption, an additional tax credit or deduction for each preschool child, regardless of the parents' work status, and a more equitable dependent care tax credit (Burton, Dittmer, and Loveless 1992:151—52). According to the MAH, the proposed tax measures would give parents the financial flexibility to choose either at-home motherhood or child care.

But for poor and very low-income mothers—those below the $20,000 to $25,000 bracket which, according to Yoest (1998:3), has "the largest number of at-home mothers"—and especially for single mothers, caring for their own children at home is not an option. Pressed by "welfare reform" to find employment—in some states without even minimal training or job search preparation—they do not have the right to choose. Their plight does not, however, concern the advocates of at-home motherhood, most of whom appear to be married and relatively stable financially. Except in the literature of the "mompreneurs" and their ilk, family income is more or less taken for granted in the form of the ever-present Dad. Fathers are at best supportive, at the least neutral, and at worst hostile toward mothers who decide to stay home, but few seem to quit their jobs or abandon their families. Unless they are laid off or fall ill, most continue to provide.[8]

The spate of books and Web sites suggests that large numbers of at-home mothers are joining forces, but they are doing so in the interest of promoting a privatized, individualistic vision of motherhood. The rhetoric repeatedly invokes the pleasures, virtues, and rewards of mothers caring for *their own* children in *their own* homes. Although advocates encourage sharing experiences and information, they disdain collective solutions to mothers' problems; "commercial child care" becomes the despised symbol of all that must be avoided.[9] Across the political spectrum, the policy reforms proposed are designed to facilitate parent "choice," but not to build public institutions and services. It is but a short step from at-home motherhood to home schooling and the further dismantling of America's already fragile welfare state. Such a politics will do little for the most vulnerable American mothers—those struggling to care for and protect their children and other family members under the conditions of poverty and discrimination.

The Impact of Social Activism on Gender Identity and Care Work

Women's Activism in the
Toxic Waste Movement

Social movement activism frequently causes an upheaval in how women activists define themselves and their roles, particularly movements formed around care work issues, such as the controversy over toxic waste. Gender identities, histories of activism, and movement experiences combine to shape and reshape gender identity. As women become active, they redefine who they are; their care work shifts as an expression of that identity change. Yet, the degree of that change varies. For example, for some women in this chapter—those experienced in activism, with gender identities rooted in public and private sphere participation— change was subtle and preceded this study, transforming at an earlier date with their *initial* activism. For other women—those new to activism, with a gender identity primarily vested in stay-at-home motherhood—the affirming experience of activism led to an expanded gender identity and shifting and dynamic care work responsibilities. These women participated in the movement precisely because of their care work responsibilities, their children and home, and they legitimized their participation on that basis. Their positive and empowering experiences with activism, however, initiated a profound but not complete transformation of their identities, as their activism became another expression of their care work responsibilities. With participation in the movement, though, their gender identities stretched to include activism on behalf of their children as *part of* their gender identity and part of their definition of motherhood and womanhood. Hence, the locus of their care work shifted.

The Impact of Activism on Individual Activists: A Review of the Literature

Activism is potentially galvanizing. While movements seek institutional change as their goal, intense participation may catalyze change in individual actors. The social movement literature is bountiful with narratives and research suggesting that the individual actors change or grow as a result of their participation. Accounts of Love Canal activism note a shift in social supports: activists were more likely to form new relationships and friendships, while nonactivists continued to rely on family relationships for social support (Edelstein 1988). Love Canal activists were also transformed in their view of their own abilities, experiencing enhanced self-worth, self-control, and personal efficacy (Edelstein 1988).

Freudenberg (1984) and Krauss (1993b) suggest that the activists become more politically aware. They may develop a critique of the political system and their own disenfranchisement. This may mark a dramatic shift in the individual's understanding of politics, power, gender, and class. Similarly, Szasz (1994) suggests activism can transform the actors' view of the world, moving them toward a radical critique of the social world, as in the case of Lois Gibbs's transformation, "from apolitical housewife and mother into dedicated activist, a leader, someone who can articulate a broadly progressive perspective" (Szasz 1994:153). According to Brown and Ferguson (1995), women toxic waste activists gain a sense of power as they become skilled movement actors and experts on toxic waste issues. That empowerment might alter care work responsibilities and arrangements within the family. Krauss (1993a) found that the white, working-class women in her study gained a sense of empowerment, became more self-confident and assertive, and, consequently, developed new relationships with their spouses and children.

Other authors point to the potentially negative consequences of activism. McAdam's (1988) study of the 1964 Freedom Summer civil rights volunteers documents the impact of their involvement on life experiences: twenty years later, Freedom Summer activists divorced at higher rates than those who signed up but did not participate. Higher rates of separation and divorce are also associated with toxic waste activism (Brown and Ferguson 1995), as is marital conflict in general (Zeff, Love, and Stuits 1989). Lois Gibbs attributes her divorce to the transformative effect of her Love Canal activism. Activism, and the time and resources devoted to it, can create a strain in marriages, perhaps leading to divorce (see Gibbs Interview, Herda-Rapp 1998).

Change may come in the individual actor's identities as well. Calhoun (1987) suggests that social movement activism provides the backdrop against which identities may be transformed. As sociologists who follow the tradition of symbolic interactionism pose identity, each individual has several shifting and dynamic identities, or self-meanings. And the individual actors have agency to define their identity against the backdrop of their social relations: "Personal identities refer to the meanings attributed to the self by the actor. They are self-designations or self-attributions brought into play or asserted during the course of interaction" (Snow and Anderson 1987:1343). Our identities do not merely emerge from the social context but are carved out by the actor in a reflexive proposition (Giddens 1991), whereby the actor constructs and reconstructs their identity in the context of their interactions. Thus, identity is an interactional accomplishment and is *redefined* with new experiences (Snow and Machalek 1984), including social movement activism. Hence, it is useful to conceptualize identity as involving a process of negotiation that takes place in the social context (Ginsburg and Lowenhaupt Tsing 1990; Howard and Hollander 1997): an active process called *identity work* (Snow and Anderson 1987).

Della Porta and Diani (1999) suggest that change can be especially profound for individuals for whom these activist experiences are new, affecting one's politics, life choices, and the organization of everyday life. As a result of activism, a new or altered identity and set of relations may be negotiated, including a newly configured gender identity and care work affinities and responsibilities. Gender identity may motivate activism — as in the case of mothers motivated to participate in the toxic waste movement because of their womanhood and care work responsibilities — and may be transformed through activism. That is, the way women view themselves and their womanhood impels their activism even as this view changes through activism. Empirical evidence from social movements suggests two possible scenarios in which gender identity can be transformed through activism. In the first pattern, *empowering* experiences in the movement lead to a critique of patriarchy and transformed care work relationships and gender identity, while in the second pattern, an *empowering* ideology but *disempowering* organizational structure likewise leads to a critique of patriarchy and changed care work relationships and gender identity.

In accounts of toxic waste movement activism and its effects, the first pattern is most prominent. Researchers of the movement contend that as women are empowered through movement activism, they come to see both themselves and the position of women differently. According to Hamilton (1990), women toxic waste activists come to the movement without a critique of patriarchy but develop their critique in practice. Moreover, the women may have been motivated by the traditional responsibility of mothers for their children's health — by their care work responsibilities — but, through activism, they develop an awareness and critique of gender roles and the division of care work within their families. Krauss (1993b) contends that the working-class women in her study (which also included the activism of women of color) often initiated a change in the distribution of power in their marital relationships, a consequence of their empowerment:

> As blue-collar women fight to protect their children and communities from hazards posed by toxic wastes, they reevaluate the everyday world of their experience. This leads to a critical examination of traditional assumptions about relationships in the family, community, and society. Traditional beliefs in the working-class culture about home, family, and women's roles serve a crucial function in this process. These beliefs provide the initial impetus for women's involvement in issues of toxic wastes and ultimately become a rich source of empowerment, as women appropriate and reshape traditional language and meanings into an ideology of resistance. (p. 115)

In altering the distribution of power, Krauss suggests, the women are undergoing a change in how they see themselves and their relationships.

Research on the movements of the 1960s, however, suggests a second pattern in which women undergo a transformation as a consequence of a discourse of empowerment and *experiences* of disempowerment, including sexism and inequality, in social movement organizations (e.g., the movement organization's gendered division of labor, as documented by McAdam [1992] and by Thorne [1975]). This inequality was logically inconsistent in the civil rights and New Left movements that espoused but did not practice equality, and as such, spurred the emergence of one branch of the women's movement.

> Feminism was nurtured in that contradiction that the intensification of sexual oppression occurred in the same places where women found new strength, new potential and new self-confidence, where they learned to respect the rebellion of strong women. (Evans 1979:54)

Similarly, Blumberg (1990) contends that women's awareness of their own subordination in the civil rights movement was a by-product of their activism in that movement. Thus, women may develop a critique of patriarchy, which is then incorporated into their gender identity, as a consequence of experiences of inequality, eventuating in transformed relationships. For this scenario to play out, however, this experience must be interpreted as inequality. Such an interpretation is promoted by a consciousness raised and shaped in the movement. Cable (1992) contends, though, that this scenario—of inequality in the movement spurring a larger critique of gender inequality—was unlikely in the toxic waste movement because the movement was not premised on equality. That is, the movement lacks the ideological framework necessary to name and interpret gender stratification in the movement as prohibitive, unequal, and symbolic of women's subordination in the larger culture. Given the absence of a rhetoric of rights, the women's consciousness of gender issues will not be heightened.

All of this suggests that activism can have a profound effect on individual activists, resulting perhaps in empowerment, personal growth, altered personal relationships, and a transformation of the self. What is not analyzed, however, is the way different activist backgrounds, movement experiences, and gender identities converge to transform different social movement actors in different ways. The effects of activism are not uniformly felt by all activists. Rather, they are mediated by past experience, the openness of opportunities within social movement organizations, and gender identity. In the next sections, I explore how toxic waste activism impacts the experienced activists' lives, gender identities, and care work responsibilities. I then inquire as to how gender identity and care work relationships are, in the case of some women activists, redefined and altered through activism, as a consequence of particular movement experiences.

Methods and Sources

The findings presented here are based on a larger study (Herda-Rapp 1998) of three Chicago-area grassroots environmental organizations active on toxic waste issues: Citizens Against Ruining the Environment (CARE), in Lockport, Illinois; the Grand Calumet Task Force (GCTF), in northwest Indiana; and the Human Action Community Organization (HACO), in Harvey, Illinois. CARE emerged quickly in 1995 in response to a proposed construction debris incinerator. HACO had been active for nearly 30 years in social justice issues but adopted an environmental justice platform in the early 1990s when a medical waste incinerator was proposed for Harvey and a municipal waste incinerator was proposed for nearby Robbins. GCTF formed in 1980 in response to pollution of the Grand Calumet River and its harm to sportsmen's activities, but has increasingly focused on a plethora of environmental issues, particularly those related to the link between human health, the river's health, and industrial contamination. Each group was different in class, sex, and ethnic composition. CARE was all white, predominantly female, and predominantly working-class. HACO's core group had an equal mix of black and white, male and female, and working-class and middle-class activists. Roughly one-fifth of GCTF's core group were black, with the remainder white, and slightly more women than men constituted the core group; most were employed in professional-managerial occupations.

The findings presented in this chapter are based on participant observation of each group's meetings and events, analysis of related documents and newspaper accounts, in-depth interviews with 34 core members of the three organizations, and one interview with Lois Gibbs, leader of the Love Canal Homeowners Association and founder of the Citizens Clearinghouse for Hazardous Waste (CCHW). To select the core members, I asked each organizational board member—and later, each interview respondent—to list those people, past and present, who were most involved in the organization. From these lists, I constructed a list of individuals to interview. When names became redundant and no new names were introduced with any recurrence, I concluded the sampling and interviewing.

I conducted one semistructured interview — via telephone or in person — with each respondent. Interviews lasted from 35 minutes to 2.5 hours. I worked from a series of open-ended questions, asking questions about respondents' backgrounds, previous activism, reasons for and the nature of their involvement, restrictions to their involvement, effects of their activism on their lives, and the level of family/spousal support for their activism. In the latter part of the interview, I asked the respondents about their views on gender, gender roles, the division of labor in the home, and gender in their respective organizations.

The Toxic Waste Movement: A Movement of Women

Much of the social science literature suggests women are the predominant actors across social movements (Brown and Ferguson 1995; Farenthold 1988; Morris 1984). The toxic waste movement is a movement characterized by a strong female presence, and, in some cases, its organizations are predominantly female (Brown and Mikkelsen 1990; Cable 1992; Cable and Cable 1995; Edelstein 1988; Hamilton 1990; Levine 1982); one source cited in Brown and Ferguson (1995) estimated that 70 percent of the activists are women. Freudenberg (1984) suggests that the typical activist in the toxic waste movement is a woman, between the ages of 26 and 40, and a homemaker. Adding to this composite, Brown and Ferguson (1995) point out that most were previously not involved in activism, particularly environmental activism. The leadership of the toxic waste movement consists primarily of women as well. The Citizens Clearinghouse for Hazardous Waste (CCHW), which works with 8,000 grassroots organizations, estimates that 80 percent of the organizations are led by women (Miller 1997). Similarly, Szasz (1994) cites an estimate of 70 to 80 percent of the leadership. Levine (1982) reported that the core group active in the Love Canal Homeowners Association was chiefly women. Moreover, toxic waste organizations mobilize around issues that have been coined "women's issues": their families' health. Women's care work responsibilities provide the impetus for action.

Across each of the three organizations included in this study, women were the predominant actors; they held the primary leadership positions and constituted the bulk of the core membership and rank and file. Most were spurred to participate because of threats to human health, often that of their own children, families, and neighbors. Marla (HACO) notes why she became involved in opposing the incinerator:

> It was health concerns first and foremost. There was little children. It was the issue of the kids. If you want to know the truth, being a mother of five, I thought about those kids. And the parents . . . some couldn't afford to move. Some don't have the luxury of moving.

Maureen (HACO) asked, "What else was the fight [against the incinerator] for if not family?" Karen (CARE) cited the higher incidence of cancer among children and the cancer of a neighbor employed at the local refinery, and others in her opposition to the Lockport incinerator. Similarly, Carol and Allyson (CARE) cited concern for their asthmatic children's health as their main fear if the incinerator were to become operational. And "Patricia" (GCTF) remarked that her involvement stemmed from the reality that "the Grand Cal River runs through my neighborhood," resulting in concern for "what was going on and how it affected me and my children, my family, and my other neighbors."

While motivated by the same concerns with human health, activists within the three groups differed in the degree to which gender identities and care work responsibilities were redefined as a consequence of that activism. For some activists, their lengthy activist histories equipped them for the demands of activism, leading to little change in their lives with this newest activist cause.

The Consequences of Activism: The Importance of Previous Activism

Activism in the toxic waste movement initiated changes in CARE, HACO, and GCTF activists, though the effects were mediated by prior activist experience and movement experiences, including the openness of opportunities within each organization. Table 5.1 illustrates responses to the questions, "Has *your life* changed in any way since you became involved in the movement?" and "Have *you* changed in any way since you became involved?"

Previous activist experience—whether the activist was a veteran or was new to activism—mediated the consequences of activism cited by individuals, and by and large, GCTF and HACO activists were veterans of activism and CARE members were neophytes. While veteran activists cited few consequences, new activists experienced many, largely positive, effects on their lives. CARE activists consistently cited the same significant number of consequences and nearly all attributed dramatic changes in their lives to their activism. Aside from the marital problems stemming from their activism, CARE members associated not just many more consequences but also largely positive and affirming consequences with their activism. For many of them, the experiences of activism were new and potentially empowering: gains in self-confidence, enhanced public-speaking abilities, acquisition of new knowledge and political awareness, a return to school. Activism led some CARE members to actively and consciously transform their lives, as Allyson's reflection suggests: "I would say any changes I've made in the last couple years has been because of my involvement with CARE."

The change was more subtle for GCTF and HACO activists and most likely preceded their current activism in the toxic waste movement. Both groups of activists were collectively more experienced in activism and consequently cited fewer consequences. Their activist histories included a range of causes: common

Table 5.1. *Emergent Categories of Activism's Consequences*

HACO (n=11)[1] (11/27)	CGTF (n=14) (7/12)	CARE (n=9) (12/42)
Changed priorities (1)[2]	Involvement in politics or government (2)	New activism/involvements (4)
New abilities (3)	Self-actualization/confidence (2)	Return to school (3)
Personal threats (3)	Environmental practices/personal habits (3)	Distrust of government (3)
Issue expansion (2)	Changed concept of leadership (1)	Speak out/assertive (5)
Financial loss (5)	Changed concept of process (2)	New public speaking (6)
Empowerment (2)	Career opportunity from leadership (1)	Confidence (3)
Personal loss (1)	New knowledge (1)	Aware of economy/politics/ environment connection (2)
More aggressive (1)		Greater political awareness (7)
Family/marital problems (4)		New knowledge (2)
Greater political awareness (3)		Aware of gender roles (1)
New knowledge (2)		Loss of free time (1)
		Family/marital conflict (5)

Notes:

1. Numbers indicate total number of categories/total number of responses.

2. Numbers in parentheses indicate number of times response was given.

Source: Author's calculations.

among them were the student, antiwar, civil rights, and women's movements of the 1960s and '70s, community activism on issues of crime and housing, antipoverty campaigns, neighborhood organizing, patient rights campaigns, and involvement in civic organizations. These involvements were so extensive and constant that one GCTF respondent, Norm, commented that, for him, "It all seems to be part of the same fabric." One HACO activist underscored this pattern when he remarked, "I just didn't become an activist; I just didn't [become] consumed all of a sudden because of an incinerator." This extensive and constant activism, however, served to prepare the members of GCTF and HACO for the effects of their participation. These veteran activists were better able to anticipate the course of their activism and divert problems associated with it. As Charlotte (GCTF) suggested, "these are intense avocations," but having been involved in activism for years, the consequences were known and anticipated. For the members of GCTF and most members of HACO, dramatic changes in their lives, their responsibilities, and their identities were uncommon. For them, participation in the toxic waste movement was just a continuation of their activist lives.

These patterned experiences with activism — new activism versus lengthy activist histories — have implications for activists' lives, for family life and care work responsibilities, and for how activists "do gender" (West and Zimmerman 1987). Changes in care work responsibilities and gender identity are mediated by previous activism, with the consequence that activists with different identities and experiences are affected in different ways. A change in gender identity and care work responsibilities was not evident among the women of HACO and GCTF, as their activism and experiences were not new nor particularly galvanizing. Moreover, these activists had worked in the public sphere, developing careers and structuring care work responsibilities around those workplace obligations.

Lin (GCTF), for instance, noted, "I was coming up [as a young activist] right when the women's movement hit. I went through all these movements. It had a *tremendous* impact on my life." With activism in that particular historical context, her gender roles and gender identity "changed along with society, as part of that process." By the date of this study, for Lin and other experienced activists, care work relationships and gender identities had already taken shape through their public sphere participation, including both activism and workplace participation.

Moreover, HACO and GCTF women's gender identities and care work responsibilities were embedded and constructed within a larger cultural context and shift. A majority of GCTF and HACO respondents, both men and women, saw their views about gender, gender roles, care work, the division of labor, and their gender identities changing with the larger social context so that any change *preceded* this relatively recent participation in the toxic waste movement. Lin's remark, noted above, points to the importance of the historical moment. Dorreen (GCTF), now in her 50s, said that her "views were molded really when I was in my twenties, reading all that feminist literature and my opinions have just been verified over the years." GCTF and HACO women's gender identities and care work relationships were carved out of the social context of their youth. As many of these women also began their activism at this time, their gender identities and care work responsibilities may have been configured via activism. As their activist histories are lengthy and few such activists noted recent consequences, it is likely that initial, galvanizing activism — not the activism observed in this study — led these activists to transform their family lives, gender roles, care work responsibilities, and gender identities.

Gender Identity Expansion and Shifting Care Work: The Women of CARE

Whereas GCTF and HACO women illustrate how gender identity and care work are less apt to change with continued social activism, the women of CARE illustrate the dynamic nature of gender identities and care work relationships as related to the newness of the women's activism. Even as CARE women were impelled to participate because of their gender identities and primary responsibility for care work, those identities and responsibilities were redefined as the women were empowered by their new activism and the open opportunities for their leadership in the toxic waste movement. They illuminate a third scenario of individual change — the expansion of gender identity and the shifting of care work responsibilities as a consequence of activism. The change, while not revolutionary, was quite profound, marking expanded self-meanings and new affinities as the women negotiated a gender identity that built public-sphere participation into their previously private-sphere-centered identity, shifting the locus of their care work responsibilities in the process.

CARE women began their activism with a gender identity rooted in the private sphere, in stay-at-home motherhood and primary responsibility for care work. The material condition of their lives shaped their gender identities: with little education beyond high school, the women faced low-wage employment and potentially high day-care costs; those with paying jobs either worked in the home (as telemarketers) or worked part-time; their spouses earned solid wages in blue-collar jobs. Thus, CARE women made the choice to remain out of the paid workforce or to work in settings that could accommodate their family responsibilities, allowing them to direct their energies toward their children and home. For CARE women, womanhood was motherhood, and motherhood mean: choosing children over a career. That particularly configured gender identity, grounded as it was in their responsibility for social reproduction of the family, mobilized CARE women to become active in the movement on behalf of their families' health. They were motivated to become active *because* of their care work responsibilities. Mary, a stay-at-home mother of five, explained her participation in a way that mirrored the sentiments of the other CARE women: "I knew . . .

that this [incinerator] would be spewing toxic garbage and I was not gonna let my children be exposed to this if I could help it." This activism marked a change in the women's civic participation; the proposed incinerator posed such a threat that the women stepped outside of their everyday roles. As Karen put it, "[The incinerator] just made me angry *enough* to do something and fight back."

With the new experiences introduced by activism, CARE women's gender identities expanded. Instead of challenging the very basis of their gender identity, the affirming experience of activism reinforced the base of their gender identity while also stretching its boundaries to include a broader identification and range of activities, though it still centered on care work. With their new activism, what it meant to be a woman and a mother expanded to now include public-sphere activism; though motivated by their private-sphere allegiances, concern for the environment, because of its implications for their families, became embedded in their womanhood. The caring work of motherhood remained central to their identities, but the areas and ways in which they expressed their concern for their families expanded. The *locus* of their care work shifted. Much of that work — activism on behalf of their responsibility for their children — now moved to the public sphere. The empowerment of toxic waste activism and new and largely unrestricted leadership opportunities for women (or at least little awareness of restrictions) promoted this identity expansion, expanded definition of care work, and shifted locus in which care work took place.

The following sections focus on the expansion and negotiation of CARE women's gender identities. Because their gender identities were not linked to public-sphere participation and because the women were new to activism, the potential for identity change was great. They represent, then, one example of gender identity reconfiguration, that of identity expansion and its negotiation.

Stretching Identity: Rock the Boat but Don't Tip It Over

The women of CARE stretched their identities and expanded the locus of their care work with this new activism, but they were no closer to economic autonomy than when they started their activist careers; they had invested heavily in their families and marriages. The combination of these two elements makes abandonment of their previous identities, with all the economic and personal uncertainty associated with divorce and single parenthood, unlikely. In addition, nearly every husband resisted new household arrangements; some resisted vehemently. Combine this reality with the above economic reality, and it quickly becomes obvious that revolutionary change in their relationships, care work responsibilities, and gender identity was highly unlikely and, indeed, unappealing. Instead the women of CARE stretched their identities, so as not to abandon their previous gender identity, nor to revolutionize their lives. This amounted to rocking the boat, but not enough to tip it over.

This stretching involved, in part, shifting the center — the locus — of their care work as those activities moved outside the home. This shift is symbolic of the shift in their view of themselves as women as well. Sandy illustrates the centrality of care work in their lives and suggests a possible decentering with their public-sphere participation:

> I believe we've always been traditional. I mean, what's more traditional than me staying home and raising my children? . . . There's still a traditional role there, but still there's that outside. . . . Maybe from that traditional role we've kind of come out within the CARE group.

Carol, after first becoming involved because she wasn't "about to subject my kids to an incinerator spewing out toxic materials," noted a shift in her gender identity and care work. She and her husband, she said,

> had made an agreement, though originally when the kids were small, that I would stay home with them because we both felt that that was an important time to be around and to be available. So, I never had a problem with that. It wasn't really until I got involved with CARE that I more or less decided that I didn't want to be at home all the time anymore.

She went on to say, "I identify with this more than I have with anything else I've ever done. . . . It has become my life." Carol rationalized her participation and the shifting locus of her care work by linking her movement activities to her private-sphere activities while giving movement activities primacy:

> When you're dealing with people being exposed to toxic materials, and they could die or have respiratory problems for the rest of their lives, how could you, on the other hand, say, "Oh gee, I have three loads of laundry to do, and dusting, and vacuuming, I better get to that first"?

By minimizing the importance of minor household tasks while simultaneously defining her participation as stemming from her private-sphere responsibilities, namely her family's health concerns, Carol can legitimize her social movement participation. In locating her reasons for activism within her care work responsibilities as a mother, Carol stretched her gender identity to include activism in the public sphere, making it part of who she was and how she thought of herself and her womanhood. Carol defined her activism as emanating naturally from her responsibilities as a mother, even as the locus of her activist energies was now outside of the home, marking a change in the locus of her mothering. Similarly, Mary attempted to convince her family that her participation in CARE was for them and that it was consistent with her job (as she saw it) as mother and wife:

"They were why I was fighting . . . and I was telling them that all the time." Her activism, however, added a new dimension to her definition of motherhood.

Carol's case also highlights how, with activism, care work shifts to include new activities (meetings, protests, petitioning, etc.) and some, but not all, old activities (as illustrated below), as care work activities are prioritized and perhaps negotiated:

> The time [away from home] factor was, I think, secondary to the fact that I wasn't doing enough of what he thought I should be doing around the house: laundry, throwing dishes in the dishwasher. I was always available to the kids, running them wherever they had to go. Very few times was I not available to them, because, to me, they're a priority over the laundry and just about everything else. To me, it was like, the laundry shouldn't be an issue because I looked at it as though the laundry and the dusting and all those factors were something that shouldn't even be brought into the equation because we're dealing with life and death.

Certain activities — cleaning, cooking, and so on — were no longer important, yet such activities as child care, playtime, and meeting their children's emotional needs remained fundamental. As the women recount it though, their husbands considered the diminishing homemaking standards to be problematic. They became symbolic of a change in their wives and a change in their own lives and the division of care labor.

CARE women's participation in the political process illustrates a dialectic in which gender identity and politics are reshaped through activism. The women engaged in activism in the public sphere because of their gender identities and social location in the private sphere, yet, their participation in the political process was unorthodox in this community and thereby worked to undermine status quo politics. With this new participation, however, the women consequently expanded their gender identities to include public-sphere dimensions, shifting the locus of their care work. Activism came to be subsumed within the realm, newly expanded, of CARE women's activities, as *part of* their care work. This new public-sphere participation (and not other types of public-sphere participation such as full-time paid employment) became a fixed part of the women's home/family (i.e., private) responsibilities and a central part of their gender identities.

These cases of Carol, Mary, and other CARE women with similarly vested identities and lives highlight, though, the reality that a shift in gender identity and care work can be contentious as it often results in change for the family unit as well. It is ironic that, for this group of women, activism conflicts with their private-sphere identification, even as their public-sphere participation is *motivated by* their private-sphere affinities.

CARE Members' Negotiation of Gender Identity and Shifting Care Work

The stretching of identity and shifting of the locus of care work was accomplished via social interaction, in the context of new and existing relationships. In our telephone interview, Lois Gibbs discussed the identity expansion she witnessed in the working-class community of Love Canal and its potential conflict:

> [The women] took the leadership, they became educated, they understood how the world worked, and they didn't want to go back, although they still maintained some of those gender roles at the same time. And they straddled that, because generally their family or their partners married them because they took on this role, because they were in that role. And so, to totally dismiss that role means to totally change their family, and most partners are not willing to do that.

For CARE women as well, the shift was laden with conflict. The expansion of CARE women's gender identities and the shift in the locus of care work were products of active negotiation by the individual women: negotiating with their husbands and children as to how they would define themselves as women and how the family would adjust to dynamic care work responsibilities.* For some of the women, this negotiation was successful; they achieved an expanded gender identity, though not without conflict. For other women, who negotiated an expanded identity but reverted back to their initial gender identification, the conflict within the family was too much. Regardless of the outcome, what is illuminating is the *process* of negotiation.

Expansion of activities and of gender identity is not an easy accomplishment. Because mothers' lives are so intertwined with those of their family, and change in one individual can affect long-established family patterns, it can be a process fraught with conflict. The perception that marital conflict is widespread among activists prompted the CCHW to address the issue in a workshop and publication whereby advice was provided for placating spouses and family members:

> There are many times when the personal relationships with the men in our lives become strained due to the fight. Personal stress, adjustments to new roles and new life styles, are hard on relationships, sometimes bending them to the point of breaking and sometimes strengthening them. (Zeff, Love, and Stuits 1989:25)

Mary suggests that change in her gender identity and care work activities presented problems in her home:

---

* For CARE women who did not have young children, the negotiation was less pronounced and less problematic.

[My husband] was used to having dinner ready, which was my job. That's what I signed on to do, raise the kids and be the homemaker, the happy little homemaker. And then when those roles were changing, he was like, 'Hey, wait a second."

Her husband complained of the time spent on her activism: "He'd say, 'Mary, I never even see you anymore. Or when I do see you, you're reading or writing letters or doing something' that didn't involve him." Previous to her activism, her responsibilities to the family took up the bulk of her day. Now, they were squeezed in between phone calls, strategy meetings, and city meetings. But her husband and her children resisted this time away; they wanted their wife and mother back. As she said earlier, being a stay-at-home mom was what she signed on to do. Now that was up in the air.

A tug-of-war commenced. Mary's husband and children attempted to pull her back to the status quo while she pushed to include activism in her life and, ultimately, theirs. Mary's stories of resistance and accommodation illustrate the push and pull of negotiation. With the children, Mary frequently backed off her activism, hoping to placate them:

There were times when I would just turn the phone off. And the kids would come home to a perfectly prepared meal and a clean house. [And they would say] "Did you quit, Mom?" "No, I took a day off." . . . I needed a reality check.

With her husband, however, a battle ensued. To appease him, she rose at 4 A.M. to make his breakfast and spend time with him before he left for his construction job. Mary told the story of one argument in which her husband started by saying that at so-and-so's house, the floors were so clean, a person could eat off of them—a reminder that she was letting her responsibilities to the house and family slide. His remark also voiced his discontent with her new sense of self and the changes in their household arrangements that symbolized that identity shift. Furious that he could not see the positive effects of her activism and couldn't put up with dirty floors for a good cause, Mary took action. As she recalled, she took his plate of breakfast, set it on the floor, and told him he was welcome to eat his breakfast on the floor. She proceeded to serve his breakfast on the floor for the remainder of the week. During their argument, she reminded him that:

"You're supposed to be supportive of me. . . . I didn't forget how to cook; I just don't have time to do it. Get off my back; I'm doing this for you." Well, he didn't want to hear that. You know, he wanted his breakfast.

When asked if anything changed after that, Mary responded by saying, "Oh, yeah, we didn't talk to each other for about a week," and laughed. She summed up the negotiation when she said, "I had to prove a point," a point about how she saw herself and who she wanted to be. She continued, however, to adapt the intensity of her involvement to the mood of her family, spending more time with CARE when her family was supportive, and curtailing her activities when they resented her involvement.

Throughout her involvement, Mary actively negotiated two potential but conflicting gender identities — that of full-time mother and that of mother-activist — each with a different locus of care work activity. She attempted to rectify the two through an elaborate balancing act. But identity negotiation is not a solitary endeavor. Because of her family's intense resistance, Mary left the organization and has not resumed her activism. Her gender identity expanded rapidly, but briefly, eventually returning to her initial identification as a full-time mother, devoting her time to meeting her family's immediate needs. Her prior gender identity had won out.

For other CARE activists, the negotiation continued, and was still continuing as I left the field. Another CARE woman, "Laura," went through a similar process, though less with her children. Before she became consumed with the fight against the incinerator, her days were filled with care of her children and home as a stay-at-home mother of small children. Initially, when she first became involved, she packed her days full of her previous care work activities and now activism as well. As she said, however, it was a tenuous balance:

> At one point, it was very hard for my husband because all I did was read. I just wanted more. And he said, "You've got a family here. You're going to have to back off just a little bit, take care of stuff here too."

Rather than back off, Laura adapted her activities to meet the family's schedule. She would do the bulk of her reading after her family went to bed at night and do as much as she could during the day when her older children and husband were out of the home. Because of her structural availability, Laura was able to closet her expanded identity, taking it out during the day or at meetings, and returning it to the closet during interactions with her family in the evening. With varying degrees of success, she attempted to split the expanded element of her gender identity from the one presented to her family. This adaptation was aided by a slowdown in the organization, however, as the incinerator that had consumed most of CARE's energies was defeated.

During the busy times, Laura simply added more and different responsibilities into her day. When I inquired if she asked her spouse to take on more household and child-care tasks, she said no. "That would have definitely been a problem. If I do more, that's OK, but don't expect him to." Her comment suggests that her identity was expanding, while his was probably not; the locus of her care work was no longer centered *within* the home, while he refused to respond by altering his care work responsibilities. An incident toward the end of the observation period made it clear her husband was not happy with her expanded identity and care work. He publicly chided her for spending too much time on the organization, taking too much time from their family. This was particularly troubling, he said, because they had defeated the incinerator, the battle was over, yet she continued her involvement. His remarks suggested that he supported her initial activism because it was in defense of her family's health *and* it was short-term. When it evolved into an element of her identity, constituting a rearrangement of her identity and threatening a new division of care labor and *their* lives, her activism was no longer acceptable. In this incident, he publicly disputed her expanded gender identity. Unlike Mary, however, Laura did not cease her involvement, though it was naturally curbed by the slower pace of the organization in the post-incinerator days. However, her case suggests that she negotiated her identity, particularly with her spouse, at times modifying her daily activities to make room for her expanded activist identification.

Carol's experience highlights the use of token gestures in the identity negotiation process. When activism became a part of her life and her identity, even as it was motivated by her social position as mother, it meant reordering her care work, shifting the locus and kind of care work to that outside of the home. But she was no longer fulfilling the particular role of mother that she and her spouse had initially negotiated. To maintain her new identity and still appease her spouse, she fulfilled token activities of her previous gender identity, as she explains here:

It's like, if he says, "You know, we really have to get going on the laundry. It's getting to be overwhelming" or whatever. It's like, "OK, fine"; that day I'll throw in a bunch of laundry. I don't even care how I'm throwing it in or what I'm throwing in. I separate whites and colors and that's it. It's like "OK, there, I did something. Now he can get off my back."

As her gender identity shifted to include care work activities outside the home to the neglect of her previous in-home care work responsibilities, Carol's husband tried to pull her back to her previous gender identity, one centered on her presence in the home. To placate him, she performed token tasks, just enough to maintain peace. As with Laura, she didn't ask him to do more. Only *her* identity and *her* care work responsibilities were being actively negotiated. She stretched her gender identity to include activism, while he attempted to pull it back. For Carol, however, the balance between *at-home* care worker and *activist* care worker, and thus, the negotiation and expansion, were more easily accomplished because her spouse worked long hours outside the home, and, at the time of our interview, her youngest child was of school age. Consequently, she could spend blocks of her day away from their home and could elicit the help of her children.

Activism's Effect on Gender Identity: A Third Scenario of Identity Change?

While the models of gender identity change presented earlier illustrate two possible scenarios, they do not fully capture the change expressed by CARE women. The first model, as illustrated in some toxic waste activism, suggests that empowering experiences may lead to a critique of patriarchy and transformed care work relationships and gender identities. The second model, embodied in women's disempowering experiences in movements with empowering ideologies such as the New Left and civil rights movements, suggests similar consequences. CARE women's gender identity expansion, however, illustrates that activism's effects are conditioned by certain factors: individual histories of activism, the ideology of the movement, opportunities within the organization, and gender identity. The women of CARE suggest that for new activists involved in a movement not premised on rights, whose gender identity is vested in motherhood and care work responsibilities, the experience is profound, initiating redefinition and expansion, but not transformative.

While restricted opportunities and experiences with sexism may have led women of the civil rights and New Left movements toward a critique of patriarchy and gender inequality, CARE women did not face those same conditions. Within the organization, CARE women faced new and largely unrestricted leadership opportunities (outside of those internally imposed by the women themselves). Those open and affirming experiences led CARE activists to cite positive changes in themselves and their lives as a consequence of their activism. For them, then, gender identity reconstitution was not a function of awareness of sexism or restricted opportunities. Indeed, any gender stratification in CARE went unnoticed by the women, a point revealed in a later phone conversation with Karen, months after our interview. *During* our interview, when I asked questions as to who wrote speeches, who delivered speeches, who spoke to the media, and so on, Karen came to realize that, indeed, CARE was characterized by a degree of gender stratification (though mostly in regard to visibility in video media). As she described it, the women did not want to deliver the speeches, appear on camera; they *chose* to remain behind the scenes. In our later phone conversation, Karen said that she had continued to dwell on the gender roles and was bothered by the extent to which the women fell into those patterns. She repeated that she just had not noticed the patterns when she was involved in CARE. Similarly, Allyson spoke of developing an awareness of gender constraints in hindsight, only after she had left the organization and had not been active for more than a year:

> *Now*, being on the outside looking in, I start to see a disrespect [from town officials and residents]. . . . Could it be because it's mostly women? That they're pulling this off, and they're doing it on camera, and they don't seem to care who sees them?

Karen's and Allyson's comments suggest that gender went unanalyzed in CARE. Consequently, a scenario premised on the galvanizing effect of sexism toward gender identity transformation quickly falls short. But neither did empowerment via toxic waste activism lead to a critique of patriarchy, the other scenario outlined in the literature, as most of the women demanded little change of their husbands, activist organizations, or social institutions.

Instead, patriarchy went unchecked, sexism was not problematized, and gender identity expanded to encompass the new responsibilities and identification with activism. Home relations changed but, over the long run, only to the extent that the women's (and not their spouses') gender identities grew to include new dimensions.* Thus, the meaning of womanhood itself was expanded to include a new range of activities. Gender identity was stretched, not usurped, and the core identification with (a particular construction of) motherhood was not abandoned. Hence, the women of CARE illustrate a third scenario of gender identity change resulting from activism: an expanded but not radicalized gender identity, stemming from positive, affirming experiences and the perception of open leadership opportunities.

Conclusion

My case studies show that activism has a strong effect on individuals, their lives, their care work, and their identities. Symbolic interactionism contends, and these case studies confirm, that gender identity is constructed and reconstructed not in a vacuum but in a specific social context: with one's spouse, children, friends, and fellow activists, and against the backdrop of movement experiences. Veteran activists anticipated these shifts and grew with these changes.

The experiences of CARE women, perhaps if only because of the recent initiation of their activism, illustrate the dynamic and shifting nature of identity and care work responsibilities. Though their gender identities expanded in an explosive and sometimes conflict-laden way, activism did not necessarily have a radicalizing effect. Because the women of CARE experienced a movement relatively free of gendered constraints and were largely unaware of the constraints that existed, the women gained a sense of power without developing an identity that incorporated feminist ideology. The CARE women went so far as to expand their gender identities and the locus of their care work but stopped short of setting aside previous gender identities and substantially altering the division of care work. With

---

* This study focused on women activists' gender identities, not their spouses'. Thus, it is impossible to conclude that the gender identities of CARE members' souses did not expand. Each spouse occasionally performed extra household tasks or took on more child care but only for short periods and with resistance.

their previous (to activism) gender identities intact, the women added a new sense of what it meant to be a woman and a mother. To that definition, they added a public-sphere dimension, decentering their care work. The CARE women's gender identities as women and mothers meant choosing to stay home, choosing to focus one's energies on one's children *in the home*. Their expanded gender identity, however, included public-sphere participation as activists, as an extension of their care work. It was added because it represented involvement on behalf of the home and children, extending private-sphere responsibilities to include *some* public-sphere participations.

But the women of CARE also illustrate the contested nature of identity. A *shift* in identity is reinforced by some (such as other movement activists) even as that newly configured identity is challenged by and negotiated with those (e.g., family) in other arenas. The CARE members experienced, to varying degrees, expanded identities as a consequence of their experiences, but it was a change that the women actively negotiated with much contention.

Public Markets/Private Caring

Public Markets/Private Caring

*G*radually, we have become aware of the dissolving boundaries between the public realm of paid work and the private realm of family or domestic work. The same acts of caring for the children, elderly, and disabled take place both within families and in the public realm and are both paid and unpaid. The blurring of this distinction, and its ramifications, are the suject of Part II. As Clare Ungerson argues, the introduction of cash into care can be problematic. Ungerson's cross-national policy analysis, which categorizes different ways of compensating care workers, reveals how the exchange of currency complicates the dynamics of the relationships between care workers and care receivers.

Often the rules and standards in the public realm do not permit the emotional subtleties that define good care within families and among friends. If time is money, as Tim Diamond documents in *Making Gray Gold*, chatting with nursing home residents to relieve their loneliness is wasted money in a for-profit market that emphasizes efficiency and cutting financial costs. Feminists are increasingly critical of the devaluation of emotional work and emphasize that care is not "good care" without it. In a series of interviews, political scientist Deborah Stone reveals how paid care workers often feel forced to violate professional standards prohibiting hugging or other emotional labor in order to provide good care, even though doing so means that they risk losing their jobs.

The increasing shift of formerly unpaid work into the paid realm is a dual-edged sword; though women are financially rewarded for the labor, it is often at low wages. Mary Tuominen's study of family day-care providers shows just how incredulous day-care providers are that virtually no one will believe that caring for other people's children in their own homes is real work. As a result, the women she interviewed strategically describe their jobs in words that stress instrumental rather than emotional aspects of the work to elevate their status as care workers.

The most pervasive fear about care work provided in the public realm is that providing financial incentives for work that was once performed solely out of love will hinder and devalue the act of caring. As Tuominen emphasizes, however, care performed for love versus care performed for money are simplistic distinctions that do not capture the true nature of the care work that women perform, whether in paid or unpaid arenas. The at-home paid day-care workers Tuominen interviewed were quick to explain that they put up with low wages and low prestige because of their love for, and their commitment to, the children for whom they cared.

In contrast to decades of thinking that presumes care work is best performed unpaid by family members, the authors in this section challenge the idea that market values will always supersede the personal values of caring by demonstrating just how effectively personal values infiltrate. Sociologist Francesca Cancian argues that at times low salaries, the desire for profits, and excessive bureaucracy reduce paid care workers' capacity to provide good care. At other times, however, organizational structures can evolve to allow, and even encourage, the provision of good care that is rich with nurturing and compassion. Most important, she reminds us that social structures can shape care work; the ability to provide good care is not predetermined as a biological trait, but is shaped and fostered by structural forces that we influence.

In our discussion of the advantages and disadvantages of market-based care work, we cannot afford to stray far from the question of "good care at whose expense?" Among the ranks of invisible, low-paid care workers are thousands of transnational mothers—women from poor and developing countries—who leave their own children to come to the United States or Europe to take jobs as nannies and housekeepers in upscale families. Sociologist Pierrette Hondagneu-Sotelo argues that this demonstrates how the commodification of reproductive services, including housework and food preparation, has reshaped the global economy. She describes an international division of labor wherein poor immigrants perform the United States' reproductive labor, from caring for children to cleaning houses, while the immigrants' reproductive labor remains neglected in their countries of origin.

Cash in Care

*T*he capturing of unpaid work as a concept has probably been one of the major successes of second-wave feminism. The impact of that idea has been profound, both in analytical and in policy terms. Within policy, the struggle to name and quantify such work has been worldwide, and the campaign to include domestic labor within public accounting has recently become an important issue both within the United States and in the United Nations (Himmelweit 1995). At national levels, too, welfare states and policy makers within them have learned to pay at least lip service to the way in which welfare delivery is dependent on the continuous presence of mothers and other caregivers within the domestic sphere (see for example in the British context, Griffiths 1988). In analytical terms, the visibility of unpaid work, which in the early days of second-wave feminism was largely construed as housework (Oakley 1974) and debated within the Marxist-framed domestic labor debate (Seccombe 1980), later came to be analyzed as personal services delivered within the household and named as care or, in the particular case of care of the disabled, informal care. There is now a very considerable literature on care, construed both as motherhood and as care of disabled people including elderly people and children with special needs (for example, within the British context, Finch and Groves 1983; Ungerson 1987; Qureshi and Walker 1989; Twigg and Atkin 1994).

That literature has been extremely important in delineating the similarities of unpaid work and paid work (Graham 1991; Thomas 1993; Ungerson 1990), and in outlining the way in which the demands and exigencies of unpaid work affect opportunities for and status within paid work, particularly for women (Joshi 1992). Nevertheless, I argue in this chapter that the dualism of paid and unpaid work is dissolving, and that we are moving into a period where the boundaries within public and private domains, so well laid down in the nineteenth century and continued into the second half of the twentieth century, are beginning to crumble away (Ungerson 1994, 1995). Nowhere is this more obvious than in the policy area of care for people with disabilities. There is evidence from both Europe and North America that welfare states are searching for ways to underwrite the provision of care within households and kin networks through cash subvention both to caregivers and to care recipients. The consequence is the marketization of intimacy and the commodification of care.

The effect of this direct injection of cash into the care relationship has as yet to be explored fully. A North American literature exists (see, for example, Eustis and Fischer 1991) but the British literature is relatively underdeveloped, relying to a large extent on Leat's work on fostering (1990), on Morris's work on the experience of the employment of personal assistants (1993), on Qureshi's work (with Walker) on paid volunteers (1989), and on largely speculative work by me (1997b). The work that has so far been done tends to look at one kind of payment for care and its consequences for the care relationship. In this chapter I attempt to unravel the complexity of the various kinds of payments that exist cross-nationally and outline a typology of payments for care. I then proceed to use that typology to consider the ways in which these different types of payments will produce varying kinds of working conditions, contracts of employment, and differential impact on the care relationship. The paper then moves on to look at one type of payment in particular—that of direct payments to disabled people, which they use to employ personal assistants, and considers the care relationship from the personal assistants' perspective. In that section of the paper I address some of the general issues of control and boundary setting and crossing.

A Typology of Payments for Care

The ways in which care, particularly informal care for disabled people, is being commodified are manifold cross-nationally. It is impossible to do justice to the nuances of the rules of eligibility, the formal and informal arrangements for payments to caregivers that prevail, or the various reasons why payments have been put in place. What follows is based on empirical, country-by-country-based work undertaken by me and others (Evers, Pijl, and Ungerson 1994; Glendinning and McLaughlin 1993) and provides a basic summary and typology of the main trends.

One thing can be said in general: apart from the countries of Scandinavia, notably Norway, Sweden, and Finland, it is striking how many of these systems of payments for care originate from the 1980s and were given additional boosts in the early 1990s. They reflect a number of strands in the politics of care, especially the recognition by policy makers of a care deficit (Hochschild 1995) and the need to find some means of reinforcing a supply of informal care in the late twentieth century. There has been not only a growth in these systems in the 1990s, but a shift in their nature. The particular feature of the changes in the 1990s has been a change of emphasis from allowances paid to caregivers to allowances paid to care users. In the case of the allowances paid to care users, these payments are often specifically intended to fund the purchase of services, especially personal care services, from an identified personal assistant. It is important to distinguish these kinds of direct payment to care users from benefits to care users that are designed to increase the incomes of people with special needs in order to protect them from the additional exigencies of their impairment, and ameliorate the particular likelihood of poverty linked to disability.

It is arguable that there has been a chronological process from benefits for care recipients, to allowances to caregivers, to direct payments to care users, which reflects a chronological shift in the politics of care and the politics of disability. During the 1970s, especially in Britain, the recognition of the extra needs of disabled people was a feature of the rediscovery of poverty within the framework of a welfare state over which there was still a broad political consensus. At the same time, a politics of disability was couched in terms of a medical model of dependency and the existence of special needs (Oliver 1990). A range of benefits payable to disabled people and designed to cover the additional costs of disability was put in place. In the decade of the 1980s, feminist claims that care is unpaid work and that the constraints imposed on women's participation in paid work should be compensated for and the actual provision of caring labor should be reimbursed came to the fore and were increasingly accounted for in a politics of caregiver support in Britain and in other countries of Europe. In the 1990s, the claims of disabled people that they have a right to independent living and the right to organize their own provision rather than depend on the decisions of professionals, began to draw the attention of policy makers. This view of care user as care consumer also fit well with other antistate and antibureaucracy arguments coming from the New Right during a period of widespread welfare state retrenchment.

It is important to devise a typology that makes some generalizable sense of the policies that are in place. In an earlier paper I made a fairly unsubtle distinction between caregiver allowances and what I called quasi-wages, where caregiver allowances are based on eligibility rules and quasi-wages on formal and informal contracts (Ungerson 1995). I no longer feel that dualistic distinction is adequate to describe the complete variance for payments for care, and I want to make some further distinctions of payments for care, but hold fast to the concept of payments that are based on eligibility criteria in contrast to those that are based on contingency and contract.

First there are caregiver allowances paid directly to caregivers through social security and tax (uncontingent, noncontractual, based on eligibility). Second, there are proper wages to caregivers coming from the state or its agents, which provide payments to caregivers, many of whom are relatives of care users, and which are based on the prevailing wage rates of state-employed home helps (contingent, contractual, with state as employer). Third, there are symbolic payments, paid by care users with their own money, or money coming in the form of benefits, in an effort to lubricate a reciprocal system within kin and neighborhood networks (may be contractual, but in a diluted form, with care user as quasi-employer). Fourth, somewhat different kinds of symbolic payment can also be found in a curious hybrid, particularly developed in Britain, called paid volunteering (contractual, with the voluntary organization or local state agency as quasi-employer). These are contractual arrangements designed to instill an element of regularity and reliability into volunteering since the short-term opportunity costs of volunteering are exceptionally high (Baldock and Ungerson 1994). Finally, there are routed wages, which are paid to caregivers from state-provided direct payments routed via the care user (contingent, contractual, with care user as employer). A typology of payments for care is:

- Caregiver allowances paid through social security and tax systems.
- Proper wages paid by state or state agencies.
- Symbolic payments paid by care users to kin, neighbors, and friends.
- Paid volunteering paid by voluntary organizations and local authorities to volunteers.
- Routed wages paid via direct payments to care users.

This typology does not have an equivalent cross-national classificatory meaning to the term *welfare regime*. Unlike welfare regime, it is not a way of describing the dominant feature of the welfare system in one particular country or group of countries. Rather, this typology is a route to understanding the way in which cash in the caring relationship impinges on and structures the care relationship itself. As each one of these types of payment enters the caring household or caring relationship, it gives rise to different working conditions. Moreover, unlike the term welfare regime these are not discrete categories: within particular countries they can and do overlap. Nevertheless, it is also possible to see that different types of payments for care are beginning to dominate in particular countries.

Care Allowances

These benefits for caregivers, paid either through tax or social security systems, are often construed as recompensing caregivers of working age for not being able to take paid work as a result of the exigencies of the unpaid work of care. These include the British Invalid Care Allowance introduced in 1977 and extended to married women of working age in 1988, the Federal Dependent Tax Care Credit available in the United States to taxpayers who are normally in paid work, and provisions under the Danish Social Assistance Act, which pays caregivers of working age full compensation for earnings forgone. The Irish Caregivers' Allowance, which dates from 1990, is payable to caregivers of all ages who are on very low incomes and is designed less as a compensation to caregivers who give up paid work than as an incentive for family rather than residential care.

What is so fascinating about these social security and tax-related caregiver allowances is that they are payable to caregivers who do not have to demonstrate that they are actually caring. It is normally sufficient to demonstrate a relationship (relational or geographical proximity) to someone who is able to produce documentary evidence of need of care — usually assessed on a medical basis. From the evidence on hand, only in the United States is additional note, in federal taxation arrangements, taken of the financial support actually provided by the caregiver to the care user. Thus, these caregiver allowances are, essentially, citizenship-based rights to income for caregivers, funded on the basis that the risks of becoming a caregiver should be pooled, and that there is a collective responsibility to alleviate at least some of caregivers' income needs. In almost all these schemes, only one caregiver is identified, and this means invariably that the payment of these social security or tax-based caregiver allowances is likely to lead to the relative isolation of the caregiver working within the domestic sphere. Moreover, given that many of these caregiver allowance schemes are intended only to compensate caregivers of working age, they tend to cease when caregivers reach the official retirement age or when they fall below tax thresholds. Thus they constitute recognition of care work, but only for a restricted category of caregivers which in particular excludes elderly retired caregivers who are likely to be caring for their spouses. It is precisely because such allowances are framed by a conception of caregivers and care recipients as citizens that they tend to be construed as compensation for not entering paid work, at least within the European context: for it is in Europe, particularly Northern Europe, that the idea prevails that welfare state citizenship is earned through participation in paid work.

Within this specific framework, how are caregiver allowances likely to affect the care relationship? In itself, recognition may make that relationship an easier one: both care recipient and caregiver may feel that their roles as citizens dealing actively with dependency have been recognized and compensated for by the welfare state. Care recipients, too, may feel that problems of reciprocity are less acute, in that their need to reciprocate within the relationship has, at least in financial terms, been dispersed and defused by state provision (although the amount of the allowance may determine how far the issue of reciprocity has been satisfactorily resolved). The additional income to the caregiver, particularly where the caregiver and care recipient live together, will raise the standard of living of that household and the problems arising out of financial stringency may be at least a little relieved. Caregivers who manage to keep the allowances for themselves rather than let it drift into general household revenues report that they much appreciate that they are granted at least a modicum of financial independence (McLaughlin 1991).

At the same time, however, it is the nature of tax and social security systems to identify a single person or claimant to whom payments are made. Thus the payment to these caregivers is likely to mean that they are identified as the person responsible for the person with disabilities, and thus it is easy to become singly identified within a wider kin network, and isolated within a caring dyad. Moreover, the amount paid may be low but nevertheless constitute enough to prevent them from job seeking, thus in effect entrapping them into the role of caregiver, sometimes for very long periods. There tend to be no additional rights attached to the receipt of such allowances. Thus, the ironic consequence of such recognition, based on a framework of citizenship, is likely to be long term loneliness for the caregiver, severe constraints on participatory and active citizenship, and engagement in an occupation that, in terms of human capital acquisition, remains entirely unrecognized in the more conventional labor market.

Of course, the income provided through such allowances is variable — from the Danish wage-equivalent allowances through the British and Irish barely subsistence allowances to the United States tax breaks which, at $1,440, are only about a quarter of the maximum declarable expenditure on care. In addition, in the United States, there are programs in individual states to supplement federal arrangements (Linsk, Keigher, Simon-Rusinowitz, and Osterbusch, cited in Keigher and Stone 1994). Some of these state-organized schemes in the United States come close to the proper wages described below.

Proper Wages Paid by State Agencies

As we have already seen in the case of Denmark, some nations pay caregiver allowances, which are equivalent to the wages that particular caregivers could otherwise earn. Other systems of payments for care are based on the direct employment of informal caregivers by the state. Such arrangements, commonly available to relatives, have existed for some time in Sweden (Johansson and Sundström 1994) and Norway (Lingsom 1994). In the Scandinavian countries, wages are usually set at the prevailing wage for home health care workers paid by the municipalities. Thus, in these situations it is possible for caregivers to become state employees. They do not appear, though, to have exactly the same status as salaried employees: it is rare, although it does happen, that they are employed full time and similarly rare that they receive the same contractual employment and social security rights as the more formal caregivers who work within the collectivized personal social services. They do not, of course, have multiple clients as other home caregivers do: their care work takes place one-to-one within a setting of intimacy and an established biography between caregiver and care recipient. Nevertheless, related as these systems necessarily are to prevailing wage rates for care work, and in countries where minimum wage laws applys, such proper wage systems are potentially very expensive. After all, they constitute a full-blown version of wages for housework. On that basis, it can be argued that they are cost-inefficient as a method of reinforcing informal care, which will come forward anyway, motivated by obligation and affect. There is some evidence that the Scandinavian systems of proper wages are in decline—for example, the number of Swedish informal caregivers employed by the municipalities declined from 18,517 in 1970 to 6,500 in 1991, and the number of Norwegian caregivers employed by the municipalities dropped from 12,749 in 1980 to 6,168 in 1992 (Lingsom 1994), and this may be a reflection of general attempts to reduce the scope of Scandinavian welfare states in the 1990s (Ungerson 1995). However, Lingsom argues that in Norway, despite 1988 legislation that made it mandatory for municipalities to have care salaries programs from 1992 onwards, the number of salaried informal caregivers has declined because municipalities have tried to professionalize and formalize their domiciliary care services. Thus salaries for relatives, while ostensibly a way of introducing surveillance of informal care, have not apparently developed into a professionalization of informal care, and have thereby failed to satisfy the criteria of policy makers seeking to introduce quality assurance in the less visible domestic world. Hence, despite procedural and legislative efforts to maintain such systems, they may eventually disappear in practice.

Proper wages are based on a loosely applied employer/employee model rather than a citizenship model. Thus employers, in the form of municipalities, will consciously seek out the most cost-efficient form of service provision, of which salaried home helpers are but one option. Employers will tend to select wages for caregivers when either there is no obvious alternative (for example, for disabled people and their caregivers living in remote rural communities) or when it is an available and cheaper option. There is evidence from the Norwegian case that salaried caregivers are very unlikely to receive formal support. Lingsom cites Nygård's 1982 study as showing that paid relatives also have substantially less informal help from other caregivers in their network, thus supporting the view that a paid caregiver, whether through allowances or proper wages, is likely to have to work alone. Lingsom suggests it may be that in a proper wage system it is precisely the isolated and unsupported caregiver who might be regarded as a suitable case for formal employment and payment. It is also of note that in the Norwegian system, certainly in the 1980s, "homehelpers typically had a limited work contract without ordinary employee rights such as job security, sick leave or employee pensions" (Lingsom 1994:7).

Indeed the Norwegian evidence appears in general to suggest that proper wages for caregivers are a somewhat inadequate way of supporting caregivers and may leave them and the person they care for more isolated and locked into a relationship of intense dependency. Nevertheless such wages do, like caregiver allowances, help to resolve the issue of reciprocity in the care relationship, and certainly constitute a strong version of recognition of care as work. Moreover, even if the Norwegian example is not a good one when it comes to the additional rights for waged informal caregivers, the fact that this is a payment for care framed within an employer/employee perspective means that there is always the potential political leverage to argue for such benefits as paid holidays for respite, coverage of social security contributions, redundancy rights, and rights to bereavement counseling when caring ends.

Symbolic Payments to Caring Kin, Friends, and Neighbors

These kinds of payment are the least visible of all payments for care, and hence there is the least documentation of them. Keigher and her colleagues are currently investigating the gray market for home care in Milwaukee, Wisconsin (Keigher and Luz 1997), and there clearly is a large contribution to care work that can loosely be called informal economic activity, which, precisely because it is informal, awaits thorough investigation both nationally and cross-nationally.

Some of this informal economic activity must be generated by and through the payment type of routed wages, considered in detail below. However, there is also scattered evidence in Britain that a considerable source of paid caring labor comes from relatives, friends, and neighbors. Such payments are made by disabled people out of the benefits that are meant to support the additional costs of their disability (Baldock and Ungerson 1994). The benefits are far too low to pay proper wages, and they become, perforce, symbolic payments used to maintain gift economy reciprocities (Cheal 1988). Further evidence is available from Lakey's (1994) study of disabled people receiving direct payments from the Independent Living Fund (a precursor of the direct payments system discussed below). She found that no less than three-quarters of the directly employed personal assistants were either relatives (34 percent) or nonrelatives previously known to the disabled person (40 percent). Such nonrelatives probably consisted largely of friends and neighbors, although some of them were no doubt people previously employed in a strictly contractual arrangement. Of the paid relatives, one-third had been paid by the disabled person before the cash from the fund became available (Lakey 1994, Tables 22, 39). Equally interesting is that all this employment of relatives subsequent to receipt of money from the fund is strictly illegal according to the fund's regulations (and strictures against the employment of close relatives have been carried through into the regulations of the new Direct Payments scheme). Not surprisingly, the rates of pay of these illegally employed family members were particularly low, and edged toward the symbolic: the median hourly rate for a relative was £2–50 compared with £5–71 for workers recruited through an agency, and for those working 35 or more hours a week, the comparable figures dropped to £1−71 compared to £4−98 for an agency worker (Lakey 1994:150−52).

Symbolic payments have the particular feature of combining the rationality of the market and the rationality of the gift. Indeed, such payments often appear to take the form of a gift. For example, in a study of discharged stroke patients undertaken by John Baldock and myself (1994) we found the following examples of gifts related to care: paying for the whole of someone's shopping when that person provides a shopping service; giving someone a car and paying the related tax, insurance, and a gasoline allowance to encourage home visits; paying for the installation and maintenance of a neighbor's landscaped garden; paying for the purchase of gasoline of a neighbor or a family member who provides help with transportation. We also found examples of the straightforward proffering of small amounts of cash, both to friends and neighbors and to family caregivers who provided regular services.

This is not only uncharted territory for researchers, it is also uncharted territory for the participants in the care relationship. While the need for reciprocity presumably drives these exchanges, there is no established economy of reciprocity where the participants know the rules of exchange and the exchange value of the services on offer. Care recipients report embarrassment and puzzlement over what to exchange and to what value, and considerable difficulty in knowing how to stop or start such informally constituted contracts. (There was in our research one example of such a gift-based exchange where the care recipients thought the service they were receiving from their daughter was not adequate and they were thinking of asking for the return of the car they had given her; in the short term they had stopped paying her £20-a-week gasoline allowance.) The one area where the rules of giving and receiving may be clearer is within kin networks where cash in exchange for care flows across generations from older to younger. Such cash flows, while dealing with the problem of reciprocity, also go with the grain of gift giving within families in later life (Finch 1989; Finch and Mason 1992). While there are elements of an employer/employee relationship here which may serve to lock caregivers into a care relationship they do not welcome, it is also likely that these kinds of commodified care relationships are more amenable to analysis within a sociology of community and a sociology of friendship framework. The isolation of the caregiver in symbolically contracted care work is probably bipolarized. Some tasks, particularly those undertaken by friends and neighbors, are likely to be discrete and bounded (such as help with shopping and transport) precisely because they are the less intrusive aspects of care and hence more acceptable coming through relationships that are normally themselves strictly limited. Hence nonrelatives who provide services in receipt of symbolic payments are probably one of a number of caregivers. The reverse is almost certainly true of kin caregivers who are paid symbolically: they are probably very isolated, with informal contracts that are especially difficult to alter or break.

Paid Volunteering

This form of paid care work is probably unique to Britain. Paid volunteering involves contracting caring labor from strangers to work in the private domain and paying them symbolic payments rather than proper wages. It is difficult for countries that have minimum-wage laws to operate such programs legally (it will be interesting to see if the introduction of a minimum wage in Britain in April 1999 causes the decline of these programs). At present, in Britain there are numerous programs organized by voluntary organizations and local authorities, which recruit volunteers to undertake care work for someone in their neighborhood and then contract them, using symbolic payments to cement the contract (Blacksell and Phillips 1994). The payments can range from £1 a visit (and there may be as many as four visits contracted per day) to a limited amount of money per week. Many of these programs deliberately target women who are seeking small additional incomes that do not push them into compulsory social security contribution bands or take them above social security benefit earnings limits (Baldock and Ungerson 1991).

Sometimes these paid volunteering arrangements are said to cover expenses rather than to represent any emolument for the actual work undertaken, but they tend to pay standard amounts (Leat with Ungerson 1993). It is likely that they will expand, particularly in countries with high unemployment: workfare programs, which make social assistance for the unemployed contingent on taking up paid work, may well spread from the United States and be used, in conjunction with voluntary organizations, to provide a reliable supply of symbolically paid voluntary care workers. By linking the work with benefits rather than wages, minimum-wage restrictions can be avoided. Whether these programs remain as female-targeted as paid volunteering currently is remains to be seen.

As far as the impact on the care relationship is concerned, paid volunteering has many of the elements of symbolic payments except that the personal exchange between volunteer and care recipient is missing. In this case, the volunteer enters a contractual agreement with the voluntary or statutory agency that introduces payment in order to guarantee reliability and control. It is not necessarily the case, though, that care recipients will be aware that the services they are receiving (for example, the delivery of a daily meal, a sitting service to provide respite for their caregiver, speech rehabilitation, being gotten up in the morning and put to bed at night) are actually being provided by a volunteer who is paid small amounts and contracted by an agency to do so. The care relationship here is more likely to resemble the relationship between a care recipient and fully paid formal caregivers with whom the care recipient will be familiar, at least in theory. The volunteers too may construe themselves as more like professional deliverers of care than as friends of the care recipient. In a major and rare study of such volunteers in one experimental project, many of the volunteers did see themselves as engaged as autonomous semiprofessionals and gained great satisfaction from doing so (Qureshi, Challis, and Davies 1989). It is interesting to note, however, that as this project progressed, the researchers reported the relationship shifted toward informal care, with both caregiver and care recipient increasingly behaving as if they were close kin or long-standing friends (Challis and Davies 1986). Thus an optimistic account of paid volunteering might present it as optimally maximizing the elements of reciprocity, informality, and professionalism within the caring dyad, while also introducing some element of control, surveillance, and support by an outside agency. It also avoids the perils (and pleasures) of long shared biography, which can intrude upon, and indeed prevent, a good-quality care relationship within a kin network. The paid volunteer is probably one of a number of caregivers and, because she works within a voluntary or statutory organization, is likely to be able to call on support when responsibility becomes irksome or the relationship difficult. Such an optimistic account does not, of course, take on board the gendered assumptions that underpin the recruitment of such volunteers, and the opportunity for introducing yet another form of very low-paid work within the care sector.

Routed Wages Paid through Direct Payment Schemes

These are systems where care users are given the means to employ caregivers directly in an employer/employee relationship. Many of these schemes seem to take their cue from early direct payment schemes developed in the United States for veterans. Started in 1951, the Department of Veterans' Affairs Housebound Aid and Attendance Allowance program provides cash grants for some 220,000 veterans. As Keigher and Stone (1994) state, "veterans are free to purchase necessary services from professional providers, pay a relative or friend for help, use the money for living expenses, or anything else they choose." These patterns of consumer autonomy, which allow care users to purchase their own services, including the direct employment of care assistants, are now being widely copied in Europe. Italy, Germany, France, Denmark, and Austria are all countries that during the 1980s introduced direct payments to the care recipient for purchase of care (for more details of specific arrangements see Glendinning and McLaughlin 1993; Evers, Pijl, and Ungerson 1994; Ungerson 1997a). In Britain, the Community Care (Direct Payments) Act of 1996 has introduced the option for disabled people under 65 (and now extended to those age 65 and over) to choose cash rather than services, and the expectation is that they will use the cash to purchase personal assistance. Interestingly, the British scheme, unlike most of the others, specifically forbids care recipients to employ their close relatives.

These developments constitute the sharp end of commodified care and marketized intimacy. The underwriting, by the state, of employer/employee relationships within the care relationship dyad is, at least for European welfare states, a radical innovation in care delivery, apparently reversing the professional and bureaucratic hegemonies in health and social care developed since World War II. Daly (1997) suggests that welfare states "are in effect distancing themselves from how care needs are actually satisfied. . . . We could be seeing the emergence of a new type of welfare citizenship." Disabled people campaigning for direct payments argue that the resourcing by the state of their effective demand for personal assistants constitutes genuine empowerment through the extension to them of contractual rights, in contrast to the purely rhetorical empowerment underwritten through procedural rights, where the gatekeepers to care resources remain social workers and health care professionals (Morris 1993). The liberation of many disabled people through direct payments is indisputable, but there is yet to be any systematic research of the motivations and satisfactions of the caregivers employed through these arrangements, or of the long-term effects on their labor market position and social security rights (Ungerson 1997b). The qualitative data that follow in the second part of this paper explore some of these issues in more detail.

Routed Wages and Personal Assistants: Aspects of the Care Relationship

British research on the employment of personal assistants paid for through direct payments exists, but all of it has looked only at the views of disabled people (Kestenbaum 1992; Morris 1993; Lakey 1994; Hendey and Pascall 1998). The difficulties and dangers, as well as the advantages, of becoming direct employers of caring labor have been well documented in these studies. No research, however, has been undertaken of the personal assistants themselves. It was partially to rectify this lacuna that I decided to conduct a very small qualitative study as a pilot for further studies, both of the care relationship between personal assistants and their employers and of the availability of caring labor of this direct kind in contrasting labor markets. The data that follow draw on that pilot study, which was based in a medium-size city on the south coast of Britain.

At this early point it was decided to restrict the pilot to the study of personal assistants only, with the intention that in later work both they and their employers would be interviewed. The personal assistants were all drawn from a register organized by the city's Center for Independent Living, a voluntary body run by and for disabled people. Since the study was a pilot it was always intended that the sample size would be small. Twenty potential respondents were selected by the Center for Independent Living (the researcher was not given direct access to the register). The center agreed with the author that the initial group should

include equal numbers of men and women, an equal spread over four age co-
horts, and some ethnic minority representation. We had hoped that at least 16 respondents would emerge from this group. However, the response was low, with
only nine personal assistants agreeing to be interviewed, of whom seven finally
appeared for the interview. The age range was reasonable, although none of the
respondents was aged over 50; there were four women and three men, and one of
the men was from an ethnic minority. The interviews took place in March and
April 1998, and were undertaken, taped, and transcribed by the author. The data
that follow reflects the nature of this study: very small, very exploratory, very
qualitative, very unrepresentative.

The in-depth interviews covered four basic areas: the respondents' occupational biographies, their experience in the work of paid care, their attitudes toward
it, and whether or not they expected to continue in the work. In unraveling the issues that the data give rise to, I have decided in the context of this paper to concentrate on aspects of the care relationship that the respondents reported. This
means that the equally rich data collected on their routes into paid care work, and
the way in which they construed the work that they did, has been left for another
occasion. Suffice it to say that the models they brought to bear on the work ranged
from the professional through the entrepreneurial to the holistic and companionate. In all these models, the question of time loomed large: in terms of the legitimacy of the length of the caring relationship, the number of hours spent caring
and at what intervals during the day, and whether or not care took place over the
day or over the night. These are issues I will want to explore in further work. It is
the relationship that I am going to concentrate on here; these issues concern the
question of control and power and the issue of boundary setting and crossing.

Control and Power

The main objective of the direct employment of personal assistants is to ensure that
disabled people, through their ability to hire and fire, acquire the power to control
the nature of the assistance they receive, its timing, and who delivers it. Thus, as
has already been discussed, this injection of cash into the care relationship is perceived to be the means to empowerment, via the development of contractual as well
as procedural rights. Those studies that have been undertaken of disabled people
who are direct employers of personal assistants indicate that on the whole this is
how disabled employers have found the system to work, particularly when compared to the disempowering delivery of care commonly found in residential institutions (Morris 1993). Nevertheless, Kestenbaum (1996), in a review of the research
findings on Independent Living, suggests that theory and practice can diverge:

> Paying a market rate for an assistant theoretically puts control in the hands of
> the employer. In practice, because of the personal nature of the work and the

relationship, the whole business of establishing mutual understanding and respect is much more complex. (p. 26)

The establishment of mutual understanding and respect can clearly be difficult and will involve carefully negotiated rule setting over a period of time. There is evidence that these relationships can involve danger as well. Hendey and Pascall (1998) report that disabled employers remain vulnerable to violent intrusion, both of their bodies in the form of physical and sexual abuse, and of their property, in the form of burglary. A context of trust is absolutely essential if these intense and intimate relationships located within the secrecy of the private domain are to work. Hence, it is not at all surprising that Lakey (1994) found such a high number of people being employed who were either relatives or had been known to their employer before the paid relationship began. Indeed no less than 64 percent of personal assistants in her study had been recruited by word of mouth (Lakey 1994:147), thus introducing some minimal risk avoidance—which is so essential to the processes of consuming personal service labor, particularly where those services are delivered within the private domain. Where knowledge of a person predates the paid care relationship, the question of power in the relationship is inevitably muddied and, as we shall see in the section on boundary setting, the containment of the relationship becomes an issue.

The recruitment of assistants through an agency such as a Center for Independent Living should at least partially circumvent risk through the screening of applicants, the monitoring of their behavior in relation to clients, and the provision of some training. The ideology of empowerment had clearly had some impact on these workers. The respondents often found points in the interview to make it clear that they understood the particular philosophy of Independent Living and respected its tenets. For example, at the end of one interview, when I asked if there was anything that the respondent wanted to add, he said:

> I think one of the things about being a personal assistant is basically enabling somebody that is disabled to basically lead as far as possible a normal life. From the earliest age of actually working for the disabled, which was when I was 17, we were actually told that the disabled do not want mollycoddling, or sympathy. They basically want people to all intents and purposes being friends that will act for them as arms and legs, where the need arises. I know there are a lot of places that have equal opportunities as far as disability is concerned, and I think really the main thing about being a personal assistant is that you are as far as possible promoting independence for that person. Because somebody can do for them so that they can work, they can do this and they can do that, where otherwise they wouldn't.

There was a sense of lip service about this statement. However, a female respondent based her comments on lived experience. She found clients both through the center and through a local nursing agency. Using these examples she was able to point up the particular feature of Independent Living as she understood it:

> I've worked out that it's a people thing and you've got to really like the people. And with the CIL [Center for Independent Living] when I get a name to go and visit, you may not like them so that's fine—we don't work. So they have a choice. With the lady at the Nursing Agency, she has no choice, whether she likes me or not I'm there. So that's the difference, and that's what the CIL is about. . . . They have it done their way. And really you're not allowed to take over.

> Q. Can you give an example of them having it done their way?

> A. You get to know what it is, but they can change it just to make sure that they're in control. And I feel that that's part of their security, I suppose.

> Q. Yes. And that doesn't worry you?

> A. It can if it's been a bad night, yeah. It really bugs me a bit. 'Cause it's hard work. 'Cause I know them , and I've got to live with them you know. It's not so easy, so you know another night, she'll say, "Well why don't you do it?" and you think, "Well, you know". . .

> Q. And what do you do then?

> A. Oh I just sort of let them do what she wants. . . . She's not easy to work for, but she's fair. And I respect her, and I like her.

Thus, there does at least seem to be some recognition that there should be an empowering practice of care, especially where disabled people have recruited their assistants through an organization that promotes a particular ideology of power and control. However, in previous speculative work I have suggested that there are material reasons why these relationships may resemble master/servant relationships since those who can hire and fire are in absolute control of personal assistants who themselves are vulnerable to exploitation because of their weak labor market position (Ungerson 1997b). I now recognize that this construction of paid personal assistants as servants is far too simplistic. First, the master/servant relationship, precisely because it involves the delivery of care within the private domain, has its own complexities involving trust and shared intimacies, but within the context of considerable social distance (Gerard 1994). Second, just as with some life-cycle servants of the nineteenth-century country house who entered domestic service for brief periods at a transition point between leaving the parental home and entering marriage and who moved from employer to employer

(Gerard 1994), so there are personal assistants who, like their disabled employers, feel they are free to leave the paid care relationship when it is found wanting. Thus some respondents reported incidents which had driven them away:

> I had a gentleman who had a stroke who didn't know a lot about the system which I knew more about. And he was really horrible by the time he'd finished. And he went through staff. . . . When I gave my notice in I found out the other staff had left as well. 'Cause he was quite mobile but he really didn't understand. . . . He thought he was in the big world, and he was going to employ us the hard way, you know . . . week in hand, and . . . he was really horrid, you know, and it got my back up really.

> Q. What did you say —"week in hand"— what does . . . ?

> A. I had to work a week and then get paid. And I thought, "Well that's not how the others pay it. You get paid when you've finished." I mean John pays me once a week 'cause I do . . . he's not going to pay me every night. And Margaret would pay me once a week if I worked two or three nights with her. And I mean I would never worry about Margaret because she'll always pay me anyway. And so would John, but . . . he was really, you know he just thought he was some . . . the big employee [*sic*]. Anyway he got rid of his staff in about two minutes flat. And then he wrote a horrible report about me, and I really worked hard for him. I really resented the fact . . . 'cause I cleaned his flat out because it was needing to be done. And I did all the hard work, really, and I felt it was unfair. So I reported him to the CIL when I'd finished.

Another female respondent described an incident which had prompted her to leave, although in this instance it was what she was asked to do and the manner of the asking that had annoyed her rather than any unfair employment practices:

> It was actually to take somebody to church. I went to church with her, I took her home. I put her to bed, and I was quite cross with this person actually because she didn't tell me about the putting to bed thing, and it was quite late, it was just after ten. And she said, "Oh I wanted a bath before but I've left it a bit late," and she had a cup of tea, and then she said, "Well, would you like to put me to bed?" And I said, "yes that's fine," you know till eleven. . . . And I actually stayed till twelve and she wasn't satisfied. . . . They phoned me up again to do this woman and I said, "no." Because she was heavily disabled. She went up through the ceiling into this room with a hoist over here, and one over there, and this sort of thing. And the actual getting her into bed—very hard work. And to get her comfortable and these cushions assembled—one underneath her. I know that's her choice but it was just. . . . I just felt that where I put the

cushion initially, after I'd moved it for half an hour it seemed to end up exactly where it was in the beginning, and I just felt that she was just very difficult. And I said to her, I said I had to pick somebody up. This was my husband. . . . I had his car and I was going to pick him up from work, and I said to him, "I finish at eleven," and he said, "Well I finish at eleven, but I'll wait for you," and it was sort of twenty to twelve, and I was still messing about with these cushions. And I said, "Look, I'm terribly sorry." I said that I cannot carry on with this. I said, "I have to go now.' And I thought, "She's only paying me till eleven anyway." I said, "I'm really sorry, but I have got my partner's car, and I have to collect him from work."

This incident clearly contains within it considerable conflict. The image of an able-bodied woman who is longing to get away tussling with a disabled woman is not a happy one. And it brings to the fore the third reason why the construction of these relationships as master/servant is too simplistic: both participants in this commodified relationship are vulnerable, although in rather different ways. The disabled employers are not supported by social distance and by deference as nineteenth-century country house ladies and gentlemen were: indeed, the social construction or impairment in itself demeans disabled people. Moreover, being undressed, or, on occasion, naked in the presence of someone who is dressed generates extreme vulnerability (which is why this situation has been used over the centuries by torturers and, in this century, by concentration camp administrators). In contrast, the vulnerability of the personal assistants arises not out of the immediacy of the relationship itself, but out of the constraints embedded in their local labor market that determine their ability to exit poor working relationships. Moreover, the receipt of low wages in the paid care sector and the casual and temporary nature of much of this one-to-one work will, in the long run, have a considerable effect on their social security rights. And, as in the case of the woman respondent quoted above, the juggling of paid and unpaid care and the demands generated by a sense of guilt coming from both directions is likely to cause acute stress in their daily lives.

Thus, the injection of cash into the care relationship does not straightforwardly shift power toward the person who employs the personal assistant. Other factors, such as management of risk, the ability of the personal assistants to walk away, and the vulnerabilities inherent in close interaction and intimacy between disabled and able-bodied people, tend to dilute the directness of the employer/employee relationship. The ideology of independent living is a useful tool in promoting the redistribution of power toward the disabled employer, but the impact of that ideology will fall away when the time demands on the personal assistant become pressing or when the time paid for is inadequate to the task at hand. The purity of the employer/employee relationship also is diluted by other factors, some of which arise out of the incentives to construct the relationship as beyond the purely contractual; these are the issues to which I now turn.

Boundary Setting and Crossing

All the respondents were asked whether they felt the relationship was an employer/employee relationship, and all replied in the affirmative. But it was in further discussion that it became clear that for some personal assistants and their employers other kinds of construction, particularly friendship, are almost as important. This in turn produced its own problems: it became unclear where the boundaries to relationships lay, and in some cases interaction with others in the household of the disabled employer also created tensions. In these employer/employee relationships of one-to-one intimacy, it seems difficult for the participants to agree on the rules of the game.

Such findings of difficulties in boundary setting are confirmed in other studies. Eustis and Fischer (1991:451), in a much larger study that included both employers and employees, found similar problems in Minnesota. As they suggest:

> Where does the professional relationship end and the personal bond begin—and vice versa? As noted, given the nature of the work setting, there is a pull toward informality and at least some degree of intimacy between clients and workers.

They go on to suggest that there are dangers in this tendency toward informality because workers can be persuaded to work beyond contract and thus be at risk of exploitation, and employers are vulnerable to loss of control over the relationship particularly as norms of reciprocity kick in. In the exploratory study discussed in this paper, the question of loss of control or exploitation was less evident than the impact of sheer embarrassment at boundaries that had been crossed. For example, one personal assistant was working for a woman whom she had met through their church—in other words, through word of mouth. The employer lived with her mother and a nephew. The assistant described the nine-year-old nephew as "the grandchild I always wanted 'cause he's interested in cooking." When the personal assistant had a big birthday party, the little boy made a cake, and his aunt, who was invited to the party, also made a dish. But when it came to the party itself, social embarrassment ensued:

A. But I noticed, and I heard back because I've got a lot of time for Margaret . . . that she really couldn't relax with my friends.

Q. What do you think the difference was?

A. Well, my friends would come up and say, "We've heard a lot about you, Margaret," and she just got defensive. And I thought, "Well, they were only saying what I would have said about you." . . . She couldn't be the friend for the night. I thought it was sad, really. I've never said anything to her but . . . my uncle specially went up to her, and he didn't get anywhere with her either. And I thought it was very hurtful really, 'cause it was . . . a social evening. And it shouldn't have been his fault.

There clearly is an additional problem here, named by Eustis and Fischer (1991) as access to what they call the backstage world. In this case, the transgressing of the boundary between the two backstage worlds of employer and employee had immediately given rise to doubts about trust, and particularly doubts about the security of confidential information.

Sometimes the relationship itself can begin to acquire backstage features about which the rules are not very clear. This same respondent has another client—John—whom she fits with a catheter every morning. She described their relationship as "not a friendship, but it is a friendship in a way." She likes him—"I get on very well with him I feel, and he, well, he gets on well with me." Later in the interview we suddenly got into very deep water while talking about the procedure of fitting the catheter:

Q. If he did have an erection would that put you off?

A. No no. Not if it's just er . . . but if it's a sexual thing . . . you know a sexual. . . . I mean I never kiss him. I mean some people you would kiss . . .

Q. Oh really! I never thought of that.

A. Oh yes. And I've never kissed Margaret! Margaret doesn't get kissed either, but I mean . . . with some people you would just naturally, I mean, you just do, don't you! You just give them a kiss and a hug, you know. . . . I kissed him for Christmas and he got such a shock! And then he felt embarrassed 'cause then he realized why I kissed him. (Laughs)

Q. And when you're kissing them, what . . . I mean is it in a sort of maternal way or a . . .

A. No, no. Just a friendship kiss like you would do for a friend. But I thought since it's Christmas I'll give him a kiss, and he got such a shock, and then he realized! (Laughs) And I thought, "Well, you won't get another one anyway." I mean I would only kiss him because it was Christmas.

In this particular case then the potential for boundary transgression was under control: meaningful physical contact had—so far—been kept to a minimum and confined to special events such as Christmas and birthdays. Indeed Christmas may be an event where formality and informality combine most easily, even though the rules of the territory remain unclear. One young man personally took cards to the elderly people he had gardened for in the summer and reported, with laughter, "They were very surprised!" Another respondent received a Christmas card from his woman employer, but by a roundabout route since she did not know his home address; he didn't send her one.

However, with some relationships, the personal assistants reported that it was precisely because there were clear rules and boundaries between employer and employee that the relationships worked. Informal care, particularly where wives cared for their husbands, could be problematic, and those problems could be obviated by the presence of another woman who was paid to care:

Q. So how was he difficult?

A. Oh he was difficult with his arm, his actual lifting, and all that sort of thing, you know, and it did affect his brain. . . . He was difficult with us, but he was never abusive, but towards his own family he was quite abusive, so . . .

Q. So in a way you were relieving the family of that.

A. Oh, yeah. Yeah, definitely.

And another respondent said that a male client showed less frustration with her than with his wife.

Q. Why is that?

A. Well (laughs) you talk nicer to the caregivers than you would to the wife at the end of a bad day.

Q. Right.

A. It's better that way. . . . If they go out she does it. But it's better that he doesn't have her bathing and doing everything 'cause obviously, you know, he's quite frustrated. . . . He's an active man that's got disabilities.

Thus, the intimacy of the paid care relationship is, apparently, not so great that it allows for total breakdown of barriers. Violence and abuse from either party in the paid care relationship is almost certainly less likely than within an informal care relationship, since the presence of the employer/employee contract means that either party can walk away. Friendship, though, is more permeable: once feelings of affection arise, then the consequences of crossing boundaries can range from the minor pain of social embarrassment to the personal risk of a broken heart.

In almost all the relationships described here, shadowy figures of significant others appeared in the interviews. Members of disabled employers' households, including, and particularly, their spouses and their children, featured in the descriptions of these relationships. The relationships with these others were not always easy. One woman personal assistant described the wife of a disabled man she puts to bed as, at their first meeting, "a bit cross with me, but understandable." But in contrast, another woman personal assistant said that the widow of a disabled man she had cared for till his death remained "a lovely friend." Sometimes the personal assistant took responsibility for providing the whole family with a meal, and housework could include washing up and making light snacks for everyone. In one situation a male respondent had been drawn into caring for the mother of the person who employed him. He had no objection, because he was paid in the form of free singing lessons! But once he managed to get a full-time job and a grant for singing lessons, he felt he had to stop the care of the mother—"I feel incredibly guilty but . . ." Thus, the backstage metaphor used by Eustis and Fischer is very appropriate, except that it must be borne in mind that sometimes the backstage can come on stage and even move into the spotlight.

Conclusion

This chapter has moved from the general area of comparative policy analysis to the very particular area of personal relationships. The comparative analysis was presented in order to tease out the differences between the various developments of paid caring that are visible cross-nationally and to develop a typology that can be used to illuminate differences in caring relationships. I have argued elsewhere that the claims that are made for the impact of cash in care tend to be far too generalized and sometimes ideological (Ungerson 1997a) and that only empirical and qualitative research can inform a full appraisal of the commodification of care and its different dimensions. Here I have suggested the complexity of the effects on the relationship of the type of payment called routed wages. My own original view of a system of exploitation has been somewhat tempered by the narratives presented by this small sample of personal assistants, most of whom had clearly made some gains beyond the merely contractual, none of whom reported a sense of exploitation and all of whom felt that eventually they were free to leave a paid relationship if they wanted. The length of time that some of these care relationships had lasted—the longest reported was four years—also indicated that the employers of these assistants had reason to be satisfied. At the same time, though, there are delicate negotiations happening here, pitfalls encountered, bricks dropped, and traps entered into. Above all, these are relationships that are newly developing and where the rules of engagement are as yet unclear.

Caring by the Book

*C*aring comes from the private world of love, intimacy, families, and friendship, but much of it is now done in the public world of work, organizations, markets, and governments. Just as farm and craft labor were once wrenched out of the family and brought into a system of work controlled from outside (Polanyi 1944), caring work is increasingly separated from the personal relationships in which it naturally arises and is performed instead in a system of managed and waged labor. Caring work is still overwhelmingly done informally by female relatives, but to a significant degree it is transforming into jobs with formal task descriptions and occupations with formal training and certification requirements. Much caring is now "produced" by organizations that manage workforces, clienteles, and the "delivery" of care. In these organizations, care is measured, allocated, and monitored by accounting systems, which fragment it into countable components.

This change in the organization of caring work represents a shift from the private to the public sphere. By public sphere, I do not mean "government" or "public sector." Rather, I use the terms *public caring* or *caring in the public sphere* to denote three conditions that make this newer caregiving politically different from its traditional private context. First, the relationship of care involves others in addition to the caregiver and care recipient. These others might include payers, such as insurance companies and government programs; for-profit firms or not-for-profit organizations that provide caregiving services; or government agencies that oversee government-funded services. Second, these external parties are at least initially strangers instead of intimate acquaintances or relatives; third, and most important, these external parties have some authority over what happens in the caregiving relationship.

In the private sphere, caring is done informally and spontaneously, mostly by relatives and friends, and it is mostly unremunerated, though not necessarily. People make up the rules as they go along, negotiating with each other about what sorts of tasks will get done. In the public sphere, caring is more formal and done by people who care for others as their primary occupation and source of livelihood. Caregivers often are, and think of themselves as, professionals or paraprofessionals instead of as ordinary friends and relatives, though a significant amount of caring work is done by women who are nominally hired as maids and housekeepers but who are asked to mind children or care for adults while they are cleaning. Unlike caring work in the private sphere, public caring work is controlled by organizations, professional associations, private firms, nonprofit agencies, and government programs, and it is regulated by rules about which caregivers and care recipients have little say. This shift from private to public sphere is especially true for care of people deemed dependent — children, the frail elderly, the disabled, and chronically ill.

When care "goes public," worlds clash. The values, feelings, and interactions that make up the relational essence of care in the private sphere are sometimes devalued, discouraged, and even forbidden in the public world. Caregivers and the people they care for are pressured by the norms, rules, and policies of the public world to make care conform to the image of work that predominates in the public world. At the same time, they struggle to sustain the meaning and value of care as they know it in their more intimate relations.

The feminist discussion about caring work has focused on three issues. First, how can caring work be rendered more visible, so that it is appreciated as a learned skill and hard work, and so that people who do it can be properly recognized and rewarded (Waring 1988; England and Folbre 1999; Steinberg and Walter 1992; Steinberg 1999)? Second, if caring work is brought into the market economy and if people receive pay for doing it, will money change the motivations of the people who do it or the character of the care they provide (Evers, Pijl, and Ungerson 1994; Waerness 1996; Folbre and Weisskopf 1998; Radin 1996; Himmelweit 1999)? And third, how can more care be shifted to the public sphere, so that women do not have to bear the extraordinary burdens of doing it alone and invisibly (Hochschild 1990; Harrington 1999)?

Recognizing that a huge part of caring work already operates in the public world and is already part of the money economy, this chapter asks a different question: what happens when care is recast in the image of work as we know it? Rather than focusing on money as somehow corrupting care, I focus on ways that professional, business, civic, and bureaucratic cultures clash with the understandings of good care held by most caregivers themselves. I suggest that the norms, ideas, and rules about care in the public world are in some ways incompatible with the norms, ideas, and rules about care in the private world. Abel and Nelson (1990:12) trenchantly articulated this theme as "the conflict between the universalism of bureaucracies and the particularism of caregiving."

This is not to argue that private, family, or informal care is always better than public, formal care. We do need more care in the public sphere, because the burdens in the private sphere are too high, and the needs are too great. But when we move in that direction, we must know how to preserve what is valuable about care in the private sphere. We need to make care public in ways that do not destroy its value. We need to make the essence of caring work visible, not so much in order to make it countable and rewardable, but rather, in order to render clear what it is that we want to provide in the public sphere.

Methods

To show how the norms and rules of public care might conflict with caregivers' ideals of good care, I use interview studies of people in caregiving jobs to learn how they define good care and its components. I then use this same material to listen for the ways they feel tensions and conflicts between their ideals and their practices, and between their concepts of good care and the requirements of their jobs. The first section of this paper describes the broad components of good care from caregivers' point of view. Subsequent sections explore the tensions between caregivers' more particular concepts of good care and public-sphere rules and norms. I have identified six tensions: 1) talk versus tasks; 2) love versus detachment; 3) specialness versus fairness; 4) patience versus schedules; 5) family relations versus work relations; and 6) relationships versus rules. There is some overlap among these categories, but separating out particular elements of the concept of good care highlights how particular aspects of public caring conflict with ideals of good care.

In this chapter, I am avowedly a "lumper" rather than a "splitter." I aim to describe the elements of good care that are common to many types of caregiving, and to reveal the kinds of tensions that arise between public care and private ideals in a variety of contexts. Thus, I include examples from mothering, family day care, child care centers, family health care at home, formal home health care, nursing homes, chronic disease and rehabilitation hospitals, group homes, and psychiatric hospitals. I include private-sphere caring in families and public-sphere caring at varying levels of "organizedness" from in-home, one-on-one care to care in large institutions.

There are, of course, important differences in caregiving among different types of clienteles (especially, differences that arise from varying degrees of dependence and cognitive function); different types of institutions (for example, care provided in individual homes versus that provided in small institutions and large institutions); and different types of labor arrangements (for example, private in-formal — sometimes underground — arrangements, private contracts, full-time and part-time work, agency employees, employees of large institutions). I ignore these differences, however, because I want to illuminate the commonalities, not the differences. My goal is to articulate a theory of how care "works" from the point of view of people who do it — what is essential about it and what are its meaning and value to those who care and those who are cared for?—and to illus-trate how the content and values of private care sometimes clash with those of public care.

I make use of several sources of interviews with caregivers. First, there are nu-merous published studies by sociologists, anthropologists, public health re-searchers, and others who have conducted in-depth qualitative interviews. By no means have I found or used them all, but they are a rich source of quasi-ethno-graphic data to learn how caregivers in all types of caring work think about what they do.

Second, I have been studying how policy changes in home health care are affecting actual care at the bedside. As part of my study, I interviewed 24 direct caregivers: home health aides (7), home health nurses (9), physical and occupa-tional therapists (5), a social worker, and two case managers. Nineteen of these people are affiliated with one not-for-profit visiting nurse association in New England, which also allowed me to observe team case conferences where clients' progress and problems are discussed. This agency is located in a small town and serves about fifteen other towns in its semirural, virtually all-white area. The other five are people I learned about through word of mouth, and they work in a large metropolitan area. I am expanding my study to interview caregivers in a large urban area so that I can capture the views of immigrant and minority women, who constitute the backbone of home health care in most big cities. So far, all of my interviewees are women, and all but one (from the metropolitan area) are white. In the text that follows, any quotations without attribution to a publication are from my own interviews.

Third, the Picker Institute in Boston, Massachusetts, graciously allowed me to use an unpublished transcript of a focus group with ten home health aides. The group was conducted in 1995 by Lisa Leroy, a Ph.D. candidate at Brandeis Uni-versity, and the discussion centered on aides' concepts of good care as well as their views of what factors contribute to or hinder good care. Quotations from this material are cited as "Picker Institute."

This kind of enterprise runs the risk of mistaking people's resigned accep-tance of the status quo for their ideals. By looking at care as it is currently done and at caregivers as they currently are, one is liable to hear what they think is possible or even only actual, rather than what they think would be ideal. Their very ideals are constrained by their socialization and by the power relationships in their jobs. In studying caregiving, there is a special danger that one might find a gendered image of care without realizing that it *is* gendered, simply because most caring work has been and still is done by women.

Although some writers on both the left and the right have argued that compassion itself is a distinctly "feminine" virtue (Ruddick 1984; O'Sullivan 1999), the ideals of good care as I perceive them from the data are not gender-specific. There are few male caregivers in the published studies, and none in my own study of home health care, so my sample is small. Nevertheless, there is a lot of similarity between the ideals expressed by men and women who *do* work in caregiving (see especially Diamond 1990; Harris 1998). This similarity may arise from the fact that because men are a tiny minority in paid caregiving work, they are socialized into accepting the female standards that dominate. But even if there is some disparity between men's and women's concepts of good care (something I do not believe has ever been documented), I suspect that the disparity between the ideals of the private and public worlds of caring is far greater than any distance between the ideals of men and women. The tension between public and private modes of caregiving is by far the more serious problem.

Last, a note about why I use the term *caregiver* instead of *care worker*, putting me out of step with the conventions of this volume. This chapter is about the transformation of caregiving from a personal and relational activity to a more routinized, managed, impersonal activity. The term *care worker* suggests the modern industrial and bureaucratic concepts that I am contrasting with the relational and personal concepts of care I believe caregivers hold. None of the women I interviewed in my home care study ever referred to herself as a "worker." They talked about themselves and each other as aides (or "girls"), nurses, and "PTs" (physical therapists). They talked about their jobs and their work, to be sure, but I think applying the term "worker" to them misrepresents how they think of themselves. I sense that the same is true for most of the caregivers interviewed in the literature I cite, though of course I cannot be sure. It may well be that in fields and regions where paid caregivers are unionized (such as home care aides in parts of California and New York), the women do think of themselves as workers in the modern, industrial sense. On the whole, however, I think most caregivers, and especially professionals with college degrees, would feel demeaned by the term.

Finding Ideals of Care

Caregivers frequently say that good care or the care they aspire to give is the kind of care they would give their own relatives. "I would like to think I would take care of my mother the way I would take care of my patients," says a home care aide, talking about what she considers good care (Picker Institute 1995:15). "My example of good care is when my mother took care of my grandmother," said another. "The way she took care of her, gave her attention. You know, she still made her feel like she was young and alive and us being around growing up and my grandmother see us grow up around her" (Picker Institute 1995:17). An aide in a long-term hospital for the chronically ill explained: "You have to be human and understand that these people are like your father and mother. They are the same. And you have to treat them exactly the same. You have to think at every moment that this is your mother, this is your father" (Glouberman 1990:35).[1] Family day-care providers consistently say that they try to treat their client children the same as their own: "I try to give them the experiences I gave to my own children" (Nelson 1995:28). The Golden Rule of caring work seems to be "Do unto others as you would do unto your own kin."

For every kind of caring work in the public sphere, there is an analogue in the private sphere that hovers around as a kind of inspirational doppelganger. Children's day care operates in the shadow of motherhood. (One wants to say parenthood, but in fact, day-care providers are almost all women, and they do use motherhood as their standard of comparison [Nelson 1995].) Home health care operates in the shadow of family caregiving. Group homes for retarded adults operate in the shadow of families and apartments housing roommates. Caregivers and care recipients seem to carry images of this other sphere and use them to compare and judge caring in the public sphere.

People in public caring jobs frequently compare themselves, usually favorably, to the even more public, more centralized analogues of their field. Family day-care providers use day-care centers as their invidious comparison. Home health workers use nursing homes. Group home staff use mental hospitals and institutions. Even people who provide care in institutions, the most public of public care settings, also frequently make invidious comparisons between institutions and more private care. They, too, seem to use the private-sphere analogues as points of reference. "It is better if they can be kept with their families, or have family care," says a nurse in a psychiatric hospital (Glouberman 1990:49). "I wouldn't put a mentally handicapped child of mine in an institution," declares a teacher in an institution for mentally handicapped children, who portrays herself as much more competent than the mother of her favorite patient (Glouberman 1990:27). "It's true that it's more natural to die at home outside an institution," asserts an aide in a long-term hospital for the chronically ill, all of whom eventually die in the institution (Glouberman 1990:39). Private-sphere caring remains the ideal, something people are willing to give up only when it becomes too burdensome or impossible.

Family caregiving is by no means a bed of roses, however (Abel 1991; Cohen 1996). A significant body of literature documents the high levels of stress, as well as physical and psychological illness, that family caregivers sustain (Abel 1991:62–68 reviews this literature). What has not been much examined are some of the intense negative *emotional* aspects of family caregiving relationships. As Sholom Glouberman says, "Private caring relationships not only have more love and hugging, they also are more challenging and have more hatred, resentment, irritation, despair and frustration than professional and public ones" (personal correspondence, 1999).

Caregivers in institutions, even while saying that they think family care at home is better, tend to acknowledge that sometimes home care can be worse than care in an institution. "I think that my training gives me some special skills that parents might not have. I don't think that parents really know how to deal with mentally handicapped children," says the teacher in an institution for handi-capped children who would never place her own child in an institution (Glouber-man 1990:27). "People can be badly treated at home as well as in an institution," allows the chronic-care hospital aide who thinks it's more natural to die at home. "For some of them, it's better to be in an institution," he adds (Glouberman 1990:39).

Nevertheless, it seems very clear that for people in all fields of caring work and at all levels of "publicness," the standard of good care they carry in their heads is an image of the care given in good family relationships. Public care, care by strangers, care by people who do it as a job rather than as a family connec-tion — that kind of care is regarded as second-best.

Beyond care provided by relatives, at home, what are the elements that distin-guish good care from second-best? A home health aide, asked to give an example of what she considers really good care, replies, "It's not always the clean bed, it's not always some food or medication, but it's a smile or I'll get that for you or I'll do that for you, and so many of us tend to forget that aspect of caregiving. I know girls that will go up and do care with not a word spoken, not a remem-brance made, not a courtesy. That is not good care" (Picker Institute 1995:15–16).

In every walk of caring, caregivers distinguish between "doing the job" and "caring," between the physical tasks and the emotional relationship, between the technical quality and the moral value of what they do. In fact, they often de-scribe good care by invoking technically good task performance as its opposite. They say that no matter how good the technical care, it is not good care if it does not include other things.

What are those other things? What are those elusive elements of caring work that make the difference between caring and doing a job?

Talk versus Tasks

A psychiatric hospital nurse describes her work to an interviewer as the most mundane list of scheduled chores. "At 11:30 one staff goes with the patients for lunch and the other stays on the ward. Between 12:30 and 2:00 the rooms are opened for the patients so they can rest" (Glouberman 1990:93). She marches

through her day, hour by hour, ticking off chores mostly in the passive voice—
patients are gotten up, patients are given medications, reports are made, the food
is brought, patients are escorted here and there, patients are counted, patients
are observed, rooms are cleaned, and on and on. Her description of her work
sounds like a manager's dream—this woman works by the book, and the patients are manipulated as passive objects.

Nothing in her account suggests any human interaction with the patients, and
in fact, she explicitly says she avoids any real involvement. "If you become so seriously involved with the patients, you have to put so much of yourself into them
that it's impossible. If you're so emotional and so sympathetic to them you can go
crazy." Yet immediately she adds, "Actually, really I am so close to our patients. I
always sit down with them, talk to them and everything. I think just two people
sitting down and conversing normally is how you have to get through to them to
gain their confidence" (Glouberman 1990:96).

Just two people sitting down and conversing normally. You will not find that
as part of the job description in any caring occupation, but it is the basic structure for every kind of caregiving. The whole time they are doing something to,
for, or with a client, caregivers are talking and listening. Often they take this
part of caring work so much for granted that they do not even see it as part of
caring. It is so unconscious that it becomes invisible, even in the private sphere
of caring within families (DeVault 1991).

Invisible and unconscious as this aspect may be, talking and listening are the
elements that caregivers consider *instrumental* in creating care. This is as true for
caring work in the private sphere as in the public. A mother explaining what it
means to make a family meal, says: "If you have a real discussion at the dinner
table, like we used to when I was a kid, you can give a person a chance to let you
in on their life. What they were doing all day when they weren't with you. You
can find out more about that person. . . . It's a time when you can show that you
really care about that person in more than just a caretaking role. I mean, I'm their
mother, so I attend to certain needs for them. But that doesn't mean I really know
them" (DeVault 1991:53–54).

Talking and listening seem to be the background, the time fillers, the inciden-
tal accompaniment to the performance of tasks, but to caregivers they are the engine, the tool, the vital force that creates care out of physical tasks. "Listen to
them, it will do them some good," says a male aide in a long-term hospital, suc-
cinctly stating the therapeutic value of listening (Glouberman 1990:35). No matter how much drudge work, medical work, or education caregivers do, and no
matter how strongly their employer emphasizes the performance of specific
tasks, they think the important stuff happens in the talking and listening.

One home health aide says meetings with "the other girls," even just casual
conversations, are extremely helpful. Asked what she gains from these meetings,
she says, "Someone might have a good idea, or tell us about a problem they faced

the day before, and will give us a little tip. If a man doesn't want to talk about something, a certain subject, make sure you don't mention that. That sort of information. I find it helps." What first comes to mind when this woman thinks of helpful collegial advice is tips about topics of conversation, not information about the skilled bodily care that is officially the heart of her job.

A day-care center aide says that before she came to work in the center, she thought the job would involve things like changing diapers and potty training. Then she took some training in early childhood education, which taught her that she could help toddlers to learn. "The classes I took helped me. They taught me how to talk to them [the children]" (Strober and Gerlach-Downie 1995:109). Implicit in what she says is her belief that talking to children is a learned skill, and it is the skill that enables her to accomplish the goal of child care, helping toddlers learn.

Wordless care is not care in the minds of caregivers, or for that matter, in the minds of most people. It is the archetypal horror story. "At the Kindercare infant room, there was more than an hour and a half on a recent Thursday morning when no one said a word to 13-month-old LaRhonda," reported the *New York Times* to illustrate a story on poor-quality day care (Lewin 1998). An academic critique of day-care centers uses similar vignettes for its "data": "Lena" (5 months) was sitting on the floor playing with some toys. The caregiver decided to change her diaper and approached Lena from behind, abruptly and wordlessly picked her up, and laid her on the changing table. . . . The caregiver did not talk to Lena. . . . A few times Lena gurgled and cooed. The caregiver did not respond. . . . When finished with the task, she put Lena back down on the floor, also without a word" (Leavitt 1995:7).

If doing tasks without words is quintessentially bad care, caregivers who work with clients who have trouble communicating think a crucial part of their job is to help them find words and to learn to understand them. "You have to figure it out sometimes for yourself," says a teacher in a hospital for handicapped children. "Some of them will make some kind of sign and then you know. But for the ones who really don't, it's a really hard thing. They all have things they want to communicate, even the ones that don't seem to know what they want" (Glouberman 1990:25). Nonverbal communication becomes as important as verbal. Like the day-care aide who learned how to talk to children, people who work with nonverbal clients consider nonverbal language a genuine skill. A nurse's aide in a geriatric care unit explains why nonverbal communication requires personal relationships: "They all have ways of communicating. . . . Sometimes it's with their eyes or a certain move. They have their ways. If you know the patients, you can communicate" (Glouberman 1990:102).

Nonverbal communication is important even when clients are perfectly able to talk. That is why, as Suzanne Gordon shows in her close observational study of nurses, face-to-face talking can elicit much more information than written questionnaires. For example, a typical question asked to find out if home health care patients need help with activities of daily living is "Do you have help with shopping?" A home care nurse explains why verbal answers are not enough: "The patient might answer, 'Yes. My son helps me.' The nurse might think, oh great, there's no problem here. But in a face-to-face conversation, the patient's hesitancy in answering a question or his body language might convey hints that he really has difficulty getting his son to do his shopping" (Gordon 1997:133–34). Here is another way caregivers find that talking, simple talking, is a tool of their trade.

But seemingly simple talking, "just two people sitting down and conversing normally," entails highly skilled, attentive listening and watching. People who do caring work are often oblivious to the real skill involved. Like the nurse who called her conversations with patients "just two people sitting down and conversing normally," sometimes caregivers are not aware of how they have learned several idiosyncratic languages to communicate with each of their clients, how they have learned to decipher sounds, facial expressions, gestures, and other body language, in order to carry on that "normal conversation."

In the public world, where people are paid for caring, the payers care about how their money is spent. The managers of caring work want proof that they are providing *something*, and often, proof that they are providing something of high quality as well. So they want everything documented. And measured. "You can't manage what you can't measure" is the mantra of management. Managers want something to *show* for their money and their efforts. Tasks show. Talk does not (Smith 1974; Diamond 1990).

Thus, for example, the agency I studied uses a "service plan" for home health aides. It is a paper that serves as the aides' "work order" and lists some 50 possible tasks a nurse might check off for the aides to do. Not one of them is talking or listening. This contrast between the formal job description and the actual practice highlights how, when care becomes public, something essential is squeezed out. Timothy Diamond, a sociologist who worked for two years in nursing homes as a nurse's aide, illustrates how tasks drive out talk with this story: "I stopped to sit with Mary Karney, a seventy-seven year old resident, who was crying on her bed. Before I could find out why she was crying, I was interrupted by my supervisor who scolded me for sitting with Mary, reminding me that I had more vitals to do before bed check. My job priorities did not include sitting with Mary Karney. . . . In this instance, the routine taking and recording of blood pressures not only took precedence, but in effect precluded, tending to Mary Karney's sadness" (Diamond 1990:176).

A home care physical therapist I interviewed worries that soon she will be required to document her time by 15-minute increments, as she already must do when she practices in a clinic. "Did you do gait training? Did you do therapeutic exercise? Did you do, you know, just PT stuff? And you don't get time for, you know—I let [someone] cry on my shoulder for 15 minutes because things aren't going as well as she wishes they were . . . or she has some concerns . . . or she's worried about whether her husband's going to be able to take care of her and can she *stay* here [at home]." This kind of thing "may be social work," the physical therapist says, "but right now *I'm* there, and she needs *me* to listen. I need to know when to refer this on [to a social worker], but sometimes I'm just there to listen."

Thus, in the public world, caregivers learn that talk is not considered work. The same male aide in the chronic care hospital who advised that listening to people "will do them so much good" went on to say, "If you're with them here you will have to do your work, and you can't stop. But they want your complete attention and at times you don't have time to talk" (Glouberman 1990:37). Here is the danger of caring work in the public world: When care becomes formal work, talk is no longer a legitimate part of it. Talking is not "doing your work." Not that talk is forbidden or that lots of talk does not happen despite the pressure to "do your work"—but talk is no longer valued for its own sake.

Love versus Detachment

In the Western dichotomy between reason and emotion, work is viewed as belonging to the realm of rationality. Its purpose is to get things done, to produce something useful or desirable to somebody else, and to meet specific goals. The emotional and spiritual parts of work—caring for one another, attending to emotions and personal dignity, maintaining bonds of loyalty, and finding and expressing meaning—are left to the realm of family and personal life. In the work world, anything that smacks of feelings, emotions, personal relationships, dating, family concerns, and most especially love is thought to disrupt the workplace and interfere with rational judgment and productivity.

Caregivers in every walk say that their training, their employers, and their professional norms all discourage "getting too close," "getting too attached," or "getting too emotionally involved" with the people they care for. Sometimes the "too" is left out, and caregivers perceive that any kind of closeness is discouraged. "Sometimes . . . we, the home health aide, are the only people they come in contact with, that they call their friend, that they talk to, telling you their personal problems. Sometimes it gets too much for you, it weighs heavy. Because they tell you, don't get involved, but how can you not get involved with a client?" (Glasser and Brecher 1997:117). As one physical therapist put it, "If you're human, you do." Clients, patients, and children get attached for their part, too. "Of course they bond," another physical therapist told me when I asked about attachment. "I mean, if you see a patient two to three hours a week, that's more than my mother sees me."

At some point, almost all caregivers use the word "love" to describe their feelings toward some or all of their clients. "I love them. That's all, you can't help it. They give you hugs and kisses and tell you how much they appreciate it. You are not supposed to take them home but you do, in your hearts you take them home" (Karner 1998:79). The deep affection that is almost taboo in the formal rules of caregiving organizations is both unavoidable and essential to caregivers. " 'Oh Rose, I love you,' I would say," a home health aide tells a journalist about her relationship with an elderly woman, as she gestures how she would embrace her client and the client would hug her back (Conover 1997:132).

Love is often a way that caregivers distinguish good care from mere technical care. Speaking about the chronic disease hospital where he works, an aide says, "Here they love all the patients. If it weren't like that I would have left, because I couldn't stand that. There are hospitals with all the equipment. They're well set up, they have everything, but they don't treat the patients well" (Glouberman 1990:38). One type of "bad" day care happens when "love fails to emerge," to use the phrase of sociologist Margaret Nelson. A family day-care provider told Nelson she had once had a boy who "wasn't lovable and I couldn't hold him and hug him. . . . I don't think there's anything wrong with having personality clashes. The thing is with a kid you don't want to hurt their feelings. I wouldn't want my kid in a home where he wasn't at least liked, let alone loved" (Nelson 1995:38). For this woman, and for many caregivers, the work of caring is similar to the world of dating or friendship, where personality clashes and special attractions are legitimate bases for deciding whether to go deeper into a relationship. Just as this woman probably would not marry someone she did not love, she thinks she ought not enter into a contractual relationship to provide day care for a child she cannot love.

The love that develops between carer and cared for is perceived as both inevitable and good. Yet caregivers are sometimes ambivalent about the love in their work. They talk about the pain of losing people they have cared for and loved. And some talk about how too much closeness can undermine their therapeutic effectiveness (personal interviews and case conference observations). Much of their ambivalence, though, comes from the clash of norms between the private sphere and the public sphere and from public caregivers' perceptions and training that attachment is wrong. There is a striking defensiveness in these caregivers' professions of love: "You can't help it," "You just do," "How can you *not* get involved?"

Because professional training and workplace culture emphasize the importance of detachment, caregivers sometimes feel badly about their strong emotional attachments. They come to see themselves as emotionally immature, professionally incompetent, and sometimes even guilty of transgressing the rules of good care. Thus, for example, a family liaison officer in a long-term hospital describes her own path toward emotional detachment as if it were a process of maturation: "I used to become very attached to patients and became quite upset when they died. Now I don't let it happen. I haven't closed myself to the patients. . . . I really love some of them—I run over and give them a hug but I think it's part of my own maturation. How long can you go on climbing over everyone you meet?" (Glouberman 1990:60). This woman seems quite conflicted about her own attachments. She says she no longer "lets it happen," then she says, in so many words, that she still does let it happen, then she makes fun of her own attachment, calling it "climbing over everyone you meet," as if her hugs and warmth were an adolescent excess.

One home health aide, when I ask about attachment, tells me that she finds it very hard when a patient is dying and that she "would never be good at" hospice care. I ask her if she has any tricks to protect herself a little from getting too attached. "That's one of my downfalls," she answers, as if not being able to stay detached is a professional failing. She says, "That's the way I am. I have always been like that all my life. . . . You know, 'cause that's one of the things on—when we do our yearly evaluations or our six months. They will ask a goal, and I've taken hospice courses through the agency and I've read books and I still, I cannot do anything to overcome how I feel. That's just the person I am, I guess."

One can understand how it would be very useful for caregivers to be less affected by the sadness of their clients' lives. At the same time, this woman's struggle captures one of the deep conflicts in caring work, the conflict between "the person I am" and the ideal work personality that professional norms seem to require.

Specialness versus Fairness

Love means special attraction, preference for some people more than others, stronger loyalty to some people than others, simply making someone else special. But specialness is taboo in the public world of caring, where fairness and equal treatment are the governing norms. In the world of work, even the words for these special bonds are decidedly pejorative—favoritism, nepotism, cronyism, and in recent political times, preference. Many caregivers talk about having "favorites," as if it is normal. "She is my favorite. . . . I consider her like a relative—like my daughter," says a teacher of a 17-year-old girl in her hospital, before she mentions her own 8-year-old daughter (Glouberman 1990:21). Others talk about having a favorite as something of a professional failing. A nurse in a psychiatric hospital says, "I try not to get too involved with the patients so that they become dependent on me." And then, as if confessing a weakness or a professional slip, "I do have a favorite patient. I guess old Martha. Other than that, no one" (Glouberman 1990:50).

Here is still another way that private norms of caring clash with public norms. Employers, supervisors, and the formal culture of workplaces discourage emotional attachment and the "favoritism" it sometimes spawns. A nurse in a psychiatric hospital, having absorbed these norms, denies any favoritism and explains to an interviewer why favoritism is wrong: "We don't have any favorites here. If we did and one client noticed it, it would be bad" (Glouberman 1990:97).

In the public sphere, caregivers are caught between the natural human experience of special attachments and the civic and professional norms of equal treatment. The norms of equal treatment are extremely strong, and certainly a forceful part of professional socialization. Caregivers often tell interviewers, "I treat all my clients the same" while they are in the midst of discussing their different feelings toward clients. When Margaret Nelson asked family day-care providers whether they feel differently about their own children and the other children in their care, "the answer [she] almost uniformly received was, 'I treat them all the same'" (Nelson 1995:33). When I ask home health workers whether their work and their relationships with clients are affected by the length of time they expect to be working with the client, they, too, are quick to deny differences in their treatment. "No, because I just give everybody the same care. I think I do my best and I give everybody the same care," says one aide. "You know I *feel* like I'm still treating them the same as I treat any patient, whether I'm going to be there for two days or whether I'm going to be there for a year. I feel like that I give the same whether or not the time is the same." Nelson (1995) says day-care providers' insistence on equal treatment is "a form of denial" that their feelings for different children *do* differ, and that the women deny such feelings because their standard of good care—motherhood—requires loving all children equally. But these proclamations of equal treatment also indicate caregivers' outward acceptance of the larger cultural norms of fairness, even when these equal-treatment norms conflict with their own strong sense that each child or client is unique and deserves *different* treatment.

Caregiving requires individual caregivers to reconcile these two conflicting norms. One norm holds that each person is unique and should be cared for uniquely. The other holds that all people should be treated alike. Caregivers in the public world are thus caught in a moral double bind. They cannot give good care by their own standards if they do not love their clients, if they do not allow themselves to let strong attachments develop, and if they do not treat each client uniquely. But they cannot be good professionals, good workers, or good citizens if they violate the norms of impartiality and equal treatment that govern public life and that have been drummed into them since kindergarten civics and before. Individual caregivers are left to reconcile these conflicting moral imperatives.

Patience versus Schedules

Every caregiver agrees that to do this job, "You've got to have a lot of patience." For starters, it takes time to build up a relationship with people before they trust you to take care of them. If somebody does not want a bath, a home health aide tells me, "If it's somebody that really says, 'No, no, no,' I say, 'Well, how about we just soak your feet?' That's not too intrusive, that's not too intimate. So we start with soaking the feet. I might be just soaking the feet for months. . . . So sometimes it's a bit of gentle persuasion, or gradually working that whole trust factor in and the person begins to feel more comfortable with you."

Caregivers see building trust as a prerequisite to everything else, so to them, it is more important to spend time building trust than doing any particular task of caring. Insofar as building trust takes time, it is often time in which the more physical and countable tasks do not get done. But while individual caregivers may have the patience for this long, slow buildup of trust, organizations usually do not. They have work to get done, they pay people to do that work, and time is money to them.

One home health aide tells me she is sometimes criticized by supervisors for taking too long with a client. For example, she says, if the aides are going into a home only to put elastic stockings on someone's legs, a supervisor might say, "Well, that should only take you 10 minutes to do, and why are you there for a half-hour or 45 minutes?" The aide then tells me: "You know, you can't just go in and get out. I'm sorry. You know, my grandmother had people taking care of her. It's like I wouldn't want them to do the same — you know, just come in and wash her up and leave. You know, they have to have some kind of relationship going." The time it takes to "get that relationship going" is essential time to caregivers and their clients; it is wasted time to organizations.

Patience is essential to good care in other ways in addition to its role in building a trusting relationship. Many caregivers define patience not in terms of time but rather as responding to individuals' needs. "Patience is understanding the individuality of all of these children," according to a family day-care provider. "I could have another 181 [children] and each one of them would be different again. There's no two that need the same amount of loving or need the same amount of reprimanding. Each one needs a little extra something of some sort which is fun finding with that individual" (Nelson 1995:32–33).

Patience is in this sense the opposite of standardization. To claim this kind of patience as part of caregiving is to claim the authority to discern clients' idiosyncratic and unique needs, in opposition to the general determination of client needs asserted by an employer or a payer. Moreover, to insist on exercising this kind of patience is to grant greater legitimacy to these unique needs than to needs as defined by a superior or an organization. Thus, for example, a nursing home might see clients as having a need for their medications at certain times during the day and night. Nurses' jobs are then defined as dispensing medications according to a schedule. But nurses typically see the patients' need for pills as part of a larger set of needs, including the need for a relationship. "I have to give medications to 50 patients on my shift, sometimes three times a shift," says a licensed nurse who works in a nursing home. "You can't just go and put the pill in the person as if they were a machine. These are human beings. They need to talk to you. They need to know what's new. They need a little conversation" (Eaton 1995:22–23).

To claim this kind of patience as essential to caregiving is also to claim a different standard of distributive justice. While an organization typically allows each client a fixed amount of time for medications, dressing, or bathing, caregivers use a concept of "to each according to his need." Caregivers' resistance to schedules is in part asserting their own authority to enact their vision of justice. One home health aide, explaining why she prefers home care, described nursing homes this way: "They're always shorthanded, they only hire the very minimum of help, and I felt like these people were assembly line. We'd have anywhere from seven to nine people to take care of in an eight-hour shift. Plus answer call bells, plus do the other things, give two baths. And I felt like I was cheating these people because I could not effectively give them the care they deserved to have that I felt that they were paying for."

In a public context, caregivers' awareness that each client is only one of many clients changes the way caregivers and clients experience time. Spending time is the major means by which caregivers can show they care about someone and the major way that they can make someone feel valued. The obvious time rationing required in most caring jobs undermines the illusion caregivers try to create that each client is special. A home health aide tells me how she deals with a client's request that she stay longer than the time she can allot to that client: "I'll say, 'Well, you *know* I can't. Such-and-such is waiting for *his* lunch, too.' And I say, 'You know how important it is.' I say, 'You're important and my next person is just as important as you are.' " The aide negotiates demands on her time by making the client feel important, and she gains the client's assent to ending the visit by getting her to identify with the next client. I ask the aide if clients accept this explanation. "Usually, if they have everything upstairs, they can be reasonable," she says. "And if they don't have everything upstairs?" I ask. She laughs. "Yeah, it is a little hard to explain to them that you have to get going. And I will just leave. I'll just say, 'I'll see you tomorrow.' And I'll go."

Not having enough time to do what you think the client needs is a source of stress and guilt for caregivers. Being unable to slow down to the client's time ("They aren't made to be rushed," one home health aide says) highlights both the client's neediness and the caregiver's inadequacy. A nurse tells of a patient with a brain tumor who has a hard time talking. "She knows what she wants to say but she has a hard time getting it out and she gets very frustrated. Sometimes you try to wait. But sometimes you sort of help her along and it makes you feel kind of bad. But you have to because you don't have the time to wait. And at times she's grateful for your help. But she's always sorry. . . . And she's sorry that she has taken so long to get things out. And you feel guilty because you can't spend the time with her that you really should" (Glouberman 1990:104).

Not having enough time is a fact of life, caregiving aside. Even in the most private of caregiving settings, the family, people have to divide their time and cannot "give" it all to one person. But time rationing becomes a more acute problem the more organized the caregiving setting. When caregivers describe their work in moderately public settings — such as family day care and home health care — they usually criticize the insufficient staffing and time rationing required in their more institutional counterparts — day-care centers and nursing homes. Good care, it seems, requires some sense of being able to allocate time according to individual needs and some sense of freedom from the control of a schedule.

Family Relations versus Work Relations

Caring for a parent, child, or grandparent, with all the love that entails, sets the standard of care for many caregivers in the public realm. If family caregiving serves as a model, the metaphor often also becomes emotional reality. When people care for strangers as jobs, they say over and over that the people they care for are "like my own family," "like a second mom," "like my own children." They often say they are treated like a member of the care recipient's family. They love and feel loved just as if these strangers were kin. They become what Tracy Karner (1998) calls "fictive kin." "We get close, very close," says a home health aide. "You are just as much a member of their family as their children or their grand-children. They spend more time with their homemakers than they actually do with their families a lot of the time" (Karner 1998:77).

Sometimes the metaphor of kinship becomes more than just emotional reality. Caregivers begin to integrate their own families and their clients in little ways. A teacher in a hospital for handicapped children talks about bringing some of the children home to her house, and bringing her own little girl to the hospital (Glouberman 1990:23). A home health aide tells me how, on her day off, she helped a client get ready for her 100th birthday party, then later picked up her daughters from school, brought them to the party, and proudly took their picture with the woman. I ask her if her girls had ever met this client before. "Yes, in fact, one time on my vacation I took a day and I made a picnic, and we came up and had a little lunch with this lady."

In the public world of caring, this erasure of the boundaries between real family and work associates is discouraged. A real mother would have her daughter's phone number and feel free to call, but agencies and organizations discourage, sometimes even prohibit, their workers from giving out their home phone numbers. John Herrmann, a sociologist at the University of Virginia who has been researching volunteer-based hospices, asked volunteers why they do not seek Medicare certification and funding (which would enable them to be paid). Among other reasons, "they note that volunteers in certified programs are discouraged from giving out their home phone numbers, and are otherwise proscribed from treating the patients like family, which is what they think they do" (personal communication 1999). Several home health aides tell me that though they are not supposed to give out their home numbers, they do it selectively, or they tell a client, "I can't give you my number, but if you want to call me it's in the book." They are also quick to tell me they do not mind that clients call them and they do not think clients ever abuse the access. When I ask what kinds of things clients call about, the aides make clear they think every call is legitimate. Someone calls to say she needs to change her appointment, or she would like the aide to come early to get her ready for a visitor, or he would like the aide to bring some milk or bread when she comes, or she wants to warn the aide that her driveway has not been plowed yet.

Aides feel that giving their clients their phone numbers contributes to good care, but it also clearly violates the rules of their employer. They understand why the agency has this rule. They usually say that the rule is to protect them from excessive demands by clients and to keep their caregiving job within the bounds of a job. But they are not sure they *want* to keep their relationship within the bounds of the job as defined by the agency, or that the agency's boundaries permit them to do the job right. They want to have discretion. "You know, we are not allowed to give our phone numbers out. Well, that should be our choice, if we want to do that, you know, we should be able to do that," one aide tells me. In the absence of discretionary authority, they simply take it. They use the phone as a way of making their client and themselves more like family.

Even agencies whose mission is to re-create home and family life for their clients find themselves operating under rules that prohibit development of familylike relationships. David Schwartz, former director of the Pennsylvania Developmental Disabilities Council, had been active in the deinstitutionalization movement and in developing group homes in the community for retarded citizens. He eagerly "developed lots of procedures and systems," while "working hard to achieve structure and organization." Then one day he got a call from a staff member in a group home. She had made friends with one of the residents and wanted to invite her home on Sundays to go to church and spend the day together. The rules, however, prevented such a breakdown of the staff-client relationship. Because the staff person was off duty on weekends, she could not take a client home and not get paid without violating federal labor law. But the agency did not want to pay her overtime (Schwartz 1997:33–34).

The problem here is that when caring goes public, when it is done as work instead of as private family or friendship relationships, it suddenly gets new and smaller boundaries. Now, everything in the relationship must be defined as part of the work. If client and caregiver spend time together, it is work time and must be compensated and regulated like the rest of work time. But people's relationships jump the boundaries. Their feelings for one other do not stay precisely modulated according to the norms of a professional or employment relationship.

Relationship versus Rules

No matter what goals and purposes they talk about, whether it is providing personal assistance, medical care, education, safety, or life experience, caregivers do what they do by making relationships with their clients. They become like family and friends, yet they are professionals or employees or both — roles that limit their ability to act as friends.

Caregivers often believe that what clients need more than anything is a relationship. When clients are elderly or disabled, they need company, they need a friend, they need simple human contact. Caregivers are acutely aware of the isolation and loneliness of their clients: "A lot of [home care clients], they have family that stop in, but they don't have just friends — people that they can tell things that they wouldn't tell their family" (Karner 1998:76). An aide in a long-term hospital says, "People sit in a chair here all day, waiting for someone to just come over and talk to them, to wash them, to give them their food. . . . They have to sit and wait for everything in this hospital. They have to wait for the world to come to them" (Glouberman 1990:35). When the clients are children, they need mothering, affection, someone who cares for them. Nelson found that family daycare providers tend to think intellectual stimulation and learning activities are secondary goals and emphasize instead goals having to do with relationships: "I'm trying to give the children a sense of family," or "I'm offering closeness and security — my motherhood" (Nelson 1995:28–29).

Company is a goal in and of itself for clients and caregivers, but it is almost never the goal of a caregiving agency or program.[2] In the public sphere, company is a by-product of other tasks that happen to involve two people being in the same room, but it is not what programs usually pay for or what agencies instruct their employees to do with their time. This conflict is evident in how home care workers and their supervisors talk about the work. A supervisor says, "A lot of [clients] see [home care workers] as a friend — somebody to talk to and they are the ones that see them everyday. We have a rule. I know it is real hard to stick with the rules, a lot of them have a very hard time as far as not talking about your personal life and not getting into the client's personal life" (Karner 1998:77). By contrast, a home care worker says, "I don't like to make them feel that I am a worker for them. I like to make them feel like I am their worker and their friend, too" (Karner 1998:76).

Why do caregivers feel so strongly about the legitimacy of providing company and friendship while formal programs and firms consider them only secondary? Caregivers see social contact as the most essential human need. Some are fulfilling their own need for social contact by caring for others. One home care aide says her patients "make me feel so good. I don't know, because I lost my husband almost two years ago and the patients is my family now" (Picker Institute 1995:44). Perhaps their own loneliness makes them especially attuned to others' needs for contact. Some see company as the essence of the therapeutic process, though they cannot express the idea in such professional terms: "It's very difficult for me to say how a kid really improves. I think there is a bond that grows between two people — that sort of thing," a rehabilitation hospital aide tells Glouberman (1990:86).

Some caregivers see their main job as preserving a client's dignity and identity, and they use company and friendship as tools to that end. For example, an oncology nurse deliberately gets an elderly doctor reminiscing about his career while the chemotherapy is dripping. She actively listens and asks pertinent questions. "When I take fifteen minutes to talk about his work," she explains, "it affirms the validity of his life. He is not just a person with cancer, he is a person who has an identity that extends beyond his illness, even beyond his death" (Gordon 1997:210–11). A hospital nurse asks a patient how he is getting along with his urinary catheter and invites a leisurely description of his daily routine for inserting the tube and cleaning the bag. "I bet you do it really quickly," she comments, triggering another round of conversation in which the man expresses great pride in his agility with a task that is otherwise a source of shame and embarrassment. In this ordinary conversation, which the man's doctor apparently deems beyond the bounds of medical care because he doesn't even ask about it, the nurse manages to rescue and reinforce the patient's dignity (Gordon 1997:67).

Caregivers typically feel that providing company is a legitimate, necessary, and therapeutic activity, but they feel constrained by agency rules and professional norms. One home health aide reveals the high value she puts on company when I ask her for an example of a time she felt really successful: "It always makes you feel good when somebody says, 'I'm really glad to see you. I haven't seen anybody all day.' And you know, OK, you're bringing a little spark into them." Later in the interview, she unwittingly betrays what's in it for the agency, in contrast to what the client wants and what she enjoys providing. If the client does not want any type of bodily care, such as a shower or shampoo or a fingernail cutting, she says, "I try to coax them into something, because I am there—in order for the agency to get paid, to pay me—I have to do some type of hands-on [care]."

Tangled in client requests, agency rules, and their own sense of what is right, caregivers often act on their conscience, but at the cost of feeling guilty and afraid of being found out. The issue of "merely" providing company is one area where caregivers' sense of what is required in a human friendship conflicts with what is required of them by their employer. One aide tells me: "A lot of these people [home care clients], they will tell you to sit down, have a cup of tea or something. What are you going to do? Tell them no? And you do, and they will keep asking you."

Gift giving is another aspect of caring relationships where private and public standards clash. Reciprocity is a strong cultural norm. Clients in all kinds of caring relationships are eager to do things for and give things to their caregivers, no matter how poor or how dependent they are. Children bestow gifts of drawings, found objects, and trinkets on their teachers and day-care providers. A home care patient greets his nurse with a shopping handout from Toys-'R-Us and a news clipping he thinks she will like. She understands that these are his efforts at reciprocity, and acknowledges them by telling him she missed the paper yesterday and will use these items (Gordon 1997:103). Gift giving is prohibited by some home care agencies, though clients and caregivers do it anyway. Nurses sometimes bring flowers, home-baked food, or small items they know a client can use. One aide told me she is supposed to refuse any gift from a client, and she told of times when a client tried to give her a gift through the agency and the agency refused the gifts, telling the client that the aide could not accept them.

Sharing stories of one's personal life is another element of friendship that is usually discouraged in formal caring jobs. One nurse recalled how she had described her own first childbirth to a patient in labor and was then reprimanded by her nursing instructor: "You should never give any personal information to a patient. Nursing is a professional relationship" (Gordon 1997:86). Describing her conversations with an elderly client, a home health aide explains to me the rationale behind the rule that aides are not supposed to talk about their personal lives: "I try not to give her *too* much information about my family, 'cause we're not supposed to, because some of these, like I said, they take everything to heart, and you don't want to bring up family problems, because pretty soon this lady, *she's* having this problem, she's taking over your problems, and it's something that you *don't do.*"

Nevertheless, home care workers do share information about their personal lives, because you cannot carry on a conversation without reciprocating. But they come to feel that they are "not professional" when they do. A physical therapist tells me that with two of her long-term clients, she really felt like she had "maybe"—she lingers nervously on the "maybe"—"gone over the bounds of being just a professional and actually become a friend. In other words, they would share their personal feelings. They would feel comfortable to cry, to complain, to show themselves, and got to know me and my family." Her idea that "showing oneself" and "getting to know" one another are beyond the bounds of professionalism highlights the profound tension of caring work when it goes public.

Touching is a complicated issue in caregiving. For home health aides, some kind of touching is the core of the job—in fact, they typically use the phrase "hands-on" as a noun to name the type of care they are supposed to perform. They cannot be paid unless they have their hands on the patient in certain defined ways. A hug or a pat does not count, but a sponge bath or a hair brushing does.

For most caregivers outside the realm of health care, physical touching is often expressly forbidden. Since the 1970s, when sexual and physical abuse by caregivers became recognized as a serious problem, institutions have developed regulations and policies to protect vulnerable populations. Partly out of this desire to protect and partly out of fear of litigation should their employees abuse a client, agencies tend to use hard-and-fast rules against touching or to define acceptable and unacceptable forms of touching. In many group homes, the residence counselors are not allowed to give so much as a reassuring arm around the shoulder (personal interview with a residence counselor). Teachers' unions are increasingly urging and training teachers to avoid physical contact with children. The Ohio chapter of the National Education Association teaches its members "how to give a non-hug . . . a sweeping motion where you put your arm around a shoulder without really touching" (Kronholz 1998). Student volunteers in Harvard University's large community service program are instructed not to touch the people they work with—no hugs or encouraging pats for immigrants they tutor, and certainly no hugs for children. "If a child asks 'Can I hug you?' or 'Can I sit in your lap and you read me a story?', we are supposed to say, 'How about if you sit down here next to me, and I'll read you a story'" (personal interview with Harvard undergraduate).

Even health care workers, who are supposed to have hands-on contact with patients, are subtly restricted in the kinds of touching they can do. Even they sometimes feel they are not permitted to touch simply to express reassurance or affection or security. A private-duty home health aide tells a reporter how she crawled into an elderly woman's bed one night to calm her during a terrified screaming fit: "Normally they train you to be so cautious, to wear gloves all the time. That didn't seem right in this situation. You want to stop the baby from crying, so you hug it, you just do it." She tells how she lay down next to Rose with her arms around her, and they both fell asleep (Conover 1997:132).

In all these ways, the standards of behavior in caring jobs conflict with the essential friendship that constitutes the caring relationship. Being with a client only for the sake of providing company is not allowed, or paid for. Gift giving is discouraged. So is sharing information about one's personal life. Touching is restricted or forbidden. Yet caring jobs encourage and stimulate the intimacy of the private sphere. Workers cannot simply turn off their feelings or their standards of human conduct. So in order to be good workers, they constantly skirt the boundaries of the permissible, sometimes crossing over.

Conclusion

The conflict between the public and private worlds of caring is not simple to diagnose. There are no easy enemies. Private ideals are protean and are shaped in part by norms of the public realm, especially those of fairness and professionalism. Public standards, rules, norms, and goals come from a variety of sources. The culture of professionalism, civic ideals of fairness, workplace culture in general, and realities of organizational and business survival all promote disengagement, distance, and impartiality. Not getting involved, however, is impossible in caring relationships as they are conceived and practiced by people who give care.

The essential elements of care can be squeezed out by the norms and rules of work in the public world. Talk gets displaced by tasks and is no longer a fully legitimate part of care. Love is taboo; detachment is correct. The idea of a client being special is wrong in the moral culture that defines fairness as treating everyone the same. Patience, the sense of devoting as much time as a person needs, is impossible when care becomes systematized and caregivers work on schedule.

Familylike relationships are forbidden in a culture that replaces real family with paid workers. And simple human relationships are hindered, discouraged, and even condemned by rules against getting close, giving gifts, touching, and sharing of oneself. In all these ways, organization, management, professionalization, and commercialization undermine good care.

Yet, when we look closely, we see that people maintain their ideals, even in the face of the most restrictive rules, the most deadening chores, and the most despairing situations of human suffering, debility, and death. They not only hang on to their ideals, they act on them in many small ways. They violate rules, professional standards, their own better judgment and self-protective impulses, all in order to provide the kind of care they think others need and deserve. They turn strangers into kin (Karner 1998; Stone 1999).

This conflict between private ideals and public practices is part of the stress that is so endemic to caring jobs. Maintaining one's own sense of human decency and rightness takes constant work — not only emotional work but moral work as well. People who must constantly violate rules, standards, and norms in order to do what they think is right must also work to fend off feelings of guilt and fears of getting caught, of losing their jobs, and of hurting their clients. In studies of burnout and high turnover among caregivers, fear and guilt management do not get much attention. The usual policy responses to burnout and turnover are to give more training to caregivers and to offer support groups. These responses miss the mark, for they do not address, or even acknowledge, the underlying moral conflicts of caring work.

The policy problem for the future is how the ideals and practices of good care can be preserved in the face of pressures from professional, civic, workplace, organizational, and business cultures. To make caring better, we need to learn from the ideals of caregivers and from their underground behavior — the ways they follow the spirit rather than the letter of their job descriptions. We need to learn from good caregivers how to provide good care and how organized, public caring work undermines good care. If we want people to enter and stay in caring jobs, we need to face up to the moral conflicts of caring work and not wish them away with training and support groups.

The Conflicts of Caring

*Gender, Race, Ethnicity, and Individualism
in Family Child-Care Work*

Martha Buxton began providing paid family child care in her own home more than eight years ago. When I asked, "What do you like least about family child-care work?" Martha responded immediately,

> Some people don't consider it work when you're at home working with child care. I mean, they sort of do. But not *really*. They think, "Well, you're at home. You're doing your *own* thing. And you just sort of have the children there." But, that's not how I consider it. The children are my work. My own things are secondary during the day when the children are here. . . . It's a low-prestige type of a job, too. It's low pay. There's no benefits. Nothing for it.

"Low prestige." "Low pay." "No benefits." "Nothing for it." These are phrases that Martha, as well as other family child-care workers I interviewed, used to describe public attitudes toward family child care and the conditions under which they work. Why do family child-care workers like Martha believe their work to be undervalued, when public concern about child care appears to be growing in the United States?

In this analysis I seek to make family child care visible as an undervalued but nonetheless substantial form of paid child care. To understand the practice of and attitudes toward family child care (what some workers call "home child care" or "family child care"), I begin with an examination of the mixed economy of child care. Additionally, I explore gender and race ethnicity as forces shaping the organization and provision of paid child care.[1] After placing family child care in these contexts, I make the daily work of family child care visible through the stories of workers and their reflections on the challenges, rewards, and conflicts in their work. The voices and experiences of family child-care workers make clear that emotional attachments and relationships with children and families complicate the sale of child-care services, as do racial ethnic and cultural safety. Additionally, we see that family child-care work is a synthesis of two worlds that have historically been viewed as dualistic and exclusionary — the historically "private" world of households and families, and the historically "public" world of the market economy. This ideological bifurcation continues to create conflicts within the work of family child care, as well as contribute to the social and economic devaluing of the labor.

The Mixed Economy of Child Care

While child care has historically been provided as invisible labor by women in households (either as slave labor or as unwaged labor by mothers), child care has become increasingly visible as middle-class mothers of young children have entered the paid labor force. By 1996 more than 73 percent of the mothers of school-age children worked for pay (U.S. Department of Labor, Bureau of Labor Statistics 1998) and child-care arrangements in the United States have undergone a major transformation in the last 30 years (U.S. Department of Commerce, Bureau of the Census 1982, 1997).

In reviewing child-care arrangements used by employed parents over the last 30 years, three factors struck me. First, child-care centers, while the most visible source of paid care for children, are not the most prevalent form of care. In fact, 70 percent of child care provided to children of employed parents occurs not through child-care centers or school programs, but through the informal networks and arrangements of relatives, family child care, nannies, and employed mothers themselves (Table 8.1). Second, the proportion of children cared for by paid, home-based workers (family child-care workers, and nannies/au pairs) nearly equals the proportion of children receiving paid care in centers. While 43 percent of children received paid care in centers in 1994, 41 percent of children received paid care in homes from family child-care workers and nannies/au pairs (see Chart 8.2). Third, among the three primary forms of paid care for children (center care, family child care, and nannies/au pairs), the proportion of children cared for in centers and by nannies/au pairs varied dramatically between 1965 and 1994. In contrast, family child care remained a very stable source of care for the children of employed parents with family child-care workers providing nearly 16 percent of care in 1965 and 15 percent of care in 1994 (Table 8.1).

Clearly, home-based child-care work is a large and stable source of paid child care in the United States. Why, then, do the workers I interviewed voice the concerns

Table 8.1 *Primary Child-Care Arrangements for Employed Parents of Children Under Age 5, United States: 1965 and 1994 (number of children in thousands)*

	1994		1965	
	Number of children	Percentage of children	Number of children	Percentage of children
Centers	2,218	21.6	243	6.4
Nursery/preschool	801	7.8		
Relatives	4,490	43.6	1,773	46.7
Family day care	1,586	15.4	599	15.8
In child's home (nannies, au pairs)	524	5.1	580	15.3
Other (school)	107	1.0	10	0.3
Self	—	—	19	0.5
Mother	563	5.5	570	15.0
Totals	10,289	100.0	3,794	100.0

Sources: U.S. Department of Comerce, Bureau of the Census, 1997, 1982

Chart 8.2 *Paid Child Care Provided to Children of Employed Parents: 1994*

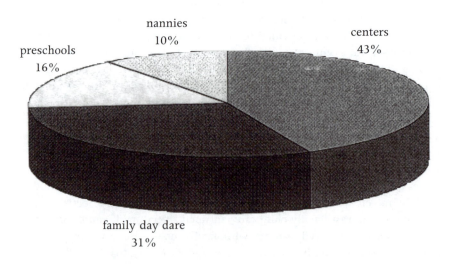

Source: Author's calculations based on U.S. Department of Comerce, Bureau of the Census, 1997

they do about family child-care work? "You're not a really employed person." "Some people don't consider it work." "You're really [seen as] just a housewife that's just watching kids."

Contested Ideologies and Practices: Gender and Race Ethnicity in Waged and Unwaged Care Work

Family child-care work, like all work, occurs in the larger cultural, political, and economic context of the gendered division of labor. The occupation is clearly organized by gender, as women comprise 98.5 percent of family child-care workers (U.S. Department of Labor, Women's Bureau 1997). In addition, a number of studies affirm that women's entry into family child care is a by-product of their commitment to the ideology and practice of the full-time, at-home mother (U.S. Department of Health and Human Services 1981; Mazur 1981; Kappner 1984; Nelson 1994). Vogel (1993:40) clearly summarizes the primary components of the race- and class-based ideology of the full-time, at-home mother: 1) motherhood is morally and practically incompatible with labor-force participation; 2) a clear sexual division of labor divides the family responsibilities of mothers and fathers; and 3) maternity and child rearing are the responsibility of individual families and these individual families are viewed within a dualistic vision of private and public social spheres.

Vogel is one of many scholars who increasingly critique the historical and contemporary reality of the ideology and practice of the full-time, at-home mother, especially for poor women, immigrant women, and women of color (see, for example, Jones 1986; Amott and Matthaei 1991; Hill Collins 1992; Segura 1994). Evelyn Nakano Glenn (1994:2–3) articulates the contradiction between the ideology of this full-time, at-home mother and historical reality when she states:

[M]othering is contested terrain in the 1990s. In fact, it has always been contested terrain. However, a particular definition of mothering has so dominated popular media representations, academic discourse, and political and legal doctrine that the existence of alternative beliefs and practices among racial, ethnic, and sexual minority communities as well as non-middle-class segments of society has gone unnoticed.

While analyses like Nakano Glenn's contribute to the contested ideology of the full-time, at-home mother, they also point out the ongoing power and implications of this ideology for women's participation in paid labor. The ideologies and practices regarding women's historically unpaid caregiving work clearly influence the contemporary public value placed on this work (Abel and Nelson 1990; Abramovitz [1988] 1996; Gordon 1990; Nelson 1990; Pateman 1988; Sassoon 1987).

Deborah Stone, for example, offers a feminist critique of liberal individualism, the well-known philosophical underpinning of the formal market economy, and its explicit values of self-maximization, competition, acquisitiveness, and the atomistic individual (Macpherson 1990). Stone (1991:547) asserts that liberal polities, and, I would add, economies "are built on the premise that their individual members are capable of caring, providing, and deciding for themselves." Therefore, liberal individualism has "no place for dependence and the caring work that goes with it" (Stone 1991:548). Consequently, the work of caregiving, work historically performed as unwaged work by women outside of the formal market economy, remains ignored in the philosophy of liberal individualism and devalued in its economic counterpart, the market economy. As an example of this devaluing, family child-care workers currently earn a median hourly wage of $4.69—less than the minimum wage of $5.15 an hour. Food service workers, service station attendants, and parking lot attendants are among those who earn higher wages than family child-care workers (Center for the Child Care Workforce 1999).

In addition to devaluing gendered caregiving labor, racial ethnic ideologies and practices also influence the status accorded women's labor. In a number of studies, scholars of race, class, and gender explore the ways in which white women transfer their domestic labor to historically subordinated women of color, thus freeing more privileged women from undesirable or undervalued labor (Rollins 1985; Romero 1992; Dill 1988; Nakano Glenn 1986). When women's historically unwaged domestic and care work enters the market economy, the gendered division of labor is also a racial ethnic division of labor infused with ideologies of status and privilege.

It is women of color who are frequently associated ideologically with domestic work, both historically as slave labor and immigrant labor and, subsequently, as low-wage workers in service occupations. These racial ethnic and gendered ideologies and practices are particularly evident in paid child-care labor. Women of color disproportionately undertake the work of providing paid child care in private homes. In addition, the racial hierarchy of women's wages reflected in employment generally (with Euro-American women, African-American women, and Latinas, in that order, representing increasingly smaller proportion's of Euro-American male wages) is reflected in the wages of family child-care workers, as well (Tuominen 1994).

Methodology

Armed with these statistics, I set out to explore the gendered and racial ethnic organization and provision of family child care in greater depth.[2] My analysis is informed by Dorothy Smith's (1987) methodology of "institutional ethnography" as well as Michael Buroway et al.'s (1992) extended case method. In interviews of family child-care workers, I listened for workers' analyses of their own lives, decisions, and options, as well as the broader social relationships that shaped their experiences of family child-care work. The workers I interviewed included 17 women of diverse racial ethnic identity (6 African-American, 4 Mexicana, 6 Euro-American, and one Asian worker) ranging in age from 25 to 48. These workers were about equally distributed among urban, rural, and small-town providers. While 13 of these workers were licensed providers at the time of the interview, 8 of them were either currently or had previously worked as unlicensed, underground providers. English was not the native language of the four Mexicanas who participated in this study, nor the Asian worker, and the interviews of the four Mexicanas were conducted with the assistance of an interpreter.

Making the Invisible Visible

The emergence of child-care work as paid work increasingly challenges historical ideologies of liberal individualism, motherhood, and care. When child care becomes paid work, caring for children, perceived to occur in the "private" sphere of families and households, enters the market economy and becomes "public" work. Work believed to be performed for "love" is increasingly performed for money. Thus, paid child-care work challenges our dualistic understanding of not only ideologies of caregiving, but also conventional definitions of "work." While family child-care workers continue to provide caregiving (work ideologically identified with women) and do so within their own homes (the historical site of both slave and unwaged caregiving by women), family child-care workers provide their caregiving for pay. As such, they challenge the ideology that child care is unwaged care motivated by women's "love" for children.

While the workers I interviewed needed to engage in paid labor to support their families (in fact, only one voiced an ideological commitment to and was economically positioned to be a full-time, at-home mother), personal values of caring and community responsibility also informed workers' decisions to enter family child-care work. The value of community responsibility for children, in particular, directly challenges liberal individualism and the gendered ideology that mothers should provide full-time care for their own children.

Additional challenges to market values and practices can be seen in the ways emotional and relational aspects of family child-care work complicate the sale of child-care services. While workers report relationships with children to be the most rewarding aspect of their work, relationships are also the aspect of the work most fraught with conflict for family child-care workers. Exploitation and conflicts emerge as a result of both empathetic relationships with the families for whom they care and ongoing ideologies regarding gender, race ethnicity, and individualism.

The Emotional and Relational Rewards and Challenges of Family child-care Work

Elisa Mendoza, a family child-care provider for the past eight years, is a Mexicana and the mother of four children who range in age from 12 to 17. Prior to entering family child care, Elisa worked as a seasonal agricultural worker in local orchards "thinning apples and picking apples . . . , then, in the packing shed for another five years." As a mother who worked outside the home, Elisa appreciates the concerns of parents in need of child care. In discussing her paid caregiving Elisa reports, "I enjoy caring for other [people's] kids. And I know how it feels to give your kids to somebody else to watch." Elisa's enjoyment of her work and her empathy for parents reflect the experiences of other family child-care workers I interviewed. And these relationships with children and empathy for their parents are the source of both the primary challenges and the primary rewards of family child-care work.

Relationships with Children

Consistently, the workers I interviewed reported that their relationships with the children for whom they cared provided the greatest reward in their work. In fact, when asked what they liked most about their work, 11 of the 18 workers I interviewed responded immediately with a phrase relating to "the kids."

Annie McManus worked as a public school teacher before she became a family child-care provider. A Euro-American woman, Annie provided underground family child care for three years before the birth of her daughter. When I asked, "What do you like most about family child care?" Annie responded without a moment's hesitation.

> I loved the children. I really love that part of it. . . . I loved talking to them. Playing with them and listening to them. I find children fascinating. And I must admit—it flabbergasts me when people don't. And I know that a lot of people don't. And I also think that children are not respected in this society. Their needs are met last, and I don't get it. . . . (Children) are the embodiment of my favorite qualities about people. They're honest. They're blunt. Their feelings are *right* there. And I appreciate that.

Other workers, while not engaging in an analysis of why they enjoyed children, nonetheless spoke clearly on the topic. "I've always loved kids. I can't explain it any other way," said Anna Burns, an African-American family child-care provider of one year. And Irene Ibarra, a Mexicana provider of eight years, spoke of the affection she receives from and gives to the children for whom she cares.

I like the job. I like the children. I like to be with the children. . . . It is rewarding when I'm in town and the children are with their parents. They see
me and they come to give me a hug. And when their parents come to pick
them up, they don't want to go home with their parents. They want to stay
here. "No, mama. No, home. Stay with Nana," they say. They call me Nana because they can't say Irene. You get attached to them. I had a little boy through
DSHS [the state Department of Social and Health Services] named Robert who
I cared for. He was really little. And the mother left the child. She left him
with her father. But the grandfather had to work and couldn't take care of
Robert. So, he left him here, day and night, and I watched him. He paid me.
DSHS paid me during the day and the grandfather paid me for the night care.
I got really attached to him.

Paula Shelton, coordinator of the state-funded Seasonal Child Care Program
through which Irene provides care, and a friend of Irene's for several years,
spoke about Irene's relationship with Robert.

She got really attached to that kid. I remember. He was like one of the family.
And she loved him. She wanted to adopt him real bad. She got *really* attached
to him. . . . Then they decided to take the boy. The grandfather moved to Ore-
gon, so he took Robert with him. . . . He took the little boy and moved over
there, and it was really hard on Irene.

Here, we begin to see the ways in which, for family child-care workers themselves, the boundaries between paid and unpaid caregiving become obscured
through relationship. While Irene provided paid care for Robert, she also developed a personal and emotional attachment to him. While the women I interviewed asserted their identities as paid and professional caregivers, I was struck
by the frequency with which they equated their work with emotional attachment and, specifically, with mothering.

Vickie Hill, an African-American family child-care worker who has provided
care for 15 years in her suburban home, spoke about her relationships with the
children for whom she cares.

And these children, they are close to you. You're like a second mom to them.
And you being there when they come home after school — you listen to the
different little things they want to talk with you about. It becomes a personal thing. Where, you know, they can't get to mom right away. But, they
can get to you. And it's nice to have those conversations. And it's nice to be
able to be trusted by these children. I think that's real important. If a child
feels that he can trust you. And he can talk to you. And you're there for him.
That's a *big* plus.

Just as Vickie spoke about being "like a second mom," Linda Menley spoke of the children for whom she cares as "like my own kids." Linda is a Euro-American woman who has been providing state-subsidized family child care in her low-income rural community for 11 years. When I asked what she liked most about family child care, Linda responded,

> Being with kids. . . . It sure ain't for the money because you don't make that much. But I think all kids need someone that they can depend on. Get the love that they're not getting at home when their parents are both working. Instead of running up and down the streets. There's too many of them kids that's left out there like that. They're like my own kids. And I try to teach them like I did my daughter.

Just as did Linda Menley, Felicia Lopez, a Mexicana family child-care provider, spoke of the children she cares for as "like my own children." When I asked why she continued in family child care after eight years in the field, Felicia stated, "Because I like children. I have children that I have cared for a long time. To me, they are like my own children."

While not all workers I interviewed likened their paid child-care work to mothering, all spoke about their long-term commitment to and emotional connections with the children for whom they cared. And, whether likening their work to mothering or not, the emotional attachments that providers establish in paid care work blur the perceived dualistic distinction between "private," emotional, home-based caring relationships and "public," formal, workplace professional relationships.

Relationships with Parents

While the family child-care workers I interviewed consistently reported their relationships with children as the most rewarding component of their work, providers identified relationships with parents as the most difficult aspect of family child-care work. I asked each provider I interviewed, "What do you like least about family child-care work?" The most consistent response to this question was "Parents." The most common concern providers report about parents was parents' labor exploitation through attempts to extract additional hours of labor without paying for them (i.e., parents who continually arrived late to pick up their children). Irene Ibarra reported, "Sometimes the parents do not pick up their children on time. I want to go buy something at the store, and they don't get here till late. And by the time I get to the store it's closed." Guadalupe Zamora, a Mexicana immigrant who has provided licensed family child care for four years, described what she likes least about her work. "The parents get off work, go home and rest for a while. Then they come and pick up their kids later. Sometimes I don't mind, but sometimes I have an appointment or something."

Barbara Brown, a Euro-American provider of nine years in her suburban neighborhood, reported

> There's a lot of parents that like to go shopping and go home after work and then come back [to pick up their children from child care]. I have a lot of that. . . . And you're at a point where you don't want the children in your home more than 10 hours. There's no need for it. . . . I have a contract that says I work 10 hours.

Barbara eventually had to confront one mother who consistently violated the contracted agreement for 10 hours of care per day.

> I even took a self-esteem class to *boost* me to be able to talk [to her]. But, she came back with "Well, I'm sorry. I'm not going to pay you overtime. And I would hate to take little Johnny out of here just because I'm an hour late."

Barbara's retort was civil but firm and to the point:

> I said, "I really love your little guy, but we *have* to stick to [the contract]." And she said, "Fine." So the last three days she's been right on time. But, the first day she was testing me again by saying, "I would *hate* to take him out because you don't want to keep him over 10 hours." So, my perfect answer was "Well, do what you feel you have to, but I think you can come back here within ten hours." So far everything is working.

The threat of the mother to remove her child from Barbara's care reflects, in a very overt form, one of the primary difficulties inherent in selling child-care labor. While providers are conscious of selling their labor, the emotional attachments that emerge in care work increase the complexity of the market exchange. Counting on workers' emotional attachment to their children, some parents seek to extract additional unpaid labor from family child-care workers. And this is the most troublesome aspect of their work for the family child-care workers I interviewed.

Workers' Responses to Families' Needs

While reporting frustration with parents who exploit their labor through extracting unpaid hours of care, some workers report a genuine concern for many of the families they serve. Vickie Hill discussed her relationship with parents.

> And in this last class I found that it's important for us as providers to set goals—to help parents be educated toward children and play. . . . There's just a

lot of things that we can do as providers to help parents out. . . . Me, myself, I'm into the kids and into the parents. I reach out there. I like to reach out. And sometimes I know if a parent is misusing me. But, if I know it's a parent that's struggling and catching buses, I'm very lenient because I believe in helping the other person. And well, I'm not into child care for gung-ho being rich. I know that these kids benefit from my care. And I'm like, "What is 30 minutes?" It's not every day. And I don't mind. Where other providers say, "Oh, no. No way."

Vickie is a good example of the interesting turn the exploitation of workers by parents takes when workers themselves adjust the terms of their contacts in order to meet the needs of the families they serve.

Six of the 17 family child-care workers I interviewed reported consciously choosing to alter the rates they charged for care in order to help meet the financial needs of the families for whom they provide care. When asked how she sets her rates, Anna Burns, who provides underground child care to subsidize her public assistance grant, explained, "With Dominic, we started out with $300 a month, but I went ahead and went down to $150." "Were you caring fewer hours for him?" I asked. "No. His mom is trying to move. And she's trying to sell all the furniture and trying to get all the bills paid before she leaves, so . . ." And so Anna, who is living below the poverty level herself, reduces her own wages out of empathy and in order to assist another member of her community.

Annie McManus told about her process for determining the rates she charged for care. "It was negotiated," she said. "It fluctuated. Especially with the two single moms — depending on what was happening with them financially." In addition to adjusting their rates based on families' financial circumstances, the workers reported additional changes they made to their contracts in order to respond to families' needs. Pam Jones, an African-American provider of licensed family child care for six years, reported,

> I prefer parents to drop off and pick up their own children. I have a mother at the present time who's having car trouble, and in order for her to get the kids here I have to go and pick them up and bring them down or else we'd have to look at her looking for other child care. And she thinks it's a temporary situation, and so I'm willing to work with her for a month. It's strenuous, you know, to have to do that. . . . It's taken a lot out [of me] right now. But we're doing it.

So, while family child-care workers identify themselves as workers and contract to sell their caregiving labor for wages, the workers I interviewed clearly experience a conflict in providing child-care services as a formal and contractual market exchange. The workers voice a conscious identity of themselves as workers and professionals and, at the same time, express difficulty in enforcing the terms of their contracts as a result of their relationships with children and their families. This conflict demonstrates the very real struggle providers experience between their roles as paid workers and as empathetic caregivers.

These relational connections that occur between workers, children, and families are, however, different from the "emotional labor" described by Arlie Hochschild in her study of emotion in paid service work. While Hochschild (1983:7) defines emotional labor, in part, as the creation of "a publicly observable facial and bodily display," the emotional qualities of family child-care work, as described by the workers, appear to go beyond the "display" of emotions elucidated by Hochschild. In contrast to a display of emotions, family child-care workers report a genuine attachment—one that complicates a straightforward exchange of their labor for wages. In the case of the family child-care workers I interviewed, emotional connections with children shaped the workers' willingness to violate their own contracts and working agreements by providing additional and unwaged labor that they perceived would benefit the children and families they served. As Margaret Nelson (1990:110), in her study of family child care, acknowledged, "[T]he challenge for these workers is to find a way to dampen acknowledged affections, to make their feelings appropriate to the structural conditions of their work."

Julie Nelson, a Euro-American licensed family child-care worker of 15 years, explicitly recognizes both the importance of and challenge to family child-care workers of doing just what Margaret Nelson says—making feelings that emerge in care work appropriate to the structure of paid work. Julie asserts that family child-care workers need to learn to establish boundaries in providing care to children and to their families. Julie reflected on the challenges of negotiating with parents around children's and families' needs.

> So, you really have to be a diplomat. You really do. And the survivors [among child-care providers] I think learn that skill. And you also need to learn when to cut it off. In terms of "I no longer have ownership of this. I've told you. I'm really sorry that you're stressed out at work, but you need to take control of this. I'm doing what I can in child care. You now need to handle it at home." It's rough. But you do learn that at some point, even though you feel bad, parents still have to be responsible for those kids. And you have to learn to turn it off. But it's hard sometimes.

The Challenges of Blending Paid Work, Home, and Family

Julie's assertion of the need for family child-care workers to set boundaries is particularly difficult given that, in family child care, one's workplace is also one's home.

That makes establishing boundaries between home and family difficult at best. And as I interviewed family child-care workers and analyzed the interviews, I became increasingly aware of the challenges of caring for one's self and one's own family in the same place where one engages in paid labor.

Caring for Others while Caring for One's Own

The assumption that women enter family child-care work because they have small children and want to be full-time, at-home mothers is not reflected in the lives of the workers I interviewed. All of the workers I interviewed entered family child care in order to support their families financially. At the same time, the women I interviewed appreciated and valued the opportunity to be available to their own children while engaged in family child-care work. As Kim Phan, a Vietnamese immigrant and an unlicensed provider of five years, stated, "I think that family child care was good for me. To make money, and I can take care of my children, also."

Pam Jones is the mother of three children. Her youngest son is six years old and, as Pam says, her son "was born into the child care." When I asked Pam what she liked about family child care she responded,

> You can be with your own kids. You can watch your own kids. And then watching them get attitudes. They get kind of jealous of all the kids loving you. And my littlest son, he says, "I don't like it when you let the other kids do this and have my stuff." Or "You hold that baby too long." Or little things like that.

Pam takes extra measures with her own children to make sure the "attitudes" don't get out of hand. With her youngest son,

> I give him his special moments. I give him his special times. As I said, I allow him to crash on my private time, too. We read that extra story or get that extra hug or treat him a little special because I know he's sharing. And then I talk to him. I say, "I know you have to share mommy right now. But when all these kids go home then you won't have to share mommy. Mommy will be just here for you."

While Pam appreciates being available to care for her own son, she recognizes the challenges inherent in caring for her own children while caring for the children of others. Other family child-care workers spoke about these challenges and the very real drain that workers experience as a result of blending their paid care work with unwaged care of their own families.

Sharon Foster is an African-American family child-care worker who provides licensed care in her urban neighborhood. She is the mother of three young children and speaks of the depletion she experiences in balancing her work in family child care with her responsibilities as a mother. When I asked Sharon if she ever thought about leaving family child care she responded without hesitation,

> Do I ever think about it? (laughter) I think about it a *lot*. In the sense that it's a lot for me because I'm a mother of my own young children. It's not like I just have child care and then it's over with. Maybe if I just worked at a child-care center it would be different. . . . I love children. And I know I want to work with children. But because my own personal children are so young, it's a lot on me right now. I had to go to school. Being licensed [as a family child-care worker] with the city — they required me to do that. When I got relicensed they required me to take an ECE [early childhood education] class. And I think that's what really wore me down because I was going to school. So I'm raising my children, going to school, and doing this child care at the same time. That is a lot.

Just as Sharon spoke of the demands of a day combining both paid and unpaid care work, Judith Dahn, a Euro-American family child-care provider, voiced the "real struggle" she experiences in caring for her own two children after a day of caring for the children of others.

> It's a struggle. It's a real struggle. It's a real dichotomy because I got into child care so that I could stay with my kids. And over four years of experience what I realize is that it's real blessing up until my own children are about 3 [years old]. And, then, I find that I'm at the short end of the stick. I mean, I see that the other parents having been out to work all through the day, they come home refreshed — fresh and really ready to see their kids and happy to see their kids. And they have the weekends to spend with their kids. And it's real quality time. But, for me, all these kids leave, and my own kids want attention. I can barely give it to them because I'm so saturated with kids. And so my need for personal time extends into their, supposedly, time with just me. And so, it's been a real struggle.

Judith articulates the very real conflicts that family child-care workers experience as a result of the literal intersection they experience between their work lives, family lives, and personal needs. While parental involvement is important and valued, one's home becomes "an open book." While family child care makes it more possible to care for their own children, workers express concern that the care provided to one's own children may be compromised. What appears, at first glance, as an opportunity to be available to one's own family proves to be, in fact, one of the most complex and formidable elements of family child-care work.

Other studies confirm the conflicts experienced by both home-based and center-based child-care workers in balancing their home and family responsibilities (M. Nelson 1988, 1990; Saraceno 1984; Tom 1992). This struggle is most pronounced among family child-care workers whose very work challenges the supposed split between "public" and "private," between work and family. While family child-care workers challenge these ideological dualisms of public vs. private through their paid caregiving work within their own homes, they do so at a price — the inability to clearly distinguish work time from family time.

Autonomy, Creativity, and Isolation

The family child-care workers I interviewed consistently spoke of the personal rewards they received as a result of the autonomy and creativity required in their work. When I asked Vickie Hill what she enjoyed most about family child-care work, she replied,

> What I like most is you can set your own pace. You can set up things the way that you want to have them set up according to whatever type children you have at that time. And I think that's important. Whereas if you're working in a child-care center you have to go by whatever *they* want you to do. You can do things the way that you want to do things. Being your own boss. To a *degree*. Sometimes I look at that and it depends what kind of parents you've got. Because they're actually the boss. Sometimes you forget that because you're working for them. You're working for yourself, but you're working for the parents to please them and see that things are set up and things are going in the right direction.

Vickie speaks of intersecting qualities that she enjoys in her family child-care work: the need for flexibility and creativity based on the needs of the children for whom she cares, as well as the autonomy she exercises in her work. However, she acknowledged a tension in "being your own boss. . . . Because parents are actually the boss."

While Julie Nelson reported a similar tension regarding independence in her family child-care work, she, too, appreciates the autonomy she has as a family child-care worker. In particular, she contrasts the constraints she experienced as a public school teacher with the flexibility she experiences in family child care — and the effects of each on her ability to provide quality care for children. I asked Julie why she continued in family child care after 15 years.

> I like my independence. Which is a real conundrum as far as talking about family child care. Because you're independent, but you're not free. (laughter) You're not. I mean, I am more free because I have somebody working for me now [Julie refers to her assistant, Debbie]. I enjoy the independence. I like being my own boss. I like deciding what is going to happen. I like the flexibility in schedules. The independence is wonderful. I enjoy working with the kids, as I did with school. But, it's just different. There's more nurturing going on in family child care.

While family child-care providers like Julie and Vickie value their flexibility and autonomy in responding to the needs of the children for whom they care, they acknowledge the downside of home-based care, as well. And one of the primary negatives of home-based care discussed by the workers with whom I spoke is isolation. I asked Annie McManus what her day was like after the last child left her family child care. "Oh," Annie's voice dropped. And then she burst out laughing.

> Hugh [Annie's husband] would come home. This was where the hard part came. I would *spew,* and we'd work on that. A *lot.* He felt like he walked in the door and I was so happy to see an adult that I would just spew. And isolation. Boy, *that's* when I felt it. I didn't really *feel* it when I was with the kids. I felt it afterwards, realizing that I didn't have co-workers to go out for tea with or people to just sit down and talk about the day and how things had gone. My co-workers (laughter) were little kids who asked me funny questions. Who asked "Why?" about everything. And the things I dealt with during the day were very exhausting. It was mentally draining. And so I needed a relief and a release for that. And Hugh was the one who got it. So that was definitely one of the hard things. And I also did not know other people who were doing at-home child care. So I didn't have anyone to share with.

While Annie speaks of the challenge of not having co-workers and not knowing other people in the profession, Pam Jones talks about how she was "in burnout mode" and "ready to quit family child care" before she developed a mutually supportive relationship with Vickie Hill.

> It's really nice to bond with somebody in this profession. Because before I had Vickie, I was taking field trips just to the store just to *talk* to another adult. (laughter) Because there's no other adults when you're in your home. So unless you have someone who's in the profession, who knows what you're going through, then it can be a lonely profession. But it's not if you can bond and relate to people.

For years, Judith Dahn, like Pam, found her one-person child-care operation to be almost unbearably lonely. Then she hired an assistant. Now Judith speaks about the ways in which an assistant in one's family child care can reduce feelings of isolation.

> And I think, probably, the main reason I have an assistant is because I have to have another adult. I think that's the main reason. Because the first two or three years, when I was by myself, it was excruciating. The isolation was excruciating. To just be with children all day. I remember just looking at 4 o'clock on my watch and thinking, "Oh, God. An adult will walk through the door any minute." And it was this hunger.

As home-based workers, family child-care providers lack the support of co-workers that is more readily available in less isolated work environments. Additionally, as self-employed workers in a home-based business, family child-care workers are particularly vulnerable when conflicts arise between themselves and the parents they serve. One of the forms of vulnerability reported by workers is that of racial ethnic and cultural safety.

Racial Ethnic and Cultural Vulnerability and Safety

Almost all of my interviews of family child-care workers took place in providers' homes during their workday. As a result, I had the opportunity to not only speak with providers, but to observe their care work and the children for whom they cared. Both interviews and observations revealed that providers most often care for families who share providers' own racial ethnic and cultural identity. Kim Phan, a Vietnamese refugee, spoke directly to the ways in which native language skills and cultural difference influenced her decision to provide care for other Vietnamese immigrant families.

> I baby-sit[2] for American children, but just part-time and just about two months [out of a total of five years of caregiving]. I wanted to baby-sit for American children also, but I felt that my English — they would not understand — and the culture difference. And that's why I was afraid. Many people asked me, but I refused because at that time I can't speak English. My English was really bad. . . . I think it's a difficult culture. I don't understand what they expect from me. Like if something happened to the children, I was just afraid that they shoot me or I'm going to get in trouble. And it's too difficult for you to explain to them. I think that's difficult for me, and I am afraid that something would happen.

Pam Jones, an African-American family child-care worker, has also seen the effects of cultural and racial ethnic differences between providers and the families they care for, and the need for providers to protect themselves from racial ethnic prejudice and discrimination.

> You know, we don't have no advocate for us. And I think that is something that is *very* needed in this profession because people can say anything. Vickie [Hill] has a cousin [who is a family child-care provider]. . . . Someone said she was mistreating kids when this one lady got mad because the provider had hired an Hispanic person. And she's prejudiced against Hispanic people, and she didn't want the Hispanic person to be in the child care, so she alleged a falsehood — that the provider was abusing kids. There's no one to stand up for the child-care providers.

Family child-care workers sell their child-care services in community-based markets and, as a result, market their services to families who are very much like themselves — with regard to social class, culture, race ethnicity, native language, and formal education. While community and neighborhood markets increase the likelihood that family child-care workers will provide care to families who are like themselves, the women I interviewed also made conscious choices to care for the children of families who shared their own racial ethnic and cultural identities. Among the workers I interviewed, their own concerns about racial ethnic and cultural safety shaped their decisions to care for families who shared, understood, and appreciated their own cultural and racial ethnic heritage.

Lynet Uttal coined the term *racial safety* in her analysis of race, class, and gender dynamics between child-care workers and the mothers they serve. In her interviews with culturally diverse mothers, Uttal found:

> Awareness of racism in U.S. society was a common topic when mothers of color talked about their childcare arrangements. Because of their own experiences with racism, they were concerned about how their children would be treated when the childcare providers were White. . . .

> Racist encounters ranged from outright hostile relations with childcare staff and other parents at the daycare to incompetent interactions with well-intentioned White childcare providers who lack experience with caring for children of color and negotiating cross-cultural interactions (1996:46, 51).

While Uttal identified racial safety as a factor considered by mothers when selecting a child-care provider, my research reveals that family child-care workers consider the same issue when choosing to provide care for children. Parents' attitudes and behaviors regarding race ethnicity and culture, as well as parents' own racial ethnic and cultural heritage are primary factors that can make a work environment more or less safe for child-care providers of color. The workers I interviewed recognized this risk and considered these attributes in deciding for whom they would provide care.

Attitudes Toward Family Child-Care Workers

Just as the home-based nature of their work contributes to isolation and vulnerability among family child-care workers, it also contributes to invisibility and a discounting of their work *as work*. Despite the fact the family child-care workers are self-employed operators of small businesses, they report that their work continues to be devalued or ignored. The family child-care workers I interviewed

spoke often of the devaluation of their work and the inability and/or unwillingness of others to recognize and respect them as skilled professionals.

When I asked Pam Jones, "What do you like least about child-care work?" she
responded without hesitation.

> The stereotype: the baby-sitter. You're a baby-sitter. You know, when you go to
> a bank and say you have a job, they say, "Oh, does your husband work?" You
> know, you're not considered a really employed person. Unless you can show
> tax receipts or someone else's signature on your stuff, you're really just a house-
> wife that's just watching kids.

Former schoolteacher Julie Nelson, who also is past president of the state Family child care Association, recounts attitudes toward family child care similar to
those confronted by Pam.

> I have the ability to present what I do with some sort of credibility outside of
> the child-care community. . . . And I dislike having to defend this as a profes-
> sion. And I *do* defend it. It's really hard to have credibility and respect. I see it
> when I go to the legislature. I see it when I go talk to the fire marshals. I see it
> in any sort of professional setting. Say I'm going to an attorney's. I went to a
> meeting with a local government association. And, I mean, it was like I had to
> try to make sure that I was coming across with big words because they would
> constantly dip down like they thought they needed to get down to my level so
> I would understand. And, yes, educated people do choose to do this. And I was
> real irritated with it. And I get a lot of that at the legislature.

Because child care is dominated by women, though, Julie is unsure whether
the condescension is a response to her profession or her gender. The condescension itself, however, is ambiguous:

> With the legislature it's—when they're trying to make a point and explain
> things to me they assume they have to (Julie begins speaking in a slow, soft
> voice) explain things and lean forward and talk a little bit slower to me so I'll
> get it. And I just—it's *very* frustrating. It's just an attitude. And maybe it's just
> because you're a woman. Maybe it's got nothing to do with child care.

Julie also detects an attitude reflecting a hierarchy of child-care arrangements in
which center-based child care is accorded more status than family child-care work.

> And referring to yourself as a business gives you more credibility. People have
> mistaken me as a center director sometimes. Because if I'm talking and they'll
> say, "What field are you in?" And I'll say, "Child care." And they'll accept that.

And the conversation progresses, and it's like "Well, typically I won't allow something like that to happen in my home." And they'll say, "In your *home*? All those kids are at your *house*?" You know, and it will degenerate. And I'll say, "Well, yes, my hours of business are from . . ." and it brings it back up again. And it's just little things that I've learned over the years. So I'm able to meet people head on and not apologize for what I do.

Martha Buxton is a Euro-American family child-care worker, a former public school teacher who has provided unlicensed family child care for eight years. When I asked Martha if she ever considered leaving family child-care work she responded "Oh yeah." "And what makes you think about leaving family child care?" I asked.

Well, low pay. That's probably the main thing. And then also there's somewhat of a—not a stigma, that isn't the word. People sometimes say, "You're doing *what*? You're doing *child care*? *Why* in the *world* are you doing that?" You know, "Your kids are on their *own*. Are you *nutty*?" You know, usually they won't say *that*—"Are you nutty?"—to your face. But sometimes they'll say, "*My* kids are gone. And now that they're gone I wouldn't tend anybody's kids for anything." And occasionally I think of that. And then I think "What *am* I doing this for?"

At the same time, Martha has a ready answer to her own question:

I think tending children is a real important job. And, in fact, I can't think of anything more important than working with human beings. Trying to make them happy and feel good and pleasant and so forth. That's what we're put here on this earth to do. To help people out. I think that's one reason I do [family child care]. I see myself as assisting people and helping people.

A Call to Serve Children and the Community

Just as Martha voices a commitment to assisting and helping others as a primary motivation for providing family child care, a number of other workers I interviewed voiced similar values. Karen Jackson is an African-American woman who has provided family child care for more than 19 years. When I ask Karen how she got started in family child-care work, she reflects:

I had always worked with children all my life. In one capacity or another. So I knew that was something I could do and live with what I was doing. Being at home but meeting someone else's need. And working with kids: it not only fulfills a need for me, but for those individual children.

As Karen and I talked further her commitment to community service, to "meeting someone else's need," became clearer. She talked about poverty, the needs of families within her community and her commitment to serving families in need.

> And so people who are trying to get off the system [public assistance] need quality child care,[3] but at the same time, it's not a whole lot of child cares that will accept state kids.[4] All of the children here come through [state-subsidized] programs. Because that's where I saw the need. I felt that, especially living in the area we live in, there were a lot of people out there who needed the assistance of the state welfare department to provide care for their children while they attempted to go back to school or go to work. . . . So that's the part I play, in providing a service, is to take mostly state kids and special needs children. The pay is *low*, but I don't think people can do this work if it's only for the pay. I think that you have to feel the *need* to help children in order to stay in a profession like this. And I could have gone strictly private [accept strictly private paying clients as opposed to state-subsidized children]. But private pay people can get child care anywhere. People on subsidies that have to use the city or the county or the state, they can't get child care just anywhere.

Asked what motivated her to provide child care for special needs kids or families who have financial needs, Karen answered:

> God. God was my motivating factor. Because I've known all my life that that's where God wanted me. There are people who are to provide care for children. There are people who will be mothers, doctors, teachers. Mine was the little small part that nobody wanted to do. And that was to provide care for kids.

Because I asked no interview questions regarding spiritual or ethical motivation for entering family child-care work, I was surprised when 6 of the 17 workers I interviewed voiced just such a motivation for their child-care work. A spiritual and ethical commitment to serve the larger community was articulated most frequently by the African-American workers in this study. Of the six African-American workers I interviewed, all but one spoke explicitly of being called to family child-care work, of the value of contributing to one's community, and of the importance of serving families in need.

This call to serve, voiced by the workers I interviewed, reflects aspects of the "ethic of care" first articulated by Carol Gilligan. Gilligan (1993) identifies women's moral thinking as based on an ethic of care that values relationship and interdependence and is rooted in empathy and compassion. She contrasts this with the male ethic of justice, which embraces the values of liberal individualism (rights, autonomy, competition). Patricia Hill Collins speaks of the importance of an ethic of care in African-American communities.

> The convergence of Afrocentric and feminist values in the ethic of caring seems particularly acute. . . . Black women have long had the support of the Black church, an institution with deep roots in the African past and a philosophy that accepts and encourages expressiveness and an ethic of caring. (1993:101)

Hill Collins's analysis is contested by scholars who disagree with the implication that all women of African descent hold similar values, including the notion of a commonly held ethic of care (see, for example, King 1992; Thorne 1992). Additionally, the concept of a gender-based ethic of care among women first articulated by Gilligan is increasingly contested by feminists and researchers (see, for example, Pollitt 1992; Kerber 1993; Puka 1993). Increasingly, scholars argue that political and economic conditions and cultural ideologies profoundly affect social life and, as a result, shape the development of an ethic of care among individuals and social groups. Thus, critics of Gilligan and Hill Collins do not argue against the existence of an ethic of care, but rather against a universal gender- or race-based ethic of care. Philosopher Joan Tronto (1993), for example, encourages us to consider that an ethic of care may be created by the social conditions of subordination — and both gender and racial ethnic identity are certainly two such historical conditions in our own society.

Understanding an ethic of care as socially constructed enables us to more fully understand the desire to serve the community through the provision of child care voiced by many of the workers I interviewed. The call to serve the community and its members, the call to care for others, enabled the women I interviewed to experience a social identity in which their contributions to their families and communities played a central role. This family-based and community-based identity affirmed their child-care work as socially valued and valuable, an alternative to the low status and stigma frequently associated with gender- and race-segregated service and care work.

While family child-care work, with its attendant low wages, sex segregation, and racial ethnic organization, can certainly be viewed as low-status work, the workers I interviewed did not perceive their work as such. While it is essential to remember that the women I interviewed needed to engage in paid labor in order to support their families, they also voiced specific rewards derived from and values associated with caring for children and serving the community. Linda Menley asserted, "I think kids need someone that they can depend on." "Children are not respected in this society. Their needs are met last, and I just don't get it," stated Annie McManus. And Sondra Altman, an African-American provider, reflecting on her provision of care to parents with a limited ability to pay, declared, "I believe that *everybody* deserves quality child care."

Conclusion

The experiences of the workers I interviewed challenge, on all fronts, the dualistic ideologies that promote a perceived division between work and family, between private and public, and between caring relationships and paid work. The workers with whom I spoke challenge the notion that work occurs in one location (deemed "public") and that family occurs in another location (deemed "private").

Analyzing family child-care work from the perspective of the workers who undertake this labor reveals three specific ways in which family child-care work conflicts with ideologies of gender, race ethnicity, and individualism. First, family child-care work overtly challenges the ideology and practice of the full-time, at-home mother. When child care becomes paid work it leaves the "private" sphere of families and households and enters the "public" sphere of the market economy. In so doing, the provision of paid child care by women challenges the notion that child care is work performed by women for love, not money. Additionally, the very existence of family child-care work challenges the ideology that only mothers should care for their children.

Second, family child care both reflects and challenges market values and practices, including the racial ethnic organization and provision of services within the market economy. Specifically, the relational quality of family child care complicates the sale of child-care services. Family child-care workers recognize their rights as paid laborers when they consistently report frustration with parents who violate the terms of their contracts and exploit their labor. However, because of relational and emotional commitments to the children and families they serve, family child-care workers frequently adjust the terms of their contracts, specifically reducing their rates or providing additional hours of unwaged care in order to assist families. This conflict demonstrates the struggle family child-care workers experience as they seek to integrate their rights as paid workers with their responsibilities as empathetic caregivers.

Additionally, the autonomy and creativity family child-care workers experience as self-employed workers is countered by the isolation they experience as home-based workers. This isolation contributes to the vulnerability of workers when conflicts arise—in particular, conflicts relating to racial ethnic prejudice and discrimination. While neighborhood markets increase the likelihood that family child-care workers will provide care to families who share their racial ethnic and cultural heritage, the women I interviewed also made conscious choices to care for the children of families who shared their racial ethnic and cultural identities. In so doing, the workers consciously reduced risks ranging from racial ethnic discrimination to cultural misunderstandings in their relationships with parents.

Third, the value family child-care workers place on children and service to the community directly conflicts with the ideologies and practices of liberal individualism. Liberal individualism, rooted in values of autonomy and competitive self-interest, fails to acknowledge the existence of dependence and hence, the existence and value of care work. In contrast, family child-care workers consistently report the pleasure and rewards they experience in both providing care and facilitating the development of those in need of care—children. Family child-care workers challenge the ideologies of liberal individualism by making dependence and the need for care visible—by bringing children and the work of care into the public sphere and by voicing the rewards and value of caring.

A number of the workers I interviewed spoke of the simultaneous value and responsibility of caring not only for individual children but for one's community, as well. These workers, primarily African-American women, viewed their provision of child care to families in need as an ethical responsibility and contribution to the community. Among the workers I interviewed, the call to serve the community and care for its children provides a valued cultural and social identity for members of historically subordinated groups. This belief in community responsibility for children and for one another certainly calls into question the liberal democratic ideology of the autonomous individual motivated by competition and economic gain in the market economy. Additionally, belief in a collective responsibility for children challenges the dualistic construction of public and private spheres inherent in the ideology of the full-time, at-home mother— the belief that children and child rearing are the responsibility of mothers under a clearly gendered division of labor provided within nuclear families.

While family child-care work challenges historical ideologies of the dualistic separation of paid work from caring relationships, public perceptions of family child-care work remain largely informed by these dualistic ideologies. Family child-care providers believe their paid caregiving work is dismissed as something other than "real" work and is not respected as a skilled profession. Karen Jackson explains:

> I don't think people realize that [family child care] is a profession and meets a need for people who hold other types of jobs. They still look at child-care providers as baby-sitters. But I don't sit babies. I provide care for children. . . . Although this is a child-care home it's still public service work.

Family child-care workers like Karen increasingly voice the public importance and value of their labor. My goal is to help make their awareness and their words motivate us to question the ideologies and practices that devalue and ignore family child-care work. The experiences of these workers and the processes that shape their labor call for a reexamination and expansion of our understanding of work, of child care, and of ideologies of gender, race ethnicity, and individualism. Such recognition requires that the wages, working conditions, and status of family child-care workers be improved to reflect the true social and economic value of their work.

Paid Emotional Care

Organizational Forms
That Encourage Nurturance

*P*aid care work often is devalued and underpaid. This pervasive pattern is documented by census data on wages and ethnographies of nurse's aides, child-care workers, and other paid care workers (Abel and Nelson 1990; Diamond 1992; England 1992; Foner 1994). The emotional or nurturant aspects of care work tend to be especially devalued. For example, nurse's aides in homes for the disabled elderly are expected to emphasize physical care and paperwork much more than emotional support. Nurse's aides who take extra time to comfort a distraught patient often are reprimanded for this deviation from their schedule (Diamond 1992).

Many lay people and social researchers are pessimistic about the prospects for improving paid emotional care because they believe that economic relations and caring are essentially incompatible. This gloomy assessment of paid care is based on the continuing influence of the ideology of separate spheres and on overly rigid models of marketplace relations and bureaucracy.

From the pessimistic perspective, good care requires the emotional bonds and deep personal commitment that we expect in families, especially from women. In the marketplace, bureaucracy and the need for profits and efficiency inevitably create impersonal and calculated human relationships that are inimical to care work. From this perspective, the quality and value of caring can be preserved only in families and other nonmarket relationships.

This paper argues that market relations and bureaucracy need not undermine emotional caregiving. Contrary to the ideology of separate spheres, good care, I believe, results from particular forms of organizing care work, not from the essential qualities of women and families. I focus on three organizational characteristics that encourage emotional care: (1) restrictions on profit making or cost cutting, (2) a structure of authority that minimizes hierarchy and rigidity and gives caregivers and care receivers considerable power, and (3) values, incentives, and training that promote nurturance and interpersonal skills, rather than just scientific and technical knowledge. Some bureaucratic, cost-oriented workplaces provide good emotional care because they exhibit these characteristics.

I begin the paper by defining caring. I then critique the assumptions that lead to the pessimistic view of paid care: the ideology of separate spheres and rigid models of market relations and bureaucracy. The remainder of the paper analyzes emotional care work in four workplaces that are organized in different ways, based on published ethnographies. I first describe two nursing homes in which emotional care is undermined by unrestricted profit making and by bureaucratic procedures oriented to efficiency and medical standards, and not to emotional care. Then I describe two institutions that encourage nurturance—an institution for people with severe mental retardation and a hospital. They encourage nurturance by a work culture that supports caring and by bureaucratic procedures oriented to emotional care.

A Working Definition of Care

My working definition of caring is: a combination of feelings of affection and responsibility, with actions that provide for an individual's personal needs or well-being in a face-to-face interaction (Finch and Groves 1983). Care work includes both feelings and effortful, goal-directed activity, and it centers on responding to an individual's needs. I use the term *the value of caring* to include both the prestige and respect given to paid and unpaid caring work, and the wages of paid care workers compared to the wages of workers in other occupations.

I evaluate care as good insofar as it meets the care receiver's needs for care. Systems of caring are likely to be a mixture of good and bad, since the needs of care receivers have many dimensions and will be defined differently by caregivers, care receivers, outside experts, and other parties. Evaluating systems of caring, therefore, will be complex and open to question, although making such evaluations is essential to organizing caring in an intelligent and morally defensible way.

Critiquing Separate Spheres, and Rigid Models of the Marketplace and Bureaucracy

The apparent incompatibility of caring and paid work partly stems from the ideology and structure of separate spheres that developed in the nineteenth century.

As economic production was separated from households, care work and paid work were socially constructed around opposing values and organizational principles (Degler 1980; Ryan 1979). The women's sphere of family, love, and caring became separated from men's sphere of work in the rationalized marketplace (Ryan 1979). Caring for others came to be seen as naturally growing from women's maternal instincts, while ruthless competition at work grew from men's natural aggressiveness. This perspective remains influential, even though it did not fit social reality very well in the past, any more than it does in the present (Feree 1990; Newman 1988). The opposition between an uncaring workplace and a caring family remains an implicit or explicit assumption of most sociological analyses, with the exception of work done by feminists (e.g., Feree 1990; Glazer 1993).

Talcott Parsons's work in the 1950s and 1960s presented a classic statement of the opposition between the caring family and the impersonal, uncaring workplace. His theory clarifies the assumptions that are still used to argue that caring is necessarily feminine and domestic and cannot be provided in the public sphere (e.g., Popenoe 1993). Parsons summarized the work of earlier theorists in his famous "pattern variables" that characterize the conflicting value orientations of the instrumental (masculine) economy and the expressive (feminine) family. Parsons argued that economic relations in a modern society are expected to be emotionally neutral, to be guided by universalistic rules that treat all relevant actors the same, and to be limited specifically to the characteristics of the person that are relevant to the transaction. Family relations in contrast are expected to be emotional, particularistic, and diffuse (or oriented to the whole person).

Parsons's distinction between expressive and instrumental action also implied that emotional caring, unlike typical work for pay, did not require extrinsic rewards. In Parsonian theory, expressive action like caring for a family member is rewarding in itself or because it contributes to a valuable personal relationship (Parsons and Bales 1955). For example, a mother responds to her crying baby primarily because the mother feels better when she does so. Instrumental action, in contrast, is motivated by extrinsic rewards such as respect, money, or efficiency in attaining another goal. The emotional or expressive aspects of caring fit the feminine role and the family, and are intrinsically rewarding; they do not require good pay or other rewards.

While the ideology of separate spheres and Parsonian theory separate affection and work, care work integrates them. Because care work includes both expressive and instrumental orientations, it is important for researchers of care work to move beyond traditional sociological dichotomies of feelings versus rationality, or private sphere versus public sphere.

Many contemporary analyses of the structure and culture of the modern capitalist and bureaucratic workplace imply a similar opposition between caring and paid work. Capitalism often is viewed as naturally tending toward unrestricted maximization of profits and efficiency, which destroys caring. For example, to raise profits, owners and managers will minimize wages by hiring few paid care workers and paying low wages; this will reduce the quality of care and the working conditions of care workers.

Analyses of bureaucracy and work organizations also tend to emphasize the contrasting systems of authority and training in large organizations and families. Max Weber, an early theorist of bureaucracy, characterized bureaucracies as organizations controlled by a hierarchy of officials who enforce impersonal rules and standards, and prescribe uniform formal procedures and schedules (Weber 1947). Training in technical knowledge and skills is required to move up the hierarchy. Insofar as bureaucracies are hierarchical, impersonal, ruled by rigid procedures, and oriented to technical knowledge, they are incompatible with good caregiving, which requires some decentralization of authority so that care workers can respond flexibly to the immediate needs of care receivers, and some training and legitimacy for skills in interpersonal relations and emotional caring. Although many contemporary sociologists point to the variation in the degree of hierarchy, formalization, and impersonality across organizations, and examine efforts to humanize the workplace, the Weberian image of bureaucracy remains very influential (Scott 1992; Rothschild and Whitt 1986; Ouchi and Johnson 1978).

Rigid models of capitalism and bureaucracy as inevitably incompatible with caregiving are challenged by considerable evidence. There are many examples of capitalist organizations and societies in which profit making is restricted by regulations and practices that safeguard care for citizens, workers, and clients. Studies of Scandinavian welfare systems and of corporations that provide day care and other employee benefits are examples (Hooyman and Gonyea 1995). Almost all capitalist societies tax profits to provide services for citizens. Many bureaucracies have moved toward less hierarchical authority structures and more flexible procedures (Jenkins 1973). In fact, some observers claim that a new form of decentralized, flexible structure is now emerging in corporate America, to encourage constant innovation and adaptation in the global marketplace (Brownstein 1997).

The assumption that families provide good care (while market relations do not) is also challenged by considerable research, although family care is not the main focus of this paper. Families often provide poor care for children or the sick. Unequal power relations in families often lead to abuse, but the misuse of power in families tends to be covered up by the emotional, particularistic quality of relationships and by romantic images of loving, selfless family care (Gelles and Cornell 1985). Family care, like paid care, can be good or bad, depending in part on how the paid or unpaid care is organized.

Before considering the impact of specific organizational characteristics on the quality of care, it is important to note the pervasive devaluation of care work across most workplaces, as indicated by the low pay of care workers compared to other workers. A substantial part of the pay gap by gender can be explained by the devaluation of nurturance, according to Paula England's detailed study of census data on wages and occupations (England 1992). "Being in a job requiring nurturing carries a net wage penalty of between 24 cents/hour and $1.71/hour," her analysis shows (p. 182). This penalty cannot be explained by cognitive or physical skill, by degree of managerial authority, type of industry, or proportion of women holding a particular job, since all these variables were controlled in her multivariate analysis. "Nurturant work is devalued in markets because of its traditional link with women's work in the home and in labor markets," England concludes (p. 182). The second important job characteristic that explains the pay gap is the gender composition of an occupation, indicating that the dominant organization of the marketplace devalues both care work and women's work.

Women's work is valued less and paid less than men's work. Caring is defined as women's work and therefore is devalued. In addition, since good wages are justified as a reward for applying specialized knowledge and skills, and caring is seen as a natural ability of women that does not require specialized knowledge or training, it appears fair to pay low wages to care workers.

Recent data on the average national wages of selected service jobs graphically illustrate the patterns that England described. As Table 9.1 shows, service jobs that focus on caregiving, such as "child-care worker," are paid less than non-caregiving jobs such as "manicurist" or "elevator operator." And jobs that are typically filled by women, like "maids," are paid less than comparable men's jobs like "janitors."

In addition to this overall devaluation of paid care work, three organizational characteristics affect the quality of emotional care: the degree of restriction on profit making, the extent to which authority is hierarchically distributed, and the value given to emotional care. I will now present four case studies that show the impact of these characteristics.

Table 9.1.   *Wages of Caregiving and Other Service Occupations in 1996 (caregiving occupations in bold)*

Occupation	Average Hourly Wage
Cooks, fast food	$5.74
Child-care workers	**$6.73**
Maids and housekeeping cleaners	$6.84
Manicurists	$7.40
Nursing aides, orderlies, and attendants	**$7.75**
Janitors and cleaners	$7.90
Psychiatric aides	**$10.19**
Elevator operators	$13.74
Flight attendants	$17.52
Police detectives	$19.84

Source: U.S. Bureau of Labor Statistics, Occupational Employment Statistics, 1997.
URL: http://stats.bls.gov/oes/national/oes_serv.htm.

Characteristics That Undermine Care: Capitalism, Medical Experts, and the Devaluation of Care

The negative impact of specific organizational characteristics on emotional care is clearly illustrated by two ethnographies of nursing homes. Tim Diamond's description of the care work of nurse's aides in three for-profit nursing homes in Illinois shows how emotional care is blocked by the capitalist push for profits as well as bureaucratic state regulations oriented to scientific, medical knowledge (Diamond 1992).

Capitalism undermines caring partly by cutting down on the time available for emotional care, as the following incident illustrates. Sara Wostein, an 85-year-old resident of a nursing home, is awake in the middle of the night. She is mentally alert, but very disabled physically. The nurse's assistant or aide, Tim Diamond, one of the few men in this job, is checking each room. "Is there anything I can do for you, Sara?" he asks. "Yes," she responds, propping herself up and looking straight into his eyes, "stay with me" (Diamond 1992:123–24). But Tim doesn't have time to stay. On the night shift he is responsible for 30 people, and is busy checking each room and entering his room checks on the medical charts, sorting laundry, getting people water, and doing other tasks. To keep profits up and labor costs down, management avoids hiring more nurses aides. As a result, aides often have too little time for emotional care because they are preoccupied with other tasks.

State regulations also take time away from caring because they involve rigid bureaucratic rules that require extensive paperwork and procedures that are often unnecessary. These rules are based on a scientific, medical model of care and contribute to the devaluation of emotional care. For example, in all three homes in which Diamond worked, vital signs — blood pressure, pulse, temperature, respiration — had to be taken and recorded for each person, several times a day, even though many residents had the identical vital signs every day for years, as their charts showed. The "Restraint and Position" sheet in each person's chart had to be filled out every two hours of the 24-hour day, as mandated by the State Board of Health. For the bedridden, this involved the important job of turning them to help avoid bedsores. For them, the medical rules were essential. But for the other residents, this procedure had little value.

Medical standards also undermine emotional caring by defining physical care and monitoring and charting medical information as much more valuable. The emotional or interpersonal parts of care become secondary or invisible. Talking to a person, holding their hand, or validating their dignity and worth is not entered in the charts, or required by management or state regulations. Emotional caring is not reported or compensated, only medical care.

Emotional caring also gets little attention in the formal training of nurse's aides, Tim Diamond reports. His training in Illinois focused on biology, anatomy, physiology, and nutrition, to prepare students for the certification test controlled by the State Board of Health. Like medical schools, training emphasized curing disease, not emotional care for the chronically ill, or care for people who are dying. Diamond learned the emotional side of care work on the job, from an experienced and skilled nurse's aide. But the value of this kind of informal learning through on-the-job apprenticeship is ignored by management.

These nursing homes vividly illustrate the negative impact of capitalism, bureaucratic state regulations, and medical expertise on emotional care.

Bureaucracy and the Devaluation of Emotional Care

Nancy Foner's ethnography of Crescent Home, a large nursing home in New York City, further clarifies the impact on care work of bureaucratic hierarchies oriented to efficiency and regulations and not emotional care (Foner 1994). Crescent Home is nonprofit and unionized. The nurse's aides receive relatively good wages and benefits, the ratio of aides to patients is relatively high, and the turnover among aides is very low. In contrast to the homes that Tim Diamond studied, at Crescent Home the main barrier to emotional care is a bureaucracy oriented to efficiency and state regulations, not capitalism, according to Foner's account.

Care work at Crescent Home is controlled by federal regulations that must be met in order to obtain Medicare and Medicaid funds. The regulations are enforced by state government officials who certify nursing homes and conduct annual inspections. A top priority of the administrator at Crescent Home is to pass the inspection with flying colors. To accomplish this, he has strengthened nurses' control over nurse's aides.

The nurse coordinator on each floor, an R.N., is the most powerful person on the floor (except when administrators walk through). Her job is to enforce the policies of the administration and the government by ensuring that aides follow proper procedures. She writes the care plan which controls the daily work schedule of nurse's aides such as when they take breaks or give baths. Any change in residents' food, medications, or physical positioning must be approved by her.

The R.N.s at the top of the nursing hierarchy have a rigid bureaucratic approach to care focused on pleasing the administrators and enforcing rules, not on responding to the emotional needs of individual patients. The aides, at the bottom of the nursing hierarchy, are much more interested in caring for patients than in complying with rules, but they have little power.

The contrast between the "best" and the "worst" aide on one floor shows how administrators and nurses value efficiency and following orders over emotional care. The nurse's favorite aide was Gloria James, an intelligent, energetic woman in her late 40s. Ms. James (as she was known) was efficient and neat and obeyed the nurse's care plan. Her rooms were immaculate. She had the beds made on schedule with decorated blankets (that she had provided) at the foot, and items neatly stored in their proper location in the drawers. She worked fast, so she was usually the first aide in the dayroom at lunchtime, preparing residents to eat. Her paperwork was done neatly and on time.

With patients, Ms. James was cruel and abusive, "truly frightening at times in her anger and vicious behavior," Nancy Foner reports (Foner 1994:59). She bullied and taunted patients to get them to eat on schedule.

> "I tell you EAT," she yelled at one woman in the dayroom. "You don't want to eat, you can die for all I care." When the woman meekly complained that she could not eat because her foot hurt, Ms. James screamed, "Shut up and eat you. Eat. You think I have all day for you." And she turned to another woman, "You're such a nasty pig. You hear me, drink." (Foner 1994:61)

Ms. James verbally abused patients in front of nurses, doctors, and administrators, yet she received the highest evaluations on the floor and was left in charge when the nurses were away. Efficiency and conformity to the rules was important, not compassionate care.

Ana Rivera was "the exact opposite" of Ms. James. The coordinating nurse judged her to be one of the worst aides, and constantly criticized her. Ana (as she was called), a woman in her 40s, was warm, respectful, and emotionally involved with residents. Nancy Foner judged her to be "one of the best nursing aides in the home and the one I would pick if I were a resident there" (Foner 1994:62). But Ana irritated the coordinating nurse because she was relatively slow and often ignored bureaucratic rules and procedures.

In contrast to Ms. James's approach, at mealtimes she gently encouraged slow eaters to take their time. One lunchtime, as Ms. James yelled at residents, "Ana quietly fed a frail and weak resident, cradling her with one arm and gently calling her 'Mama' as she coaxed her to eat" (Foner 1994:62).

Ana's style of care conflicted with rigid schedules and fixed rules. She often was the last one in the dayroom at lunchtime and failed to complete her paperwork on schedule. Sometimes she broke the rules and challenged the authority of the coordinating nurse to protect the welfare of her patients. Ana's style of caring—emphasizing responsiveness to the immediate, individual needs of residents for emotional and physical care—was ignored or punished by her superiors.

Crescent Home and the homes studied by Tim Diamond show how organizations undermine care work by maximizing profits, creating hierarchical systems of authority that give little power to care workers, enforcing rigid procedures and rules, and promoting a system of values, incentives, and training that recognizes only medical knowledge. These cases justify a pessimistic view about the possibilities of good paid care. I will now describe two workplaces in which care workers have more power and have attempted to change the dominant system of organizing work. These cases clarify the organizational characteristics that encourage emotional care.

Encouraging Nurturance through Care Workers' Autonomy and Nonmedical Standards of Care: The 'Psych Techs"

Women (and some men) enter caregiving jobs in part because they enjoy responding to the needs of others. But at work they often are blocked from attending to the needs of clients or patients because of cost-cutting policies, bureaucratic rules aimed at fulfilling government regulations, and the devaluation of caring. Some care workers respond to this frustrating situation by trying to change the workplace so that it supports caregiving. Among low-status, relatively powerless workers, directly challenging the institution probably would fail and might get them fired. Collective action through a union would be more likely to succeed, but unions typically avoid the issue of giving greater value and pay to the emotional caregiving component of jobs, as Karen Sacks has pointed out (1988).

Instead of directly challenging bosses and managers, some low-status care workers have developed alternative work relations by taking advantage of their relative autonomy from management. The psychiatric technicians that I will now describe are spatially separated from administrators or managers who enforce capitalist or bureaucratic norms of work, and are relatively free to enforce domestic norms of caring.

Southern California Hospital and Developmental Center is a large state institution that cares for 1,100 severely retarded adults (Browner, Ellis, Ford, Silsby, Tampoya, and Yee 1987; Lundgren and Browner 1990). The hospital is divided into 35 residential units, each staffed by about 25 "psych techs" (psychiatric technicians) plus three psych techs who have advanced to be supervisors or "shift charges" by passing exams and proving their proficiency on the job. Psych techs, 80 percent of whom are women, provide most of the hands-on care at the hospital. While the hospital administrators emphasize balancing the budget and complying with government regulations, the psych techs "placed the highest priority on meeting residents' emotional and physical needs, and they resented anything that interfered with their ability to do so" (Lundgren and Browner 1990:156).

Many psych techs are emotionally attached to the residents and enjoy interacting with them and meeting their needs. "I have fun here, actually, but I make it fun," a psych tech explained. "I come in, I greet my kids, I hug them and kiss them, you know. I play my music with them. . . . I try to make the best possible times I can" (Lundgren and Browner 1990:158). (Psych techs refer to residents as "kids," a sign of their domestic image of care work). Psych techs often touch and hold the residents. They initiate eye contact and interaction, even with the most retarded, and use their own money to buy room decorations, stuffed animals, and bedspreads for the residents.

Many psych techs were attracted to their jobs for altruistic reasons. As one said, "Something in our life seems to lead us to this type of work. You know, wanting to help people . . . it's kind of our nature" (Lundgren and Browner 1990:158).

The work culture developed within the residential units by the psych techs includes informal rules that help them to provide better care, improve their working conditions, and encourage mutual support. They help each other evade administration policies that seem unreasonable or against the interests of the residents. They have developed a custom of being able to "walk" or leave the unit for a few minutes or hours when the stress becomes unbearable. And psych techs "run interference" for each other and intervene when one of them is about to lose self-control.

A psych tech described how she got help when she was about to lose control after a resident spat on her.

> I was so infuriated that I started to assault the resident. The supervisor saw what was happening and wrote out a requisition for a box of Kleenex. Then she handed the slip to me to go get it. I knew that the supervisor couldn't do anything to get me off the resident so she redirected my attention instead. By the time I got back with the Kleenex, I had calmed down. (Lundgren and Browner 1990:164)

Yet the caring culture of the psych techs is limited by the hospital administration's focus on finances and bureaucratic rules. Periodic budget crises result in hiring freezes that leave the psych techs short-staffed. Then work pressure increases and psych techs often lack the time to care for residents the way they would like to. Charting and other paperwork required by the administration or the state consumes large amounts of time.

The quality of caregiving may also be limited by some of the negative features of domestic caring, such as the tendency to dominate or infantilize care receivers. Although sociologists like Parsons assume that the organization of families is ideally suited for care work, the emotional, particularistic, and diffuse character of family relations can encourage domination or even abuse of care receivers and self-exploitation of care workers. For example, Lundgren and Browner report that the psych techs successfully opposed the administration's effort to reduce the psychotropic drugs given to residents, on the grounds that with fewer drugs, the residents would need more physical restraints, which would interfere with residents' social development. Although the psych techs believed their actions were for the good of the residents, perhaps the psych techs also were serving their own needs for playful, "caring" interaction with residents.

But despite these limits, the psych techs are able to maintain a culture of caring that elevates their work from custodial services to caring with affection and respect,

Lundgren and Browner conclude. By doing so, they give their own work meaning and value, and they transform "the residents from social outcasts to human beings with special qualities of their own" (Lundgren and Browner 1990:161).

In this case, the strategy of withdrawing from the system and developing a relatively autonomous work culture of care was fairly successful in increasing the value of emotional care, raising the quality of care for residents, and improving some of the working conditions for care workers. However, since the workers lacked authority within the hospital as a whole, they could not address issues such as wages or the overall organization of the hospital.

Encouraging Nurturance by Bureaucratizing Emotional Care: The Clinical Practice Model of Nursing

Higher-status, semiprofessional care workers, like nurses and social workers, have more freedom to directly challenge official values and practices. The Clinical Practice Model of Nursing, developed by Bonnie Wesorick (1991) and used in several hospitals, encourages emotional care by changing the authority structure, training, values, and formal procedures of nursing care. Directly challenging the medical model of care and the subordinate position of nurses, it gives nurses new authority to diagnose and treat social and emotional problems, includes emotional care in the formal record keeping system, and revamps the training of nurses. This strategy uses central features of bureaucracy such as formal training and record keeping to encourage emotional care.

The Clinical Practice Model was developed in opposition to the medical model, which defines nurses' care work as following the doctors' orders and monitoring patients' physical condition, and is aimed at curing illness and avoiding pain and death. In contrast, the Clinical Practice Model emphasizes nursing care that is independent of doctors and more holistic, although it also includes the traditional tasks of nursing. Nurses independently diagnose and help the patient cope with their emotional and social concerns, as well as their physical problems. Independent nursing "assures patients that when a nurse enters the room, he or she will never again be seen as a heart, a lung, a kidney, or as a medical diagnosis—a treatment. Each person will be seen as a unique individual who has a physical, psychological, sociocultural, and spiritual dimension" (Wesorick 1991:141).

Bonnie Wesorick changed the bureaucratic structure in several ways to support independent nursing. Through a shared governance system, nurses gained more autonomy to diagnose and treat patients needs, as well as time to carry out these functions. Nurses' training was redesigned to produce nurses who valued holistic care and rejected the medical model.

A new system of charting patients was developed that included the patient's personal history, religious values, family situation, and individual concerns. Attached to the standard chart focused on physiological information, this revised chart "became a daily visual reminder to all staff" of the importance of emotional care and the power and autonomy of nurses in providing such care (Wesorick 1991:144). A new format for writing the Plan of Care was developed, "documenting the patient's needs, concerns, problems, and describing personalized approaches to reach desired patient outcomes" (Wesorick 1991:145). For example, a female patient was hospitalized with pneumonia. Her chart included not only physiological information, but additional notes to facilitate caring for the whole person: "dysfunctional grieving related to loss of husband two years ago, no support system, living alone, frequent use of Valium 'to treat feelings'" (Wesorick 1991:146). The Plan of Care included decreasing the use of Valium and notifying a volunteer companion and the Widow Support Group.

This model adapts care work to the modern workplace by bureaucratizing and professionalizing it. Caring is treated as an "art and science" based on specialized knowledge that requires specific training. The knowledge in this case is the body of theory and research written by the network of nurses focused on caring. From Wesorick's perspective, "nursing is the professionalization of the human capacity to care through the acquisition . . . of knowledge, attitudes, and skills required for nursing's prescribed roles" (Roach quoted in Wesorick 1991:137). Wesorick asserts that nurses must "clearly articulate what their unique services are, and value and deliver them with the same expertise that they deliver medical services" (Wesorick 1991:137).

This strategy for raising the value and quality of emotional care seems both very powerful and very problematic. It is likely to produce significant, long-term change, since it combines changing values through redesigned training with raising the power of nurses and using record keeping to enforce policies that encourage emotional care. The Clinical Practice Model suggests that bureaucracy may not be as incompatible with emotional caring as some scholars believe. Emotional caring does not have to be treated as a natural emanation of a woman's personality. It can be redefined as a body of knowledge or set of skills and treatments that can be taught in schools, charted, and evaluated.

On the other hand, bureaucracy can undermine caring, as the ethnographies of nursing homes demonstrate. Emotional care requires a personal relationship, a flexible response to an individual's unique needs, and an element of egalitarian "listening" to the wishes of the care receiver, instead of imposing authoritative "help." This kind of care is undercut by defining caring as expert knowledge and incorporating caring into predetermined categories and rigid procedures.

Moreover, professionalizing and bureaucratizing emotional care may incur special risks of violating the rights of care receivers, because emotional care entails close personal relationships and a blurring of the limits of appropriate interventions.

Cases of psychotherapists abusing their patients suggest that this risk is substantial. On the other hand, the benefits of therapy for many people show that professional emotional care can be very effective.

By redefining emotional caring as expert knowledge controlled by powerful professionals, nurses run the risk of dominating patients and intruding on their personal lives. For example, the widow described above might have a strong personal need or commitment to mourn her husband for a long period of time. She might feel that the nurse was being intrusive and manipulative in contacting the volunteer and the support group. The nurse certainly seemed to be judgmental in labeling her grief as "dysfunctional." The description of the Clinical Practice Model shows no awareness that people from different cultures or religions might object to the nurses' values, nor is it clear that patients entering this hospital consented to receiving emotional or psychological care. To counteract these problems, bureaucratized, professionalized emotional care needs to be tempered with programs to articulate the perspectives and interests of care receivers.

Conclusion

The quality of emotional care that is produced by paid care workers depends in large part on specific characteristics of the organization in which the caregiver works. Even though the dominant organization of the United States economy devalues care work, as indicated by the relatively low wages of care workers, alternative organizational forms support caring. Descriptions of nursing homes illustrate how care work is undermined by unrestricted profit making, hierarchical authority structures that give little power to care workers or care receivers, and values, incentives, and training that promote scientific and technical knowledge but ignore interpersonal skills. In contrast, the care work of the psych techs indicates that good paid care can be produced by workers if they have some autonomy from supervisors and administrators, and if they develop a work culture that supports emotional care. The Clinical Model of Nursing illustrates a very different kind of organizational structure that encourages emotional caregiving by bureaucratizing it.

Paid emotional care will become increasingly important in many societies as the use of day care and nursing homes expands. Caregiving organizations will become a larger segment of our economy, and women probably will continue to do most paid care work. Understanding how specific organizational characteristics affect the quality of care is essential to understanding economic organizations, and to improving the quality of care and the lives of women in the labor force.

The International Division of Caring and Cleaning Work

Transnational Connections or Apartheid Exlusions?

As many of the articles in this volume attest, the work of caring and cleaning continues to fall disproportionately to women. But, we might ask, to which groups of women? When transformed into paying jobs, the tasks of cleaning homes and caring for children, the elderly, and the sick have usually fallen to poor women of color. As many observers have noted, to accommodate their employment responsibilities in other people's homes and their care work for other people's children and elderly kin, paid domestic workers have often found themselves trying to squeeze in the care of their families, or forfeiting their own care work and their own family lives altogether.

Today in the age of globalization and international migration, domestic jobs in the United States—especially in cities such as Los Angeles, Washington, D.C., and New York—are disproportionately held by immigrant women. These women, many of whom are Caribbean and Latina, are disenfranchised by race, class, gender, and increasingly, by citizenship. The incorporation of immigrant women into paid domestic work in the United States is accompanied by a new pattern: many of these women experience long-term spatial and temporal separations from their own families. It is not unusual, for example, for Central American or Caribbean immigrant women to live with their employer family in the United States while their children remain in their countries of origin. While many nanny/housekeepers initially envision these to be temporary arrangements, 10 or 15 years may pass before they once again see their children.

This is not a case of United States' exceptionalism; it is a development that is occurring around the world. Just as paid domestic work has expanded in the United States in recent years, it has also grown in many other postindustrial societies, such as, for example, the newly industrialized countries of Asia, the oil-rich nations of the Middle East, Canada, and parts of Europe. In all of these places, immigrant women are the primary recruits to paid domestic work. Nations that "import" domestic workers from other countries do so using vastly different methods. Some countries, such as Canada, Hong Kong, and Singapore, have developed highly regulated, government-operated, contract labor programs that have institutionalized through formal channels the recruitment, bonded-servitude, and transnational family arrangements of domestic workers (Bakan and Stasiulis 1997; Constable 1997; Yeoh, Huang, and Gonzalez 1999). In the United States, by contrast, a laissez-faire, informal pattern predominates. Regardless of the differing degrees of governmental organization of paid domestic work, paid domestic work worldwide continues its long legacy as a racialized and gendered occupation. In today's global market economy, however, there is a new twist: the divisions of nation and citizenship are increasingly salient. Around the globe, Caribbean, Mexican, Central American, Peruvian, Sri Lankan, Indonesian, Eastern European, and Filipina women predominate—the latter in disproportionately great numbers—as the cleaners and the care workers. Rhacel Parrenas (1998), who has studied Filipina domestic workers in Rome and Los Angeles, refers to this development as the "international division of reproductive labor," and Anthony Richmond (1994) has referred to this as part of a broad new "global apartheid."

In this chapter, I take inspiration from these compelling concepts, as well as from the transnational migration scholarship, to discuss the case of Latina immigrant women who work as private house cleaners and nanny/housekeepers in Los Angeles, while their young children remain in Mexico, El Salvador, or Guatemala. My primary focus concerns the relationship between changing economies, gendered labor demand, and changing family forms. I argue that the way much paid domestic work is organized and remunerated in the United States today institutionalizes, albeit informally, "transnational motherhood." Immigrant women who work and reside in one nation while their children remain in their countries of origin constitute one variation in the organizational arrangements, meanings, and priorities of motherhood. Elsewhere, a colleague and I focused on some of the emotional consequences of this pattern, and more specifically, how the meanings of motherhood are rearranged to accommodate these spatial and temporal separations (Hondagneu-Sotelo and Avila 1997). In this chapter I contrast this new contemporary pattern, common to postindustrial societies, with patterns of contract labor which prevailed in earlier historical periods in the western region of the United States.

Research Description

The argument and the reflections expressed in this essay derive from my readings of secondary historical research and from my primary research on Latina immigrant women's paid domestic work in Los Angeles. For an occupational study of paid domestic work, I conducted in-depth, audiotaped interviews with 68 people. These included interviews with 23 domestic workers (20 of whom were Latina immigrant women), 37 employers of various racial ethnic and class backgrounds, three attorneys specializing in legal issues surrounding private, paid domestic work, and with five individuals who owned or worked in domestic employment agencies. I also spoke more casually — without my tape recorder and interview guide — with many more domestic workers, employers, and several organizers and attorneys.

The materials also include data from a survey questionnaire I administered to 153 Latina immigrant domestic workers at a public park, at bus stops, and at evening English classes. Finally, the primary research includes limited ethnographic observations made in public and private sites, such as public parks, buses, bus kiosks, legal clinics, waiting rooms of domestic employment agencies, and meetings and informal gatherings of the Domestic Workers Association, an advocacy group of Latina immigrant domestic workers.

Below, I begin the discussion of contemporary paid domestic work, reproductive labor, and transnational motherhood by noting some of the parallels between today's labor and family arrangements with earlier programs of contract labor. These programs responded to demands for male labor, primarily in agriculture, but the effects of these institutionalized programs, which recruited bracero workers, are very similar to those we see today among female domestic workers.

Contract Labor: The Externalization of Labor Reproduction Costs

Until the twentieth century, most non-European people who came to the United States were incorporated into the nation through coercive systems of labor that denied the right to family life (Dill 1988, 1994). Chattel slavery is the paradigmatic example. Under that system, marriages were not legally recognized, family members were bought, sold, and torn apart from one another, and slave women raped by their owners. African slaves experienced many atrocities and indignities, including the institutional control and denial of daily, face-to-face caring for their own family members.

Contract labor constitutes another primary mode under which non-Europeans were incorporated into the United States. From the late nineteenth century until well into the twentieth century, men from Mexico, China, the Philippines, and

Japan were recruited and contracted to work under particular constraints for specific periods of time. Members of these groups were brought to work in plantation agriculture in Hawaii and in agribusiness, railroads, forestry, and mining throughout the western and southwestern parts of the United States. Under systems of de jure and de facto contract labor, family members—typically women, children, and the elderly—remained in the countries of origin.

Although there were no significant exceptions to this pattern, from the late nineteenth century to 1964 the direct recruitment of Mexican male contract laborers prevailed. In particular industries and contexts, however, employers did informally recruit Mexican women and entire families. As economist Paul Taylor (1983) documented, in the sugar beet fields of Colorado in the early twentieth century, employers deliberately recruited Mexican families in an effort to discipline the male workforce and induce geographic stability ensuring the men would remain to constitute the following year's labor force. With entire families present, growers believed that male workers would be less likely to enact militant labor strikes. In some instances, the presence of women and entire families was thought to discipline male workers away from rowdiness, drinking, and prostitution. In the early twentieth century, agricultural growers also benefited by using entire families as sharecroppers, as this allowed for the exploitation of labor in the field by women and children. Family unification rendered more productive yields than did individuals. In some instances, employers invited the presence of women and families, using this as a way of disciplining the men.

Industrialization in the United States and ongoing disruption caused by the Mexican Revolution also challenged the pattern of male sojourner, contract labor. During the 1920s, the permanent settlement of entire Mexican families accelerated and Mexican barrios took shape throughout the Southwest. By the 1910s, and increasingly in the 1920s, emergent Mexican urban centers formed in Texas in San Antonio and El Paso and in Los Angeles. These patterns of family unification and transnational families co-existed, so that the urban centers often came to serve as centers of community and as points of labor distribution for solo-male workers headed for jobs in the fields (Romo 1983). In many instances, daily face-to-face caring and interaction between contracted workers and their family members were effectively restricted.

Contract labor programs incorporated men as pure workers, not as human beings enmeshed in family relationships. In the aftermath of the Mexican-American War and the Treaty of Guadalupe Hidalgo in 1848, the United States annexed approximately one-third of Mexico's territory. The extraction of raw materials to fuel industrialization in the Northeast and the development of transportation and trade infrastructure followed at a clipped pace. In this project, employers were primarily interested in minimizing labor costs. With chattel slavery a distant option by the late nineteenth century, capital sought other ways to minimize labor costs. Contract labor provided the solution.

Labor demand was both gendered and racialized. The vast majority of labor contracts went to men. Although it is probably obvious, it is important to underline that the jobs the Mexican braceros were recruited to perform were jobs socially constructed as "men's jobs." These jobs entailed heavy, physical labor in the building and maintaining of railroad lines, in agriculture, mining, and forestry. In the Bracero Program, which was initially prompted by wartime labor shortages, most contracts involved agricultural work; it is important to recall that most contracts were authorized well after World War II had ended (Garcia y Griego 1983).

The racialization of contract labor was also key to this process. The hiring of nonwhite, "racialized" Mexican and Asian workers allowed for the omission of the "family wage," a wage substantial enough to support the family of a male breadwinner. These higher wages were to be reserved for only white male citizens employed in industrial manufacturing.

Various government-regulated programs served to calibrate labor flow and to limit the growth of permanent communities of Mexicans and Asians. Relations of power among nations, as well as race and gender, were fundamental to this recruitment. Only the less powerful, colonized nations could effectively be tapped, as these governments could not effectively protect the rights of citizens (Chan 1990). A series of deliberate exclusion and deportation programs and legislation—among them, the Chinese Exclusion Act of 1882 and the Repatriation Programs that targeted Mexicans in the 1930s—ensured that immigrant workers could not remain in the United States. In effect, these were gendered and racialized programs of deportation and exclusion, but they targeted only immigrants from particular nations (Hondagneu-Sotelo 1995).

One important mechanism in the effort to diminish expenditures on labor was labor elasticity. As many commentators have noted, the "revolving door system of labor" allowed capital to keep labor costs down. Under systems of contract labor, male workers were recruited during times of seasonal labor demand, or for the building of a particular project, and then immediately discarded and sent home when labor demand diminished.

Workers' own patriarchal cultural notions of gender also supported these programs. In the case of the Chinese, for example, patrilocal marriage patterns and strong expectations that younger women should assist their mothers-in-law helped to forbid immigration for women. With the exception of the wives of well-to-do Chinese merchants and some prostitutes, Chinese women did not accompany the Chinese male workers. In the Mexican case, restrictions on women's spatial mobility away from home, ideals of premarital virginity and self-effacing motherhood, and the belief that women needed protection from dangers resulted in arrangements where women were not easily accorded access to men's social networks (Hondagneu-Sotelo 1994).

Contract labor programs were also cost-effective because they externalized the costs of socially reproducing the next generation of employees (Burawoy 1976;

Glenn 1986). The families and children of contract laborers remained in the other society. All costs spanning from prenatal and postnatal care of dependents — nutrition, education, health, and job training — were borne by the other nation. While the contract laborers worked to maintain themselves in the United States and to support their families "back home," remittances were not always forthcoming (Hondagneu-Sotelo 1994). Feminist scholars have pointed out the corollary beneficiaries in the society of destination. As the next section suggests, as the economy has shifted, so has gendered immigrant labor demand. The global commodification of care work and cleaning and the more general expansion of services have encouraged new transnational family forms.

From Extractive Industries to Care Work and Cleaning

In European, Asian, and Middle Eastern nations, as well as in the United States, we have witnessed some dramatic transformations in the international demand for immigrant labor as already noted. In the United States during the late nineteenth and early twentieth centuries, the period during which the various contract labor programs were put in place, the economies of the Southwest and West relied on primary extractive industries, such as agriculture and mining. During the mid-twentieth century, mass production and mass consumption reigned, and federal government investment in various Cold War industries characterized the region. Defense and aerospace manufacturing prevailed, providing many unionized jobs. With the exception of the Bracero Program, which primarily funneled Mexican men to agricultural field jobs until 1964, the mid-twentieth century constituted a hiatus in United States immigration.

As the twentieth century turns into the twenty-first century, the United States is once again a nation of immigration. This time, however, immigrant labor is not primarily involved in extractive industry. While agribusiness continues to be a financial leader in the state of California, relying primarily on Mexican immigrant labor, only a fraction of Mexican immigrant workers are employed in agriculture. Labor demand is now heterogeneous and structurally embedded in the economy of California (Cornelius 1998). In the current period, which some commentators have termed "postindustrial," business and financial services, computer and other high-technology firms, and trade and retail prevail alongside manufacturing, construction, hotels, restaurants, and agriculture as the principal sources of immigrant labor demand in the western region of the United States.

We now see a diversity of gendered immigrant labor demand in many industries, and parallel diversity on family immigration patterns. On the one hand, there is increasing permanent family settlement of Mexican immigrants in California cities, suburbs, and even in rural areas (Chavez 1990; Hondagneu-Sotelo 1994; Palerm 1994). Altogether, about seven million Mexican immigrants reside in the United States (Baker, Bean, Latapi, and Weintraub 1998). Simultaneously, we see a continuation of solo, male sojourners who work in California, while their families reside in Mexico. Due to the Salvadoran civil war (1979–1992) and the longer-running militarized conflicts in Guatemala, hundreds of thousands of Central Americans fled to the United States in the 1980s and early 1990s, many of them "without papers." According to one estimate, about one-sixth of El Salvador's population now resides in the United States (Mahler 1999).

A new related but distinct pattern is that as the demand for immigrant women's labor has increased, so too has the increasing regularity of Mexican and Central American women who leave behind their families and young children to seek employment in the United States. Women who work in the United States in order to maintain their families in their countries of origin constitute members of new transnational families, and because these arrangements are choices they make in the context of very limited options, they resemble apartheidlike exclusions. These women work in one nation-state, but raise children in another. In the next section, I show how this pattern is related to the contemporary arrangements of social reproduction in the United States.

Commodified Dirty Work and Transnational Mothers

The remainder of this paper will focus on the relatively new pattern of immigrant women leaving behind their families in order to work in the United States. This arrangement is associated with the changing labor demand in the global economy. The exponential growth in paid domestic work is due in large part to the increased employment of women, especially married women with children, the underdeveloped nature of child-care centers in the United States, and patterns of local income inequality and global inequalities.

Several commentators, the most notable of whom is Saskia Sassen, have emphasized the expansion of jobs in personal services in the late twentieth century. Sassen located this trend in the rise of new "global cities," which serve as business and managerial command points in a new system of intricately connected nodes of global corporations. Accordingly, cities such as New York—as to a lesser extent, Los Angeles—serve as home to a host of financial and business services—such as insurance, real estate, public relations, and so on. These industries, together with high-tech and entertainment industries in Los Angeles, spawn many high-income managerial and professional jobs, and the people who hold these high-income positions require a good deal of personal services that are provided by low-wage immigrant workers. Sassen provides the quintessential New Yorker examples of dog walkers and cooks who prepare gourmet take-out food for penthouse dwellers. The Los Angeles counterparts might include gardeners and car valets, jobs primarily filled by Mexican and Central American immigrant men, and nannies and house cleaners, jobs filled by Mexican and Central American immigrant women.

Before moving into a discussion of the concrete jobs involved, I want to suggest moving away from the concept of "personal services," which seems to imply services that are somehow private, individual rather than social, and superfluous to the way society is organized. A feminist concept that was originally introduced to valorize the nonremunerated household work of women, "social reproduction" or, alternately, "reproductive labor," might be more usefully employed. Replacing "personal services" with "social reproduction" shifts the focus by underlining the objective of the work, the societal functions, and importantly, the impact on immigrant workers and their families.

In their classic article, Barbara Laslett and Johanna Brenner (1989) define social reproduction as those activities that are necessary to maintain human life, daily and intergenerationally, and they underline that the way a society organizes social reproduction has far-reaching consequences for macrohistorical processes. The activities of social reproduction encompass how we take care of ourselves, our children and elderly, and our homes. Food, clothing, and shelter must all be prepared for human consumption. As Evelyn Nakano Glenn (1992:1), another important contributor in this arena, put it, "Reproductive labor includes activities such as purchasing household goods, preparing and serving food, laundering and repairing clothing, maintaining furnishings and appliances, socializing children, providing care and emotional support for adults, and maintaining kin and community ties."

Racial divisions of reproductive labor have been largely ignored, Glenn (1992) argues, by both race relation scholarship that tends to be androcentric, and by Marxist feminists who focus on women's unpaid labor in the home and assume that women share universal experiences. Glenn uses the example of paid domestic work to show how many American-born women of color exited jobs as private housekeepers and maids, only to enter other types of reproductive work in more public venues, such as working in organizations as hotel maids, licensed clinical nurses, or cafeteria workers. Racial divisions of reproductive labor in the California landscape are certainly not new, but Glenn's study reminds us that they do not remain static, but change over time.

Similarly, the standards of social reproduction—how we should maintain human life—are also fluid. These standards are culturally and historically determined. For example, conceptions of childhood, child rearing, and who should do the work of child rearing have changed over time. While in an earlier era, aristocrats routinely relied on wet nurses to feed their infants, that notion today sounds not only strange and foreign, but consistent with notions of child abuse and motherhood deficiency. Yet in this area of dual-career families, a common family-work practice may relegate young, preverbal children to the care of a nanny for 65 hours a week. Other elements of social reproductive labor may reflect regional idiosyncrasies. The automobile culture of Los Angeles, for example, has led to the fetishization not only of automobiles as status symbols, but clean, polished, hand-detailed status cars. Drawing on primarily Latino immigrant workers, the car wash industry in Los Angeles has become a labor-intensive one, and one that is relatively affordable for mass consumption.

The connection that I wish to draw between social reproduction and the jobs performed by Latino immigrant workers is this: there are a series of products and services now available for purchase in Los Angeles, and more generally in the Southern California region, that did not exist 20 to 25 years ago to the extent to which they do today. These include products and services for high-income elites as well as for the masses. Many of these services and products are dedicated to social reproduction, and they are often connected as part of the informal, unregulated economy. New Latino immigrant women and men are doing the work, and for many of them—particularly the women who work as nanny-housekeepers—the job requires that they leave their children behind in their country of origin.

An entire series of food preparation services may be categorized under the rubric of social reproduction. Certainly restaurants, which employ busboys, car valets, cooks, dishwashers, and wait staff, are among the most public and visible locales. But there are more private, virtually invisible occupations as well. For example, the "baby greens" salads that began appearing in upscale restaurants several years ago are today sold as prewashed, prepackaged leaves in plastic bags sometimes labeled as "Euro Salad." These are available at virtually any supermarket because Latino immigrant workers have been incorporated into jobs not just in harvesting, but now in washing and packaging agricultural products. Cultural taste dictates new products, and these generate new labor demands.

Some of these cultural products are distinctively gendered. In recent years, the manicure seems to have emerged as the most important symbol of emphasized femininity in Los Angeles, and commensurately, the city has witnessed the expansion of the number of nail parlors. Korean immigrant women seem to be disproportionately represented as owners and workers of these nail parlors. Asian immigrant women perform the manicures and pedicures, and not surprisingly, these labor-intensive manicures are now a relatively low-cost item in Los Angeles, available for $7 to $10. Products and services once affordable for only the elites are now accessible to the masses.

Meanwhile, other services remain in the home but are commodified. Many of these reproductive labor jobs are constructed as "feminine," as jobs requiring women workers. These encompass a number of domestic work tasks, including house cleaning, laundry, child care, elder care, and meal preparation. Male immigrant workers are incorporated into many home services, principally as gardeners or as the occasional handyman, furniture mover, or painter, but in general male immigrants are hired for jobs that require less time and less intensive face-to-face contact. Male day laborers, for example, might be occasionally hired to clear hillside brush or paint houses, but they are hired "casually," not regularly incorporated into the household-service routine. Gardeners do provide weekly services, but given the way gardening is organized in Southern California today, this generally involves a quick, 15-minute team effort of "mowing and blowing" lawns.

The incorporation of Latino immigrant workers into paid social reproductive services has been relatively overlooked in literature. There are several explanations for this. First, much of this work is conducted as part of the informal economy, as unregulated uncounted work; it is not well captured by the IRS, nor by the Census Bureau or Labor Department statistics. Furthermore, households, not business firms employ these workers, and as they perform their duties as nannies, housekeepers, cleaners, gardeners, handymen, or painters, they are not directly involved in capital accumulation. No product is made available for sale or profit.

Alternatively, while a numerical minority of Mexican immigrants in California are working in agriculture, that sector commands attention because it remains a primary financial sector of the state's economy. Yet it appears to directly incorporate a relatively small proportion of Mexican immigrant workers in the state. Similarly, Latino immigrant workers who are employed in social reproductive services that occur outside of the home—say, in car washes or restaurants—are also overlooked because they work in small, competitive businesses that are generally not highly capitalized.

In the late twentieth century in Los Angeles, and elsewhere in the United States, paid domestic work is virtually institutionalized as a Latina immigrant woman's job. Historically, as in the contemporary period, paid domestic workers have had to limit or forfeit primary care of their families and homes in order to earn income by providing primary care to the families and homes of employers, who are privileged by race and class (Glenn 1992; Rollins 1985; Romero 1992). What appears to be new today—on the East Coast with Caribbean domestic workers, throughout Asia, Europe, and Canada with Filipina domestic workers, and in California with Central American and Mexican domestic workers—is the regularity with which immigrant women leave behind their own children in their country of origin to pursue paid domestic work.

Paid domestic work is organized in various ways and there is a clear relationship between the type of job arrangement women have and the likelihood of experiencing transnational family arrangements with their children. Although there are variations within categories, I find it useful to employ a tripartite taxonomy of paid domestic work arrangements. This includes live-in and live-out nanny/housekeeper jobs and weekly housecleaning jobs.

Weekly house cleaners work in different houses on different days according to what Mary Romero (1992) calls modernized "job work" arrangements. These contractual-like employee-employer relations often resemble those between customer and vendor, and they allow employees a degree of autonomy and scheduling flexibility. Weekly employees are generally paid a flat fee, and they work shorter hours and earn considerably higher hourly rates than do live-in or live-

out domestic workers. By contrast, live-in domestic workers live and work in isolation from their own families and communities, sometimes in arrangements with
feudal remnants. There are often no hourly parameters to their jobs, and as our
survey results show, the majority of live-in workers in Los Angeles earn below
minimum wage. Live-out domestic workers also usually work as combination
nanny/housekeepers, generally working for one household, but by contrast with
live-ins, they enter daily and return to their own home in the evening. Because of
this, live-out workers resemble industrial wage workers (Glenn 1986). Live-in
jobs are the least compatible with conventional mothering responsibilities. Only
about half (16 out of 30) of live-ins surveyed have children, while 83 percent (53
out of 64) of live-outs and 77 percent (45 out of 59) of house cleaners do. As Table
10.1 shows, 82 percent of live-ins with children have at least one of their children
in their country of origin.

In the United States, there is a long legacy of Caribbean women and African-
American women from the South leaving their children "back home" to seek
work in the North. Since the early 1980s, thousands of Central American women,
and increasing numbers of Mexican women, have migrated to the United States
in search of jobs, many of them leaving their children behind with grandmothers, with other female kin, with the children's fathers, or sometimes with paid
caregivers. In some cases the time and distance of separations are substantial—
10 years may elapse before women are reunited with their children. In another
publication, Hondagneu-Sotelo and Avila (1997) analyzed Latina transnational
mothers currently employed in Los Angeles in paid domestic work, one of the
most gendered and racialized occupations. No one knows the precise figures on
the prevalence of transnational motherhood, just as no one knows the myriad
consequences for both mothers and their children. However, one indicator that

Table 10.1   *Domestic Workers: Wages, Hours Worked, and Children's Country
of Residence*

	Live-in (n=30)	Live-out (n=64)	House cleaners (n=59)
Mean hourly wage	$3.79	$5.90	$9.40
Mean hours worked/week	64	35	23
Domestic workers with children	(n=16)	(n=53)	(n=45)
Percent with all children in the United States	18	58	76
Percent with at least one child "back home"	82	42	24

Source: Author's calculation based on survey research

hints at both the complex outcomes and the frequencies of these arrangements is that teachers and social workers in Los Angeles are becoming increasingly concerned about some of the deleterious effects of these mother-child separations and reunions. Many Central American women who made their way to Los Angeles in the 1980s, fleeing civil wars and economic upheaval, pioneered transnational mothering, and some of them are now financially able to bring to the United States the children whom they left behind. These children, now in their early teen years, are confronting the triple trauma of simultaneously entering adolescence—with its own psychological upheavals; a new society—often in an inner-city environment—that requires learning to navigate a new language, place, and culture; and new families that do not look like the ones they knew before their mothers' departure. Their families may include siblings born in the United States, new stepfathers, or new boyfriends of their mothers. In a previous article (Hondagneu-Sotelo and Arlin 1997), we examined how their meanings of motherhood shift in relation to the structures of late-twentieth-century global capitalism.

Like other immigrant workers, most transnational mothers came to the United States intending to stay for a finite period of time. As time passes and economic need remains, however, prolonged stays evolve. The separation of work life and family life constitutes the separation of labor maintenance costs from labor reproduction costs (Burawoy 1976; Glenn 1986). According to this framework, Latina transnational mothers work to maintain themselves in the United States and to support their children—and reproduce the next generation of workers—in Mexico or Central America.

Transnational mothering is different from contract labor arrangements of the late nineteenth and mid-twentieth centuries, as it is now women with young children who are recruited for American jobs that pay far less than a "family wage." When men come north and leave their families in Mexico—as they did during the Bracero Program and as many continue to do today—they are fulfilling familial obligations defined as breadwinning for the family. When women do so, they are embarking not only on an immigration journey, but on a more radical gender-transformative odyssey. They are initiating separations of space and time from their communities of origin, homes, children, and sometimes husbands. In doing so, they must cope with stigma, guilt, and criticism from others. As they do care work and cleaning for others, they lose the right to do care work and cleaning for their own families.

Conclusion

Taking a long view, we see in retrospect that preindustrial economies were characterized by the household unification of production and reproduction. Industrialization brought about divisions between public and domestic spheres, with some men going off to work and women doing reproductive work in the domestic household. For many Asian and Mexican men who were incorporated into industrialization and extractive, primary industries in the western region of the United States, this involved not a cross-town journey to the factory but a cross-national, long-term sojourn to California, Hawaii, or other western states. In the current postindustrial context, many reproductive services are commodified, removed entirely from the household (e.g., fast food, dry cleaners, car washes), or they are now performed for pay in the household. While this scheme glosses over important nuances and may be too linear to capture what is, in fact, a more complex transition, I believe it is suggestive of an historical trajectory. The work of caregiving and cleaning, once relegated to wives, mothers, and grandmothers, is increasingly commodified and purchased on a global market.

The commodification of social reproduction is bound on a global scale with the international migration of women and their employment in domestic work. Immigrant women from Sri Lanka, Indonesia, the Philippines, and various Caribbean nations, like many Mexican and Central American women, migrate internationally for work in commodified social reproduction. Many of them leave their children and other family members behind in their country of origin, assigning the reproductive work of caring for these dependents to family members and paid care workers.

As a result of this international division of cleaning and caregiving, we now see in California dual-family forms among Latina and Latino immigrant workers. On the one hand, the last 20 to 25 years have witnessed the consolidation of Mexican and other Latino immigrant families in the United States. This trend toward permanent settlement has fueled the demographic transformation of California, and signifies the absorption of costs (e.g., health, education) of reproducing the next generation of Latinos in the United States. Yet on the other hand, we see the continuation of the separation of labor maintenance and labor reproduction, a pattern made historically familiar to many Mexican families through various male contract labor systems. Paid domestic workers have historically forfeited much of their own family lives to serve other families. What is new are the dimensions of these separations brought about by international migration. Contemporary Mexican and Central American domestic workers in Los Angeles, and Filipina and Caribbean domestic workers elsewhere, now include women who experience long-term spatial separations from their children as an effect of their wage employment in the United States. A key feature of this arrangement is that these women are employed in jobs where they do other people's reproductive work for pay. These contemporary arrangements of social reproduction will have far-reaching and long-term consequences for the demographic composition, culture, and politics of many regions.

These transformations in labor demand and family forms have fallen like cat's paws in comparison with the clamor that has rightly surrounded restrictionist immigration legislation such as California's Proposition 187, a 1994 ballot measure which proposed to deny publicly funded schooling and medical care to the children of undocumented immigrants. The voters of California voted in favor of this measure, but Proposition 187 was finally deemed unconstitutional by the judicial system. Perhaps Proposition 187 was not necessary, as the new international division of reproductive labor and its commensurate transnational family forms resemble precisely the type of apartheid system that immigration restrictionists advocated. Proposition 187 may be illegal, but it is already institutionalized in the family lives of many Latina immigrant domestic workers.

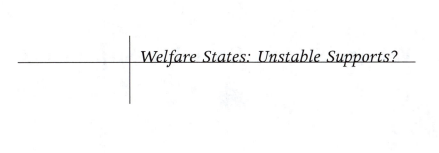

Welfare States: Unstable Supports?

Welfare States: Unstable Supports?

Welfare states vary markedly in their capacity to support women's choices to perform care work or shift it to other sources. Socialist and radical scholars and policymakers have long declared that the most stable and equitable arrangement for providing care to our dependents was through universal welfare state programs that distribute the burden across families rather than concentrating it within families (Korpi 1998). But before most Western nations ever implemented a full slate of programs, landmark retrenchments began, causing programs that tended to be stable, if meager, to become unstable. As the authors reveal in Part III, families who relied on these safety nets found themselves in unstable care working situations at best.

No welfare retrenchment has proved more telling, or more chilling, than the effort in the United States to "end welfare as we know it." In 1996, the president and Congress signed into law the Personal Responsibility and Work Reconciliation Act (P.L. 104-193), thus abolishing Aid to Families with Dependent Children (AFDC) and the notion of guaranteed support for children and the parents, largely mothers, who raise them. Welfare rolls have plummeted across the country, and we are just beginning to see the consequences of a leaner welfare system. Proponents of reform have hailed declining rolls as signs of success, while others question this definition of success. Do declining rolls mean that former recipients are in the workforce and that their wages are pulling their families above the poverty line, or are they simply cut loose without stable supports?

Historically, AFDC was created precisely to allow women who did not have other financial supports the ability to stay home and raise their children. Yet, by the 1980s these same mothers had been redefined as "welfare queens" who were lazy and irresponsible. According to many scholars, what became critical to this shift was precisely that the mothers were no longer white women left destitute by a husband's death, but were instead single poor black women (Quadagno 1994; Mink 1998). While white middle-class women were critiqued for putting their careers ahead of their children, poor single mothers who chose to stay out of the paid labor force and focus solely on raising their children were critiqued for failing to be self-supporting.

In her 1998 book *Welfare's End*, Gwendolyn Mink points out that this reform revealed the true divides that exist among American women in terms of class and race. Four of the five Democratic women senators and 26 of the 31 Democratic women representatives, most of whom were white and middle-class, voted for the 1996 reform which so disproportionately affected poor black women. Mink (p. 26) emphasizes that many feminists "conflated their own right to work outside of the home with poor single mothers' obligation to do so." The reform systematically ignored class differences among women. Middle-class, largely white, women can afford quality day care and often employ low-wage women of color to perform domestic labor to help balance work and family obligations. Poor women, however, do not have the same resources to balance these obligations. Child-care quality is directly correlated with cost. Leaving children in an environment that is mediocre at best and unsafe at worse contradicts mothers' values of caring and motherhood.

The first two chapters in this section explore how this reform has affected poor single and divorced mothers and the communities of which they are a part. Sociologist Stacey Oliker argues that the shift from AFDC to Temporary Assistance to Needy Families (TANF) forces mothers to prioritize paid work over care work, damaging the domestic moral economies and reciprocol care-taking networks that she documented in poor neighborhoods. Long a trusted source of free or low-cost child care for poor women, informal care networks are likely to weaken under TANF, stripping low-income families of yet another key social resource.

The supports for divorced mothers may be increasingly unstable as well. Presently only one-third of single mothers receive child support. Sociologist Demie Kurz criticizes policies that emphasize the pursuit of resources from absentee fathers rather than implement a public source of guaranteeing income to dependents. Kurz argues that while the government is tracking down deadbeat dads, it should pay child support to the women and children who rely on those funds, thereby stabilizing their financial security. Recent policy in the United States is guided by the inherent irony that while it specifically targets poor mothers, arguing that they are irresponsible and lack a work ethic, it is largely mothers

"Of course, our ultimate goal is to refer all our Medicaid patients to their mothers — then whatever the individual medical problem is, the mother can kiss it and make it all well."

who are already assuming full responsibility for children because so many absentee fathers fail to do so.

Long term care for the elderly is another arena in which the American welfare state fails to shape care as a community responsibility rather than as an individual responsibility. Economist Jennifer Mellor points out how present market-based solutions to alleviate the burdens of long term care for the elderly, particularly providing tax incentives to encourage the purchasing of long term care insurance, will not relieve this burden from the shoulders of most American women. Sociologists Madonna Harrington Meyer and Michelle Kesterke-Storbakken show how recent cuts in Medicaid reimbursements to nursing homes have made access to this care increasingly difficult for low-income older citizens. They show how the tangle of Medicaid regulations, particularly below-market rates of compensation, lead many nursing homes to refuse to accept patients who are unable to pay out of their own pockets. When no beds are available to Medicaid recipients, such patients must be cared for at home—and the burden falls predominantly on their wives and daughters.

As welfare reform reveals, the welfare state has the ability to shape care work, either easing or increasing the burdens placed primarily on women. Recent policy trends reveal a move toward the retrenchment of the welfare state, viewing it as an "impediment to the market" (Quadagno 1999:4). Policy makers are increasingly transferring social welfare needs that were once the responsibility of the state to the individual, reviving American exceptionalism (Quadagno 1999). The above 1991 cartoon from the *Fort Worth Star-Telegram* shows just how obvious attempts to push care work from the state to individual families have been.

Examining Care at Welfare's End

P atterns of caregiving depend on context. The ways poor single mothers care for their loved ones depend on their resources, which include time, money, and so-cial support. Arrangements for gathering these resources are changing. In 1996, the United States Congress abolished Aid to Families with Dependent Children (AFDC), ending the federal welfare "safety net" for poor single mothers and their children. Before it was abolished, the AFDC welfare system influenced the ways poor mothers balanced the tasks of earning and caring. How will caregiving change at welfare's end? How will this policy change affect caregiving of children, elders, and others in poor communities when single mothers must work or risk losing their families?

We are already beginning to learn what happens economically to single mothers who leave welfare, and we are positioned to learn more, for we have adequate research formations in place to answer questions about jobs and wages. We are not well positioned to learn about changes in caregiving. This paper suggests questions, conceptual frameworks, and directions for research on caregiving at welfare's end. Using my qualitative study of how urban single mothers balanced earning and caring in the last years of AFDC, along with others' work on kinship and personal networks, I consider how the end of welfare might reshape the ideas, commitments, and capacities that influence relations of care.

My focus is on the contexts of caregiving, and my conceptual framework is social network analysis. I consider how the end of welfare and the gradual implementation of Temporary Assistance to Needy Families (TANF) restrictions might alter the contexts in which poor single mothers draw resources for care and form strategies of caregiving. The three contexts I describe are family moral economies,[1] personal networks, and local — in this case, urban — environments.

Frameworks for Examining Families at Welfare's End

To prepare a framework for examining the contexts of care at welfare's end, I draw from the literature of welfare policy research, the work-family nexus, families in poverty, and social network analysis.

Ending Welfare, Mandating Work

The new federal policy that replaces AFDC devolves authority from federal government to the states, mandates work, sets maximum time limits on receipt of federally funded services, and caps future federal spending in state programs. Each state will determine standards of eligibility for the programs it sponsors; these programs and benefits will vary greatly. Since the federal government ordered the end of welfare, a few states have moved much faster than others to implement the new law. The state of Wisconsin, for example, had received federal permission to institute mandatory work before AFDC ended. After the end of AFDC, Wisconsin, which was previously a high-benefit state, abolished income grants altogether and required full-time employment for all welfare claimants with children more than 12 weeks old. The rolls of Wisconsin's postwelfare work program register a 77 percent decline in cases, placing the state second only to Idaho in cutting out welfare (Janofsky 1999). Though most states have moved slower to cut cash grants, sooner or later, everyone who receives federal benefits will face the end of welfare.

What will happen when welfare AFDC is phased out and TANF is fully phased in? Most predictions pertain to employment. Studies have already documented dramatic increases in employment among people who previously used welfare. About two-thirds of those who left welfare have found jobs (Goldberg 1999). Yet, labor market analysts remind us that those who leave welfare fastest tend to be people who are better prepared for the labor market; they have more education and job experience and fewer children than those who remain in programs. Analysts also raise questions about the stability of jobs in the low-wage job market that former welfare recipients enter, the insufficient incomes and benefits unskilled new labor market participants will bring home, and the low-mobility jobs that will keep them poor (Blank 1997; Burtless 1998).

As of now, we have only scattered state reports of the economic impact of welfare's end (U.S. General Accounting Office 1999). A study of single parents leaving AFDC in Milwaukee County, Wisconsin, for example, reported that they had high rates of employment, but also high rates of turnover and unemployment. Most jobs were in sectors that feature short-term or high-turnover jobs. Nine months after leaving the rolls, a third had no earnings, and only 10 percent maintained earnings above the poverty level for six months (Pawasarat 1997). Various state studies in 1999 also suggest that approximately a third of welfare leavers have no jobs, and most of those who are employed do not leave poverty (Goldberg 1999; U.S. General Accounting Office 1999).

Labor market analysts anticipate shortages of jobs appropriate for the skills of former welfare recipients, and barriers to employability among sectors of the welfare population (Blank 1997; Burtless 1998). In Wisconsin's booming economy, for example, economists estimate there are between two and three low-skilled workers for every low-skilled job opening (Kleppner and Theodore 1997).

In the absence of a social safety net or a wage-earning partner, single mothers now must provide financially for their children or risk losing them. Unlike many mothers, single women with young children do not have the option of limiting their work involvement or work hours. They are not free to trade income or job opportunity for flexibility to meet domestic needs. Even those who maintain steady employment may not achieve occupational mobility or family economic self-reliance (Blank 1997).

The Work-Family Nexus

In the public debates that preceded the repeal of welfare, virtually everyone agreed that poor single mothers should work for pay. The exemplars were the "other working mothers" of the country, who managed to balance family and employment responsibilities. The unitary ideal of the working mother suggested that balancing work and family is the same for the affluent and for the poor.

In contrast to the welfare reform discourse, sociological literature on the work-family nexus has increasingly taken into account how differences in families' social location — along dimensions like class, race, and parental structure — diversify the ways family members balance the obligations of work and family caregiving. The meanings and strategies of care differ, depending on parental resources and the environment of care (Glenn, Chang, and Forcey 1994; Collins 1990; and Cancian and Oliker 2000). Ensuring children's safety, for example, is a more time-consuming daily care task for parents who cannot provide their children with safe neighborhoods and schools (Furstenberg 1993; Rosier and Corsaro 1993).

Meanings and strategies of work also depend on resources and alternatives. Mothers' education, occupational rewards and conditions, and domestic supports influence their work commitments and their views of substitute care (Bielby 1992; Hochschild 1989; Voydanoff 1987). Long-standing orientations to work or parenthood are often reshaped by opportunities and constraints, which are "packaged" by social structures that pattern the workplace, marriage, and divorce (Gerson 1985).

Poverty and Family Networks

In the absence of a social safety net, wage-earning partners, stable employment, and family-supporting wages, single mothers are likely to depend on informal supports through their personal networks. What effects will ending welfare have on personal networks? And what effects will network changes have on caregiving? Sociological and anthropological studies of poverty and of social networks suggest how we might pursue these questions, though findings both converge and conflict.

Ethnographies of Families in Poverty

An array of ethnographic studies, most of them conducted in the '60s and '70s, showed that poor and minority families were embedded in close-knit, kin-based networks of support (Stack 1974; Martin and Martin 1978; McAdoo 1986). Carol Stack's 1974 classic *All Our Kin* vividly portrayed how female-based domestic networks of kin and nonkin, who may not live together, constituted the family in the poor, African-American inner-city community of The Flats. Exchanges of shelter, child care, domestic services, and economic, emotional, and moral support created stable family lives in a community where poverty threatened subsistence for isolated mother-child families.

Countering a view of impoverished families as disorganized and damaging to children, ethnographic work emphasizes the ways that extended networks organize family functions, like parental authority and child socialization, albeit differently from the middle-class nuclear family ideal. Such work highlighted communal capacities of nurture and care across the boundaries of households (Stack 1974; Martin and Martin 1978; McAdoo 1986). And though only some ethnographies compared poor families with the affluent, their influence on family studies was a sense that the poor are richer than others in kin support (Rochelle 1997).

Some recent ethnographic studies, however, question the extensiveness of kin support for poor families. Studies of teen mothers, new immigrant families, and urban single mothers suggest that, regardless of ideals of "familism" in poor communities, many families lack the support of kin or close friends. Authors of these studies often interpret their findings as suggesting a decline in extended family and communal support, rather than a challenge to earlier studies (Kaplan 1997; Mahler 1995).

Large-Scale Surveys of Kin Support

Quantitative analyses of large, national, representative-sample surveys, conducted in the '80s and '90s, uniformly suggest that the poor are not richer than others in support from kin. To the contrary, they find that families in poverty, and minority families in particular, have smaller networks of extended kin. Affluence, not poverty, increases the size of networks of support, the frequency of contact with kin, and the amount of help and economic and emotional support that families receive from others (Rochelle 1997; Hogan, Hao, and Parish 1990; Hogan, Eggebeen, and Clogg 1993; Hofferth 1984). Moreover, the poor who receive support are more likely than the nonpoor to give support to others. That is, they have greater burdens of reciprocation (Rochelle 1997; Hogan, Eggebeen, and Clogg 1993).

The large-scale studies do confirm that single mothers are more likely to live with kin than are married mothers (and minorities more likely than whites) (Hogan, Hao, and Parish 1990). While many single mothers receive some kind of support from parents, one-third receive none (Hogan, Hao, and Parish 1990; Hogan, Eggebeen, and Clogg 1993). Though the large-scale studies are persuasive, they may distort patterns of economic support because of the way they measure exchange. Some measured financial exchange with questions about who gave or received a minimum of $200, thus missing the small exchanges of money that help make ends meet among the very poor (Stack 1974). More important, few measured frequency of exchange (see Rochelle 1997). Frequent exchanges may create stabler bonds than infrequent ones (Wellman and Wortley 1990). Ethnographic studies, like Stack's, emphasize the way frequent, small exchanges constituted stable core domestic networks (1994).

Though these shortcomings may limit the usefulness of the large national sample studies, the same studies repeatedly identified the poor among those who had *no one* with whom to exchange advice, child care, or household help. Since these are important supports for caregiving, the studies suggest that a substantial minority of the poor are without these kinds of support. Taken altogether, studies of families and kin in poverty suggest we look closely at the ways poverty both elicits and limits reliance on kin supports.

Social Network Analysis

Scholars who study the dynamics of social networks rarely have a substantive interest in poor single-mother families, but their research offers suggestive ideas for those who do (see Uehara 1990; Wellman and Wortley 1990). Social network analysis explores how the *structure* of social relationships influences action (Wellman and Berkowitz 1988). Examining a person's network of ties to others, network analysts might investigate the effects of having a loose-knit network (where members of one's network do not know each other) or a dense one (like a kinship network, where a person's network members know each other well). They might study the multiplexity of one's ties (whether, for example, one just socializes with network members, or also receives or lends money, child care, or emotional support). In structural dynamics, kinship networks are likely to operate differently than friendship networks, not just because of cultural family norms, but because dense and multiplex networks are sturdier and better able to enforce norms (Feld 1981; Uehara 1990; Wellman and Wortley 1990).

Social network researchers also might pay attention to the *content* of network exchanges; for example, the kinds of resources that are exchanged, such as emotional support, information about jobs, help with care, or beliefs about caregiving. Yet, their interest in structure often leads them to look at how networks link people who offer exchanges of various contents.

A main *principle* of exchange identified by network theorists is reciprocity, which is the expectation that what individuals give and receive from network ties is commensurate (Fischer, Jackson, Stevve, Gelson, and James 1977; Wellman, Carrington, and Hall 1988; Uehara 1990). Drawing on varieties of exchange theory, network theorists distinguish between dyadic and generalized reciprocity. Dyadic reciprocity involves quid pro quo expectations of accountability between exchanging actors and creates emotional vigilance, mistrust, and fragile ties (Uehara 1990).

Generalized reciprocity among several people diffuses reciprocation among them over time, and creates trust and stable relations. A person who receives from someone in the network will, in time, give to another. While people expect to give and receive commensurably ("what goes 'round, comes 'round"), they do not expect immediate reciprocity or strict reciprocity in all of their ties (Uehara 1990). Cultural ideals make generalized reciprocity a foundation of kinship, but kinship networks vary in the extent of dyadic and generalized reciprocity within them. Structural characteristics of networks, like density of ties, and content characteristics of ties, like intimacy, favor generalized over dyadic exchange in kinship or friendship networks (Uehara 1990; Wellman and Wortley 1990).

Social network analysis suggests that if welfare's end encourages single mothers to seek more help from kin and friends, then we should examine the changes in their social networks, the dynamics these changes trigger, and the changes in obligations and resources that work and network changes entail.

The Proximate Contexts of Caregiving

I drew on approaches of welfare policy studies, research on families in poverty, on the work-family nexus, and social network analysis to plan and interpret a qualitative study of how single mothers who participated in work-welfare programs balanced their obligations to work and family. Thus, I assembled accounts of how mothers approached earning and caring in the years just before welfare ended, when AFDC gave poor single mothers some discretion to withdraw from or limit employment.

Many women I interviewed had used welfare to allow them more time for caregiving of children and close kin. All of them had also worked at paid jobs in the past; many still worked part-time, at unreported jobs; all of them intended to invest more time in employment in the future. AFDC had enabled them to make decisions about how best to allocate their time and efforts when conflicts between caring and earning emerged. Welfare enabled some women to work part-time and continue to qualify; some had left jobs to stay home full-time; some had voluntarily moved in and out of jobs, depending on their situation at home; and others had risked being fired for absences and tardiness, slighting job responsibilities in favor of responsibilities at home. These work patterns were not made up simply of attitudes and calculations about work; they emerged from strategies of balancing work and family.

Using single mothers' accounts of how they experienced the demands of providing, the demands of caring, and how they resolved conflicts between them, I identified the "proximate contexts" that influenced the strategies that poor single mothers used to sustain family life (Oliker 1995a). I focus on proximate contexts because macrosocial forces, like the economy or welfare policy, influence individuals *through* social relationships, including those that are morally and personally important, like family members and kin. The same set of job opportunities will look different to a mother who has help with baby-sitting than to one who does not; or to a mother who is the only daughter of a sick elder and one who has sisters in town. I identify proximate relations as those that are nearest in time, space, personal investment, and moral priority. I use the term "context" to evoke the structural patterning of personal relations and of the social relations in which they are embedded.

The focus on proximate contexts allows me to contend with economistic rational choice accounts of the work behavior of low-income single mothers, which conclude that the "welfare dependent" are irrational and demoralized (Mead 1992). The choices and strategies of mothers on welfare appear both rational and more intelligible when one considers pecuniary and nonpecuniary motives and the social contexts of economic action.

While examining patterns of balancing work and family in the period before welfare ended, I identified three kinds of proximate context. Examining *moral economies*, I look at how mothers' allocations of resources and effort are shaped by family commitments and communal values, as well as economic pressures. Focusing on *personal networks*, I examine how patterns of personal relations of dependence and exchange shaped single mothers' strategies of earning and caring. Under the rubric of *local environments*, I examine the urban ecologies of family life and personal networks. After I describe my data and methods, I employ these rubrics of proximate context to suggest how personal networks, urban environments, and moral economies may change when welfare ends, and how altered contexts of family patterns may affect caregiving in poor families.

Data and Methods

The primary data I employ are interviews and observations from my qualitative study of how single mothers on welfare balanced work and family obligations

(Oliker 1995a, b). These obligations derived from welfare policies that mandated work preparation and search, as well as from communal norms and personal priorities.

Between 1987 and 1993, in the last decade of AFDC, I visited welfare-to-work programs. I interviewed program workers and single mothers on welfare in two states' largest cities. I observed case meetings, orientations, job search and training programs, and I talked with hundreds of participants and program workers. I ultimately interviewed, in depth, 30 single mothers.

I chose to interview women whose range of demographic and neighborhood characteristics were suggested by the literature on single-mother poverty. All of the women I interviewed were required to participate in welfare-to-work programs in order to receive AFDC. Half of them acknowledged earnings from work, but most of the work was part-time, "off-the-books" jobs done at home, like baby-sitting or hairdressing, which the women did not report to welfare authorities. Though women on AFDC could declare earnings and still qualify for welfare, those who worked half-time or more were exempt from mandatory participation in the programs from which I selected respondents.

Most of the mothers I interviewed were in their 20s and 30s. Sixty percent were African-American, 30 percent European-American, and 10 percent Latino. Forty percent had not finished high school, half were high school graduates, and a few had some community college.

Both states in my study paid higher than average AFDC grants. Both cities were smaller and less plagued by crime than the nation's largest cities. Few participants with serious mental health or substance abuse problems agreed to be interviewed. In short, the women I interviewed may have had more resources to draw on in caregiving than many women facing welfare's end.

In the following sections, I use my qualitative study of single mothers, along with findings in studies discussed above, to project how the end of welfare might affect the caregiving patterns single mothers described before welfare's end. I begin with the moral economic context of care.

Moral Economies

Johnetta B. (not her real name) held down a number of factory jobs until child care became unmanageable. At the time I met her, she was a 40-year-old, divorced, African-American mother of three—one child grown, one eight years old, one six and disabled. She had also unofficially adopted Troy, a toddler whom her drug-addicted niece, the mother, had neglected. Johnetta had resigned herself to being the only plausible caregiver in her heavily drug-involved extended family: "What can you do? You can't just walk away and say, 'Well, I don't give a damn.'"

Troy had been evicted from one day-care center for uncontrollable rages, and Johnetta feared that his current center would do the same. She was already in trouble with her work search program because her disabled child's school often called her in to assist. Johnetta's older daughter moved back home and was helpful when she was off work, but she was pregnant and would soon need Johnetta's help and give less to Johnetta. "You get to the place where you can't rest, and then I start having those bad headaches and chest pain."

When I interviewed Johnetta, she had not abandoned the idea of finding the part-time job she was required to seek ("I would have to try to do it at night"), but her practical priority was caregiving. If her work plan failed because of health and family problems, she would lose her own AFDC grant but not her children's. It seemed likely that Johnetta and her daughter could keep their family afloat with the help of AFDC. Without that help, their success is not as likely.

Household economies are moral economies. In allocating resources and efforts, parents are guided by communally negotiated and reinforced commitments to care, including orientations to particular family members' needs, as well as to economic gain or self-interest. Rather than following a superordinate ethos of maximizing economic well-being, the single mothers I interviewed organized their resources and their efforts to pursue morally invested priorities centered on the well-being of their children.

Children's interests favored economic-maximizing effort, but they also favored investment in caregiving. Children's needs for material provision and their needs for attentive caregiving were frequently at odds, so mothers reallocated their efforts in shifting particular circumstances, armed with shifting and unstable resources. For example, the job that one woman held on to through her child's first years seemed impossible to face after she was switched to night shift and then fell asleep when she was bathing the toddler. Another woman left a night job when a neighbor reported that her teenage son had friends hanging around all night when she was gone. Yet another had ambivalently chosen employment instead of the after-school supervision she thought her preadolescent children needed because "if they go totally without [things that other children have], their character starts to change."

Though I emphasize moral commitments to caregiving here, both obligations to work and obligations to care sometimes took priority for purely pragmatic or self-interested reasons. One mother, who much preferred employment over full-time care of three children, quit her job to keep neighbors from informing her landlord and police about her children's destructive behavior when they were on their own before and after school. In general, though, the needs of others justified actions of many mothers.

Although welfare in the United States had never moved many families out of poverty, it ameliorated poverty enough to permit poor families to embrace the broader social ethos of attentive and nurturant child care.[2] Women I interviewed elaborated this ethos, for example, in describing how they kept children at home until they could talk, so they could use their children's accounts to monitor the quality of day care. They recounted why they left jobs they wanted to keep, in order to respond better to a child's needs for more intensive care. They evoked the desirability of responsive care when they explained why they personally cared for sick kinfolk. The absence of subsidized institutional alternatives was not always a factor; when it was a factor, it was rarely the only one. Among African-American mothers, for example, protecting children or vulnerable elders from the injuries of racism and racist neglect by institutional caregivers frequently entered moral economic calculations.

The women I interviewed took for granted their responsibility for children in their care. Poor prospects for good pay or mobility rarely placed these women's interests in self-development in conflict with family commitments. For many of them, the balance between earning and caring periodically had tipped toward work, when jobs seemed secure, appeared to be steppingstones to better jobs, or when a Christmas without gifts loomed. So mothers recounted times when, for the children's economic benefit, they denied their needs for attention or supervision, nursed them by phone from work when they were home sick, or refused schools' demands to retrieve an unruly student.

Often, the mothers I encountered felt that every choice they made seemed too costly to loved ones, and they regretted past decisions they had made. Nonetheless, the safety net of welfare, by permitting withdrawal from work, permitted some discretion to decide how to work and how to care. Discretion is a moral grounding and a constitutive ingredient of care.

A Repeal of Discretion

Reforms in the last years of welfare increasingly mandated work search or preparation. Sanctions for failing to comply with work-welfare mandates, however, were often weak. When sanctions were enforced, mothers forfeited their own share of the AFDC grant, but not their children's. Before welfare ended, women had very little discretion to place caring above earning in priority, but that small space for discretion was the arena for construction of moral economies that routinely took account of the personal needs of children and close kinfolk.

Before welfare ended, women risked losing jobs, or lost them, when they arrived late because the baby-sitter was late, they refused a shift where no child care was available, they decided to take care of a mother who was dying, or one child passed the flu to a sibling. That small space of discretion to make decisions about work and care will no longer be available when welfare ends. Although this loss of discretion may appear small, revoking parental discretion in matters of care may have far-reaching effects.

The end of welfare makes getting a job and keeping it an inevitable priority. Work or children do not eat, they lose their home, or mothers lose their children. With the new policy of heavily sanctioned mandatory work, children's needs for care, however valuable, must now take second place. This is not likely to be a simple matter of grimly installing a survival-centered family life, however. It entails forswearing caregiving practices that are invested deeply with meaning — practices that are normative, constitutive of identity and standing in a community, understood to be beneficial, and unlikely to be replaced.

Renouncing the priority of care may require psychological denial to cope with the pain of loss and failure, and this bears study. Whatever psychological motives emerge, however, the need to subordinate caregiving to earning is likely to encourage those who believed in doing otherwise to minimize the damage this causes.

Of the mothers I interviewed, those who had previously held jobs had pulled their children out of bad day care, thrown out boyfriends who reneged on promises to watch their children, or refused to leave children with sisters whose alcoholic boyfriends hung around. At welfare's end, mothers who previously reviled their child-care options may come to view poor day-care centers or care by irresponsible relatives as adequate.

I spoke to mothers who, before welfare had ended, had taken off work when crime close to home had made a child fearful and anxious about being alone after school. I spoke to others who had decided that the meager income advantages of work were costing troubled and angry children the attention that might resolve their problems. At welfare's end, mothers who fear leaving children alone or who worry about children's needs for attention may find that, helpless to act on their concerns, they supress them. Studies of life after welfare should aim to capture changes in attitudes toward care, as well as changes in caregiving practices.

When the guiding principle of moral economies is the needs of children, and mothers have normative and practiced strategies of subordinating economic interests to caring, their inability to allocate time and energy to care may affect more than the quality of caregiving. It may affect individual attitudes toward care and the communal ethos of caring. We will more easily conceive of plausible changes in communal dynamics if we look at the personal networks that reinforce such commitments.

Personal Networks

In welfare reform debates preceding the end of welfare, policy experts frequently invoked the supports available through the personal networks of single mothers on welfare, arguing that families could cope with needs for child care that would accompany mandatory work (Mead 1992; Kaus 1992). This optimism found a defensive echo after welfare's end when advocates for the poor asserted that poor communities would effectively "pull together," as they have always done in adversity. Both sides thus evoked the strengths of extended family networks.

Instead of assuming the capacities of personal networks to cushion adversity, however, we should examine the effects of welfare's end on networks of support. A range of recent studies of kinship exchange and of dynamics in social networks suggest we might find damage to personal networks and personal relationships, which could threaten families' capacities to care. The damage might take the forms of constriction and greater fragility in networks, the replacement of caregiving with support for subsistence, and a decline in communal commitments to care.

A majority of single mothers I interviewed before welfare's end received numerous supports for care from kin and others close to them. Supports for care included money, goods, and services that helped with subsistence; emotional succor, advice, and encouragement that helped mothers shoulder single parenthood; and care itself, primarily in the form of child care. Although a few of the women participated in large, extended networks of kin and friends, most had small kinship-based networks of support, centered on the mother-daughter relationship.

Kin

The kin who were most involved with the women I interviewed were their mothers, adult daughters, sisters, fathers, brothers, and aunts, in that order. Their own mothers were the primary adult relationships in many single mothers' lives. Their mothers both anchored the exchange of help and care and linked single mothers to other sources of support (for example, to their maternal aunts). Two-thirds of the mothers I interviewed maintained close ties with their mothers; half received care, help, goods, or money (both proportions are higher than large-scale studies report). Whether or not they were part of the household, women's mother's frequently provided regular or emergency child care and participated in the homemaking rituals of everyday life. Mothers were likely to identify only their mothers, along with their children, among those who are most a part of their lives.

Observers of the poor are quick to praise the richness of close kin networks. Invoking the homily "What goes 'round, comes 'round," admirers of poor people's networks pay most attention to what comes around. That rich supports must go around again in reciprocation is easily forgotten. Giving is as constitutive of communal networks as getting (Stack 1974; Uehara 1990; Hogan, Eggebeen, and Clogg 1993; Rochelle 1997; Schweizer and White 1998).

In the accounts I collected in the years before welfare ended, single mothers gave frequent help and care to network members who gave them help in caregiving and supports for care. One mother, for example, cared for her brother's children anytime he "dumped them," because she needed his car to get to her night job. She had been dropped from a training program that provided her with child care because she had stayed home too often with her nephews. Less instrumentally, several women had cared for sick or dying mothers, leaving jobs to do so or losing them in the process. Others had taken in the children of siblings who were disabled by alcohol or drug addiction, or young relatives who had fled domestic abuse or conflict. These additional burdens of care had interfered with their employment.

In some of these examples, obligations to give care reciprocated the woman's previous receipt of care or support. In others, reciprocation by the care receiver would not soon follow. Patterns of generalized exchange made it possible for some mothers, particularly those of very young children, to receive help from kin, expecting that their main obligations to others would come later. For others, particularly mothers whose close-knit networks consisted of people who were also poor, there were burdensome obligations to reciprocate, as well as unreciprocated obligations (see also Rochelle 1997). (In kinship-based networks, such unreciprocated obligations are often reinforced by those to whom one is much obliged, as when a maternal grandmother asks a single mother to care for her sister's troubled grandchildren.) In the years before welfare ended, single mothers measured these obligations against the work obligations imposed by work-welfare programs. They sometimes decided to use welfare, for a time, to meet their commitments to kin, and to accept the economic sacrifice that entailed.

When welfare ends, single mothers who are compelled to find work or face losing their children will be less able to find the time to reciprocate the help others give them. The low-wage job market they enter will leave most of them no more financially able to replace the care they once provided with purchased services, like home health aides or taxi fares. Will increasingly asymmetric exchanges in close kin networks damage relationships and constrict networks? The answer may be no in the short run. In the long run, however, stark asymmetries may undermine close ties. Those who give a lot but do not receive begin to feel exploited, or they just "burn out" (Stack 1974, 1994; Minkler and Roe 1993).

What other changes may unfold in the roles that caregiving grandmothers play? Once government support has ended, and work is scarce and low-paying, committed grandmothers may, in the interest of children, invest more time in earning, rather than caring, just as mothers will. Such a strategy may secure subsistence but drain the family's store of attentive, loving, and flexibly arrangeable care.

Another likely change is "doubling up" to share housing expenses. This is typically the first step homeless families take before they lose all shelter (Rochefort 1998; Torrey 1997). In Milwaukee, Wisconsin, it appears that this transition has begun. Local landlords have coined the name "W2 stacks" (W2 is the nickname of Wisconsin's postwelfare law) to complain about the increased doubling up of households that they began to witness after welfare ended (Derus 1998). Also in Milwaukee, homeless shelters report increases in the numbers of single-mother clients, who enter shelters alone after leaving children with kin (Huston 1998).

If existing patterns indicate future ones, single mothers will most often take their children and move in with their mothers. This strategy might be generally cost-saving, but for many families, it will yield few additional hours of grandmother's child care. (The benefits to care are most likely to concentrate among whites, who are now less likely than members of racial minorities to reside with kin, and who might, proportionally, have most to gain by this change (Hogan, Hao, and Parish 1990; Hogan, Eggebeen, and Clogg 1993; Hao and Brinton 1997; Rochelle 1997). Among the large minority of single mothers who already depend on their own mothers' care, co-residence may net little more. Those mothers who have not secured help from their mothers, despite past need for more child-care help, may not receive help after moving in with their mothers.

The stresses of co-residence and crowding may displace the opportunities for care created by economic improvement. Among the women I interviewed who had previously lived with their mothers, conflicts had overwhelmed the advantages they gained in living together. Some had sacrificed their mothers' child-care help to escape the conflict, but considered their children better off. Single mothers are more likely than married mothers to live with kin. Yet, like other families, single-mother families have steadily abandoned the practice of living with kin over the last half-century (Ruggles 1994). Economic pressures may encourage dependencies that deplete, rather than augment, domestic care.

Fathers and Boyfriends

Few of the women I interviewed considered the fathers of their children as a part of their family networks because their contributions were so irregular and undependable. Many preferred this erratic, but occasionally substantial, unreported support to the $50 a month they would receive from the state, in place of whatever child support the state collected from the father. This system encouraged both mothers and fathers to favor informal child support (see also Edin and Lein 1997).

The end of welfare may encourage more mothers to use the government to secure formal child support from fathers, if they are now allowed to receive the money fathers contribute. Moreover, irregular contacts and contributions are ties that may potentially be convertible to steadier and more beneficial ones during times of great need. The end of welfare deepens mothers' economic interest in activating relationships with children's fathers, which could involve more fathers in active care, as well as financial support of children. This strategy of extending networks of support around children can secure support and care from fathers' relatives as well as fathers (Stack 1974).

Although involving children's fathers may increase child care and support, single mothers who do this also stand to lose authority over children to formerly uninvolved fathers. In the welfare era, irregular, unreported support by fathers allowed fathers to control paternal support, but their distance enabled mothers to maintain authority over children. A greater involvement of fathers in mothers' and children's networks may also revive relationships of conflict, abuse, or exploitation that had been severed by separation (Garfinkel, McLanahan, Meyer, and Seltzer 1998). To secure more support from fathers, mothers may risk the harms to themselves and their children that the breakup of partnerships had eliminated.

Greater involvement of children's fathers also risks alienating boyfriends. In my study, mothers' boyfriends were steadier contributors of cash and material goods to households than fathers were. Only a few of my respondents' boyfriends contributed regular child care, but boyfriends were an important source of emergency care. Boyfriends, like fathers, are network members whose roles mothers might successfully expand amid altered family circumstances at welfare's end. Boyfriends, however, crowd single mothers' accounts of damaging dependencies, which they sometimes used welfare to end. Women who become less able to expel exploitive or abusive boyfriends may experience these relationships as the main source of damage to their children and to their own capacities to care for and protect them.

Friends and Neighbors

I have focused on kinship networks, rather than friendship networks, because women in my study did not report extensive exchanges with friends, beyond emotional support and sociability. Among network members who were not close kin, older women neighbors helped more with care of children than friends did. Women sometimes reciprocated older neighbors' help by paying, driving them to appointments, or buying them groceries with food stamps. Friends were more likely to be peers who also had children, so receiving a friend's help with child care nearly always required reciprocal care. Most women I interviewed were hesitant to ask for child-care help or money from friends, because the burdens of repayment might be more than they could manage. Rochelle's large-scale study shows single mothers are more likely than married mothers to exchange child-care help with friends, but those who receive child-care help from friends also give it (Rochelle 1997; see also Hogan, Eggebeen, and Clogg 1993).

The Network Solution to Crisis

The end of welfare could have a number of effects on networks of close kin, friends, and neighbors. Families and communities do tend to "pull together" during crises, so we may expect intensified exchange and sharing in the support networks of single mothers. It is even possible that the large minority of single mothers who have poor networks of support will be embraced by their communities and drawn into networks of support.

The literature on poverty and social networks discussed earlier suggests otherwise. Although ethnographic studies of the poor have documented vital networks of kin and kinlike relationships, large-scale studies of kinship and social networks suggest these are rarer than earlier ethnographies indicated. If the consistent conclusions of large-scale surveys are correct, then ideals of extended family support may not be realized for many single-mother families. Most poor families will have small networks to rely upon, and some will have none. Few resources of help and money will circulate through many mothers' networks, even kin networks. And many mothers who receive help, especially those who come from the poorest communities, will have burdensome obligations to those who help them. Moreover, if writers who interpret these findings among the minority poor as a "demise of social support networks in minority communities" are right, then the end of welfare may augment forces that are eroding ties and accelerate the demise of networks (Rochelle 1997:149).

Even among single mothers who participate actively in kinship networks, welfare's end and mandatory employment may deplete the ability of single mothers to reciprocate material support and caregiving; this may, over time, undermine the material and moral capacities of networks of exchange. Overtaxed network members may bail out; networks may constrict; relationships may "burn out." And relations of "community" in networks of generalized exchange may become increasingly pervaded by instrumental, rather than altruistic, motives.

If networks of flexible, generalized exchange constrict, and single mothers attempt to rebuild networks of survival among kin and others, immediate obligations to reciprocate are likely to intensify, and these will be harder to meet under a regime of mandatory work. Desperate network builders will inevitably draw in others desperate enough to depend on mere velocity of exchange.

The ideal of solidarity—voluntary networks among neighbors and friends—is admirable and constructive, and most adaptable for community organizations seeking to fortify caregiving in the civic realm. For individuals whose personal networks are formed outside organizations, however, the networks that result from the constriction of older networks and pressing need are likely to be more heavily composed of people who are not bound by the moral obligations of close kinship, and who consistently have few resources to share.

Voluntary networks, like friendship networks, are harder to build and to sustain among people who have desperate instrumental needs of each other. One mother framed her mistrust this way: "I don't socialize with too many people. The less company you keep, the better off you will have your stuff in your home." Friends are more likely to expect strict reciprocity than kin are. Moreover, friendship networks are likely to be looser-knit than networks of kinship, and looser-knit networks break down more easily (because, for example, there are few members who can fill the role of the aunt who seats feuding adult siblings together at the holiday dinner). In the looser links of such networks, capacities of communal reinforcement weaken, which may in turn weaken the communal ethos of care. In this dynamic, both the structural and communal supports for care erode.

Even the optimistic vision of networking in times of crisis—in which kinship networks persist and caring others join them—could negatively affect care while supporting subsistence. If the end of welfare creates routine economic crises for families, committed network members will want to give more material support; in low-income networks, efforts to supplement material support may displace care. Like single mothers and their mothers, other network members who want to help may invest time in earning instead of caring.

The content of caring exchanges in an interdependent community may also change in ways that reinforce a decline in care. As the ability of families to give care declines and family crises threaten the possibility of government intervention to protect children by removing them, network members who are intent on keeping families together share the mother's incentive to redefine adequate care.

That is, if children cannot be nurtured, supervised, taught, and protected, communities and individuals who want to keep families together can help to do so by revising norms of care and perceiving that children can do all right without these privileges. This is not to say that poor communities will cause the resulting decline in caregiving. But if communal networks cannot prevent a decline in care in poor families, their interests in keeping families whole may favor silences, or even revised norms of care. We could see fewer reports of child neglect and abuse, even as rates increase. For researchers, the usual ways of registering change—whether by respondent accounts or official data—may fail us.

Finally, since I concentrate on personal networks formed outside of organizations, readers may respond that religious and charitable voluntarism might provide stable, beneficial, and communal ties that replace or regenerate single mothers' networks of support. This may happen. Yet, the capacities and influences of these organizations are likely to be limited where poverty is more geographically concentrated than churches and charities, which is the situation in most big cities (Hodgkinson 1995).

Urban Environments of Care

Low-income single-mother families live in the poorest and most dangerous city neighborhoods. A number of child-care patterns are shaped by the need to adapt to these dangerous and disruptive surroundings. For example, in poor neighborhoods, staying home and keeping children indoors are widespread modes of protecting homes and children, concentrating parental influence, and mediating negative peer influences (see also Anderson 1990; Kotlowitz 1991; Rosier and Corsaro 1993; and Furstenberg 1993).

According to mothers and work-welfare program workers I interviewed before welfare's end, women often left jobs or work programs when a wave of crime swept through their neighborhood or after their homes had been burgled. They also left after learning that children who had been ordered to stay home after school had ventured out, or after children were frightened on the streets when they headed home after school. One woman, who had held on to a job even through her son's hospitalization with serious injuries, became too anxious to stay at work after a fire displaced them to a more dangerous neighborhood.

Women I spoke to repeatedly said meeting the school bus before and after school was a vexing obstacle to employment—even more so than after-school care, since many felt their children were safe alone, once they were at home. By requiring mothers to work or search for work, the end of welfare may clear responsible adults out of poor neighborhoods precisely at a time when deepening poverty would increase the local dangers and, thus, the incentives of single mothers to try to be home with their children after school.

If the end of welfare is not accompanied by the kinds of changes in government or charity programs that would supervise and protect children when mothers are at work, we should expect declines in these forms of care. Although some states will extend child-care provisions, few programs are likely to be better than Wisconsin's, where large increases in state child-care spending have been accompanied by deregulation of care, pay cuts for providers, and reductions in the ages of children qualifying for after-school care. Even without changes in protective policies in areas such as child care and public housing, front-line social service workers could begin to relax enforcement of child-care ratios or rules against crowding, for example, to allow the desperate to have some benefits, albeit perilous ones.

Although some single mothers might use employment to finance moves to safer neighborhoods, most who were on welfare cannot expect wages that will enable them to move up (Blank 1997; Burtless 1998; Goldberg 1999). Instead, moves are likely to pursue survival rather than improvement; for example, when unsteady incomes prompt eviction. This kind of forced mobility pulls families out of whatever neighborhood networks offered them support. Moreover, my research suggests that employed mothers may be less able to cultivate the kinds of neighborhood relations that help to protect children than those who used welfare. Those who worked full-time knew fewer neighbors who could keep an eye on children. Mothers on welfare who were at home with children may have made neighborhoods safer.

Few existing public programs serve children who, in safe neighborhoods, are old enough to look after themselves. The public views such programs as "recreation," since children who are not poor live in communities in which concentrations of young people are much lower. There, the invitations to trouble are sparser, and temptations for illegal and illicit behavior are limited by the ways such behavior risks promised futures. Single mothers I interviewed had sometimes used welfare to leave jobs temporarily, when trouble threatened for their teenage children. They remained at home after school to supervise teenagers, to limit the use of their homes for troublesome activity, and to personally carry out their threats to punish misbehavior.

The end of welfare threatens increased want for many older children, as well as increases in maternal stress. It seems likely that we will see increases in domestic conflicts involving older children, as well as problems associated with the absence of supervision. As crowding and shortages in food and money make domestic life more tenuous, it seems reasonable to predict that families will increasingly push out their unproductive teenagers, and that more teenagers will seek to leave home. In short, it seems likely that older children will be the first to be liberated from receipt of caregiving. The public may register the effects of welfare's end in encounters with teenagers in the schools and on the streets.

Finally, Kathryn Edin and Laura Lein (1997) suggest that although criminal opportunities were available in poor neighborhoods, single mothers on AFDC avoided the most lucrative forms of crime to avoid risking custody of their children. If the end of welfare changes the calculus of risk, the poorest single mothers will be well positioned, in urban environments, to find high-risk opportunities.

Conclusion

I have used the accounts of single mothers I interviewed in the years before welfare ended, along with studies of kinship and social networks, to suggest where we might look for changes in care at welfare's end. In the final years of meager federal safety net entitlements, when work mandates increased dramatically but single mothers retained some discretion to decrease or decline work commitments, many single mothers used welfare to give brief or long-term priority to caregiving. They built strategies of care in the context of their job markets, their networks of personal exchange, their urban environments, and their moral priorities. I have drawn attention to these proximate contexts of decision making as a source of strategies of care.

When welfare is no longer available, but wages are insufficient to purchase good substitute care, the domestic moral economies that favored caregiving over earning may be impossible to re-create. Personal networks of support may weaken, as the capacity of single mothers to reciprocate care declines. The close-knit networks that remain may concentrate on the exchange of material subsistence rather than care. The norms of care that personal networks transmit and reinforce in an era of meager social provision may change once provision ends. Communal support for subsistence and keeping families together may become paramount. Reliable strategies of care in poor urban neighborhoods may become less accessible. Through such dynamics, caregiving declines as does the social ethos of care.

Paying for Care

Child Support Policy in the United States

T hose who study care work should focus greater attention on the issue of child support. Child support is money paid by a noncustodial parent, usually the father, to the custodial parent, usually the mother, for the care and financial support of a child or children from whom they are living apart. Child support is regulated by the state in the interests of ensuring that children born to single mothers or divorced parents can be adequately cared for and will not suffer economic hardship. In recent years, the issue of child support has received increased attention from policy makers who want single-parent families, many of whom are poor, to receive less money from the government and more from private sources, particularly in the form of child support from the noncustodial parent.

The case of child support is very useful for analyzing how policy makers conceptualize the care work of mothering, for showing how mothers do and do not receive compensation for the care work they do, and for providing evidence that this work is continually devalued and made invisible. This issue is particularly interesting for examining assumptions about care work that become embedded in contemporary social policy, as well as for understanding how problems in the implementation of care work policies can undermine reforms intended to support care work and those who do it.

It is also important to study child support because it is a critical social policy issue affecting children who need care and their caretakers, usually mothers. The number of single mothers has increased as the divorce rate has risen and as more

unmarried women bear and rear children. Many cannot find jobs that pay a sufficient wage for themselves and their children, provide health-care benefits for
themselves or their children, or enable them to cover child-care costs. These
mothers risk poverty. Families headed by females are five times more likely to be
poor than families with married couples: forty-seven percent of all single mothers (and 39 percent of all divorced mothers) live below poverty levels (Rotella
1995). Women of color experience disproportionate levels of poverty. About half
of all families headed by black and Hispanic women are poor compared with 28
percent of families maintained by white women. The figures are considerably
higher for families with children under the age of 18 (Rotella 1995).

Mothers' poverty also affects children. While children in married, two-parent
families have a poverty rate of 12 percent, 54 percent of children in families
headed by mothers live in poverty (Sidel 1996). As in the case of their mothers,
minority children face the highest levels of poverty. More than 46 percent of all
black children and 41 percent of all Hispanic children lived in poverty in 1993,
compared to 14 percent of all non-Hispanic white children (Sidel 1996). The majority of these children are from single-mother homes.

Child support can be critical to help single mothers and their children escape
poverty. Researchers have established that regular child support payments would
improve the standard of living of women and children and would lift a number of
them out of poverty (Nichols-Caseboldt 1992). This is as true for the divorced
mother as for one who never married. While in theory divorced women have available to them various resources from their ex-husbands and from their marriages —
child support, a share of the marital property, and spousal support — most women
do not receive property or alimony of any significant value (Seltzer and Garfinkel
1991). The primary resource available to divorced women is child support, which is
critical for improving their standard of living as well as that of their children.

Because of its potential to keep mothers and children out of poverty, child
support is a key part of the new welfare reform bill, the Personal Responsibility
and Work Reconciliation Act (P.L. 104-193). The new welfare bill ends the entitlement of poor women to state support and seeks to ensure that women support
themselves through private rather than public means. The current plan for poor
single mothers, as embodied in the new welfare legislation, is that single mothers
will support themselves and their children through a combination of paid work
and child support from the father(s) of the children. While policy makers and the
media have focused mainly on the work requirements of the bill, child support is
a crucial part of the reform plan. The assumption is that child support will make
up for what women do not get in wages and will ensure that children are adequately supported.

This attention to child support is long overdue. Less than one-third of single
mothers receive regular child support (U.S. Bureau of the Census 1991).[1] According to the U.S. Government Accounting Office (1994),

Of the nearly $35 billion in child support payments owed nationwide under the Child Support Enforcement Program, more than $27 billion remained uncollected at the end of fiscal year 1992. During that year, more than 5.7 of the 8.5 million non-custodial parents owing child support made no payment on the amount owed.

Nor have child support awards been adequate; funding formulas have been inequitably applied across states, and those women who do obtain child support have received relatively small awards (Garfinkel, Melli, and Robertson 1994; Roberts 1994). Further, women have found it extremely difficult to obtain increases in their child support awards as their children grow older and their expenses increase (Garfinkel 1992:98).

While the attention of policy makers to child support in the welfare reform bill and in social policy in general are positive developments, I challenge the assumption that women will receive enough income from child support and from their wages to support themselves and their children. Although improvements in the child support system will result in many more women receiving child support and in their receiving higher awards, I argue that women will not receive as much child support as they should, and that a large number of women will continue to receive none at all.

The analysis of child support policies presented here underscores the importance of examining the assumptions underlying care work policies and the implementation of these policies, to see whose interests they actually serve. I demonstrate the limitations of recent child support policy in terms of how child support is determined as well as in terms of the implementation of child support policies. I will first analyze child support guidelines, or formulas for determining child support awards, that have been developed in recent years to address the problem of low levels of child support. I will then examine recent reforms to improve the enforcement of child support awards, including income or wage withholding, a system whereby child support payments are automatically deducted from the wages of the noncustodial parent and sent to the custodial parent. In the case of reforms concerning both guidelines and enforcement procedures, assumptions are made about women and women's work that seriously disadvantage mothers and that ignore the realities of their lives. To demonstrate the limitations of these reforms, I will present data from my study of a diverse group of divorced mothers and their experiences with the child support system (Kurz 1995).

Child Support Guidelines and the Establishment of Child Support Awards

One of the most serious problems with the child support system is that the awards are inadequate, and are a major contributing factor to the poverty of mothers and children. In this section I will analyze why this major type of care work—the care of children by single mothers—is not supported in child support awards.

The basic reason that child support awards are so low lies in how they are calculated. The dominant approach to allocating resources for child support continues to be a "percentage of income" approach. The goal of this approach is to ensure that the noncustodial parent, typically the father, contributes the same proportion of his postdivorce income to his children as he did during the marriage (Rhode 1989:151). Policy makers have developed formulas for computing child support awards based on this approach.

The most serious problem with these guidelines is that they do not consider the nonmonetary costs of child rearing. Most important, they do not compensate women for the time they invest in child rearing. Women get no recognition for the tasks of mothering, which remain "invisible work" (Daniels 1987), despite their difficult and time-consuming nature. Further, there is no recognition of forgone earning opportunities. Mothers often reduce their work hours or do their work part-time in order to care for their children, or they take lower-paying jobs that provide more flexibility for combining work and child care. Thus, the percentage-of-income approach has serious limitations, both from the viewpoint of mothers and from the viewpoint of those who wish to give more support for care work. As it is currently structured, the child support system recognizes the needs of the object of care—the child—but not the caregiver or the work of caring.

There are additional problems with these guidelines. The methods of calculating these child support guidelines are based on the costs of raising children in a two-income family. They do not take into account that divorced single mothers have many additional costs in establishing a new household. Further, the percentage-of-income approach excludes savings and investments from its formulas and does not include some important expenses, such as educational costs (Goldfarb 1987). In many states, when the children turn 18 years old, fathers' financial obligations end, and they have no obligation to contribute to their children's college educations (Goldfarb 1987). Thus, a mother can be left with many expenses as her children finish college.

The only proposed alternative approach to the calculation of child support that would begin to address the needs of the caretaker is an "income equalization" approach, which would ensure that children continue to have the same standard of living as the nonresident parent (Sawhill 1977). Because it is impossible to separate the standard of living of the child from that of the resident parent, income equalization attempts to establish some rough parity in the postdivorce standards of living of the fathers' and mothers' households. It adjusts for the "economies of scale" of the marital unit: after a divorce it takes more money for a parent to live alone with a child than it did for a couple. An income equalization approach would greatly increase the child support obligation of most upper-middle- and upper-income nonresident fathers, and raise the standard of living of mothers and their children.

While an income equalization approach would definitely be a better system for calculating child support, it still does not explicitly acknowledge the contribution of the caretaker—the mother—to the child's life and well-being. This method of calculation does not challenge the conventional division of labor between mothers and fathers and the income differentials that this division of labor creates. It supports the traditional assumption that the father's income is his alone, even though it is the mother's invisible labor of care that has typically enabled the father to earn this income.

Unfortunately, however, while there is evidence of some public support for larger child support awards (Bergmann and Wetchler 1994), there is currently no jurisdiction that would favor the income-equalization approach. State authorities undoubtedly hold attitudes similar to judicial authorities, who have been more concerned with enabling fathers to start new lives than with compensating mothers (Weitzman 1985). They also share the widely held belief that the income that fathers earn belongs to them, and are reluctant to rule that a larger share should be transferred to former wives, even if the money is for the children. Thus, for the foreseeable future, the income-shares approach will remain in place.

The federal government has introduced some reforms in the system of determining child support awards. The Family Support Act of 1998 mandated that states develop standardized formulas or guidelines to set more uniform and fair levels of child support awards. The goals of this legislation were to make the awards conform more closely to the actual costs of raising a child, to eliminate inconsistencies between the awards of people in similar circumstances, and to decrease the time delays in processing child support awards (Garfinkel, Melli, and Robertson 1994). Most states have adopted guidelines, which apply to all women except those on government assistance.

While the establishment of guidelines is an important step in improving the child support system, initial evaluations of the impact of child support guidelines are mixed. On the one hand, an early study of their impact in three states showed that the implementation of child support guidelines resulted in awards that were 15 percent higher—a positive development (Thoennes, Tjaden, and Pearson 1991). This increase in the size of awards is far short of the 70 to 100 percent growths some had predicted, however. Further, according to this study, the main effect of the guidelines has not been to increase all child support awards, but to raise the substandard award levels found in some jurisdictions to more average levels. The other main effect, according to the study, has been to increase the number of noncustodial mothers paying child support to custodial fathers.

Why did the levels of child support not rise to projected levels under this new legislation? First, there are some loopholes in the law that contribute to lower awards. Guidelines have often been set in accordance with vague standards that permit the courts to decide what is "reasonable and just." Garfinkel argues that "because courts are permitted to depart from guidelines when the outcome is deemed to be unfair to any of the parties, it is possible that this loophole will be used to undermine the intent of the law" (Garfinkel 1992:72−73). Second, for women who have some type of joint custody agreement, courts may reduce the support award, reasoning that because the custodial parent, typically the mother, is getting more help from the noncustodial parent in raising the children, they should receive less child support. This kind of reasoning, however, fails to take into account the lower earnings of the mother and her need to maintain an adequate standard of living, and the high fixed costs of having children and the costs of maintaining two homes (Thoennes, Tjaden, and Pearson 1991). Finally, again, these reforms do not compensate mothers in any way for the work of mothering.

While fundamental reforms that would seriously take into account the interests of women and children seem unlikely in the near future, Garfinkel believes that adoption of the "percentage-of-income standard," the percent rate for child support described above, is an achievable goal. For one child, a noncustodial parent would pay 17 percent of his income, an amount that would increase proportionately with the number of children to be supported. Whether 17 percent of the noncustodial parent's income would cover the mothers' costs of her care work is a question that Garfinkel's proposal does not address. Nor does this proposal take into account the value of mothers' care work. Garfinkel focuses on the fact that this standard is easy and efficient to use, and also that it provides for automatic adjustments in awards as the noncustodial parent's income increases or decreases (Garfinkel, Melli, and Robertson 1994), something which current law does not do. Ultimately, however, to truly reform the child support system, there will have to be a radical change in how society views care work. Policy makers will have to better understand the nature and scope of this work, take it seriously, and see that mothers are compensated for the work they do.

Problems Negotiating for and Enforcing Child Support Orders

I will now turn to issues of the enforcement of child support awards. As will be demonstrated, by failing to provide adequate mechanisms by which mothers can receive the child support they are due, the state is again failing to support the care work of mothers.

As noted earlier, rates of child support enforcement are low. Forty percent of all custodial mothers and 28 percent of divorced mothers do not have child support awards, and only half of those with an award receive the full amount; this is the same rate of collection as that of 20 years ago (U.S. Bureau of the Census

1991). After noting recent reforms in the child support enforcement system, I will describe the experiences of the women I interviewed, to demonstrate the failure of these policies to overcome basic gender inequalities.

Reforms in Child Support Enforcement

The most important and effective reform for child support enforcement enacted to date is income withholding. This is a procedure by which an obligator's employer (typically the father), withholds payment from his paycheck and then sends the money to the state child support agency (U.S. Department of Health and Human Services 1993). The Family Support Act of 1988 required that by 1994 all states adopt laws that contain a provision for immediate wage withholding for the amount of child support awarded (Garfinkel, Melli, and Robertson 1994). An initial evaluation of 10 counties that instituted routine income withholding showed that withholding increased child support payments by between 11 and 30 percent (Garfinkel 1992). Garfinkel estimates that income withholding will "increase the national amount of child support collections out of total child support obligations from 59 percent to between 65 and 77 percent" (1992:47).

In addition, many states have established other procedures for strengthening the enforcement of their child support orders, including measures that would have been unimaginable until the recent change in attitude toward child support. Laws now mandate referring difficult child support cases to the Internal Revenue Service for collection, imposing liens on real and personal property, and reporting arrears to credit agencies (Roberts 1994). Some states, such as California, withhold state professional licenses when a parent is in arrears. Others, among them Virginia, even refuse to issue driver's licenses, car registrations, or hunting and fishing licenses to those who are behind in their child support payments and have made no arrangements to meet their obligations. Vermont has gone so far as to seize lottery winnings (Roberts 1994).

While these reforms are important for increasing the number of women who receive child support, at the same time, according to the figures of Garfinkel (1992:47) which were previously cited, between 23 and 35 percent of women will still not receive child support after income withholding is instituted. What accounts for this high percentage of women who will not receive any child support? First, there is no child support enforcement system for women whose ex-husbands or former partners are self-employed. Income withholding legislation dictates that employers withhold child support from the income they pay to their employees; there is no comparable child support enforcement mechanism for men who are independently employed.

Second, collecting child support is a problem in interstate cases, which comprise 30 percent of all child support cases (Garfinkel 1992:76). Until recently, only $1 out of every $10 in child support had been collected from an interstate case (Garfinkel 1992:76). Fortunately, federal legislation, particularly the Personal Responsibility and Work Reconciliation Act of 1996, has created new enforcement mechanisms for interstate cases. The effectiveness of the new regulations, however, depends on the ability of state child support agencies to take action on individual child support cases. Unfortunately, at this time, state agencies are underfunded and labor under very large caseloads. Thus, enforcing interstate cases will remain a problem.

In the course of my research, I found other problems that will continue to prevent mothers from obtaining child support, even after the introduction of income withholding. Some of these problems have been invisible to child support authorities and policy makers, while others have been ignored. In the following section, based on the experiences of the women in my study of divorced mothers, I address the problems that women will continue to face in negotiating for child support and enforcing child support orders, even after the passage of recent child support reforms.

Methods and Sample

The data reported here are based on an interview study of a random sample of a diverse group of 129 divorced women with children, drawn from the 1986 divorce court records of the County of Philadelphia, Pennsylvania. The larger study focused on a variety of topics, including how women viewed the ending of their marriages, how they managed on their reduced incomes, how they negotiated for resources from ex-husbands and the state, and what custody and visitation agreements they made (Kurz 1995).[2]

The mothers in this sample received child support at a rate similar to national averages (U.S. Bureau of the Census 1991). Of those women with a child support order, 56 percent received child support regularly, 23 percent received partial support, and 21 percent received none at all. Seventeen percent of the women had no child support order, although roughly half of them reported that they did receive child support informally. In addition, 29 percent of the women in this sample had income-withholding arrangements, so it is possible to draw some tentative conclusions from these data about the possible successes and limitations of this new form of child support collection enforcement.

In their negotiations for child support, the women in this sample reported four serious problems: 1) difficulty securing legal help; 2) inability to collect child support from ex-husbands who can evade the child support system; 3) fear of reprisals from their ex-husbands; and 4) their ex-husband's inability to pay child support. The data show that due to these problems, some women have difficulty negotiating their initial child support awards, updating these awards at a later time, and enforcing them. These problems demonstrate how within the current system, men can use their power to further their interests, while women and their children remain vulnerable. Despite the fact that, as Arendell (1995) describes, men feel they have lost power at divorce and that their former rights and prerogatives have been stripped away, they still have many advantages in the negotiations for child support.

Lawyers and Legal Assistance

Under current procedures, to obtain child support and other resources women must go through a process that entails negotiations with different parties, particularly with their ex-husbands, sometimes with court personnel, and frequently with lawyers. In some cases, a couple determines the amount of child support together with their lawyers before going to court. In other cases, the couple goes to court with or without a lawyer and the award is determined at a support conference or a pretrial hearing. A minority of women in the sample—typically middle-class women—had their lawyers negotiate child support agreements with their ex-husbands' lawyers. The majority went to Family Court where they had to negotiate with a hearing officer, a judge, and other court personnel.

Whether a woman has a lawyer negotiate her settlement out of Family Court or she negotiates a settlement in Family Court, when women begin the process of obtaining child support, they have almost no information about how to navigate the child support system. Almost all of the women in this sample wanted to retain lawyers who would provide them with information and assistance to guide them through the process of negotiating for resources, which they saw as difficult. Most of them were overwhelmed at the prospect of collecting all of the appropriate information and believed that lawyers could be very helpful to them. Lawyers can benefit women in many ways, such as by helping them to determine their own and their ex-husband's assets and to establish whether there may be any concealment of assets. Research shows that divorced persons with lawyers secure more assets from the marriage (Seltzer 1991) and have a greater chance of securing favorable custody arrangements (Maccoby and Mnookin 1992).

The women in this sample faced major problems obtaining good legal advice, primarily because of the high cost of good lawyers. Seventeen percent of the women in the sample had no legal assistance, and there were dramatic class and race differences in the remaining women's use of lawyers. While 81 percent of middle-class and 83 percent of the working-class women had their own private lawyers, only 29 percent of poverty-level women had private attorneys. Those who had no lawyers gave two different reasons for not having them. First, they said they could not afford a lawyer. Second, some believed they didn't need a lawyer, either because there were no resources they could get from their ex-husbands or because their ex-husbands were paying on their own. Most of this group regretted their decision and now wished they had hired a lawyer because their ex-husbands did not follow through on the promise to pay child support.

Many women complained about the cost of their lawyers. As in other metropolitan areas, divorce lawyers charged anywhere from $125 to $350 an hour (Kurz 1994:55). Some women complained that their lawyers did not inform them of how much their divorces were costing until the fees had become very high, and that they never received itemized bills from their lawyers. Some divorced women in other locations complained of being exploited by lawyers, and a New York state judge issued a rule requiring divorce lawyers to provide itemized billing and forbidding lawyers from taking women's homes when legal fees are not paid (Dao 1993).

The cost of lawyers has several other serious consequences. Another group of women initially had lawyers, but said they could not afford to hire a lawyer to go back to court and raise their child support awards. In theory, with new legislation mandating the periodic review and updating of child support awards, women should have an easy time securing increases in their awards. In practice, however, as Garfinkel has argued, the courts are free to depart from guidelines if they think it would be fairer to one of the parties (Garfinkel 1992:74). This may enable some husbands and wives who have legal assistance to take advantage of loopholes in the law.

Another problem for women is that the high cost of lawyers means they are unable to retain the kinds of lawyers who will give them high-quality service. A few women — particularly middle-class women — express satisfaction with their lawyers. They look carefully before they choose a lawyer, they pay their lawyers large amounts of money and, in return, learn about their rights and receive a lot of advice. Many women, however, state that they had to rely on the cheapest legal advice they could find. Some obtained the services of a lawyer as a favor and complained that because of this, they felt they could not ask things from their lawyer that they would have liked to ask. Many of these women believed that the fact that they had to settle for whatever lawyer they could get put them at a disadvantage in negotiating for child support, and that they did not get the information they needed. A few women reported that their lawyers did not show up in court. "The lawyer had a clerk do it," said a 28-year-old white medical secretary, married six years with one child. "He just didn't keep me informed, he didn't know what was going on. When you pay a lawyer, you expect him to know what's going on. For example, he didn't tell me how to go about getting child support."

Evasion

It has long been known that many women do not receive child support because their ex-husbands successfully evade paying it. Recent child support reforms have tried to address this problem. One of the major reforms in the area of child support is income withholding, mandated in the Family Support Act of 1988. Income withholding authorizes employers to automatically deduct child support from the wages of the obligor (usually the father) and forward it to state child support agencies. This system should greatly reduce the ability of fathers to evade paying child support because payments are automatically issued and are not dependent on actions taken by fathers.

Unfortunately, however, the experiences of women in this sample indicate that even with income withholding, some women will not get child support because their ex-husbands will be able to successfully evade the system. In my study, which took place before this legislation was passed, 29 percent of the women had income withholding arrangements for obtaining child support. At the time these interviews were conducted, Pennsylvania courts were supposed to automatically withhold child support payments from the wages of the noncustodial parent if they had failed to pay 30 days' worth of child support. Of those women who had income withholding agreements, 27 percent received no child support—a figure consistent with Garfinkel's estimates that 23 to 35 percent of women nationally will still not receive child support even with income withholding (Garfinkel 1992). The experiences of these women give us an indication of the promise and the problems of income withholding procedures and show why, even with income withholding, there will be mothers who will not receive child support and have inadequate incomes to raise their children.

Evasion was the major problem reported by those women who had income withholding agreements and were not receiving child support. Said a 31-year-old mother of two who had been married seven years, "I got the wage attachment. When he found out he was going to court, he quit his job. He started dancing; he makes money under the table." Another said, "My ex-husband doesn't pay child support at all. I've contacted the court. They say they've written him and that they're going to attach his wages. When my ex-husband found that out, he called me and said he would make sure his employer said he didn't know him" (34-year-old black women, day-care worker, married eight years with one child).

Nineteen percent of women who have wage attachments receive only partial amounts of their child support awards and also report evasion as a problem. A 28-year-old white mother of one has had to get her ex-husband's wages attached several times. She has tracked him down through several states and several different jobs. She has written the court again and again to tell them where he is working. She says, "I don't like the system. It's the woman that has to do everything." One woman stopped receiving child support when her ex-husband became unemployed. She is now trying to arrange to have his unemployment check attached.

Those women who had income withholding agreements but who did not receive child support experienced the same problems as all the other women who did not receive child support. In addition to being paid "under the table," lying about their financial circumstances is a common ploy of ex-husbands trying to evade child support. Although they work full-time, they tell the court that they are not working or work part-time. Frequently, women cannot provide any evidence that the fathers are earning income because they are working in the underground economy.

Fathers' ability to evade the child support system can also result in women receiving a lower child support award than what they are entitled to. Some women complain that their awards are inadequate because their ex-husbands were paid under the table and did not report their full income. As one woman said, "I don't know if the child support award is fair. I don't want to really rob him. I guess if I thought he could afford more I wouldn't think it was fair. But I don't know how much he earns because his overtime, which he gets every other weekend, is off the books." Finally, some women who have income withholding agreements report that their ex-husbands have gone to another state and are impossible to locate. The court told one woman that it could try to locate her ex-husband through the IRS, but he had never paid taxes, so this did not work. In some cases, the court makes an effort to find these men. In other cases, it does not.

Fortunately, some states have developed measures to reduce fathers' ability to evade paying child support, such as requiring employers to report all new hires or rehires. Some states also include a new-hire report as part of the W-4 reporting system that employers already use for collecting tax-related information. Other states have developed child support registries to collect abstracts of support orders and financial data about parents. Employers send support payments to the central registry with a list of the parents from whom the support was withheld, and the registry credits the proper account and disburses payments (Roberts 1994:22–23).

Wage withholding, computerization, and employer reporting systems will markedly improve the child support system. Some men, however, will continue to go to great lengths to avoid paying child support. Arendell (1995) found that some fathers in her sample withheld child support as a way to exert their power. Angered by their loss of authority and by the ability of the court to order them to pay child support, they refused as a kind of symbolic act of resistance. Several remained unemployed or underemployed to avoid paying child support. Some reported working in the underground economy to avoid child support payments. They shared a view that child support was "their" money. Refusing to pay it was resisting an unjust authority.

Feeling Fearful and Avoiding Conflict

Thirty percent of all women in my sample stated that they were fearful during their negotiations for child support, with few race or class differences among them. There is overlap between those who report being fearful while negotiating for child support and those who report being fearful during negotiations for custody and for property. Of those fearful during the latter, 74 percent were also fearful during negotiations for custody and 62 percent during the negotiations for property.

These women's fears are strongly related to their experience of violence during marriage. There is a statistically significant relationship between women's fear during the negotiations for child support and their experience of violence during marriage and separation. Further, women's fears during child support negotiations are related to the frequency with which they experienced violence during marriage. The more serious or frequent the violence these women experienced, the more fearful they were during negotiations for child support.

Some women are also fearful because of their experience of violence during the separation. Increasing numbers of researchers are concerned about high levels of violence during separation or "separation assault" (Mahoney 1991). Some believe there may be even more violence during periods of separation than during marriages (Ellis and DeKeseredy 1996; Ellis and Stuckless 1992; Johnson and Sacco 1995). Seventeen out of 129 women in this sample reported experiencing violence during the separation period. Six additional women reported an immediate threat of violence during the separation. Many more women experienced violence during their marriages. Fifty-four percent of the women reported several acts of violence during their marriage or the separation, and 19 percent of women said they left marriages because of domestic violence.

There are strong indications that their fears prompted some of these women to reduce their demands for child support. There is a statistically significant relationship between feeling fearful during negotiations for child support and receipt of child support. Only 34 percent of the women who reported being fearful received regular child support, in contrast to 60 percent of those who did not report fear during negotiations for child support. The qualitative data confirm that women are fearful about getting child support. One woman, on welfare at the time of the interview, said, "I felt that if I had pushed him for things, he would have beat me up. I also figured he never would pay." A middle-class woman told her ex-husband that she would give up her demand for child support if he would stop harassing her. According to her, "The money is not worth the harassment of it all. I find the money very useful. It helps pay the bills. But nothing is worth the harassment. I get terrible headaches, terrible ones. I get very tense."

While some women who were fearful gave up trying to get child support, others reported receiving a lower child support award than they wanted. Several women who were trying to obtain increases in their child support awards at a later time when their expenses for their children had increased mentioned their fear of violence. Several other women were explicitly fearful of trying to get more child support because they were afraid that their ex-husbands might take the children. One woman was afraid for her life. Another woman, advised by the court to file to increase her child support order, declined, saying, "After we came out of court the last time, he said he was going to kill me. He ran at me, and my lawyer stopped him."

Thus, fear is a strong factor in women's ability to obtain child support. Because of the factor of fear, it is very important that abused women not be forced to negotiate

for child support with their abusers. For example, the 1996 welfare reform bill required mothers who wish to receive welfare payments and child support payments to cooperate with authorities in identifying the fathers of their children, a
procedure called "paternity establishment." Fortunately, amendments to the bill
have provided waivers so that abused women who qualify do not have to identify
the fathers of their children, which might put them in danger (National Resource
Center on Domestic Violence 1997). It is critical that states, which are responsible
for enforcing most aspects of the welfare bill's child support provisions, support
the waivers. Unfortunately, it is not clear how generous or understanding states
will be in the situation of abused women. States are now under heavy pressure to
reduce their welfare caseloads. This means they must help women gain access to
the only other potential sources of income available to them — jobs and child support from their children's fathers. Thus, given that states now want to ensure that
fathers pay child support as a way to get women off the welfare rolls, they may not
view protecting abused women as a high priority.

Ex-Husbands' Inability to Pay

Finally, some of those women in my study who received no child support reported that their ex-husbands could not afford it. Primarily, poverty-level
women reported this problem, particularly those on public assistance and minority women, who described their ex-husbands as not employed or not having any
money. These men are more vulnerable than others are to unemployment and discrimination. They are also typically ordered by courts to pay proportionately
more child support than other men (Garfinkel 1992:76–77). In addition, proportionately more poor fathers are sent to prison for evading payment of child support (Garfinkel 1992:76–77). However, it is also the case that of the women on
welfare in this sample, the ex-husbands who had an income averaged $14,100.
This is similar to national figures, where the average income of fathers whose former partners are on welfare is $13,000 to $21,000. This is still considerably
higher than $7,872, which is the median income of their former wives (Roberts
1994:37).
    What should be done when fathers' incomes are very low? Whose responsibility
is it then to ensure that children are able to have an adequate standard of living?
Different approaches to calculating the child support obligations of low-income fathers have been suggested. One is that noncustodial fathers whose children are receiving welfare should provide 25 percent of their income to support two children,
or for those at the lowest end of the scale, $2,000 a year (Roberts 1994:37). Gar-
finkel, Melli, and Robertson (1994:92) argue that the percentage-of-income approach would also help address the problem of fathers with low incomes. If the
father is poor or unemployed, under the percentage-of-income approach, he will
have a low child support obligation.

Another way to increase the ability of noncustodial fathers to contribute to their children's support is to improve the job prospects of these fathers. In the 1980s some localities, such as Maryland's Prince George's County, began to offer education and training opportunities to low-income fathers who were unable to meet their child support obligations (Roberts 1994:37–38). The idea of assisting low-income fathers so they can support their children was adopted by Congress in the Family Support Act of 1988. This law authorized several demonstration projects to test approaches to training and employment for fathers with children receiving Aid to Families with Dependent Children (AFDC) benefits. The problem with this approach is that funds for such training programs are usually limited and unpredictable. Others have suggested different approaches, for example that teen parents "pay" their child support by going to school, attending parenting classes, and baby-sitting, rather than with cash (Roberts 1994:37–38).

In conclusion, the experiences of the interviewed women show that new reforms, particularly wage withholding, will greatly facilitate the payment of child support to divorced women with children; fewer men will be able to evade paying child support; and women will be less constrained by fear. However, these data show that the problem of evasion is far-reaching and cannot be overcome by wage withholding — some fathers will be able to evade the system by disappearing or being paid under the table. Other mothers will get no child support because they are too afraid to demand it, or because their ex-husbands are not working. Finally, women will continue to have less power in their negotiations with their ex-husbands as long as they do not have access to adequate legal services.

Conclusion

Child support is critical for keeping divorced and single mothers out of poverty. Unfortunately, however, there are serious problems with the adequacy and enforcement of awards, and most women will not receive the child support that they need. One of the major problems with child support awards is that they do not recognize the care work of mothering. Rules for determining child support focus on how to divide responsibility for expenses between custodial parent (usually mothers) and noncustodial fathers — the care work that mothers perform is not taken into account and is virtually invisible. This lack of compensation for their care work directly contributes to mothers' poverty, as many mothers adapt their work schedules to take care of their children and, as a consequence, receive lower pay at their jobs.

Further, the government is not taking adequate steps to ensure that women receive their child support awards. Despite introduction of reforms such as wage withholding, as the data presented here demonstrate, a variety of obstacles will continue to prevent some women from getting child support: lack of legal services, evasion, fear, and the low income of the child's father. The current child support system is still a private transfer of funds and, as such, is contingent on the noncustodial parent having a sufficient income and on a certain amount of goodwill on the part of ex-husbands. Thus, current reforms cannot guarantee mothers the child support that they are due, and other measures must be taken to increase the independence and security of divorced women and other single mothers with children.

The problems with the child support system in the United States demonstrate that we must adopt a child support assurance system, as some European countries have already done (Kamerman and Kahn 1988). Such a system guarantees that if a woman does not receive all of the child support she is owed, the government will make up the difference to her while trying to collect child support from the father. A few people have made the case for a child support assurance system in the United States, arguing that it would reduce poverty and promote security and independence for single parents (Garfinkel 1992). Unfortunately, given the desire of many policy makers in the United States to privatize social problems rather than build an adequate social welfare system, the development of a child support assurance program will not take place here soon. However, it is important to keep the pressure on policy makers to adopt such a system. While child support by itself will not solve the economic problems of single mothers, it is a critical tool for keeping mothers and their children out of poverty.

Filling in the Gaps in Long Term Care Insurance

Policy Implications for Informal Care Workers

*I*nformal care, defined as unpaid care or care that is provided outside of the market, comprises a significant portion of all long term care of the elderly. Most informal care is provided by family members, and among family members, daughters are the largest source of this care. Daughters are more likely than sons to be the primary source of care, and on average provide more hours of care than do sons. In addition, the wives of frail elders provide a substantial portion of informal care. These facts imply that women, to a greater extent than men, play an important role in the long term care of elderly family members. Research findings suggest that more than half of all women will provide care for an ill or disabled person at some point in their lives (Robinson, Moen, and Dempster-McClain 1995). Over time, women's participation in elder care has remained significant, despite increasing pressures on women's time from career and family obligations.

This chapter examines the connections among women's roles in the provision of long term care, the structure of the health insurance system for the elderly in the United States, and the policy options for reducing the burden of long term care. The first part of the chapter deals with the characteristics of the provision of long term care in the United States. In particular, I discuss how existing public and private insurance options fall short of covering all long term care needs, and the degree to which women participate in the provision of informal care. I use the term *caregiver* when citing previous research studies that employ this term to refer to those who provide informal care. Because many providers of informal care do so at a serious cost of their time and well-being, I use the term *care worker* elsewhere.

I next turn to the question of how current policy solutions may alter the dynamics of informal care. Policy solutions to the burden of long term care have the potential for serious changes for care workers. Of the leading policy options, private insurance is seen by many as the best way to shift the burden of care from families and Medicaid to the paid private sector. Current attempts to increase private insurance include tax incentives for long term care insurance and public-private partnerships for long term care. Despite the focus on private insurance, there is much evidence that private insurance lacks the potential to alter long term care coverage on a large scale. For this reason, policies to increase private insurance coverage are unlikely to significantly reduce the burden of care work on family members.

A second policy option for long term care is social insurance. Social insurance for long term care is subject to many criticisms. One such criticism is that compulsory social insurance programs may actually make individuals worse off, if they would prefer that family members serve as a form of "insurance" for long term care. The evidence, however, fails to support this criticism of social insurance for long term care. The cost of social insurance for long term care is also thought to be prohibitive, but the high cost of informal care work for those who provide it must also be considered. If the United States considers reducing the burden on care providers to be a policy goal, then these types of evidence suggest that the current form of market-based policies aimed at increasing private insurance will have limited effectiveness. Other forms of market-based policies or social insurance options need to be explored.

Insurance for long term care in the United States

Despite the presence of an entitlement program for acute care, the United States health insurance system is characterized by serious gaps in the coverage of long-term care for the elderly. The gap begins with the Medicare program, which is the major source of health insurance for nearly 40 million Americans over age 65. Medicare covers most acute care needs, but does not include coverage for chronic care such as nursing home care. The exception is when an elderly person is released to a skilled nursing facility (SNF) directly from an inpatient hospital stay and under physicians' orders. In this case, only the first 20 days of care in the skilled nursing facility are covered. With the purchase of supplemental insurance for Medicare — or Medigap — individuals have the option of additional coverage for SNF care. Three-fourths of all Medicare recipients own Medigap policies, and three-fourths of those policies include an option for additional coverage for skilled nursing home facility care (Rice, Graham, and Fox 1997). Although these statistics suggest that Medigap coverage for nursing care is widespread, this type of coverage is inadequate. It covers a maximum of 100 days of care in a skilled nursing facility, and then only when preceded by a Medicare-covered hospital stay. Most important, the care provided in skilled nursing facilities is distinct from the custodial or personal care provided in nursing homes, which includes the kind of assistance with eating, dressing, and bathing that is often required by those in need of long term care. It is expected that many elderly are unaware that Medicare and Medigap fail to cover nursing home costs and other long term care expenses. In the absence of these types of coverage for long term care, many must choose between "spending down" their assets to become recipients of Medicaid or purchasing expensive private insurance.

Medicaid

The cost of a year of nursing home care averages around $40,000 in the U.S., and varies significantly by region. Paying for this type of care out of pocket can quickly exhaust the savings of many elderly persons. When their assets are near depletion, many recipients of long term care become eligible for the Medicaid program, the means-tested public health insurance program for the poor, disabled, and medically needy. Under the eligibility criteria of the program, assets can be no greater than roughly $2,000, excluding the value of the individual's home. Any monthly income in excess of a small nursing home allowance — typically $30 a month — is transferred to the state to compensate for part of the cost of nursing home care. For many of the elderly, public programs such as Medicaid are the primary means of financing long term care needs. Of the $115.1 billion spent on long term care in 1997, 60 percent was financed by the federal government and states (Health Care Financing Administration 1999a). In 1997, 14 percent of all public medical expenditures on health care went toward nursing home care or home healthcare (Health Care Financing Administration 1999a).

While Medicaid pays a substantial share of the costs of long term care, there are many concerns about the quality of care received in Medicaid-affiliated institutions. The low reimbursement rates set for nursing homes by Medicaid have led to concern about uneven care and inadequate medical attention (Institute of Medicine 1986). In addition to concerns about quality, the elderly and their families may also be concerned about the stigma attached to participation in Medicaid, known as a welfare-related insurance program for the poor. Medicaid is also biased toward institutional care. Almost three-fourths of Medicaid spending on long term care in 1996 was directed toward institutional care, with the remainder going for community-based care (Health Care Financing Administration 1998).

Private Insurance for long term care

Privately purchased insurance policies can cover long term care costs without requiring the insured to deplete private assets or to enter a Medicaid-affiliated institution. These types of policies are relatively new products and are still not widely held. The market for private long term care insurance came into existence in the mid-1980s, and it is estimated that about 4 to 5 percent of the elderly hold such policies. There is a great deal of variation in the features of private long term care insurance policies. Policies usually cover stays in nursing homes, and sometimes cover home care, community care, or adult day care. Benefits usually become payable when the insured person is unable to perform certain activities of daily living, such as bathing, dressing, and eating, although some policies require medical certification or prior hospitalization before benefits are triggered. Policies also vary in the length of the elimination (waiting) period, which may mean that benefits begin between 20 and 100 days after the insured enters a nursing home. Once the insurance company begins making payments, payments may cover only the services specifically defined by the policy, or the insurer may pay benefits to the insured regardless of the specific services received. In most cases benefits are paid out daily or weekly (to coincide with the daily or weekly rates of nursing home care) and up to some lifetime maximum amount. Some policies are sold with inflation protection, which allows benefits to increase with inflation.

One suggested explanation for the low coverage levels of private insurance is the size of the premiums. In 1995, the average annual premium for a standardized individual long term care insurance policy, including inflation protection and other options, was $2,560 for a 65-year-old; the annual premium for the same policy purchased by a 75-year-old individual was $8,146 (Coronel and Kitchman 1997). Many elderly may forgo the purchase of insurance because they lack information about insurance policies or about their own future needs. In addition, the availability of insurance policies for long term care may be limited. Insurance companies may be wary of the costs of offering this type of insurance since it holds greater appeal to those already in need to care.

In summary, while the Medicare program addresses the acute-care needs of the elderly, it does not provide the long term care that an estimated 7.3 million Americans over age 65 need. Medicare supplemental insurance does not provide coverage for chronic care either. Private long term care insurance is available; however, it is not very common, and the policies can be very expensive. Private insurance is often unavailable to individuals who are already in poor health and appear to need care in the near future. Companies will inquire about previous hospitalization or wheelchair use before issuing a policy; they may also review medical records and physician assessments of the individual's health. Coverage is often refused for persons with serious conditions that indicate nursing home use in the near future; individuals with other pre-existing conditions may have difficulty finding coverage or receiving benefits. The high cost of private insurance options, in conjunction with the quality concerns associated with Medicaid and institutional care in general, could explain in part the prevalence of informal caregiving by family members.

The Prevalence of Informal Caregiving

In contrast to statistics that suggest low levels of formal (market-based) insurance for long term care, many studies have noted the prevalence of informal caregiving. Approximately 80 to 90 percent of the care provided to impaired elderly persons is carried out by family members (Cantor 1989:106–7). Early studies, based on the 1982 National Long Term Care Survey, indicate that daughters and wives are especially involved in the provision of care. Stephens and Christianson (1986) found that daughters spent six hours per day providing care, while sons spent about four hours (46–47). Similarly, Stone, Cafferata, and Sangl (1987) found that caregivers are predominantly female (72 percent) and that daughters were more likely than sons to assume the role of caregiver. A large majority of caregivers (90 percent) provided care without the assistance of formal services. Many caregivers were also employed in market work at the time they provided care; more than 40 percent of daughters and 50 percent of sons had paying jobs. Almost one-third of these caregivers reported family incomes that were below or near the poverty line.

Analysis of more recent data has been consistent with earlier evidence of a greater level of involvement by women and daughters in caregiving activities. Three-quarters of primary caregivers sampled in the 1989 National Long Term Care Survey were female (Doty, Jackson, and Crown 1998). The care recipients in this survey were predominantly low income. Nearly 73 percent had incomes under $15,000 a year, which suggests serious financial constraints for the 40 percent of primary caregivers who are spouses, as well as other family members. Analysis of data from the 1993 Study of Asset and Health Dynamics of the Oldest Old showed that daughters were 9 percentage points more likely than sons to provide care, controlling for characteristics of the care recipient and the caregiver (Wolf, Freedman, and Soldo 1997). When care was provided by both sons and daughters, daughters provided between 10 and 18 more hours of care per month than sons. Even when differences in past receipt of financial support from parents are taken into account, daughters remain more likely to provide care to parents than sons (Henretta, Hill, Li, Soldo, and Wolf 1997).

Spitze and Logan (1990) summarize several explanations for the difference in caregiving efforts between daughters and sons. Leading explanations include society's assignment of gender roles, which designate nurturing activities to women more than men, and the stronger emotional bonds between daughters and their parents. Economic factors may also explain the larger role of women in the caregiving process. Women face a lower opportunity cost of providing care because fewer women than men work outside the home, and their wages tend to be lower. Differences in caregiving efforts remain, however, when labor market status is held constant (Stoller 1983).

The burden of informal caregiving may be even greater among women of color. Previous research has found that blacks use fewer days of nursing home care than whites, either because of discrimination by nursing homes (Falcone and Broyles 1994) or because blacks have been shown to have a greater availability of unpaid caregivers among family members (Burton, Kasper, Shore, Cagney, LaVeist, Cubbin, and German 1995). A survey of caregivers conducted by the National Alliance for Caregiving and the American Association of Retired Persons (AARP) reported that caregiving was slightly more prevalent among Asian, African-American, and Latino families than white families (National Alliance for Caregiving and the AARP 1997).

The persistent finding of women's significant role in the provision of long term care has motivated much research on the effects of caregiving on women's work patterns and well-being. The causal relationship between care work and employment has been difficult to identify empirically because of the possible existence of reverse causality (that is, employment status may shape one's decision to engage in care work), and the inability to control for certain factors that may affect both employment and care work decisions simultaneously. As a result, the research in this area often reports mixed results, depending on the choice of econometric techniques and other differences in data sets and time periods. Of the many studies on the linkage between care work and employment, only a subset specifically address the problems of causality or simultaneity. Wolf and Soldo (1994) reported that among married women, caring for an elderly parent was not associated with reduced employment or hours of work. In a similar study using different data, Ettner (1995) found that for women ages 35 to 64, living with a disabled parent led to a significant reduction in hours worked. Using three years of data on caregiving and labor force participation, Pavalko and Artis (1997) found that caregivers experienced a reduction in the number of hours in paid employment when care work began, and that when care work ceased, there was no increase in hours of paid employment.

Studies of caregivers also reveal serious behavioral health consequences. Gallagher, Rose, Rivera, Lovett, and Thompson (1989) reported that 49 percent of female caregivers were clinically depressed, and George and Gwyther (1986) found that caregivers of demented adults used prescription drugs for depression, anxiety, and insomnia at two to three times the rate of the rest of the population. In economic terms, the cost of the time spent providing informal care is substantial.

Estimates of the opportunity cost of informal care services based on the minimum wage suggest that providing informal care for an elderly person with a problem in at least one activity of daily living can cost between $7,280 and $10,403 a year (Robinson 1997:245). Estimates based on the market value of informal care services (the cost of informal care were it purchased in the market) are similar, and are as much as $7,680 a year (Harrow, Tennstedt, and McKinlay 1995). As would be expected, the value of informal care for persons with Alzheimer's disease is much greater, and has been estimated to be $34,000 a year (Max, Webber, and Fox 1995). Ward (1990) estimated that the total value of uncompensated care provided by family members, in terms of forgone wages, may be as much as $18 billion a year. Thus, in terms of the opportunity cost of time and in terms of psychic costs of illness and stress, informal caregiving places a high cost on those who provide it.

A variety of demographic trends suggest that the burden of caregiving on women will increase. The population aged 65 and older numbered 34.2 million in 1995 and is projected to be about 60.8 million by the year 2025. Gains in the life expectancy of 65-year-olds, from 14 years in 1980 to a projected 15.6 years in 1999, imply that the duration of caregiving may lengthen. Finally, the trend toward smaller family size, from 3.6 persons in 1970 to 3.2 persons in 1995, implies that there will be fewer caregivers available in the form of family members. These demographic trends together suggest that the demand for long term care will increase in the near future while the supply of informal care providers decreases (U.S. Bureau of the Census 1997; Health Care Financing Administration 1999b).

Policies to Address the Burden of long term care

The low level of private coverage for long term care is associated with high levels of informal caregiving by family members, and also with high levels of public expenditure by the federal government and the states. The costs of long term care borne by the Medicaid program totaled more than $69.1 billion in 1993, and long term care spending by Medicaid grew at an average rate of 13.2 percent a year between 1989 and 1993 (U.S. General Accounting Office 1995:8, 13). Only a small fraction of total long term care costs (0.2 percent of $100 billion) was paid by private long term care insurance. In an attempt to keep these costs under control, several policies have been considered or are being evaluated. While the control of formal costs is the primary motivation for these types of policies, increasing coverage for private long term care insurance may provide some relief to care workers themselves. In the United States, current policy initiatives for long term care have focused primarily on using the market for private insurance as a way to reduce public costs. These policies include tax incentives for long term care insurance and public-private partnerships for long term care.

Tax Incentives for Long Term Care Insurance

There have been various attempts to use the tax code to create incentives for the purchase of private long term care insurance, dating back to its emergence on the market. In 1988, the House of Representatives considered legislation to align the tax treatment of long term care insurance with the treatment given to health insurance plans, and to offer tax credits to individuals who purchased long term care insurance. This attempt at legislation failed, as did similar legislation introduced in 1991. In 1994, calls to change the tax treatment of long term care insurance appeared in the Republicans' *Contract with America*. These were followed in 1995 by proposed legislation to exclude employer contributions to long term care from employer and employee gross income and to treat long term care expenses as medical expenses, thus making them tax-deductible. Finally, with the passage of the Health Insurance Portability and Accountability Act of 1996 (the Kassebaum-Kennedy legislation), Congress successfully enacted tax incentives for long term care insurance. Effective January 1, 1997, taxpayers could deduct qualified long term care expenses as itemized medical expenses. The allowable deductions include the premium for long term care insurance coverage. In addition, employer contributions toward the cost of group long term care insurance became a tax-deductible expense for employers.

Proposals to increase long term care insurance through tax incentives have been openly criticized. In their 1994 book *Sharing the Burden*, authors Wiener, Illston, and Hanley include a detailed discussion of the shortcomings of allowing employer contributions and the taxpayer purchase of long term care insurance to be tax-deductible. Taxpayer deductions of the cost of long term care insurance are equivalent to subsidies for long term care insurance premiums, where the size of the subsidy increases with the marginal tax rate. This type of subsidy is regressive, in that it benefits higher-income households more than lower-income households. As a result the benefits of tax incentives are much smaller for the members of low-income families who provide a disproportionate share of unpaid care work and who face the greatest challenge in affording this type of insurance.

Wiener, Illston, and Hanley also state that the effect of deductions for long term care insurance on long term care coverage is limited by the fact that few taxpayers itemize deductions. They cite statistics showing that only 29 percent of tax returns included itemized deductions, and only 4 percent included itemized medical deductions in 1993. The authors also estimate that the costs for each additional person with long term care insurance under tax policies similar to those included in the Kassebaum-Kennedy legislation would be quite high, and would exceed any Medicaid savings. They also suggest that those most likely to benefit from these tax policies are individuals who would have purchased insurance in the absence of subsidies (Wiener, Illston, and Hanley 1994:85–86).

Tax deductions for employer contributions also have limited ability to change coverage of long term care insurance. Wiener, Illston, and Hanley write that the financial problems associated with employer-sponsored health insurance plans for retired workers have led many employers to cut back on retiree benefits. They view this trend as a sign of the limitations of the interest and ability of employers to contribute to long term care insurance plans, especially since employees don't derive the benefits of long term care insurance until years after having left the company (1994:84–85).

Public-Private Partnerships for Long Term Care

A second method for increasing private insurance coverage for long term care is currently under evaluation in four states. "Public-private partnerships" for long term care combine private insurance with liberalized Medicaid eligibility, making public insurance easier to access for individuals with some private coverage. In the early 1990s, the partnership program began when the Robert Wood Johnson Foundation, a national philanthropy focused on improving health care, solicited the participation of various states. The public-private partnerships for long term care promote the purchase of private insurance to cover the initial costs of long term care services. Each participating state must alter Medicaid program rules so that participating individuals can become eligible without spending down their assets entirely. The goal is to motivate insurance purchase by creating complete or partial asset protection with limited private insurance coverage. For example, an individual might buy private insurance to cover $50,000 of long term care costs. When the private insurance coverage runs out, the individual can retain $50,000 of his or her assets and still become eligible for Medicaid. Such a plan is referred to as a "dollar-for-dollar" approach, where every dollar of private insurance coverage protects one dollar of assets. Three states (Connecticut, Indiana, and California) have implemented dollar-for-dollar approach partnerships. A fourth state, New York, has implemented a public-private partnership that offers total asset protection with the purchase of limited private insurance coverage.

As is the case with tax incentives for private insurance, many criticisms have been directed toward the public-private partnerships. Because the partnerships work by allowing insurance purchasers to protect assets, authors have raised concerns about the limits of asset protection as an important consideration in the purchase of long term care (Wiener and Hanley 1992; Wiener, Illston, and Hanley 1994). Wiener and Hanley (1992) cite a statistic from a survey of long term care insurance policyholders that shows that only 14 percent of the respondents listed protection of assets as the "most important" reason for buying insurance. This suggests that changing asset-protection limits will not induce sizable numbers of individuals to purchase private insurance. Critics also dispute the cost-effectiveness of the partnerships, arguing that the program is not, as suggested by their proponents, budget neutral. If the individuals who purchase insurance would have purchased insurance without the partnerships, then Medicaid costs could actually rise. The partnership programs' ability to increase insurance coverage may also be limited by the welfare stigma associated with Medicaid. In a survey of individual motives for purchasing long term care insurance, 91 percent of respondents replied that avoiding Medicaid was either an important or very important motivation for buying a policy (Life Plans Inc. 1995).

Recent Initiatives: The Clinton Proposal

Efforts to increase private insurance coverage for long term care continue. In January 1999, President Clinton announced a new initiative for long term care. Two of the four major components of the initiative would encourage the purchase of long term care insurance. First, to signal the importance of employer involvement, Clinton's new plan calls for a long term care insurance benefit for federal employees. Second, to educate Medicare beneficiaries about options for financing long term care, the plan introduces a national campaign to provide information about long term care insurance and other options.

Critics of the proposal have commented that the emphasis on education about private insurance is a "gimmick . . . intended to offer a concession to the insurance industry," as opposed to a working solution (editorial by Robert Kuttner, the *Washington Post*, January 8, 1999). While the new Clinton initiative may continue to reflect the government's interest in solving the problem of long term care through private insurance, the plan also places emphasis on alleviating the burden of care workers. A new National Family Caregivers Support Program would be established to provide information, referrals, and respite care to caregivers. Finally, to provide financial support to persons in need of long term care or family members who provide such care, a central part of the plan calls for a tax credit of $1,000 to compensate the disabled and their families who care for them for their formal and informal caregiving costs. This proposal represents a recognition of the value of informal care services and the value of in-kind services in addition to out-of-pocket costs. The long term care initiative would credit taxpayers who made out-of-pocket expenses for formal care such as adult day care and home health care. For the first time, taxpayers could receive a credit for the value of time lost due to the provision of informal care during unpaid leaves from employment.

The initiative isn't the first to use tax credits to benefit taxpayers providing long term care. The existing child and dependent care tax credit allows taxpayers to deduct up to $2,400 in out-of-pocket expenses for the care of a disabled dependent, such as a parent in need of long term care. The child and dependent care tax credit is restrictive in that a low-income dependent must live with the taxpayer and receive at least 50 percent of his or her support from the taxpayer, and the care expenses must have been incurred so that the taxpayer could continue working. Proposals to extend the dependent care tax credit during the 105th Congress were unsuccessful.

President Clinton's initiative differs significantly in that the proposed $1,000 credit would apply to informal care costs in addition to out-of-pocket expenses. This proposal takes an unprecedented step to recognize the value of informal costs, and builds on efforts to lessen the burden of providing care for families through the Family and Medical Leave Act of 1993. The initiative nonetheless has its limitations. A $1,000 tax credit is only a fraction of the total cost borne by those who provide informal long term care. Estimates place the informal care anywhere from seven to ten times that amount, and as much as 34 times that amount in the case of caregiving for persons with Alzheimer's disease. Another limitation is the use of tax credits to recognize the costs of long term care. Kuttner states in the *Post* editorial that the income of 40 percent of the elderly is so low that no income taxes are owed; these needy elderly would receive no benefit from a tax credit. Finally, similar to the dependent care tax credit, the proposed program requires that the caregiver reside with the recipient of long term care. So, for approximately 32 percent of all providers of informal care who live apart from the care recipient, the tax credit would not apply (Doty, Jackson, and Crown 1998).

Compulsory Social Insurance: The Case of Germany

While the United States has focused primarily on reforms in the private insurance market for long term care, other countries are taking bolder initiatives to control long term care costs. In 1994, Germany passed legislation to enact a compulsory social insurance policy for long term care. Prior to the enactment of this law, Germany addressed such needs with a combination of short-term nursing home coverage for those covered by national health insurance, long term care insurance benefits for public servants, and a means-tested program that paid for long term care if individuals became impoverished paying for home care or nursing home expenses. The Statutory Long Term Care Insurance Act, which went into effect in 1995, established a new branch of the social insurance system specifically for long term care insurance. All German citizens must enter into the program, unless they can provide evidence of a private policy that provides benefits similar to the social insurance program. The program is financed by employer and employee contributions of 1.7 percent of payroll.

Germany's social insurance for long term care places special importance on allowing persons in need to remain in the community as long as possible. To that end, monthly cash benefits or in-kind benefits provide coverage for home care up to set limits. Professional caregivers are offered relief nurses for up to four weeks a year. In order to provide incentives for caregiving from family members, nonprofessional caregiving is treated as market-based employment by the pension program. When institutional care becomes necessary, the social insurance scheme allows for a monthly payment to cover nursing home stays (Schulte 1996).

Potential Impacts of Policies on Care Workers

Attempts to increase private insurance coverage for long term care have been greeted with skepticism. A subsidy for long term care insurance would be regressive, may benefit individuals who would have bought insurance anyway, and would be of value only to the minority of taxpayers who itemize deductions. The public-private partnerships for long term care would make Medicaid-provided nursing home care easier to access, when many of those interested in private insurance wish to avoid Medicaid. Preliminary statistics on the number of new policies purchased through the partnership programs have been referred to as "disappointing" (Wiener 1998).

The partnerships rely on asset-protection motives to entice people to buy long term care insurance policies. As stated earlier, some have questioned how important these motives are in the decision to buy insurance. In my own work, I find that assets do have a strong association with owning insurance for long term care, but only when assets are above $200,000 (Mellor 1999a). This finding suggests that private long term care insurance is considered an option for those with substantial resources, and that the partnership program is potentially a vehicle to provide the well-to-do with Medicaid coverage.

The many criticisms and limitations of private insurance options to reduce the financial burden of long term care can be extended to their ability to reduce informal care burden. If tax incentives for long term care insurance are severely limited in their ability to increase long term care insurance coverage, then it follows that they are limited in their ability to alleviate costs to the public through Medicaid programs, and also to reduce the burden of care workers providing informal care to those without insurance.

Substitutes for Insurance

Social insurance programs, such as the one enacted in Germany, appear to hold greater promise for alleviating care worker burden than do market-based policies aimed at increasing private insurance for long term care. The German program provides comprehensive coverage for long term care to all citizens, and provides relief for professional caregivers and pension benefits for nonprofessional (informal) caregivers. Not surprisingly, however, social insurance for long term care does not appear to be a politically viable option in the United States in the wake of the failed proposal for universal health care in the early part of the Clinton administration.

The concept of compulsory social insurance has among its critics those who believe that social insurance can actually make an individual less well-off from an efficiency standpoint. Economists Peter Zweifel and Wolfram Strüwe (1998) offer such a criticism of Germany's social insurance program. Their theoretical model of a parent's propensity to purchase long term care insurance suggests that when children with low wages are available as potential care providers, the purchase of insurance will result in welfare loss for the parent. Zweifel and Strüwe's interpretation of their theoretical results leads them to suggest that compulsory social long term care insurance programs will have adverse consequences for welfare.

This interpretation is based on the notion that children and insurance are interchangeable—that is, children are substitutes for insurance. This concept has been expressed in previous literature, especially with respect to developing countries, but the question of whether the elderly do not buy insurance because of the availability of children (i.e., potential caregivers) had not been tested empirically until recently. In recent work (Mellor 1999b), I found that neither the presence of children, nor the presence of female children specifically, reduced the extent of coverage for long term care insurance. In some cases, the opposite relationship was observed—some parents with children who were potential caregivers were more likely to have private insurance for long term care. These findings are in contrast to the notion that family members serve as substitutes for long term care insurance, and refute the specific criticism that social insurance programs for long term care are inefficient because they require the purchase of unwanted insurance by persons who would rather use children to substitute for insurance. While many concerns about social insurance for long term care remain, notably the costs of such a program, at least one such criticism should be ignored.

Conclusion

The current provision of long term care is characterized by low levels of private insurance, high Medicaid program costs, and a substantial contribution by informal care workers. The United States is currently addressing the financial burden of long term care by opting for market-based policies to increase private insurance. Yet, as presented here, there are a number of reasons why tax incentives and public-private partnerships would have limited effects. Taxpayer deductions of the cost of long term care insurance are equivalent to subsidies that benefit those with higher incomes far more than the poor. Using public-private partnerships for long term care insurance may increase coverage by appealing to those with high levels of assets to protect, but this approach is far less appealing to the poor families who are bearing a sizable burden of unpaid care work. The current market-based policies offer the greatest benefits to those with higher incomes and asset levels, the same individuals who have options for the provision of long term care other than informal care work. The population in greatest need for better access to long term care insurance — the low-income women and minority family members who are providing care at a significant cost of their time — are offered little relief by the current market-based policies.

The emphasis on market-based approaches is not unique to the problem of long term care; instead, it echoes a larger trend toward using market principles to approach the reform and provision of social programs. Other examples of this trend are exhibited by the emphasis on privatization as a means to save Social Security, and the reform of Medicare through managed care. This trend, documented and critiqued by Jill Quadagno (1999), is based on the idea that the welfare state is an impediment to market performance. The problem with applying market-based approaches to social problems, according to Quadagno, is that since they rely on the tax system and private investment they can create a two-tiered society, where "the welfare state would consist of an investment class and a class of those too poor to invest" (Quadagno 1999:8).

Returning to the case of long term care, the use of social insurance programs, such as that enacted in Germany, is largely overlooked as a viable option in the United States. Some criticize social insurance for long term care on the grounds that it is inefficient when family members prefer to provide care. First, one must challenge the notion that family members are the preferred providers of care, in light of surveys in which elderly people reveal their desire to avoid burdening family members with the responsibility of care work (Life Plans Inc. 1992:28). As is more likely to be the case, children are forced into the position of providing care because other options do not exist: Medicare does not cover long term care, and private insurance is costly and difficult to get for those with pre-existing conditions. Moreover, recent research rejects the criticism that social insurance is inefficient on these grounds, finding that children are not substitutes for insurance.

Social insurance for long term care is also said by some to be at odds with the fiscal realities faced by the United States. Social insurance for long term care in the United States would undoubtedly share some of the same budgetary concerns that are apparent in the current debates over Social Security and Medicare financing. However, an important element of the cost of long term care has been overlooked. When the cost of informal care work to those who provide it is taken into account, social insurance may be less costly than the current approach. Government decisions to save money using policies to encourage private insurance that appeal to the wealthy and those in higher income levels may have been made without considering the value of time contributed by care workers. Finally, consideration must also be given to equity. The current system, which places the burden of long term care largely on women, is far less equitable than a social insurance system that spreads the burden across society.

In the absence of broad federal policies, many state and local agencies have developed programs to assist care workers in a variety of ways. These include attempts to help care workers deal with stress and policies to provide respite care or subsidized paid care. Subsidizing formal care raises questions about whether family members will use formal services as substitutes for the care they provide. A reduction in effort could potentially increase government expenditures dramatically. Substitution is a complex issue; it is difficult to measure empirically, and some degree of substitution is actually intended as respite or relief. While no easy solution to the rising costs of both formal and informal long term care is at hand, evidence points to the limitations of private long term care insurance policies to dramatically improve coverage among the elderly. Current market-based approaches do not offer targeted relief to the low-income providers of informal care, and as a result, other policy options need to be considered.

Shifting the Burden Back to Families?

How Medicaid Cost-Containment Reshapes Access to Long Term Care in the United States

*I*n this paper we explore the ways in which the U.S. long term care system shapes care work provided by families of frail older relatives. Welfare state policies distribute social resources in accordance with principles ranging from more to less inclusive. These underlying principles shape the experiences of the beneficiaries and their families. Benefits distributed on the principle of *universality* tend to maximize the amount of assistance the welfare state provides, spreading the risks and costs of dependency or illness *across* families. All are eligible for and receive benefits, regardless of class, employment, or marital status (Harrington Meyer 1994b; Esping-Andersen 1989; Myles 1988). By contrast, benefits distributed on the principle of *targeting* tend to minimize the amount of assistance the welfare state provides, concentrating the risks and costs of dependency or illness *within* families. Only those who meet the requirements for eligibility, usually defined by economic need, receive benefits.

Currently, the long term care system in the United States includes a hodgepodge of several different payment sources with rules that vary markedly by state. Roughly 95 percent of those age 65 and older in the United States are covered by Medicare, a universal health care program for the old and permanently blind and disabled. But Medicare specifically excludes most long term or chronic care (Siegel 1993; Hooyman and Gonyea 1995). Most older people have one, two, or even three Medigap policies to fill in where Medicare is lacking, but privately purchased Medigap policies typically exclude long term care as well

(Commonwealth Fund 1987:28). A growing fraction of older people purchase long term care insurance that covers nursing home care, but most of these plans have, in addition to sizable premiums, substantial deductions and co-payments, as well as frequent lapses in coverage (Wiener and Illston 1994; U.S. House of Representatives 1993). The result is that most older people in need of chronic long term care must pay for these costs out of pocket or attempt to spend down to eligibility for Medicaid—the targeted, means-tested health care program for poor persons of all ages.

By default, then, Medicaid remains the primary method through which the welfare state distributes long term care in the United States. Table 14.1 shows the proportion of persons from the 1995 National Nursing Home Survey in each payment group at admission to the nursing home: twenty-five percent rely on Medicare, 9 percent rely on private insurance, 26 percent rely on their own income, and 39 percent rely on Medicaid. Does payment source affect access to care? There is growing evidence that it might.

In recent years, skyrocketing Medicaid costs, as well as reports that middle- and upper-class elderly are sheltering their assets and relying on Medicaid to cover their nursing home bills, have prompted the 50 states and the federal government to emphasize cost-containment and gatekeeping efforts (Georges 1995; Lavin 1993; Ferguson 1992; Moses 1990; Wessel 1991; Katz 1986; Hooyman and Gonyea 1995; Katz Olson 1994; Harrington Meyer 1994a, 1994b; Margolis 1990). Even with a plethora of eligibility criteria, Medicaid is one of the most expensive programs in the United States welfare state. In 1998, the federal government spent $104 billion, and the states collectively spent an additional $80 billion on Medicaid to provide health care for the poor (U.S. House of Representatives 1998). Medicaid monies go disproportionately toward the aged. The aged comprise 12 percent of the population of the United States and nearly 12 percent of all Medicaid recipients, yet they account for 30 percent of the Medicaid budget. The proportion of the total Medicaid budget dedicated to nursing home care has

Table 14.1   *Percent of Current Residents in Each Payment Category at Admission to Nursing Home*

Medicare	25
Private Insurance	9
Out-of-Pocket	26
Medicaid	39
Other	1

Source: 1995 National Nursing Home Survey, weighted estimates based on nationally representative sample of 6,753 current nursing home residents who are age 65 and older who have provided information on payment source at admission.

dropped considerably below its all-time high of 42 percent in 1991 to 26 percent in 1994. Still, nearly two-thirds of all Medicaid monies spent on the elderly go to nursing home care (Georges 1995; U.S. House of Representatives 1994).

The main mechanism for controlling access to Medicaid is through the eligibility rules. Federal guidelines set *asset* limits for a single applicant at $2,000, including savings, checking, bonds, stocks, and insurance policies. Certain assets may be excluded, including the home, car, some life insurance, and burial space and funds up to $1,500. *Income* limits are complex and vary by state. Generally states are required to provide coverage to the *categorically needy*, or those eligible for Supplemental Security Income (SSI), with incomes averaging below 75 percent of the federal poverty line. States may also provide coverage to the *medically needy*, those whose incomes exceed state guidelines but who become eligible when their incomes minus their medical expenses fall below state guidelines (Neuschler 1987; Harrington Meyer 1994a).

Gaining access to Medicaid coverage of nursing home care may be more complicated than these eligibility guidelines suggest, however (Harrington Meyer 1994a, 1994b; Margolis 1990; Neuschler 1987). Some studies report that heightened gatekeeping efforts are increasingly problematic for many poor older persons and their families (Hooyman and Gonyea 1995; Margolis 1990; U.S. House of Representatives 1993; Rivlin and Wiener 1988). A 1990 U.S. General Accounting Office study found that in five of the nine states they examined, Medicaid patients wait at least two to three times as many days as private payers to gain access to nursing homes. The reason the Medicaid daily reimbursement rate is lower than the private pay rate for nursing home care. Ettner's 1993 analysis of the National Long Term Care Survey showed that nursing home operators, particularly those in counties that are wealthier or have low supplies of beds, tend to preferentially admit private pay patients. A report by the U.S. House of Representatives (1993) cautions prospective Medicaid applicants that there are disadvantages to trying to shelter assets because persons relying on Medicaid at the time of admission may not be able to enter the nursing home. Medicaid officials in Illinois warned that there were not many cheaters, but that efforts to tighten the rules "would hurt the vast majority of honest, poor people who need medical care" (Hilkevitch 1993).

If relying on poverty-based Medicaid benefits does interfere with access to long term care, who is picking up the slack? Currently, family members provide the bulk of long term care in the United States. Studies show that some 60 to 70 percent of all long term care is performed informally by family members; that roughly 70 percent of all caregivers are women—mainly wives and adult daughters; and even though caregiving can be rewarding, lengthy performance of intense caregiving activities adversely affects the economic, physical, and social well-being of caregivers (Hendricks and Hatch 1993; Cantor 1983, Hooyman and Gonyea 1995; Stone, Cafferta, and Sangl 1987). Cost-containment debates rarely take into account either the financial or the human service costs borne by families that provide infor-mal care. Studies by Estes and Swan (1993) and Glazer (1990), however, show that efforts to contain costs, such as the implementation of the Medicare Prospective Payment system since 1983, have transferred work and costs out of the paid arena and into the unpaid informal caregiving arena. Estes (1989) estimated that in just the first five years, diagnostic related groupings (DRG) shifted 21 million days of care work from hospitals to family members. Glazer (1990) estimated that the med-ical industry had saved $10 billion a year in wages because of the highly technical work that had been shifted to unwaged informal caregivers. Are Medicaid gate-keeping efforts transferring work to family members?

Methodology

Medicaid policy varies markedly by state, thus research must be conducted on a state-by-state basis. Because we wanted to see whether recent cost-containment measures had affected access to long term care among Medicaid recipients, we fo-cused on two states that had announced cost-cutting measures: Illinois and Ten-nessee. We selected Illinois because it announced a three-year Medicaid rate freeze to control costs. Tennessee was analyzed because Medicaid officials intro-duced a more extensive Medicaid preadmission screening form to control costs. We conducted nearly 100 telephone and face-to-face interviews with Medicaid officials, nursing home administrators, and nursing home residents and their fam-ilies in the two states. Table 14.2 shows the number of each type of interview we conducted.

In addition to the interviews, we read dozens of policy and annual reports, ex-amined state-specific policies, and made numerous phone calls to Medicaid offi-cials in each state to augment or verify information contained in these reports. Finally, we searched relevant national and regional publications such as *The New York Times, The Wall Street Journal, Time, Newsweek, Atlantic Monthly, New Re-public,* and *The Chicago Tribune* throughout the last decade to obtain information on policy changes and political debates surrounding Medicaid.

Table 14.2   *Numbers of Each Type of Interview, 1996–1997*

State	Nursing Home Administrator	Applicant/ Family	Medicaid Officials
Illinois	37	17	10
Tennessee	15	7	9

Source: Prepared by authors

The Medicaid Rate Freeze and a Preference for Private Payers in Illinois

As in many states, Illinois policy makers were concerned because daily Medicaid reimbursement rates to nursing homes had doubled from an average of $34 a day in 1986 to $70 a day by 1995. In response, the state of Illinois froze Medicaid reimbursement rates for three years. In an interview, Sharon Woods, director of the Illinois Public Aid Bureau of Long Term Care, explained that as recently as 1990 the Medicaid reimbursement rate in Illinois averaged 95 percent of the private pay rate. But because private pay rates continued to rise after the Medicaid rate freeze, the Medicaid rate averaged only 70 percent of the private pay rate by 1996. Indeed, the average daily private pay nursing home rate in Illinois was $100 a day, compared to $70 a day for the average Medicaid reimbursement. This differential between public and private pay rates could never have happened in Minnesota, where an equalization law requires nursing homes to set private pay rates identical to the Medicaid rate—both rates averaging $96 a day in 1995 (Minnesota Departments of Health and Human Services 1996:23). But there is no federal equalization law, and we found no evidence that Illinois has ever seriously considered implementing such a policy.

The impact of the Illinois Medicaid daily nursing home rate freeze has been substantial. We spoke to administrators at 37 of the 500 skilled nursing facilities in Illinois, and many told us that they have either stopped taking Medicaid patients altogether or have changed their admissions procedures to give priority to private payers over public payers.

> Many people want to live here because this is a nice nursing home. Yet, we routinely turn people away . . . we refuse admission if someone is on Medicaid even if we have empty beds. It is a calculated risk. We would rather have the bed empty.

> We give preferred admissions to private payers, I have to admit that . . . we keep two waiting lists.

> Depending on the census, I try to be consistent and fair to both, but if there is a private pay and public aid, I would take the private pay.

> Two public aid residents were recently admitted. One resident admitted who was public aid eligible upon admission was an ex-employee. Knowing her personally made it hard not to admit her. The other . . . had terminal cancer. Sometimes we admit public aid eligible residents right away if it does not look like a long term admission.

> Everyone who walks through the door needs placement. . . . I have to say, "You can't come because you don't have the funds." People seeking nursing home

placement act out of crisis. Then, they come in and find that there is a financial requirement.

About 10 percent of nursing homes in Illinois accept no Medicaid patients, and nursing home administrators in those homes told us that private payers who spend down their assets and become eligible for Medicaid must leave.

> There is a two- to three-year waiting list for public aid. (If they start as private payers and spend down) they can stay if we have a public aid bed available. . . . If there is no bed, we would transfer them to another facility.

> We do a screening because we don't take public aid upon admission. There is about a two-year waiting list for public aid beds.

More common, however, are nursing homes that theoretically take Medicaid recipients, but in fact refuse admission unless an incoming resident has sufficient assets to cover one to two years of private pay or can make a three-month deposit.

> The resident has to have two years of private pay funds. We never accept any public aid residents upon admission because of corporation policy. If the family says mom does not have two years of assets, then we have the family sign a contract that they are responsible for the payment.

> We require $80,000 or two years' private pay to be admitted. After that they can apply for public aid.

The administrator of a not-for-profit nursing home told me that while they are expected to take a greater share of Medicaid recipients, they still have to make money to put money into the facility. They do this by "raising the private pay rate to make up for the difference" and by requiring a deposit for each person admitted.

> We ask for a six-month deposit, and we try to *get* at least a three-month deposit. We work with the family to see if they can pay privately for the first few months.

Even nursing homes that have always taken Medicaid patients, some reporting as high as 80 to 90 percent of residents on Medicaid, have either capped the number of Medicaid patients they will accept or are considering a cap. No matter how they felt about such discriminatory action, nursing home administrators controlled the number of Medicaid admissions for fiscal reasons:

If I budgeted for 45 percent public aid, and we had 60 percent, that was serious trouble. I had to control the waiting list so that I had enough private payers there to pay bills.

There is a big difference between having $70 and $100 a day to care for someone.

Discrimination is not supposed to occur, but we did it ourselves. If you had a public aid and a private pay, you made excuses for putting someone off . . . there was over a $20 a day difference, and you had to meet the bills.

It made me feel guilty. I still feel guilty. I felt so sorry for some families, for keeping the public aid patients waiting.

A few states, notably Minnesota, Florida, Ohio, and Connecticut, have either prohibited or limited discrepancies between private and public pay rates, and as a result, admissions discrimination against Medicaid recipients is infrequent in those states (U.S. General Accounting Office 1990). But in the vast majority of states, the daily rate discrepancies persist and lead to widespread discrimination in admission procedures. Given that the average daily Medicaid reimbursement rate in Illinois is $70, each additional month that a Medicaid applicant waits on the list saves the state $2,100 in costs. Each additional month that a Medicaid applicant stays on the waiting list shifts 30 care work days from paid nursing home employees to unpaid informal caregivers.

Preadmission Screening in Tennessee

Another gatekeeping mechanism that has been implemented in recent years involves preadmission screening. Prompted in part by reports of unnecessary institutionalization (Kane and Kane 1985), but also by demands for cost containment, most states provide applicants with a form that either their doctors or nursing home admissions supervisors are required to complete. The screening form asks a series of questions about health and functional ability designed to determine whether the applicant's condition is serious enough to warrant nursing home care. As a result, applicants for Medicaid-covered nursing home beds must meet not only income and asset guidelines, but also strict criteria for medical eligibility.

Tennessee has conducted preadmission screening since 1982, but in 1992 Medicaid officials switched to an intensive screening process using an eight-page form. As a result, the preadmission screening rejection rate jumped from less than 10 percent to an average between 20 and 30 percent (confidential interview with a TennCare preadmission screening nurse). That means that among those who were deemed *financially eligible* for Medicaid, about one-fourth were deemed *medically ineligible* during the screening process. The reasons for denials were mixed; the applicant may not have met the criteria, provided proper documentation, or obtained the proper signatures. On average, one-half of those who were initially denied were approved when they resubmitted the forms. Those who were refused upon both the initial and secondary applications were permitted to appeal, and at least one-half of those were then approved on appeal. Thus, roughly three-fourths of those who were initially declined were eventually approved.

The process of applying for medical eligibility proved difficult for the families we interviewed, even when they had professional assistance. One son told us how home health care aides helped him apply for medical eligibility for his mother, but she was nonetheless denied.

> My mother had a stroke and was getting where she could not take care of herself. She was paranoid. She could not cook meals very well or take care of her house. She needed someone to check on her twice a day. If she did try to cook, she would burn things. She had bladder accidents. I went by after work every day to check on her. Home health was coming every day. The home health aide helped with the paperwork. I put in a request for a bed in the nursing home, and we waited several months. Home care botched a lot of paperwork and lost things. The doctor did not send enough information for Medicaid to accept her. We were sent a letter saying she was not eligible. Several times we had to redo paperwork and go back over things.

The impact of medical rejections can be monumental for families. In the cases we studied, the care of elderly people who were denied Medicaid coverage of nursing home care fell to families. These families faced great difficulties providing care to their frail older relatives, and perhaps even greater difficulties appealing the denials. Most applicants whom we interviewed were eventually accepted, though in some cases, the acceptance came after the applicant had died.

One disabled adult daughter described how she cared for her frail mother for more than two years. But when the mother's condition worsened and the daughter no longer felt able to provide the level of care needed, they decided it was time for a nursing home. The mother was deemed financially eligible for Medicaid in a nursing home, but medically ineligible for nursing home care. Thus, she was not permitted to enter a nursing home in Tennessee. The daughter was incredulous:

> She has been with me every day since she was sick. During the last two years, she has been in my house seven days a week, 24 hours a day. I know what I dealt with. . . . She was in the emergency room, she had a leg ulcer and fell, which created another ulcer on her ankle. She has been treated for symptoms

of congestive heart failure. She is a diabetic. . . . She has had a few mini-strokes. Her mind has deteriorated, she is confused. She cannot cook for herself, or get down into the bathtub. She does not drive, and does not have energy to go to the grocery store. But the hospital said they did not see those things. It is hard to get them into a nursing home if they are not completely bedridden.

Because her mother was refused admission to a nursing home in Tennessee, the daughter moved her to a nursing home in Virginia. There, the rules were sufficiently different that she was admitted. But the long-distance placement has created another type of hardship:

There is a nursing home within five miles of my house, but she is ineligible in Tennessee. I have to pay long distance to pick up the phone and talk to her. I also have to ask someone to drive me to see her. I don't drive anymore because of my disability.

Another adult daughter told us that her mother had taken care of her frail older father for years, but then the mother's health declined as well. At one point the parents had hospital stays just two weeks apart. The daughter told us:

I called to get him in at one of the nursing homes, but they said he did not qualify medically. This was an extremely frustrating time for me. As long as you can, you try to take care of him at home, but in the back of your mind, you think you can always put him a nursing home. But, when you are raw, they tell you that . . . he is not sick enough. He had been bedfast 75 percent of the time for three years. He is on oxygen all of the time, which limits his ability.

Another adult daughter told us of the difficulties she faced trying to pull together a mix of home care services that would enable her to continue working even though her father had just been deemed medically ineligible in Tennessee.

He had visiting nurses daily to give him a bath. . . . As far as food, they did not help. At the end they cut down to three times a week. They took his blood and inserted his catheter. . . . There was not enough of us to take care of Daddy. We all work and have to think about our pensions, too.

Because the preadmission screening device focuses on physical and functional abilities, those with dementia, particularly earlier stages of Alzheimer's disease, have difficulty qualifying for medical eligibility. An adult daughter described the frustration of repeated attempts to qualify her mother, only to have her pass away just months after receiving the benefits.

The way the doctors had written up the order did not qualify her the first time. She had dementia. . . . She needed other physical health problems to come into play. They resubmitted her application two times, and she was finally approved. However, there was a lot of anguish in the meantime — like what are we going to do? Her health eventually declined some more so she could qualify . . . she went on oxygen therapy. She gradually went downhill until July, when she passed away.

Another adult daughter told us of her summerlong struggle to get her father approved for Medicaid in a nursing home — only to face his death before he ever received Medicaid benefits:

We had to find a nursing home which accepted Medicaid. They all want private pay because it is less hassle. We put him on waiting lists. He was number 296 to number 151 on various lists. As we talked to the administration in each nursing home, we made lists of what they told us. . . . They all want the private pay because it's less hassle. The supervisor at the Department of Human Services confirmed what I was told. He said that this is not the rule, but it is the reality that you have to, in nursing homes, private pay for a few months before going on Medicaid. I started the process to qualify my father financially at least three months in advance. I thought this would be the hardest part. Then we heard about medical necessity. . . . Page 2 says, "The patient is confused and disoriented x number of times a week." Without realizing that he was really screwing up, Dad's physician answered two or three times a week. However, he answered based on just those two to three stories we told the doctor. My father had been totally disoriented 24 hours a day for the last two years. My sister and I paid until the middle of October. He died on October 4.

As in Illinois, each additional month that Medicaid applicants to nursing homes are denied access, the Tennessee Medicaid program saves more than $2,000. Each additional month that Medicaid applicants are denied access shifts 30 days of intensive care work to family members, who must then balance long term care work with their own waged work and their other unwaged care work responsibilities. As in Illinois, these are families with few resources to spare — the applicants have already passed Medicaid's strict financial eligibility tests, but they have been unable to prove that they are sufficiently impaired to require institutionalization.

Discussion

Medicaid is the primary mechanism through which the welfare state distributes long term care benefits. Because it is targeted rather than universal in nature, the program emphasizes gatekeeping. Recent cost-cutting efforts have caused many nursing homes to stop taking Medicaid patients altogether, to assign Medicaid applicants to longer waiting lists, or to refuse admission to Medicaid applicants who have not been deemed sick enough. Older people who rely on Medicaid for long term care are increasingly likely to see access to care denied or delayed. This transfers the cost — and the work — of providing care from the state sector to private families. The result is that families, mainly wives and adult daughters, perform more intense care over longer periods, at an even greater financial, physical, and emotional cost.

Admission discrimination against Medicaid applicants is not confined to the two states we examined. The U.S. General Accounting Office (1990) study found evidence of discrimination in five of the nine states it assessed —Medicaid recipients were denied access to many nursing homes, waited a significantly longer time to gain admission to other homes, and tended to be relegated to less desirable nursing homes. One of the largest nursing home chains, ManorCare, reports that across the nation it receives about $30 less per day for a Medicaid patient than for a private pay patient. "It's no secret," says CEO Stewart Bainum Jr., that the strategy is "to focus on the higher-revenue patients." In states that permit it, ManorCare takes no Medicaid patients at all (Ferguson 1992).

Table 14.3, which is based on the 1995 National Nursing Home Survey, shows that while about three-fifths of current nursing home residents received Medicaid during their stay, two-fifths were already eligible for Medicaid upon admission to the nursing home. That means nearly 40 percent of all nursing home applicants faced the possibility of being denied access to nursing home care because they relied on the poverty-based Medicaid program.

The impact of discriminatory admissions policies varies significantly by gender and race. Table 14.3 shows that older women, blacks, and Hispanics are significantly

Table 14.3 *Percent of Current Nursing Home Residents in Each Payment Group by Race and Gender*

	Total	White		Black		Hispanic	
		Men	Women	Men	Women	Men	Women
Medicaid at Admission	38.7	33.8	37.4	57.2	63.7	52.7	61.7
Medicaid Spend Down	21.9	20.3	23.0	22.8	22.1	23.3	22.8
Never on Medicaid	39.4	46.0	39.6	20.0	14.2	24.0	15.6

Notes: N=1,307,610. Chi Sq. Pr. <.0001, totals may not add to 100 due to rounding error.

Source: 1995 National Nursing Home Survey, weighted estimates of nationally representative sample of current nursing home residents, age 65 or older, who have provided information on payment source at admission.

more likely than men, or whites, to rely on Medicaid when in nursing homes. Among older men, 34 percent of whites, 53 percent of Hispanics, and 57 percent of blacks are on Medicaid at the time they are admitted to nursing homes. Among older women, 37 percent of whites, 62 percent of Hispanics, and 64 percent of blacks are on Medicaid at the time of admission to the nursing home. That means women, blacks, and Hispanics are considerably more likely to be turned away at the nursing home door because of their payment source. To the extent that Medicaid recipients are refused or delayed admission to the nursing home, reliance on Medicaid *prevents* rather than *promotes* access to needed health care among frail older women and persons of color.

Those who are unable to gain entrance to a nursing home generally turn to family members for care, but many families have already provided extensive long term care and may find it difficult to provide even more. To place an older relative in a nursing home is often quite difficult for families, but to be unable to place an older relative may be much more devastating. Studies show that families routinely wait until they have exhausted their economic, physical, and emotional caregiving resources to apply for nursing home coverage under Medicaid (Brody 1981; Cantor 1983; for review, see Hooyman and Gonyea 1995). If their older relative is denied admission because of Medicaid eligibility, families that have already shouldered considerable informal caregiving burden will be called upon to shoulder more.

By permitting private and Medicaid rates to vary, and by requiring screenings of Medicaid but not private pay patients, many state Medicaid policies are encouraging nursing homes to discriminate on the basis of payer source. This discrimination hits families who are at or near the poverty line and are therefore least able to afford or arrange alternative methods of long term care. Moreover, because the tendency to rely on Medicaid coverage of long term care varies significantly by gender, race, and class, Medicaid promotes discriminatory practices that particularly affect older women, blacks, and Hispanics. Medicaid cost-cutting efforts shift the costs out of the public sector into private families, shifting the burden of long term care onto lower-income families, and in particular onto the women in those families.

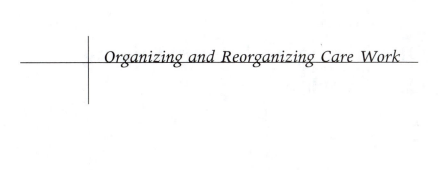

Organizing and Reorganizing Care Work

Organizing and Reorganizing
Care Work

*B*ecause of the paucity of low-cost or highly stable care options, care work is often performed in a state of flux. It is organized and reorganized due to changing political climates, concerns of fiscal austerity, the success of political interest groups, or changing social conditions that cause us to redefine and rebuild family networks. In Part IV of this book we look at both unsuccessful and successful attempts to reorganize care.

One of the primary motives for reorganizing care work at the welfare state level is to reduce budgets. Social scientist Trudie Knijn shows that the shift toward privatization of public services is occurring internationally, even in countries that have historically been committed to social insurance programs that spread the risks, burdens, and responsibilities of social problems throughout their larger community. The consequences of this shift are larger workloads for low-paid care workers and, consequently, increasingly poor and limited care for care recipients.

The needs of the care worker and care recipient can clash when the burden of care falls to one group. Social scientist Rannveig Traustadóttir explores the tension between quality of care for recipients and the cost of providing this care for workers. She assesses the reform movement for people with developmental disabilities, showing how attempts to better integrate the disabled shifted an even greater burden for care work onto their care providers, most of whom are women.

While Knijn and Traustadóttir examine situations where care is intentionally reorganized, Assata Zerai's study of cocaine-exposed children and the grand-mothers who rear them reveals care reorganization that often occurs out of sheer necessity. What happens when parents can no longer parent? Due to strong famil-ial networks, many African-American grandparents assume primary care-taking responsibilities for their grandchildren. Plagued by guilt that they might have failed as parents the first time around and are thereby somewhat responsible for their children's shortcomings as parents, they pick up the pieces and care for their grandchildren. They do so, however, with little public recognition or sup-port. Indeed, institutional structures, particularly state and legal, do not support this reorganization of responsibility, making it difficult for grandmothers to pro-vide care efficiently and effectively.

The most successful attempts at reorganization reveal the necessity of involve-ment by the broader community to provide good care, both for the sake of care workers and care receivers. Studies routinely show that among care workers, in-creased isolation leads to depression and anxiety, which can lead to abuse or ne-glect of care recipients (Hooyman and Gonyea 1995). A supportive community is critical to providing quality care and simultaneously reducing the emotional, physical, and financial burden of care for individual women. The organization of care work actually shapes the act of caring for the care worker and care recipient.

Thus we conclude with a heart-warming example of how effective care work can be when it is properly supported. Brenda Krause Eheart and Martha Bowman Power describe the emergence of "Hope for the Children," a multi-faceted com-munity network that provides permanent families for foster children who have suffered years of abuse, neglect, and upheaval. With the help of government funds, teams of social workers, elderly volunteers, and families willing to adopt foster children, Eheart and Bowman worked to transform an old military base into a supportive and stable community of care. Imagine if these forms of support were provided routinely, in all types of care situations, on a national scope through welfare states.

Marketization and the Struggling Logics of (Home) Care in The Netherlands

*I*n many Western welfare states, marketization has been announced as a potential solution for almost all of the problems in the field of social care. The logic of the market was rhetorically very successful, and it restructured care in a managerial way, although it did not result in cost reduction or efficiency. Instead, it destabilized former logics of care—the fragile balance between the bureaucratic administration of public services, the professional system, and private care arrangements.

Marketization is only one of the forms in which restructuring of care, a trend in many European welfare states, takes shape. It can be distinguished in a structural and a social-cultural dimension. On one hand, it is part and parcel of an overall shift in the relationships between the three institutional pillars of welfare: the state, the market, and the family. On the other hand, it reshapes the character of public services by introducing market principles in former bureaucratic/professional organizations (Daly and Lewis 1998). In Figure 15.1 I outline the structural dimension of marketization in relationship to other possible directions of welfare state restructuring.

When I use this structural framework, the term *marketization* should be reserved for those processes of redistribution in which the state transfers public services to the market. This can be done by contracting out specific services and provisions, by giving private instead of public responsibilities to purchasers of services, and by withdrawing state support from specific welfare provisions. Marketization could also be viewed as a form of privatization (see Fraser 1990),

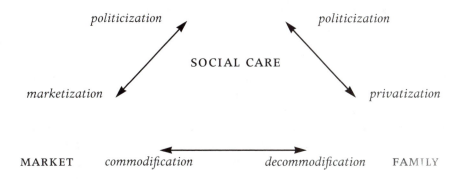

Figure 15.1

the decrease of state involvement. In Figure 15.1, however, I reserve the concept "privatization" for those processes that substitute public services with family or other volunteers. This is the case when public services cannot any longer fulfill the needs of those who depend on care and welfare. Marketization and privatization are opposed to the politicization of services. Politicization takes place when, for instance, child care is defined as an area of public interest and governments are investing in public child care. In that case, new laws and social policies are developed. Transfers between the family and the market are also captured in Figure 15.1. In the domain of care, such shifts involve the commodification of care work by payments and parental leaves and child care by employers or the reduction of withdrawal or those payments (decommodification).

All such processes actually happen in Western welfare states. For instance, in the United Kingdom the substitution of public care for the elderly by familial care work and from service provision to cash benefits is a major tendency (Ungerson 1997). In Finland, the substitution of public services by private entrepreneurs draws attention (Simonen and Kovalainen 1998). In Sweden there are some traces of a decline in public services, although it cannot be expected that marketization and privatization of care for children and the elderly will soon replace public services (Szebehely 1998). In contrast, Germany is involved in a process of "welfare dualism" where the better-off will continue to enjoy earning-related benefits and high-quality provisions, while others have to cope with deteriorating basic provisions (Ostner 1998). In The Netherlands, the same developments take place in social security and in the only recently growing field

234   *Trudie Knijn*

of public child care. However, with respect to care for the elderly, marketization has taken a quite different shape. Instead of being added to or replacing public services, it perverts them by the introduction of market principles (Knijn 1998). That is the second social and cultural dimension of marketization.

Welfare State Systems: Struggling Logics of Care

Marketization of care disrupts the equilibrium reached by the three systems that made up welfare states: the bureaucratic administrative, the professional, and the familial systems of care work. As we shall see, this will lead to an introduction of a new way of thinking about the quality of care, the quality of care work, and the relationships between care workers and care recipients. In the field of home care in The Netherlands, this new way of thinking and doing has disastrous consequences in particular for care workers and care recipients. Before paying attention to these developments, we first will outline the framework of the former balance between the bureaucratic administrative, the professional, and the familial systems of care work and see why it is so problematic that the logic of the market perverts these systems.

Marketization disrupts the balance between the former care systems by introducing a new vocabulary to the field of care, that is, the vocabulary of the consumer who buys, say, the car he needs at the market. In addition, this new vocabulary is not only added to the former vocabularies. It transforms them. In the bureaucratic system, the care recipient is a citizen vis-à-vis the welfare state. This includes the rights and duties belonging to that position, such as the right to be treated fairly and equally, the duty to pay premiums and taxes, and the access to primary goods of the care system. In the professional system, care recipients are seen as clients, demanding an approach based upon professional expertise and ethics, including a one-to-one relationship with the care worker. And finally, as a member of the familial system, the care recipient is supposed to be connected to his or her significant others on the basis of reciprocity and moral, often gender claims, that is, the assumption that women perform the unpaid care work within the family. Each of these systems has its own logic of assumptions, mechanism of control, and its own interpretation of care recipients and care providers, which I summarize in Figure 15.2.

How could the former balance of bureaucratic, professional, and familial care be disrupted by the introduction of market principles, and what are the consequences of this disruption? The main answer to this question is that the alliance of the three former systems of care was subjected to two critiques which mutually enforced each other — welfare state services are said to be too costly and lead to care dependence.

For a long time the bureaucratic administrative system formed the heart of welfare states and was designed to promote the efficient and impartial provision

	Care Recipients	Care Providers	Assumptions	Control
Bureaucratic Logic	Citizens	Public Services	Justice and Fairness/Equal Treatment	Supply Side/ Democratic Control
Professional Logic	Clients/ Patients	Professionals/ Experts	Expertise/ Personal Treatment	Professional Ethics/ Standards
Familial Logic	Kin/ Significant Others	(Female) Relatives/ Volunteers	Social Bonds/ Reciprocity/ Moral Claims	Social and Personal Control
Market Logic	Consumer/ Customer	Entrepreneurs	Efficiency/ Effectiveness/ Profit	Demand and Supply/ Managerialism

Figure 15.2

and administration of public services. As citizens of the welfare state, care recipients have a social right to certain welfare services, though these will be routine, standardized, and predictable. Moreover, these bureaucratic administrative systems should guarantee that clients are treated fairly, because the fair division of (often scarce) welfare services is their reason for existence. Bureaucratic administrative rules are under democratic control of the governments of the welfare state. These systems developed well in the rise of the welfare states after World War II. Actually they formed the heart and the body of the developing public services.

The advantage of the bureaucracy-provided services in comparison to the former charity- and community-provided services is that budgets, classification of needs, as well as categorization of potential recipients have to be legitimized democratically. Besides, the bureaucratic and impersonal routine is developed to guarantee citizens' rights, which might be preferred above the favoritism and moralism of charity. The disadvantages of bureaucracy are well-known. Weber has argued against the "iron cage" of impersonal procedures and rationalized control, and how they dismiss personal treatment and individual human behavior. Indeed the technicism of this system inevitably enforces standardization of needs in fixed classifications (Weber 1964; Henshel 1990). Habermas (1981) criticized bureaucratic interventions because they lead to the "colonization of the lifeworld," operating through the practice of transforming daily life experiences into strategic goals. Administrative systems tend to subordinate norms, values, and everyday life practices to their imperatives by offering standardized roles and services. To gain access to public services and social provisions, citizens increasingly transform their needs into the categories and rules accepted by the bureaucratic systems. They may begin to perceive their own needs in terms of the standardized categories of the bureaucratic logic, resulting in reification of these needs, which ultimately undermines "communicative acting," that is, reproducing oneself on the basis of personal and collective identity.

However, this depersonalizing tendency of bureaucratic administrative systems has been softened in the developing welfare states because bureaucracies did not solely govern public services. Bureaucratic systems went along with professionalism, which had its own distinctive logic. Professionalism is a system of expertise and skills, based upon professional and scientific knowledge and protected by professional ethics. Care recipients are clients of professionals and can expect to be treated in a personal relationship in regard to diagnoses and indications. "Where bureaucracy is concerned with predictability and stability, professionalism stresses the indeterminacy of the social world as necessitating the intervention of expert judgement" (Clarke and Newman 1997:6). Maybe the most important distinction between both logics concerns the autonomy of the expert. The bureaucratic administrator must, above all, follow strict procedures or combine several incentives in a transparent guideline. Professionals, in contrast, claim autonomous judgments, based upon skills, expertise, and scientifically proven methods of intervention. Clarke and Newman (1997:7) state that in the development of welfare states, professionalism and bureaucratic administration had to balance their interests. In the development of mass education, national health systems, and social security, both kinds of expertise and coordination of the services were presupposed, and they mutually influenced each other.

> The Welfare state, then, developed around a double logic of representation of the public. On the one hand, bureaucratic knowledge (either of rules or specific expertise) is involved in the service of the "public interest." On the other hand, professional knowledge is constituted as the engine of social progress and improvement, which would enhance the "public good" (Clarke and Newman 1997:7).

No welfare state, however, no matter its stage of development, could do without the provision of care and welfare by the family or kinship networks. This familial care provision is often neglected in analyses of the welfare distribution, but since the 1970s it has been well documented by feminist scholars (Balbo 1987; Wilson 1977; Finch and Groves 1983; Waerness 1984; Finch 1989; Ungerson 1983). The familial logic of care can be distinguished from the professional and bureaucratic logic because it mainly operates in the private, instead of the public, sphere. The implication is that because it is by principle not submitted to quality control or rules of justice, rights of care recipients are all but guaranteed. From a familial perspective, care recipients are kin, significant others, or friends. Care is provided on the basis of reciprocity, because of moral (often gendered) claims or because of altruism.

Different interpretations of the coalition between the three systems of care can be made. First of all, the familial care put high burdens on the shoulders of women as unpaid care workers. Borderlines between public care services and familial care are diffuse in all welfare states; women's unpaid care work forms always and everywhere a reservoir for filling the gaps of the public services. This gendered patchwork of care (Balbo 1987) is one of the main pillars of welfare states' gender structures, although the weight of the burden is less in those welfare states which developed good care services, such as some of the Scandinavian countries (Hernes 1987; Leira 1990; Lewis 1998). The second comment on the coalition of the three systems of care is related to the continuous claims of professionals to extend their particular areas of intervention. This resulted in an enormous expansion of services, as in health care. Professionals are never satisfied — they always discover new problems to solve, and when they are operating in the context of public services, each group of professionals will claim a larger part of the budgets for their own specific field of expertise. Although this is not true for all professions — claims of medical experts are, for instance, much more valued than claims of care experts, the latter being in majority women with lower professional status — it cannot be denied that the combination of the principle of doing justice to all claimants and the professionals' drive to expand their services contributed to the "overspending welfare states" (Hoggett 1994; Clarke and Newman 1997). Nevertheless, until the mid-1970s this coalition seemed to stabilize post–World War II welfare regimes.

The Balance Collapsed

In the 1980s, however, the balance collapsed. Due to economic crises, demographic developments, and changes in the relationship between the institutional pillars of the welfare state — the state, the family, and the market itself — a restructuring of social care took shape. On an ideological level, the driving force existed in the combination of comments on the interventionist and the "overspending" welfare state. First there was a shared analysis of what went wrong in the relationship between states and citizens. Many scholars and politicians concluded that welfare states failed because they turned into monolithic bureaucracies whose inhabitants transformed into calculating citizens knowing the way to get their wishes fulfilled, even when no real needs existed. Social scientists criticized the welfare state because of its creation of care-demanding citizens who have become dependent on an "overprotecting state."

The second comment on welfare states in the 1980s, which gave rise to marketization tendencies, is an economic one. In this perception, welfare states failed because they are too costly; public expenditures went beyond their approved limits. This argument is in some way connected to the first one, but while the first has to do with intervention and the power of state bureaucracies, the second is about cost reduction and effectiveness. Interestingly enough, these comments on welfare states were put forward in almost all Western countries, no matter how bureaucratized the specific welfare system or how high public expenditures actually were. The strength of these rhetorics was improved more by their combination than by their relationship to reality. In the context of the neoliberalist 1990s, when the economic argument dominated, the antibureaucratic comment proved to be an adequate vehicle for promoting the market as an alternative for tutelage and intervention. It operated as a vehicle for the client-consumer who would finally be able to negotiate his or her needs and the prices of fulfilling them. When the marketization of care was introduced as an alternative, both comments on welfare systems were presented as complementary: what the market could offer would not only be less expensive, but also in the best interest of the care recipient. The rhetorics of those who criticized the welfare state bureaucracies for interventionist reasons and those who criticized it because of budget reasons found each other in the ideas that the market of care is better suited to fit supply and demand, that it would operate more efficiently and even more effectively, and that this would lead to a reduction of budgets and ultimately to more satisfied citizens.

At this moment we can conclude that market principles have yet to fully control the field of care anywhere in the European welfare states. This does not mean, however, that market principles can be denied. Even though the free market of care is still far away, market principles are transforming relationships among the vested actors in the social services. The introduction of market principles — whether by the entrance of for-profit organizations in the field of care or by the restructuring of public services — redefined clients, relatives, and citizens as consumers and customers. Instead of providing care and welfare on the basis of reciprocity, moral claims, professional diagnoses, or redistributive fairness, it provides services on the basis of contracts while supply and demand are the main principles for delivery. In the market of care, democratic control is limited to preventing fraud and maltreatment and does not concern issues of social policy any longer.

Despite market logic, the transformation of the national rail company or the national telephone and post company into privatized for-profit firms differed considerably from the transformation of national health care, social care, social security, and education. Nevertheless, some similarities are striking. For instance, in hardly any welfare state or field of public services are the monopolies of (former) public service institutions broken down. This is crucial from an economic perspective, because it implies that the market principles of supply and demand have to operate under monopolistic conditions, without price and product elasticity. In other words, consumers have to buy their public services in a market where no competing suppliers are offering alternative goods. Moreover, rather than decentralizing bureaucratic control, many governments kept central direction by introducing new managerial procedures. Budgets were replaced by methods of output-financing and detailed procedures of monitoring "products and prices." The introduction of market principles gave governments new methods to control public services. By forging temporary contracts, addressing public services as if they were firms, and monitoring their outputs and continually transforming directives and procedures, managerial control replaced the former bureaucratic public administration (Clarke and Newman 1997). These developments have severe consequences for the already uneasy equilibrium of professionalist, administrative, and familial logics governing the provision of public services. Such consequences not only vary per country due to path dependency and political decision making; they also vary per care and welfare domain within countries (Jamieson 1991; Baldock 1993; Alber 1995; Lewis 1998). In the next section, I will illustrate some of these consequences by describing transformations in the field of home care in The Netherlands.

Market Principles in a Corporatist Welfare State

Home care in The Netherlands is, as in many other welfare states, given in addition to informal unpaid care by relatives or volunteers, the majority of whom are women. The receivers of this kind of care are for the most part elderly, sometimes handicapped, and persons with chronic or terminal illnesses. Home care is provided by a home care office, which decides on the kind of care to be given and is paid by collective health insurance. In all welfare states, home care is only a marginal part of the field of (health) care and welfare. Even when it is a recognized part of the public sector, as in Denmark, Sweden, and Finland, its budgets are much lower than that of its counterpart in the care sector, health care. In The Netherlands, it is only 6 percent of the budget of health care (Sociaal en Cultureel Plaubureau 1996:64). Home care workers have a low professional status, and the field confronts the universal problem of distinguishing itself from privately given care or unpaid care in the community. Nevertheless, this sector did not escape from the overall effort to introduce market principles.

When the Dutch government implemented market principles in home care, the service was organized according to the best principles of the Dutch welfare state. Like other areas of importance for care and welfare (e.g., social security, welfare, and education), its organization, provision, and purchasing structures had the characteristics of the social democratic and corporatistic hybrid which forms the composition of the Dutch welfare state. This implies that on the one hand it is organized according to corporatist principles, characteristic for many continental European welfare regimes as Germany, Belgium, Italy, and Austria. These principles say that public care services are only additional to the care the family can provide. In addition, this corporatism implies that the welfare state delegates the responsibility for the provision of care services to private non-profit organizations, which in the case of The Netherlands, originally were connected to different religions and political ideologies. These corporatist principles and organizational structures of home care went along with social democratic principles, implying that although the provision of home care should be minimal, they should at least be available for every client to the same degree. In terms of the logics of care, we could say that when people need care, the familial logic receives priority. Those who are in need of care must first attempt to get this care within their familial networks. Only when families fail to provide care will professional care be available, and this care is provided according to the principles of equal distribution of scarce resources (bureaucratic logic). How did these principles work out for the provision of home care in The Netherlands?

The corporatist principle saying that the smallest possible unit is responsible for care means that it is the family who provides home care, then the community, and finally the state. In contrast to other public services, such as education and medical health care, home care is perceived to be primarily the task of the family, specifically female relatives. Home care was originally meant to assist those families in which the mother was not able to fulfill the tasks accorded to her. It was only in the context of family policies in the 1950s when home care was perceived as an instrument to improve the quality of family life, that home care workers received occupational training, and that their profession was described in sharp contrast to the work of housekeepers.

> The care for families by skilled and trained workers, employed by a professionally directed organization, who substitute, help, or advise the housewife who is not able to fulfill her task properly because of physical or mental illness. The care is given to maintain or reshape a healthy family life. (Neij 1989:317)

In those days the professional status was protected by the government and employers (mainly religious organizations) who as purchasers (health insurance companies), as well as providers (home care offices), have their separate histories in the old pillarized structure of Dutch society. After World War II, when the number of home care offices steadily increased from 259 in 1948 to 979 in 1962 (Los 1997), each religious pillar had its own local home care office as well as its own national organization. These pillarized national organizations together formed the National Council for Home Care, which was the recognized advisor of the government until 1990. In 1990 this council merged with organizations for district nursing and maternity care to become the National Association for Home

Care. The increase of home care offices in the first postwar decade and the recognition of the importance of this kind of care made the government change the financial structure of home care. From 1955 on it was no longer paid by (members of) churches, but by state budgets and health insurance. In 1994 the Dutch government paid 10 percent of the budget of home care, while private insurance paid 13 percent, and the national health insurance paid the rest. Nevertheless, the corporatist structure remained very powerful. The Dutch government cannot change any aspect of the system of purchasing and providing home care without receiving the consent of the "Health Insurance Council" (Nationale Ziekenfondsraad), in which all providers and purchasers are represented.

After the government took the responsibility for home care in 1955, several attempts were made to balance budgets and needs, but no government succeeded in getting a grip on the budgets. One effort to control the budgets forced the home care offices to merge in order to develop large-scale home care centers. This strategy was partly to neutralize the influence of the former (religious) pillars, but the main purpose was to reach efficiency and effectiveness by scaling up. Finally, blunt budget reductions were presented during the 1970s and 1980s— every four years a new administration reduced the amount of money available for the sector. In 1992 the number of home care offices was reduced to 450. These offices operated in much larger regions than the former ones and developed hierarchical managerial procedures to balance supply and demand of care.

Another strategy to reduce the budgets for home care as practiced by the government was deprofessionalization of care workers. While in other domains, such as education and medical health care, professionals formed a strong agency in dealing with bureaucratic claims, in the field of home care such "expertocracy" or the power of the professionals (van Doorn and Schuijt 1978) did not develop. Professionalism is not only a matter of developing strict occupational expertise, skills, and a code of conduct, but also of getting one's professional status accepted. In this respect home care workers did not succeed. In a slow but steady process, the education requirements disappeared. The first step in this process was accepting unskilled part-time workers. This measure increased the supply of care workers because it brought an influx of homemakers who were looking for part-time jobs. The number of home care workers increased from 16,588 in 1968 to 26,935 in 1970 (Ministrie van Cultuur Recreatie 1973:51; Los 1997:719).

The next step was the introduction of the infamous "alpha-help" in 1975. The alpha-help are care workers who are mediated by the home care office and get a contract with the client. To help reduce the costs of such care workers, it was declared that they are not permitted to work more than two days or 12 hours per week. This implies that they cannot meet either the standards for paying taxes and premiums or for receiving a minimum wage, unemployment benefits, illness benefits, and pensions. Despite the resistance of the women's movement and of home care workers themselves and their representatives in the home care offices, the trade unions agreed to this arrangement because the home care workers who did not become alpha-helps were promised pensions and better payments (Maessen 1989). Reduction of budgets finally forced home care centers to increase the number of alpha-helps.

The postwar history of home care in The Netherlands therefore can be read as a continuous effort of the government to control the budgets by getting a grip on the home care offices (forced mergers) and on the payments and work conditions of the home care workers (deprofessionalism). The counterargument might be that this is done in order to provide at least a minimum of home care to everyone who is in need of care—that is the social-democratic aspect of the Dutch welfare state regime. In order to guarantee good health care, every citizen is insured. Premiums for private health insurance are paid by employers and by employees who meet a certain wage level. National health insurance covers everybody who does not meet these levels. Their premiums are much lower and also include all kinds of benefits such as pensions, unemployment benefits, and social assistance. This implies that every Dutch citizen has his or her compulsory health insurance and in principle, receives the same quality of care. With regard to the right to health care, the Dutch welfare state shows its social-democratic face—(health) care is of good quality, and it has a high rate of eligibility. No citizen is excluded for reasons of poverty, and income is no obstacle to getting good-quality care. Home care is part of the health care system and is nowadays described as "a service of caring, nursing, treatment, and guiding in order to support a person to stay at home as long as possible" (Nationale Raad voor de Volksgezondheid [National Council for Public Health] 1992:122).

In 1990 about 110,000 home helpers took care of about 190,000 people (80 percent of whom are 65 years and older) and about 125,000 nurses gave semi-medical aid to 865,000 people at home (Boot and Knapen 1993:131). However, despite the general assumption that everyone who needs home care should in principle receive it, and despite the fact that everyone pays his or her premiums for additional health insurance, long waiting lists exist, and many people do not get what they need. Entitlement to care is not the same as a right to care in The Netherlands (Boeije, Dungen, van den Pool, Grijpdonk, and van Lieshout 1997).

Market principles were introduced in the 1980s to this context of continuous mergers and reorganizations, to a strong corporatist structure of the organization of health care, including home care, and to a weakly developed professionalism at the level of the work itself.

Markets against Vested Interests

At the end of the 1990s we could read the following headlines in the Dutch newspaper, *De Volkskrant*: "Money leaks away because of marketization of home care"

(July 6, 1997); "Public services meet the borders of commercialization" (April 9, 1997); "People don't get the care they need" (May 15, 1997); and "Home care should listen better to the customer" (March 13, 1997). What has happened in the 10 years since the introduction of market principles in home care?

The expectations were all but modest — marketization of home care would help to reduce the budgets because the market was supposed to work more efficiently and effectively than were home care offices regulated by a bureaucratic. It was also expected that the supply of home care could be increased sufficiently to meet the demands of the graying population — and the number of elderly is increasing in all European countries (Jamieson 1991). Moreover, marketization would help to develop "tailor-made care" to meet the individual care recipient's preference for more choice and diversity — they could even expect a flexible and individual mixture of care in line with their individual needs. From the beginning though, it was clear that the Dutch government did not intend to bring home care entirely to the market.

Regulations would still be necessary to guarantee equal access to home care and to keep the budgets under control. Both criteria are related to the fact that all Dutch citizens, employed or unemployed, pay their compulsory additional health insurance to contribute to the home care budgets, while the government legally has to keep these budgets under control. The minister of care and welfare, therefore, prefers the concept "regulated competition" above "commercialization." Regarding these restrictions, four new principles were introduced to promote competition among the suppliers of home care, to extend free choice to recipients, and to develop efficiency in this domain of social care. These principles are 1) substitution of expensive forms of care by cheaper ones; 2) so-called individualized budgets; 3) permission for private home care organizations to provide care; and 4) tailorization of care. Ten years later, at the cost of care recipients and care workers, only the first and the last principles have really been worked out.

Substitution of Expensive Forms of Care by Cheaper Ones

This principle was already formulated in the first advisories on the social policy of care in the 1980s (Hattinga-Verschure 1981; Commissie Structuur en Financiering Gezondheidszorg 1987). Hospitals, for instance, were advised to concentrate on their core business, namely to cure. Patients should be sent home as soon as possible after their operations. In case of a high-care need, home care offices were expected to fill the gap. The same process took place in the care of the elderly — the principle of "staying at home as long as possible" before going to a home for the elderly or even a nursing home was advocated. Advisory committees promoted this principle, but it was also very much agreed upon by many elderly and their relatives. This substitution process was, however, in contradiction to Denmark, for instance (Jamieson 1991), not guided by an extension of the home care budgets. The consequence was that as increasing numbers of people in need of care applied for home care the waiting and lists expanded. In the beginning of the 1990s, 20 percent of clients with an official indication for home care did not receive any care at all. Fifty percent of elderly people age 75 or over who are in need of care receive only informal care from relatives or voluntary networks (De Boer, Hessing-Wagner, Mootz, and Schoemakers-Salkinoja 1994; Boeije, Dungen, van den Pool, Grijpdonk, and van Lieshout 1997). The substitution of social care, by consequence, does not stop where home care begins; it is crossing the border between formal and informal care workers, mainly women.

Individualized Budgets

Individualized budgets are paid through the additional health care insurance to clients who are indicated for home care. These allowances differ from the British care allowances because the Dutch allowance is paid to the care recipient instead of to the care worker (see Ungerson 1997). The motivation of the "individualized budgets" is that they stimulate care recipients to select the kind of care which best suits their needs. Initially it was thought that this budget would improve the consumer awareness of care recipients; they would use it for getting the best quality of care for the lowest price. These budgets would also empower care recipients; they would have a greater say in negotiations with home care officials, and consequently, home care offices would be enforced to offer higher-quality care. In a relatively short time, these individualized budgets became very popular among care recipients; they indeed experienced a greater say about the quality of care, the work schedules of the care workers, and also used the money to pay informal care workers. Because of this popularity and the strictly limited budgets, the yearly budget was already spent in the first four months of the year in some of the cities where experiments were held. Despite that fact, these individualized budgets are currently highly contested for two reasons.

First, the vested organizations — home care offices and health insurance companies — could not agree with this shift from the supply to the demand side of the "market of care." They feared losing their control on home care and decided that it was not in their best interest to have to deal with real "care consumers." The second reason is that care recipients increasingly use the budgets to pay their relatives, friends, and other informal care workers. Also, private home care offices are more in demand than the recognized home care offices. This move away from the public home care offices is occasioned by the fact that they still do not provide high-quality care and have waiting lists that are too long.

Nevertheless, in the corporatist structure of the Dutch welfare state these offices still have a great deal of say and use their power to prevent care recipients from using their "individualized budgets" to buy alternative kinds of care. The paradox is that those who have vested interests in the provision of care (the settled home care offices) argue that they fear a lack of quality in care and working conditions when this will be offered by former informal care workers and private home care offices under the conditions of market principles, while at the same time, they are not able to improve the quality of care they themselves provide. This is why in 1999 the individualized budgets still are very limited to 200 million Dutch guilders a year. Care recipients receive only 200 Dutch guilders a month to spend freely, while the rest is paid directly to care offices. The individualized budgets, ultimately, are not introduced at the scale that care recipients would like.

Private Care Providers

Private care providers who work for profit are introduced because they are viewed to be real competitors to the too expensive, bureaucratized, nonprofit home care providers. These private home care offices are increasingly directed by the same rules as the nonprofit home care offices, although they initially seemed to get more freedom and flexibility in how to run their care services, in which clients they would accept, and in negotiating their costs with the health insurance companies. Again, the national organizations of home care offices and the insurance industry reacted very defensively. On the one hand, many vested home care offices immediately started their own privatized home care offices as subdepartments. A few years later some of them got into big trouble with the National Treasury because the management, as well as the bookkeeping, of both subdepartments was in disarray. On the other hand, they furiously resisted "newcomers" in this field and blamed them for "creaming off" the easiest, and thereby cheapest, forms of care. The government finally decided to stop the growth of private home care offices until 2001 and to demand strict control on those already in operation.

Tailorization of Care

This strategy proved to be successful, albeit not from the perspective of care workers and care recipients. Tailorization calls for the fragmentation of care into clear, well-defined, and manageable "products." Several "care products" can be distinguished; the main categories are housekeeping assistance, general assistance, semimedical care, and long- and short-term care. All care work is split up into activities such as feeding (15 minutes), insulin injection (10 minutes), packing off or on to bed (10 minutes), and so on. This tailorization is now established; care indicators of home care offices are diagnosing the needs, care workers administrate their activities in terms of the delivered "care products," and insurance companies pay per treatment. This success of this marketlike restructuring of the level of the real home care work has been disastrous. Care workers have lost good social contact with the care recipients, and the number of clients they deal with per day has increased dramatically. They literally are full-speed biking from one client to the other in order to stay on schedule. Because of the declining importance of the social aspect of the work, the one-to-one relationship of the client and the care worker has disappeared. For care recipients this means that they will often meet new care workers and are sometimes visited by five different women a week. They get only very restricted care for a few times a day, if they get care at all, since the waiting lists still have not shortened. The result is that home care has lost its appeal as a nice job for less-educated women. Burnout among home care workers is enormous; their absence rate for reasons of illness is among the highest of all professions, and every year, one out of every five home care workers quits the job (Vulto and Moree 1996; Boeije, Dungen, van den Pool, Grijpdonk, and van Lieshout 1997).

Conclusion

To say that the introduction of market principles in home care has not been very successful is an understatement. First, its own objectives were not realized— cost-efficiency, organizational effectiveness, and a free market of competing home care offices. Second, care recipients have not experienced a greater choice in selecting their "care products," in the quality of care, or in care packages. On the contrary, available care has become more limited; the care the clients receive is more and more time-restricted; clients encounter long waiting lists and have been confronted with higher costs due to the introduction of private contributions. They also experience a complete lack of clarity with respect to the responsibilities for care. Hardly anyone knows where to go when in need of care, which is currently illustrated by the fact that organizations of the elderly and relatives of potential care recipients are going to court to claim the right to receive care. In these cases it becomes clear that no rules are available on who is responsible for providing home care—the state, the health insurance, or the home care offices. From the perspective of professional care workers, this chaos is very dissatisfying. Home care workers complain about the lack of time to spend on each client individually; they work under high pressure, and long for a return to the days when professional ethics dominated over managerial procedures. Their dissatisfaction results in a high rate of burnout and job diseases and becomes visible in the growing shortage of home care workers in a decade in which female unemployment is increasing.

The logic of the market is introduced in the field of home care by the substitution of expensive forms of care by cheaper ones, by a limited introduction of individualized budgets by which care recipients could buy the care they need, by a limited introduction of for-profit private home care offices in order to improve competition; and by tailorization of care in order to treat care as if it were a product with a fixed price. All these market principles together should result in a better quality of care and in the improvement of the care recipients' free choice, in more competition and a better relationship between the supply and demand of care, while the budgets would not increase. These logics of the market were thought to overcome the obstacles and disadvantages of the former balance of professional, bureaucratic, and familial logics which were evaluated as too costly, too standardized, and too often resulting in sustaining care recipients on the welfare bureaucracies. That the introduction of the logic of the market in the field of home care ultimately created chaos has to do not simply with mismanagement, making wrong decisions, or resistance of vested organizations.

Explanations have to be found in the struggle underlying the managerial, market, and professional logics of care. Each of these logics include different perceptions of care—recipients (citizens, consumer, and clients respectively) maintain different criteria for supplying care (bureaucratic but equal treatment, supply and demand, and professionally determined needs) and have their specific systems of purchasing and providing (large organizations, competitive forms, and expert client relationships). When the Dutch government underlined principles of equality and justice in the access of services which should be guaranteed, these social-democratic principles made managerial control more, rather than less, necessary especially when they are implemented in a corporatist structure of provision and purchasing. This case shows that regulating market logics while maintaining corporatist monopolies and social-democratic principles of equal access is no less complicated than regulating the combination of professional and bureaucratic logics.

In addition, it can be concluded that new forms of managerial control actually seem to upset the performance of caring work, which might be due to the rather fragile character of this highly gendered work. Precisely because the border between public care services and familial care provided by female relatives still is rather diffuse, it has been possible to substitute public-provided care with familial care, to maintain long waiting lists, and to tolerate the fact that care recipients use their individual budgets to pay their informal caregivers. The assumption that this highly gendered familial care will always be available is, in my opinion, one of the reasons for the slovenly attitude toward the public provision of high-quality home care. The same argument is carried for the deprofessionalization of home care by the process of tailorization. The relatively weak position of the less-educated women working in this field might be seen as a reason for the deterioration of the quality of their work, their working conditions, and their payments (in particular with regard to the alpha-help).

On the other hand, however, these processes met resistance and led to new efforts for the reprofessionalization of home care work. Overall, there is a growing consciousness for home care workers to organize into unions that seek better pay and working conditions. Such unions have developed independently of the traditional trade unions, which did not represent the interests of women in traditional female occupations very well. Efforts are also under way to develop new standards for professionalism, first by advocating for "case management" forms of integrated care, and second by developing qualifications for home care work distinct from those for ordinary housekeeping. Reports and studies stress the specific skills and qualities needed to take care of deteriorating nonrelatives on a regular basis (Vulto and Moree 1996). Finally, a public debate developed about the "ethic of care" concerning the criteria for "good care" whether professional or informal, whether paid or unpaid. So, in the shadow of marketization, new standards of professionalism are emerging. Whether or not they succeed depends entirely on how soon the failure of marketization is accepted.

Disability Reform and Women's Caring Work

*T*his chapter examines women's contribution to the current reform toward the full inclusion of people with developmental disabilities in everyday community life. Women constitute the vast majority of those who carry out the day-to-day work of facilitating the acceptance and inclusion of people with disabilities and perform the work necessary to enable them to be part of families, neighborhoods, schools, workplaces, and other community environments. Despite this, there have been few attempts to examine women's contributions to the reform. Women's role in carrying out the reform remains largely invisible and unstudied. The reform seems to depend upon the availability of women's unpaid labor in the home and low-paid labor within the service system, without mentioning them.

In examining women's contribution to this reform I combine two fields of study: disability studies and feminist scholarship on women's paid and unpaid care work. To gain a comprehensive view of women's care work with people with disabilities I conducted a four-year qualitative study where I examined their caring and relationship building in three different arenas: in the family as mothers of children with disabilities, in the human services system as paid workers, and in the context of friendship.

The study of disability reform and women's caring work has two main purposes. First, by focusing on the caring work and relationship building women do with people with disabilities, my goal is to make visible the important but unacknowledged contributions women make to the lives of people with disabilities and to the field of developmental disabilities. By making visible the role of women in carrying out the reform aiming toward acceptance and inclusion of people with disabilities in community life, this study attempts to contribute to our understanding of the activities, processes, and contexts of support networks in the lives of people with disabilities.

The second goal is to analyze the gendered nature of care work in the field of developmental disabilities and explore the social organization of this work as "women's work." The disability field has not acknowledged the gendered nature of caring for people with disabilities. As an activity and an emotion, caring is strongly associated with women, sometimes even to the extent of being perceived as the essence of female identity: to be caring is to be feminine. For generations women have been seen as the "natural" caregivers, and in today's Western industrialized societies women's everyday lives are still centered on care work. In an attempt to explain why women constitute the majority of those who care for people with disabilities, I trace the broader social relations that shape women's lives and draw them into relations of caring and service for people in general and people with disabilities in particular. By examining caring as a gendered activity the study contributes to our understanding of the nature and significance of caring in women's lives.

Disability Reform

The field of developmental disabilities is in the midst of a period of reform characterized by new ways of serving people with disabilities. The focus has shifted from providing services within segregated institutional settings to providing services in the community. Recently, however, the reform efforts have been criticized for failing to achieve full inclusion of people with disabilities into the fabric of ordinary community life (Bogdan and Taylor 1987a; Braddock and Hemp 1997; Bulmer 1987; Smull and Bellamy 1991). Critics argue that while community-based services have been successful as an alternative to institutional services, there are serious problems in community programs. As Taylor, Bogdan, and Racino (1991) point out, community placement does not necessarily mean community participation, and studies have found that some deinstitutionalized people are as isolated from the community as they were when they were living in institutions. Community-based services have been able to assist people with disabilities to be *in* the community, but they have not managed to enable them to become *part of* the community (Bogdan and Taylor 1987a).

These problems in community programs have led to a call for a shift in service delivery. Because community services experience such difficulties in facilitating connections between people with disabilities and other community members and have often failed to achieve social integration, the emphasis on relationships with nondisabled people and connections to what are seen as "natural" community supports are at the heart of the current trends in the field. The critics suggest radical changes in service delivery and have outlined an alternative to the traditional approaches in community programs. The new approach starts with the person and an examination of his or her social networks and informal community supports. And formal support interventions should build on and strengthen natural networks in the community (Hagner, Rogan, and Murphy 1992; Schwartz 1992; Taylor, Bogdan, and Racino 1991). This new emphasis has led to a growing interest and appreciation of the importance of informal supports and relationships in the lives of people with disabilities (Amado 1993; Bogdan and Taylor 1987b; Hutchison 1990; Lutfiyya 1991; O'Brien and O'Brien 1996; Taylor and Bogdan 1989). The criticism of community-based programs has also led to a growing interest in exploring how to integrate formal supports (provided through service agencies and programs) and informal supports in the community (based on personal ties and social relationships) (Taylor, Bogdan, and Lutfiyya 1995; Bulmer 1987; O'Brien and O'Brien 1996).

These new approaches in service delivery have been accompanied by a call for a new role for human service workers, especially those who work directly with people with disabilities (Gardener and Chapman 1992; Kaiser and McWhorter 1990; Knoll and Ford 1987; Racino 1990). For example, Knoll and Ford (1987) argue that in order to provide adults who have severe disabilities with the necessary support to become actively involved in home and community, we need to reconceptualize direct-care workers as facilitators of relationships. The most important part of the new role of direct-care staff should be to work toward "natural support" through assisting people with severe disabilities to form nonpaid relationships with regular community members (as opposed to relationships with workers who are paid to be with the person), as well as helping people maintain existing relationships with family and friends.

Because women constitute the great majority of workers within the human services, they will be the ones to carry out the day-to-day work of the new approaches. Despite this, limited attention has been directed to the women who carry out the reform. The literature on community-based services, personnel preparation, and reform rarely mention the fact that the majority of the workers are women. The reason for this invisibility of the women who bear the brunt of the daily work of reform seems to derive from the power of the stereotype of women as caregivers. Women are seen as "natural" caregivers, and it is taken for granted that women occupy caring roles within the human services as well as in other spheres of life. Women are seen as having naturally endowed skills to nurture and care, and their paid care work in the human service work is usually viewed as naturally female rather than competence-based performance.

Although it is often unclear what "natural support" consists of, it usually refers to some form of assistance from a person who is not a paid human service worker

(Knoll and Ford 1987; Nisbet and Callahan 1987; Hagner, Rogan, and Murphy 1992). This form of support is often solicited through the facilitation of friendships between people with and without disabilities (Knoll and Ford 1987). Although not conclusive, research indicates strongly that women constitute the majority of those who become friends of people with disabilities (Hutchison 1990; Krauss, Seltzer, and Goodman 1992; Traustadóttir 1993).

The new approaches within the field of developmental disabilities place an increasing emphasis on the importance of families in the lives of children with disabilities, and many authors advocate for more family support programs that build on families' strengths, empower families, and assist them to keep their children at home (Farber 1986; O'Connor 1995; Sherman 1988; Singer and Irvin 1989). While this interest in families should be applauded, this literature raises concerns due to the lack of critical examination of gender in families of children with disabilities. These studies usually treat the family as the smallest unit of analysis, and the differences in activities and experiences of individual family members are routinely ignored. This practice of ignoring gender as a socially important factor hides the difference between mothers' and fathers' experiences within the family, as well as the gendered nature of care work in families.

Women are surrounded by widespread, powerful, and pervasive expectations that they will care for others and are seen as having a "natural" ability to do so (Abel and Nelson 1990a; DeVault 1991; Traustadóttir 1995). The reform's emphasis on the importance of "natural supports" to fill the gaps left by the service system (or to replace publicly funded services) will probably reinforce women as the natural caregivers of people with disabilities.

Women's Care Work

To argue, as I do, that caring is women's work is partly because of the gendered pattern of this activity: women do most of this work and continue to feel responsible for caring. Caring, however, as DeVault (1991) has pointed out, is a gendered activity on a more profound level. Because caring has become so closely associated with women, it has become one of the major ways women have to construct themselves as female. West and Zimmerman (1987:126) have coined the term "doing gender" whereby they mean that instead of viewing gender as a property of individuals, gender should be analyzed as "a routine, methodical, and recurring accomplishment." Under this perspective, "doing gender" is an ongoing interactional process where people collectively produce themselves as "proper" and recognizable men and women. As long as caring is viewed as something that is more "womanly" than "manly," it will constitute an activity that provides a way for people to construct and reaffirm their gender. Some researchers have found that caring is so closely associated with women that when men take on the responsibility for caring activities they may be called into question for "unmanly" conduct (Coltrane 1989; DeVault 1991). Women, on the other hand, have been raised, trained, and encouraged to attend to the needs of others and care for them. If women resist doing this work, they may be called into question for not being "womanly." Women have learned to associate caring with their identity; to be caring is to be feminine and, for most women, caring has become something that seems to be a "natural" part of a gendered self.

My analysis de-emphasizes caring as a personality trait, and locates it in social interaction. I strive to understand how caring becomes "women's work." That is, I attempt to examine the processes whereby women are constructed as caregivers, and how caring comes to be defined, not only as a womanly activity, but as a part of womanly nature. Some feminist analyses of caring have been, in my opinion, overly psychological and have overemphasized the emotional aspects of caring and caring as a woman's personality trait (e.g., Chodorow 1978; Gilligan 1982). Those who take this perspective argue that although being caring and nurturing is not "natural" to women, these are specific female characteristics developed through gender socialization (Chodorow 1978; Gilligan 1982). I agree that formation of gender identity in early childhood may be an important aspect of women's socialization for care work. My analysis, however, suggests that the processes that recruit women for care work are continuing and may be equally powerful in later years long after early personality formation. The social construction of women as caregivers continues through adulthood. It is therefore not just early psychological development that creates women's predisposition to caring and connection. This perspective moves the primary focus of change from early childhood socialization and draws attention to the importance of recognizing the possibilities for change by influencing the ongoing recruitment processes that draw women into activities of caring.

Other analysts of caring have pointed to the power of social arrangements that draw women into caring and service for others. Graham (1983) argues that theories that explain women's predisposition to care as a part of a feminine personality trait mask the way caring is socially organized and constructed through a network of social and economic relations. Graham also points out that a focus on the emotional aspects of caring, and caring as a personality trait, hides the work of caring. DeVault (1991) takes a similar position and argues against theoretical explanations that present women's caring and nurturing as an aspect of female identity. Instead, DeVault emphasizes that caring is socially organized and constructed as women's work, and it is the power of this social construction that draws women into and recruits them for caring.

Researchers have found that many caregivers in the waged labor force are drawn to their jobs in part by their desire to provide service (Fisher 1990; Lundgren and Browner 1990) and derive their job satisfaction primarily from their emotional attachment to the people they care for (Abel and Nelson 1990b). While these findings have been confirmed in the present study, I would caution against too much celebration of the personal fulfillment women derive from caring because it can easily turn into celebration of differences that serve as a rationale to keep women in an inferior position. As Abel and Nelson (1990b:7) point out, "Most caregivers are members of subordinate groups, who provide care from compulsion and obligation as well as warmth and concern."

The fact that women continue to make a strong commitment to the caring work that often contributes to their subordination suggests that they have strong views about this work as important and necessary. I would argue, however, that the organization and allocation of the work needs to change. Caring is essential work necessary to sustain life as we know it. But this necessary work should be shared more equally and be better supported by society's institutions so that women are not expected to provide life-sustaining services to others at the expense of equity.

The Study

The analysis in this chapter draws upon a qualitative study carried out in the United States during my doctoral studies at Syracuse University (Traustadóttir 1992). Data were collected over a period of four years, between 1987 and 1991. The main methods of data collection were in-depth interviews and participant observation (Bogdan and Biklen 1998; Taylor and Bogdan 1998). This was a comprehensive study of the care work and relationship building that women do with people with disabilities, and it focused on three groups of female caregivers: women who have children with disabilities; women who work in the disability services; and women who are friends of people with disabilities. The 32 women who were the key informants of the study were interviewed at least once and some up to four times. I also spent two years of participant observation in a support group for parents of children with disabilities and conducted long-term participant observation (up to two years) with women who worked in the disability services. In addition I encountered, and in some cases interviewed, numerous other people who also provided insights and information which I draw upon in the analysis. Most important of these other informants were the people with disabilities cared for by the women in the study.

The Problem of Categorizing Participants

Each of the 32 women who are the key informants in the study have been identified as falling into the three categories of mothers, workers, and friends. The task of selecting informants according to these three categories seemed simple enough at the outset. I quickly learned, however, that the lives of the women in this study did not fall neatly into these three categories. Women's caring activities are not confined within categories such as "mother" or "worker," and they transcend the boundaries of "public realm" and "domestic domain."

In their everyday lives the women in this study crossed the boundaries of the categorization of human service worker, friend, and mother. For example, three of the women who were selected for the study because they had children with disabilities — and were therefore in the "mother" category — worked in the field of disability. Furthermore, two of the mothers in the parent support group had paid jobs within human service organizations. Thus, five of the "mothers" could also be categorized as "workers." Further, one of the mothers in the support group could also be in the category "friend," as she had a couple of close friends with disabilities. The same was true of the women who were selected as "friends" or "workers." One of the women in the "worker" category had a child with a disability. One of the women who was selected as a "friend" worked in the human service system, and another was a student in special education preparing to become a professional in the field. Finally, one of the women workers turned out to be a close friend of one of the persons she worked with.

This problem of categorizing women's caring activities reflects the complex composition of women's lives and the fluid boundaries of women's care work. The particular problem encountered here in terms of categorizing women's experiences is informative as an example of a more general problem: the difficulties of placing boundaries on their care work as it constantly shifts between domains in women's lives.

Analysis

My analysis begins with the everyday activities and experiences of caring, drawing on the detailed accounts based on the women's own words and observable behavior as the basis for the analysis. Following Smith's (1987) advice, I attempt to make visible as "work" the processes of caring, by examining in detail women's everyday activities and experiences. I started out by observing the women's care work with people with disabilities and asking them about their caring. This resulted in a wealth of descriptive materials about the everyday work processes of caring and the context of these practices. Although I carefully begin with particular activities and experiences of caring, I locate these activities in the context that organizes them.

While rooted in the everyday, this analysis moves beyond the actual activities in an attempt to examine how the everyday world is organized, shaped, and determined by social relations that extend beyond it. The strategy of moving beyond particular experiences to examine their embeddedness in the social relations is a way of focusing inquiry. This approach serves as a guide to discover how our everyday lives are organized by larger complex social relations. Smith (1987) urges us to trace the complex ways women are drawn into social relations of inequality, which perpetuate their subordinate situation. Analyzing the social organization of women's caring work and explaining the social relations that shape this work provides an opportunity to understand how women are being recruited for care work and makes visible how women are drawn into social relations that construct and perpetuate their own subordination and servitude. In moving beyond the day-to-day experiences of caring, I analyze the social organization of caring as women's work, and the social relations that contribute to the social construction of women as caregivers.

Care Work and People with Disabilities

This study accounts for women's care work with people with disabilities in three domains: in the family, in human service organizations, and in the context of friendship. One of the major findings of the study is how strikingly similar women's care work is across these three domains. Although many scholars have argued that women's caring activities transcend the differentiation between the private and the public (Abel and Nelson 1990b; Graham 1983), these similarities have rarely been highlighted because most studies of women's care work have examined women's caring in a particular domain; for example, in the family (DeVault 1991; Hicks 1988) or in human service organizations (Fisher 1990; Lundgren and Browner 1990). Or they have examined women's care work in the capacity of a certain role, for example, as daughters taking care of their elderly parents (Abel 1991; Lewis and Meredith 1988; Norris 1988), as mothers of children with disabilities (Baldwin and Glendinning 1983), or as wives of disabled husbands (Oliver 1983).

The care work that women perform for people with disabilities is labeled in various ways in the three domains in this study. In the family, the work mothers do is most often referred to as "caring," in the human services it is often called "formal support," "formal care," or "care work," and in the context of friendship it is usually referred to as "informal support," "informal care," or, simply, "friendship." Despite the different names given to the work, the basic components are the same across domains.

In my analysis of the women's care work I tried to rid myself of my own commonsense understanding and listened carefully to what the women said about caring. This approach revealed caring as a complex phenomenon that had at least three different meanings: "caring for," which refers to the care work, "caring about," referring to the emotional aspects of caring, and "extended caring" when the women extended their caring to a broader societal concern. These three aspects of caring, outlined below, were first identified as the most important components of the mothers' caring work but turned out to be very similar for both the workers and the friends.

Feminist scholars have developed numerous terminologies to analyze and describe caring. My analysis can be compared to those of Abel and Nelson (1990b), Fisher and Tronto (1990), Graham (1983), Noddings (1984), and Ungerson (1983).

Caring across Domains

Below I draw out the parallels in the caring mothers perform for their children with disabilities, the work of female human service workers, and caring in the context of friendship.

Caring for: Work

When the participants in the study talked about caring, they most commonly talked about "caring for" or "taking care of" the person with the disability. The mothers used this phrase to describe their care work, which could be extremely hard and demanding. Part of this work was the same kind of caring all mothers do when they care for their children. But when caring for a child with a disability this work often required specialized knowledge and techniques that are usually associated with professional work, not traditional housework or "mothering" work.

The caring work in the human services had many similarities to the mothers' caring in the family. This was particularly true in those parts of the service system that are deliberately designed to be homes, or at least "homelike." These programs are usually referred to as residential services and are based on the household model of caring. These residential services may be institutions, nursing homes, group homes, or other small residential facilities. The work performed within these facilities is very similar to traditional housework and mothering work: preparing meals, making beds, taking care of people's personal needs, planning outings and vacations, keeping in touch with relatives, and so on. Much of this work is the same as mothers do with their children with disabilities within the home and the family, and is similar to women's traditional caring activities. Even the professional or technical aspects of the work within residential facilities are similar, or even the same, as in the mothers' care work with their children at home because the technical work usually associated with professional practice is often carried out in the home by the mothers. It was common that training, therapy, systematic teaching according to written programs, and treatment of a medical nature shifted back and forth between the home and formal service organizations. This work was alternately carried out by mothers and by human service professionals, and there seemed to be no clear lines about the location of this work. As a result, many aspects of the mothering work within the home and the family were very similar to the professional work within the human service system.

Like the mothers, many of the female human service workers and the friends spent a great deal of their time facilitating the acceptance of people with disabilities within a social context. Just as the mothers worked toward having the child with the disability accepted within the family, the workers and friends worked toward the acceptance of people with disabilities within their own social networks, as well as in workplaces, classrooms, and various community places.

The similarities between the mothers', friends', and the workers' caring work also extends to the focus on other people's needs and the subordination of attention to self. Much of the care work performed by female workers and friends was aimed at enabling others to take part in certain activities or social contexts. This is very similar to the mothers' work in enabling other family members to take part in the action outside the home. It seems that women, across domains, are the means to other people's enterprises, instead of pursuing their own.

Caring about: Love

Women typically experience caring as a labor of love and have a hard time distinguishing the activities of caring from the emotional aspects (DeVault 1991; Graham 1983). This was also true for the women in this study, particularly the mothers, who used the word *caring* interchangeably for activities and emotions. Often, however, they used the phrase *caring about* when referring to relationships and emotions. The mothers talked about caring about, that is, loving the child. These two meanings of care, the love and the work, were often intertwined, and in most cases the mothers did not distinguish clearly between them. The fact that the word caring was used to refer both to the work and the love had some unfortunate consequences for the mothers. For example, if the mother thought it was unfair that she should take the main responsibility for caring for the child (doing the work) and wanted other people to share the work with her, it could easily be interpreted that she did not care about (love) the child. Not only could other people use this to pressure the mother to continue the care work, it could also create tremendous feelings of guilt within the mother.

Although not to the same extent, the female human service workers and friends also used a language of love and affection when talking about the people with disabilities with whom they worked, or were friends with. The female human service workers usually expressed emotional closeness to all the people with disabilities they worked with; they often, however, expressed particular fondness for certain people, or a particular person. The workers who developed close emotional ties to one person often established a long-lasting friendship with the person. These friendships usually lasted beyond the duration of the job; the workers kept in contact with the person after they quit their jobs. This emotional closeness and the friendships that developed between the female workers and the people with disabilities made it hard for the women to distinguish between the activities and the emotions entailed in caring and blurred the line between the role of a worker and a friend.

Because the work of caring and the emotional aspects are so intertwined, the language used by the women in this study was often unclear, and they went back and forth between talking about the work and the love. This reflects the complex nature of caring where both love and labor are fused together, and where both parts inform each other. It was primarily the emotional aspect of caring, along with the closeness of the relationship with the person being cared for, that made the caring work rewarding for the women in this study. Not only was this true for the mothers but also the workers, who derived a great deal of satisfaction from the emotional closeness with the people they worked with. When the workers developed such emotional closeness, their caring work changed. A close emotional relationship created a particular knowledge of the individual, which derived from the special attention that accompanied emotional closeness. This is similar to the "attentive love" that Ruddick (1989) describes as an integral part of maternal thought. When such attentive love informs women's caring activities, their practices change.

Thus, although it is possible to distinguish between the emotions and activities of caring, they are, in practice, often not easily separated. Moreover, these two components of care — the work and the love — are so closely intertwined that many of the women found it hard to distinguish between them. One thing was clear though — the women in this study were seen as the "natural" caregivers, both in terms of doing the work and giving the love.

Extended Caring

Some of the mothers of children with disabilities extended their care beyond their own child to a broader community or societal concern. That is, they started caring about what happens to people with disabilities in general and the way society treats them. I have chosen to call this third meaning of care *extended caring*. An example of this was when the mothers went beyond their own children and became advocates for change on behalf of people with disabilities in general. They went to meetings, lobbied legislators, pressured school boards, argued with government officials, organized parents' groups, and so on. These are usually not seen as traditional female activities, but when performed by mothers of children with disabilities they are seen as an extension of the mothers' caring and an expression of the mothers' devotion to their children. Thus, some of the mothers extended their caring to activities that were more like a professional career than traditional mothering work.

Many of the women workers and friends in the study also extended their caring beyond their day-to-day work to a community or societal concern, in a very similar way as the mothers, and cared about what happened to people with disabilities in general. Many of these women saw social change aiming toward more acceptance and inclusion of people with disabilities as the ultimate goal of their efforts.

Most of the women workers and friends shared the sentiments behind the mothers' extended caring. The work they performed within the field of disability often grew out of a commitment to people who were subject to oppression and injustices, and an identification with the powerless and excluded. Their work was often performed within a vision of a better world. The difference between the mothers and the workers was not whether they had a broader social justice framework or not. The difference was rather that most of the mothers developed their broad societal perspective over a period of a long time, while it was common for the women who worked in the field to enter their work, or professional training, with this framework.

Like the mothers, the workers in this study were also trying to change the disability service system. For example, Elanor and Johanna (teachers in an integrated classroom) were working toward changing the way children with disabilities are educated. Both entered their professional training determined to make changes in the way children with disabilities are treated. Heather Williams was another example of a human service worker who had extended her caring. Besides being a job coach (finding jobs for people with disabilities and supporting them at work), she went to schools to talk to teachers and parents about new integrated employment options for young people with disabilities, instead of the sheltered and segregated work that traditionally waits at the end of high school. Heather was also trying to change the vocational rehabilitation system that channels young people with disabilities into segregated sheltered work.

The majority of the mothers, workers, and friends who participated in this study had a vision of a better and more just society. They were on a mission to change things: they wanted to create a society where people with disabilities are welcomed, accepted, and included.

Disability Policy and Women's Care Work

The current disability reform has been carried out without much conscious awareness or understanding of the important contributions women have made to the reform. Despite the fact that women perform the vast majority of the day-to-day work of the reform, their contributions remain unnoticed and invisible. In this section I discuss some of the findings of my research in relation to disability policy. I first address family policy, followed by a discussion about human service workers and friends.

Family Policy

Current disability reform has been accompanied by a growing interest in families of children with disabilities. While this interest should be welcomed, the lack of critical examination of gender in relation to these families is disturbing. Most disability family policies and practices reflect the cultural stereotype of mothers as natural caregivers and assume that women's primary orientation is toward family and motherhood. Service providers seem to have different views and expectations of mothers and fathers. The mother, who played a central role in the care work, was typically also the main contact person for the service providers. While service providers and professionals did not see themselves as having authority over fathers and were reluctant to put demands on fathers, they were less reluctant to put pressure on the mothers. They routinely demanded a certain level of cooperation and performance from the mother, and most of them saw it as their duty to influence what she did with her child with a disability. This raises concerns about the way family support services influence and control the lives of mothers who have children with disabilities.

At least two of the rationales used in favor of family support policies are based on assumptions that are problematic for women. The first rationale is economic and asserts that family support services save money because they prevent costly out-of-home placements and may encourage families to take their children home from institutions and nursing homes (Taylor, Racino, Knoll, and Lutfiyya 1987). This rationale is supported by cost studies of services. When researchers compare the cost of residential placements and the cost of home care, they find enormous savings when the care is provided in the family (Bradley 1988). The second rationale is ideological. Family support services are seen as supporting traditional American family values, and the main goal of many family support services is to support the family as a unit, keep families intact, and help families take care of their own. These two rationales have been used to provoke policy makers and service providers to fund and provide family support services and are viewed as powerful arguments in favor of family policy directed toward families of children with disabilities (Taylor, Racino, Knoll, and Lutfiyya 1987).

A critical examination of these two rationales raises serious concerns about the underlying assumptions about mothers of children with disabilities. The first concern is related to the cost savings of family support services. Why do these services save money? Given the gendered nature of caring in families, consequence will most likely mean increased responsibility for caring for women, and family support services save money because mothers provide much of the care work needed by their children at no public cost.

The other concern relates to the idea of "traditional family values." There are many different definitions of traditional family values, and an appeal to them without further clarification of what that means raises concern because, for many people, traditional family values bring to mind the culturally sanctified female role of caretaking and selfless giving. Traditional ideas and values about women's and men's roles in the family assign the responsibility for housework, child care, and other care work to women, and women continue to perform large amounts of unpaid work in the family (Waring 1988). These traditional values also assume that women's primary orientation is toward family and that they have little commitment to paid employment. The reality today, however, is that the majority of women are trying to negotiate their caring work within the family with work outside the home (Berg 1986). An uncritical emphasis on these two rationales may lead to some serious dilemmas or conflicts, and we must ask if we are basing family support services on an outdated understanding of women in today's society. We should also consider to what extent current disability family policy assumes and depends on the substantial and consistent input of women's unpaid work in the home.

Policy makers and service providers need to become aware of the stereotypical assumptions underlying disability policies and practices. In particular, they need to recognize gender as a critical issue when policy and practices are formulated, instead of approaching families with a view that ignores gender, thereby reinforcing women's subordinate position in society.

The past few decades have seen a revolutionary increase in women's participation in the labor force. Women are no longer confined to the domestic realm but have moved into the public domain (Gerson and Peiss 1985). It is commonly assumed that women have permanently moved the boundaries that previously confined them to the home and the family. While the majority of women have managed to enter the public arena of paid work, education, and other activities outside the home, these new and expanded boundaries of women's lives are very fragile. As soon as there is an increased demand for traditional women's work within the home — such as caring for a child with a disability — the boundaries shift and women come under tremendous pressure to leave the public arena and go home. While a significant number of women have crossed the boundaries of the home and entered the public world, they seem to have done so without the support of larger structural changes. Women's primary responsibilities are still considered to be within the family, and the bulk of housework, child rearing, and caretaking remains women's work. The changes in women's opportunities and activities outside the home do not reflect lasting structural changes, only a change in some women's behavior.

The wage structure is a good example of how the changes in women's opportunities outside the home lack support in the social structure. When the parents in this study made the decision that the father would be the breadwinner and the mother would stay home because the father could earn a better living, the family was, in fact, being forced into this pattern by the social structure. The family had, in most cases, little choice of which of the parents would work outside the home and were forced to respond in a certain way because of the wage discrimination against women in the workforce, since women only earn about 60 percent of what men earn (Brown and Pechman 1987). Thus, what was often seen as a practical solution to a particular problem was, in fact, an example of how social relations shape the everyday lives of families and individual family members.

As traditionally structured and presently idealized, the institution of the family has come under wide-ranging criticism from scholars in many fields. The last two decades have seen a wealth of literature that has critically examined the traditional pattern of family life expressed by the families in this study. This literature has explored gender within the family (Dornbusch and Strober 1988; Thorne and Yalom 1982), the meaning of motherhood in the lives of women (Rich 1986; Trebilcot 1984; Wearing 1984), and the work of mothering done by women (Ruddick 1989; Smith 1987). Most disability family studies have been conducted in isolation from contemporary theory and research in other disciplines concerning women, and the critical approaches found in those disciplines rarely find their way into disability studies. Disability research plays an important role in informing disability policy and practices. It is therefore imperative that researchers adopt an approach to family studies that places importance on gender, instead of an approach that makes invisible the differences between mothers' and fathers' experiences within the family. As it stands today, disability research and disability policy are among the forces that perpetuate and legitimize the traditional family pattern and gendered division of labor found in families of children with disabilities.

Workers and Friends

The goal of the current reform in the field of developmental disabilities is the full inclusion of people with disabilities into all aspects of community life. Yet, many people with disabilities continue to be isolated, lonely, and with few friends. This has resulted in a growing emphasis on the importance of relationships in the lives of people with disabilities (Amado 1993; Forest 1989; Lutfiyya 1991; Perske 1988; Taylor and Bogdan 1989). The increasing awareness of the limitations of the service system in connecting people with disabilities with ordinary community members has led to a call for a personal commitment on behalf of nondisabled people to establish social relationships with people with disabilities. Implied is the belief that such personal relationships will fill the gap left by the service system and serve as a basis for the supports necessary for people with disabilities to participate fully in community life.

The belief that true inclusion of people with disabilities can only be achieved through supportive personal relationships with nondisabled people is beginning to influence policies and practices in the field of developmental disabilities. For example, during fieldwork in human service organizations I found that many of the workers in the field, especially those who work in direct services—and the vast majority of these people are women—are now being encouraged to establish personal relationships with the people with disabilities with whom they work. I also found that within some service agencies it has become a measurement of a "good worker" whether she has made such a personal commitment or not. As a result, an increasing number of women have made commitments to people with disabilities that go far beyond the formal requirements of their jobs.

During the course of this study I also learned that a new language has emerged to describe these workers and what they do: they are "committed and involved." The language of "commitment and involvement" has not only been adopted by those who work within the field of developmental disabilities, it is also used within the institutions that train professionals for the field. For example, during the process of soliciting nominations of female workers and friends to participate in the study, many of the people I talked to used this language, including administrators, professionals, and college professors. The women who were nominated for the study and described as "very committed and involved" had established a friendship with a person with a disability, which was the main reason for describing them in this way. Often there was no mention of these women's performance in other areas. The language of "committed and involved" has become so widespread that it has come to be commonly understood to mean "committed to people with disabilities" and "involved with people with disabilities in a personal relationship." Sometimes it even seems to be a test of people's "political correctness" whether they have a friend with a disability. "Personal involvement and commitment" have become the most important qualities professionals and paraprofessionals in the field of developmental disabilities can have, at least in those service agencies that consider themselves to be progressive. This is in sharp contrast to the old language of "professional distance" and "impartial treatment" that used to be considered to be among the highest professional qualities.

From the time we are little girls, women are trained to be nurturing, caring, and attuned to the needs of others. This makes women particularly susceptible to arguments that encourage them to make personal commitments to people in need. In addition, at the heart of many women's work with people with disabilities is the desire to change the injustices experienced by people with disabilities, and their work is often performed in the context of a vision of a world where people with disabilities are welcomed, loved, and included. All of this makes women who work in human services easy targets for the pressure to make an even stronger commitment and become even more involved.

Current disability policy has clearly had a strong impact on the women in this study, and all of them have made personal commitments to people with disabilities that far exceed the formal requirements of their jobs. This is one more example of the continuing process of the recruitment of women to care for others, a process that starts in childhood and continues throughout women's adult lives.

This pressure on women to make a personal commitment to at least one person with a disability and to become involved in the life of that person beyond what was required by their job has made it hard for women to place limits on their working hours. This has also made it hard for women to distinguish between what is "work" (paid human service work) and what is "personal commitment" (unpaid care work based on personal relationships). As a result of these fluid boundaries of women's human service work, many of the women have experienced a conflict in terms of the various demands on their time and caring work. They are torn between demands from their families, on the one hand, and demand on their time from their human service work and commitments, on the other. The difficulty women have in placing limits on their human service work brings economic benefits to the service system. The care work these women perform in the name of personal commitment is no longer defined as "work" if it is done outside their working hours. Instead, it is defined as "friendship" or "commitment."

It appears as if current disability policies are moving the boundaries of women's responsibilities within the human services in a way that creates pressures on women to increase the work they perform, without being compensated. It is no longer enough for women to perform their jobs well. If they want to earn the highest praise in the field — the praise of being "committed and involved" — they have to go beyond the formal job requirements and make a personal commitment to become involved in the lives of people with disabilities outside their paid working hours.

The current trend in the field may, in reality, consist of the recruitment of women to perform significant amounts of care work for people with disabilities without being paid for it. In times of recession and budget cuts, this transfer of paid work over to friendship is convenient for the human service system. When accompanied by suggestions that "natural support" should replace some of, or most of, publicly funded services, current disability policies place women in a position to be exploited.

Invisible Work

That something as obvious as the fact that women dominate the care work for people with disabilities has gone unnoticed for so long is quite amazing. There are, however, complex reasons for this invisibility of women's work (Traustadóttir and Taylor 1998). Below I account for some of the ways in which women's care work is made invisible.

Women's Caring Activities Are Not "Work"

Many of women's caring activities are not acknowledged as "work." This is particularly true of the mothers' care work for their own children, where their efforts are viewed as an expression of their "love" rather than as "work." Similarly, the support women provide to their friends with disabilities is not viewed as "work," but as "friendship." And the volunteer work women perform with people with disabilities does not qualify as "work" because it is not paid for. The fact that what these women do is very similar — or even the same as — the work that is paid for when it is performed in the human service system does not seem to make a difference here; if it is not paid for, it is not regarded as work. Michelle Bauer, a 21-year-old college student who participated in the study, provides a good example here. One of the assignments in her special education course, described as a "volunteer program," was to spend time with a person with a disability. That is how she met Susan Clark, a 19-year-old high school student with severe disabilities. The two young women got along very well, and Susan's parents hired Michelle to spend time with Susan. When the two young women became friends, it seemed wrong to Michelle to take money for being with Susan. She stopped receiving payments but continued spending time with Susan. Throughout she performed the same kind of care work for Susan, but the meaning of the work — and the payment — changed with changing definitions of whether she was volunteering, working, or being a friend.

Other analysts of women's invisible work (Daniels 1987, 1988) have raised similar issues and have argued that one reason for the invisibility of women's work is that the folk concept of "work" associates work with activities we get paid for in the male-dominated public sphere. But in the private worlds of family, household, and friendships, where women predominate, no monetary exchange takes place, and the activities — even if they are the same as in the public sphere — are not defined as "work." Daniels (1988) also points out that some activities in the public sphere, such as volunteer work and community service, are usually not viewed as work because they are not paid for.

Women's Caring Is an Expression of a Womanly Character

Apart from ceremonial recognition, women's work in the family, as volunteers, and in women's occupations is devalued, receives low status and low or no pay, and is usually seen as of little importance. The closer the work is to traditional female activities of nurturing, comforting, encouraging, and facilitating interactions, the more closely it is associated with women's "natural" or "feminine" qualities and therefore regarded as a natural expression of women's character, not as a learned, skilled, or professional performance. Not only do men view women's work in this way, women themselves have learned to regard what they do in this way. For example, one of the female workers in this study, Joan Gilmore, believed that her skills in working with children with disabilities were a "natural talent" she was born with, a "gift" she may have inherited from her mother. Such views make it easy to disregard women's caring activities as learned and skillful work.

Women's Caring Work Can Be Literally Invisible

As DeVault (1991) points out, part of what makes women's caring work invisible is the fact that some of this work is "literally invisible." Examples include the work of managing a family meal, which "looks like simply enjoying the companionship of one's family" (DeVault 1991:56), and the work of planning, which is largely mental work and cannot be seen. Parts of the work of caring for people with disabilities are invisible in this same sense. This was obvious in Heather Williams's work as a job coach for people with disabilities. Her work of selecting a nondisabled co-worker to be a support person for a new worker with a disability looked like socializing with the employees—which in part it was. And the work of planning how to bring them together was invisible mental work.

The More Skillful, the More Invisible

Finally, the invisibility can be built into the work. That is, when the work is skillfully done, it does not seem to be work at all. An analysis of the work of facilitating the acceptance and inclusion of people with disabilities gives insight into this kind of invisibility. For example, Lori Salerno's (a personal care attendant) work of facilitating interactions between Melvin White (a severely disabled older man) and other people enabled him to become part of a social context. When this work was done skillfully it became invisible, and the invisibility of the work was part of doing it well. The work only became visible when it was not done, or when it was done in a clumsy way. The better women are at this part of the work, the less visible it is. This invisibility—as a central feature of a skillful performance—was also a part of Heather Williams's work of facilitating interactions between a new worker with a disability and the nondisabled co-workers. When Heather tried to incorporate a worker with a disability into the social context of a workplace, she tried to make the nondisabled worker feel like the interaction was spontaneous and "natural." Heather therefore hid the "work" she did in bringing people with and without disabilities together, and the invisibility of her work became a central part of a successful practice.

The complex invisibility of women's work is gendered, since it is primarily the caring and nurturing aspects of the work that are invisible. As other authors have pointed out, these are the skills that are associated with and seen as "natural" for women, but not for men (Coltrane 1989; Daniels 1987; DeVault 1991). The multiple ways women's work is made invisible underscores the importance of reconceptualizing the concept of "work" to include all the activities performed by women in the home, in the volunteer world, in the labor market, and in the context of friendships and relationships.

One of the main goals of this study is to make visible women's contributions to the reform toward community inclusion of people with disabilities. Beginning from the standpoint of women has brought into view the competent, skillful, and often artful ways women facilitate the acceptance and inclusion of people with disabilities and support them in becoming a part of everyday family and community life.

Merely drawing attention to this work and bringing into view its invisible parts does not change the devaluation of the work or the way it is organized. It is, however, the first step in recognizing the importance of this female activity and a necessary prerequisite for the changes in policy and practices to support and recognize the importance of this work.

Conclusion

The service system's failure to achieve social integration and connect people with regular community members has led to an increasing interest in what is often called "informal" or "natural support" to fill the gaps left by the service system. Some advocates even suggest that we do away with paid support and rely instead on unpaid, or "natural," supports (McKnight 1987, 1995; Wolfensberger 1987), and some advocate for the development of friendships rather than services (Hutchison 1990). The majority, however, suggest that we replace some services with "natural supports" (Bogdan and Taylor 1987a; Taylor, Bogdan, and Racino 1991).

Given how similar women's caring activities are across domains, this trend suggests that women will come under an increased pressure to provide unpaid "natural" care. The similarities in women's care work across domains also means that it may be relatively easy to shift this work back and forth between domains so that the same work will be alternately paid work in the services system, or unpaid work outside human service organizations, in families, communities, workplaces, and so on. There are already signs that this transfer of care work between domains is taking place. An example is a deinstitutionalization program in the state of Idaho. As a way of scaling back the population in one of its institutions for people with mental retardation, the state encouraged the workers in the institution to quit their jobs and become personal care home providers. Instead of caring for the clients in the institution, they would care for them in their own homes. Many of the workers accepted the state's offer, took the clients home, and became personal care home providers for the same people they used to work with in the institution (Traustadóttir 1987). Although the personal care home providers received some compensation for their work, the new arrangement made the distinction between "work" and "natural support" unclear.

What places women at an increased risk of being recruited to provide unpaid support is how intimately the work of caring for others is associated with female identity. This understanding of caring makes it is more likely that the work will be shifted back and forth between women's spheres, rather than becoming a male responsibility.

How to integrate formal and informal support is currently a much-discussed topic among policy makers, professionals, and researchers (Bulmer 1987). My analysis of women's care work across domains indicates that the distinction between formal and informal care is unclear, and that women's activities clearly transcend the distinction between formal and informal care. For example, women who are employed by the human service system to provide formal care to people with disabilities as paid human service workers frequently do the same things with the same people outside their paid working hours, as friends. The new trends in the field of developmental disabilities toward increased reliance on informal unpaid support places women in a position of being at risk of being exploited. Before we go further down the road toward replacing publicly funded services with "natural supports," there is an urgent need for an analysis of the effects these new policies and practices may have on women's lives.

Although I have highlighted the similarities between women's caring work across the three domains I studied, I do not want to leave the impression that there is uniformity in all women's care work. On the contrary, there are considerable differences in women's caregiving both within and across domains. The main differences across domains are between the mothers, on the one hand, and the workers and friends, on the other. Compared to the workers and friends, who usually spend a limited amount of their time caring for people with disabilities, caring for a child with a disability often fills up the mother's whole life and leaves her with little room to pursue other activities and interests. The differences within domains are largely determined by social relations of class, race, age, and education. The diversity among female human service workers is primarily influenced by their level and kind of professional education. Among the women who are full-time housewives and mothers, I found a wide range of differences in the condition, practices, and organization of their caregiving work. There was also a range in the mothers' attitudes to their care work, and whether they embraced, surrendered to, or resisted it varied greatly (Traustadóttir 1991).

Instead of treating caring as women's identity, I view caring as a socially organized activity that, to a large extent, determines women's place in society. In this study I have attempted to convey the complex nature of caring and the similarities in women's activities and experiences of caring across domains. Caring, which sometimes appears as something women do for themselves to achieve their femininity, is better understood as something women do for others to keep them alive. Caring is more than feelings women have; it is a specific kind of labor women perform that requires that women constantly organize and arrange their lives to meet the needs of others. In my analysis, caring appears as a life-defining phenomenon in women's existence and a medium through which women are accepted into and feel they belong in the social world. It is through caring that women gain recognition within the home, the family, and the world outside the family. Rather than seeing caring as being on the periphery of the social order, this view of caring recognizes it as a part of society's most powerful social relations; caring marks the point where social, economic, and gender relations intersect.

"Making a Way Outta No Way"

Grandparenting Cocaine-Exposed
Grandchildren

O ne relatively unexamined consequence of the contemporary crack cocaine episode is the increasing incidence of grandparents acting as surrogate parents for one of this society's most vulnerable groups: cocaine-exposed infants and children. A national advocacy organization for older Americans estimates that 353,000 middle-age and older adults are rearing their grandchildren, great-grandchildren, nieces, or nephews in households with no parents present (Rovner 1995). In 1997, the latest estimate available, approximately 3.9 million children or 5.5 percent of all children under age 18 lived in grandparent maintained households, a 76 percent increase since 1970 (Casper and Bryson 1998). The Current Population Report from the Bureau of the Census estimates that 1.5 million children reside in the grandparents' homes with neither parent present (Bryson and Casper 1999). This trend is especially pronounced for younger children. In New York and California the number of children under three years old living with grandparents increased by 379 percent between 1986 and 1991, compared to a 54 percent increase in regular foster care. A significant share of these children were exposed to cocaine prenatally (Ross 1995). Proportionately more African-American (12.3 percent) than European-American (3.7 percent) or Latino (5.6 percent) children live in households headed by grandparents (Jendrek 1994).

The analyses in this chapter are grounded in a systematic inquiry into the personal and social experiences, community-level support systems, and public policy issues that affect African-Americans' successful grandparenting of cocaine-exposed children. For the purposes of this project, cocaine-exposed children are defined as those exposed to cocaine in utero as well as those who, while not exposed in utero, suffered abuse, neglect, abandonment, or trauma associated with their parents' drug use. Successful "grandparenting," for purposes of this chapter, will be defined as surrogate parenting that promotes maximum development for children and enhances the physical and emotional health of both the grandparents and the grandchildren.

The central research question is: how do the social context, the application of relevant laws and policies, individual socioeconomic characteristics, social support, and family circumstances shape care work performed by people who are raising their cocaine-exposed grandchildren? This chapter looks specifically at the ways that institutional arrangements limit the agency of custodial grandparents.

It is worth noting the extent and effects of in-utero cocaine exposure. A study conducted in 1992–1993 by the National Institute on Drug Abuse shows that of 4 million women who were pregnant that year, about 1 percent or 45,000 women used cocaine sometime during their pregnancy. Dicker and Leighton estimate that only about one-half of the children exposed to cocaine in utero were drug affected (1994). The effects of maternal drug abuse on infant health occur in two distinct time periods. The first occurs while the fetus is developing. The final result of this short-term effect is the birth outcome, including perinatal morbidity and mortality. The second occurs later, extending from the late neonatal period up to the first birthday and beyond. "The most frequently described consequence of in-utero cocaine exposure [is] low birth weight" (Bandstra 1992: 215). Low birth weight (less than 2,500 grams) infants are either small for gestational age or premature (less than 37 weeks gestation length). Intrauterine growth retardation or underdevelopment often accompany low birth weight. This particular condition is associated with stillbirths, premature births, and pregnancy complications (Bandstra 1992; Barton, Harrigan, and Tse 1995; Vega, Kolody, Hwang, and Noble 1993).

There is still much to be learned about the effect of cocaine exposure because few studies control for the pattern and the timing of drug use, and often the lack of prenatal care is not accounted for as an intermediate variable. Studies that do control for these factors point to two things. One, that biological effects are not as great as researchers originally believed; and two, that social effects of cocaine exposure, such as living in a chaotic environment, might be more forceful than biological factors (Johnson and Rosen 1990). Even less is known about long-term effects of cocaine exposure on children beyond infancy. The resilient children who, as a result of stability and nurturing home and community environments, "manage, despite the adverse factors they experience to 'work well, play well, love well, expect well' " (Johnson, Glassman, Fiks, and Rosen 1988:524) provide evidence that social factors may determine child health and well-being more powerfully than cocaine exposure, however. Though statistically significant biological effects appear minimal, the social stigma the mothers, their children, and the children's grandparents potentially endure is real. The stories related in the analysis below show how grandparent caretakers attempt to buffer the effects of social stigma on their grandchildren's well-being.

Theoretical Considerations for Analyzing African-American Grandmothers as Caretakers

Patricia Hill Collins's (1994:45) "Shifting the Center: Race, Class and Feminist Theorizing About Motherhood" demonstrates the usefulness of using an intersectional approach that examines the ways that race, class, and gender work in concert to produce differential mothering experiences. Or as Collins says, "racial domination and economic exploitation profoundly shape the mothering context . . . for all women." Viewing caretaking from the perspective of African-American grandmothers provides a unique angle of vision that elucidates the agency of custodial grandparents on many levels. Collins (1994:47) discusses how "women of color have performed motherwork that challenges social constructions of work and family as separate spheres, of male and female gender roles as similarly dichotomized, and of the search for autonomy as the guiding quest." For instance, "different institutional arrangements emerged in these mothers' respective communities to resolve the tension between maternal separation due to employment and the needs of dependent children" (1994:51). An example of this is the extended family structure that affords grandmothers the opportunity to become primary caretakers of their daughters' and daughters-in-law's children. Grandparents' agency is evident in their attempts to support their children's struggles with recovery from drug addiction, in their willingness to take on primary responsibility for the care of their grandchildren, and their membership in grandparent support groups that provide emotional support, education, and the opportunity to advocate en masse for themselves politically.

As Collins argues, women are not powerless in the face of racial and class oppression. Depending on their access to traditional culture, they invoke alternative sources of power. She says that mothers and children empower themselves by understanding each other's position and relying on each other's strengths. Grandparent families' very existence draws upon African-American creative family arrangements forced by slavery, the need to pool resources under the sharecropping system and later northern migration, limited access to gainful employment for male heads of household, the need for African-American women to work outside the home to make ends meet, urban deindustrialization, and the influx of drugs into African-American communities. While nuclear families have been the dominant form in which African-American families have arranged themselves, alternative forms have not been stigmatized within the African-American community because its members understand the ways in which institutional arrangements have shaped families (Franklin 1997).

This suggests that structuralist understandings of this social phenomenon are more prevalent from African-American perspectives. This does not essentialize the African-American community. In studying racial differences in grandmothering, Kivett (1993) uses a cultural variant view of racial difference. This view purports that "racial deviations from the norms of dominant culture (are) adaptive mechanisms" (1993:165). Instead of suggesting that family arrangements, viewpoints, and other characteristics of African-Americans are somehow essential to their nature, this view seeks to demonstrate that social forces that have shaped African-American lives have led to a preponderance of similar beliefs, adaptive strategies, and outcomes.

Structuralist researchers argue that social structure determines family structure and family life. For instance, Rodrick Wallace and his colleagues look at ways that economic and political circumstances affect communities, so that community decay is shown to be antecedent to familial peril. For example, they show how the rise in the number of burned-out abandoned buildings is a result of a decrease in firehouses in New York neighborhoods in which people of color live. Crack cocaine trafficking and use easily flowed into these communities immediately after these buildings were abandoned. Wallace and his colleagues further show how these circumstances decrease the cohesion of communities and break down extended family and other formal and informal social support structures. The work of Wallace and colleagues not only describes structural limitations to families' survival, but also the ways in which family and community agency have been disrupted as a result of structural limitations (Wallace 1990; Wallace, Wallace, and Andrews 1995).

Women's "motherwork" requires collaborating to empower mothers and children within structures that oppress (Collins 1994). Grandparenting support groups are a prime example of such collaboration. As will be shown below, support groups provide a space in which grandparents can be self-reflective about their parenting mistakes and successes, so they can decide how to adapt to their custodial grandparenting role. Grandparents' advocacy has earned them the eligibility to be considered foster parents. Until 1979, grandparents and other relatives could not be considered foster parents for any related children in their custody. Political work by grandparenting support groups and others led to a 1979 decision, in the case of *Miller vs. Youakim*, in which the Supreme Court ruled that relatives could not be excluded from eligibility as foster parents for minor family members.

Agency approaches promoted by researchers including Robin Jarrett, Kathryn Edin, and Laura Lein have demonstrated the importance of "bringing people back in" as a complement to structuralist approaches to social science phenomena such as the relationships between poverty, family structure, and race (Jarrett

1994). Jarrett shows how single parenthood is a strategy that makes sense for African-American mothers whose children's fathers have few economic options. Edin and Lein demonstrate that the "fundamental economic reality" of the lives of mothers on welfare, that "neither welfare nor low-wage work gives single mothers enough income to meet their families' expenses," means that women must find alternative ways to provide for their children (1997). As I will show below, grandparents' agency allows them, at times, to defy the determinism of structures because they are able to win small battles with the system and obtain care for their grandchildren despite educational and social service policy and legal impediments.

Grandparents' agency has its limits, however. Below I demonstrate that a focus on caretaking from grandparents' perspectives helps the social scientist to better understand the extent to which institutional arrangements do finally limit choices, resources, and the ability for grandparents to successfully raise their grandchildren.

Research Design and Qualitative Data Collection

In this study, which is based on original research conducted in an urban north-eastern community, the experiences of grandparents who currently take care of grandchildren or who have taken care of grandchildren in the past are examined. *Caretaking* is conceptualized to encompass housing and taking responsibility for the daily living routine of grandchildren for at least one month or intermittently for more than one two-week period over the course of two months or longer. Because the topic of grandparenting cocaine-exposed children is a new one, my co-investigator and I pursued an exploratory research design. A four-part research plan (including focus group discussions, a survey of community resources, a household enumeration survey, and in-depth interviews with grandparents) was executed in our study site. The analysis centers on focus group discussions with grandparents who are taking care of grandchildren. A grandparent support group was identified in our research site. Grandparents from this support group agreed to participate in three focus group discussions: two pilot focus groups that took place during their support group meetings in 1996 and 1997 and then a separate discussion set up apart from the regular meeting time in 1998. The purpose of the focus group discussion was to verify our conceptualization of "successful grandparenting" by finding out the ways in which grandparents themselves define the term. The analysis below is based on the last discussion.

One of the anticipated difficulties was finding grandparents to talk about their caretaking role and their relationships with cocaine-abusing children and their offspring. Grandparents often encounter problems with social service agencies and have difficulties gaining legal custody of their grandchildren. We were con-

cerned that they might feel that they could jeopardize the caretaking arrangement by speaking to interviewers at length about their grandchildren. We were
also sensitive to the fact that custodial grandparents are quite busy and may have
limited time for focus group discussions.

However, studies to date indicate that grandparents want to speak as their
own advocates (Minkler and Roe 1993). To put the grandparents at ease, personal
referrals from the project's resource person, who was affiliated with the support
group, were expected to overcome grandparents' potential reluctance in confid-
ing with interviewers. Access to grandparents was enhanced by assuring them of
confidentiality. Focus group discussions conducted in their communities were designed to make the researchers more accessible to prospective participants. A two-
year span allowed us to build rapport with the group. For example, I was pregnant with my first child during the second focus group discussion, and the
grandparents were adamant about seeing pictures of the baby when we returned
for the 1998 discussion. The fact that the co-investigators are African-American—
and that one is the same age as some of the grandparents and the other (the author) is the age of some of the grandparents' adult children—also fostered trust,
familiarity, and open communication between grandparents and investigators.

The support group setting in itself was an easy place to conduct focus group
discussions. Because most of the grandparents knew each other and were aware
of each other's stories, the discussion took the form of a rap session. Robin Jarrett
writes about the focus group discussion as a rap session and the ways that it re-
laxes participants, encouraging them to share their experiences (1993). She elucidates the performative aspect of the discussion, and the fact that accounts are
sometimes exaggerated in order to highlight what the group members believe to
be the most salient meanings attached to their experiences. Our focus group discussion was similar to what she described. Finally, the support group provided
very helpful administrative assistance. The resources of the group were used to
recruit participants, and the grandparent support group facilitator arranged for
participants' transportation. As a small token of our gratitude, our project provided funds for a luncheon and a respondent fee to participants.

Seven grandparents, one great-grandparent, the author, and her co-investigator participated in the focus group discussion. All respondents were members of
a grandparent support group, though not all were members of the group hosting
our discussion. According to information they supplied, their ages ranged from
51 to 70 at the time of the interview; two did not report their date of birth. Three
were in their early 50s and the rest were age 57 and older. The mean age was 58.
The great-grandparent in the group was amongst the oldest. All participants
were African-American women.

We did not ask their educational or occupational backgrounds, but it is safe to
assume that most if not all of the women completed high school and some had
college experience. One woman is a retired schoolteacher. Another talked about

the fact that she and her husband had paid off their home. Inferring from our conversation, it appears that the group is mostly working-class. Many are retired or on disability and spoke as if they had more economic resources during their working lives than they did at the time of the interview. Two discussed living in public housing, and one discussed her difficulties with public transportation. Half of the women mentioned husbands. We, however, did not directly ask about their marital status.

The majority of the grandparents in the group were taking care of their grandchildren because of their adult children's drug-involved past either directly or indirectly, as a result of involvement with an addict who shared parentage of the child, usually the child's mother. Finally, grandmothers participating in the focus group discussion were taking care of one to four children. The children's ages ranged from 6 months to 13 years old; the children's mean age was 8 years old. The children's ages clustered at ages 6 months to 3 years, 6 to 10, and finally 12 and 13. The widest age span of any grandparent's charges was between preadolescent and adolescent years.

In the quotes from the transcription below, I attempt to be as faithful to the words of the focus group participants as possible. Fortunately, I had both fieldnotes and taped discussions. It was difficult for the graduate student hired to transcribe the tapes to decipher every spoken word. The recorder did not pick up women's voices when their volume diminished and the European-American graduate student was unable to translate some peculiarities of African-American speech. In retyping the transcription, however, I was able to combine the notes and the sometimes inaudible taped discussions to get a more complete rendering of the grandparents' voices. Words written in parentheses in the quotations below indicate paraphrases of some of the grandparents' words, either because they were inaudible on the tape or in order to shorten the quote length. Ellipses indicate either information that is not relevant to the idea I wanted to draw out from the quote, or places where it is hard to hear or understand the respondent.

Qualitative analysis of the data reveals ways that grandparents dynamically adapt to provide care for their grandchildren. It also reveals how institutional constraints, such as the type of financial assistance available, determine the lives of the custodial grandparents under study.

Agency: Grandparents' Self-Reflection and Action

According to Johnson and Rosen (1990), to understand the outcomes of maternal drug abuse during pregnancy, research must address "several important risk factors—poor prenatal nutrition, poor prenatal care, (and) chaotic home conditions (that are) inextricably intertwined with maternal drug abuse in the population studied. . . . The data reflect the impact of the mother's life-style, which exposes the fetus and developing child to multiple risk factors" (281–82). The multiple risk factors include not only maternal behaviors, such as prenatal care and nutrition, the mother's home conditions, but also include the socioeconomic environment in the mother's community. These work in concert to affect the infant's risk of ill health early in life. The same sorts of factors affect the health and well-being of older children who experience social exposure to illicit substances.

Grandparents who offer to care for their drug-abusing child's infant have the potential to step in and have a positive impact on a child born into such precarious life circumstances. For example, a mother may ask that such surrogate parenting be provided to the child while she attempts to recover from her cocaine addiction. This adaptive behavior and the support provided by grandparents have received little attention (a notable exception is Minkler and Roe 1993). Further information about the effects of the social environment on grandparents who are potentially stigmatized as a result of their children's addiction has not been studied in any systematic way. This research attempts to explore the lives of grandparents caring for cocaine-abusing children's offspring in the context of their neighborhoods.

It is important to this analysis to listen to an "organic" definition of successful grandparenting, one that comes from the grandparents' own expectations and experiences. They reveal that grandparents have high hopes for their grandchildren. Making such hopes a future reality was one indicator of successful grandparenting discussed by the group. One grandmother we spoke with said that she wants her grandchildren

> to be responsible and to make the right choices, to get a good education, go to church, and be loving and understanding of other people. (And I hope that they) always strive for perfection if possible.

Another grandmother's revelation:

> I think I would like for mine to have . . . good morals, good values, to be God fearing. . . . I want them to have all of those characteristics so they can deal with things that happen in life. (I also want) the best education (for them and) a long life.

Grandparents in this study expressed upwardly mobile hopes and dreams for their grandchildren. Their indicators of success are no different than those of traditional values: to strive for educational achievement, to have strong moral fiber, to be virtuous, and to be able to accept the challenges life presents.

These women want to model for their grandchildren the cohesiveness of and the importance of family as expressed by this grandmother:

> It's not always possible to raise kids in this day with two parent(al) figures, but I would like them to learn the importance of family and what it means to be a family.

Another supported by adding:

> I want (my grandson) to know he has a mother and I am his grandmother. And
> for him to know that (his mother) has a problem and that she is not able to take
> care of him. . . . . (I hope) that he would be accepting of her.

In her introduction to a set of articles published in *Qualitative Sociology* in 1997
on "New Family Forms," Janet Giele says that "the distinctive characteristic of
families that sets them apart from [other social institutions and nonfamily
groups] is their intimacy, informality, and particularity of relationships" (p. 150).
These characteristics are important in the grandparent families we studied as
well. The grandparents themselves found these characteristics to be crucial for
their grandchildren to succeed in life, or as Giele puts it, "Children and parents
need family support to do well in the public world." One of the mechanisms that
allows children to do well, which grandparents assumed that family provides, is
self-worth. As one grandparent says it:

> He has to know his worth. He is loved and wanted. It is nothing he has done
> (that has led to me taking care of him and not his mother). (With family) he has
> something to build his life on. (I want him to know that) he is loved and
> needed. And he is a part of a family.

In addition to the traditional indicators, including educational achievement, strong
values, and valuing family, grandparents indicated that it was important for their
grandchildren to be independent thinkers.

> (I want them to) have the power to decide what their life is going to be in spite
> of education, in spite of what life has handed them, in spite of what their
> grandmother is able to provide for them. I want them to be strong enough to
> know their self-worth. And . . . to take control, and determine what their life is
> going to be.

Or as another grandparent put it:

> Sometimes you've got to walk away from a situation. 'Cause I talk to my grand-
> child, my granddaughter, and my grandson, the older one, a lot; and I've found
> out, you know, that a lot of time it's peer pressure and sometimes, like I say,
> "you've got to say no to things." I tell them that all the time. "A lot of things,
> you've got to say no and stick to that," and I would like to see them grow up to
> be independent, successful young adults.

Independent thinking was an important quality for grandparents to nurture,
given that some of the children's parents were unable to stop the spiral of drug

addiction that led to the grandparent ultimately taking responsibility for rearing the present generation. Grandparents were further concerned about the potentially dangerous influences that could come from the children's peers at school.

In speaking about indicators of successful grandparenting, our respondents noted the importance of breaking patterns that were established when they were parenting their own children.

> (Of course I) want to be a successful grandparent. (But) a hundred times of day it calls into question (whether I) was a successful mother.

Or as another stated:

> I'm in the process now of trying to break generation curses. I want it to stop with this generation. I don't want my grandkids to go on and do the things that (their parents did). So I have to start dealing with my mind, changing my attitude and my ways. So I have to take some of the old and some of the new and mix it together and come up with a new formula.

Finally:

> I don't like to say I'm a successful or unsuccessful parent or grandparent. But did I survive? And sometimes it's hard to just keep on going. So if I can just do the best I can with it (then that's all I can do). So I don't want to set up the pattern so that when my grandchildren have children that they're going to have to take care of the grandchildren. I don't want that pattern to repeat itself. Just do the best you can.

These grandparents are clearly self-reflective about their parenting and the ways that it molds the people their grandchildren are becoming.

Structural Conditions: Family, Migratory Dislocations, and Institutions

Self-reflection about the grandparents' present family circumstances within the context of the support group helped participants to begin to see structural influences in their lives. Questioning how mistakes in parenting their now-adult children led to custodial grandparenting, and experiencing self-doubt as one of the unfortunate by-products of such self-reflection, was the beginning to such revelations.

> I used to doubt myself as a parent. I used to doubt myself a lot. But I was sitting down talking to my brother one day, and he said, "You know what? . . .

Our mother raised 13 children, and she never had to visit the jail, she never had to visit the hospital." . . . (My brother) says, "We wasn't rich, but we learned one thing: how to love each other." . . . My father was a coal miner. . . . Momma never worked (outside the home) a day in her life. She took care of us kids. But there's a difference in raising your child in (the South) and raising your child in (a northeastern city). I learned that. I had to learn it because . . . when they got grown, (my kids) learned from the streets. . . . Well, I never learned from the streets. And when I found out about drugs I had teenage children. Then I . . . learn(ed) about cocaine, reefer, this and that. It was like I had been kept in darkness.

Grandparents report their understanding of how micro-structural events and macro-structural processes impeded their ability to successfully rear their now-grown children. The above participant adds that both she and her husband worked after migrating to a northeastern city of residence. While one income was sufficient in her family of orientation, two incomes were necessary in her procreative family. Familists might say that her commitments to the labor market kept her from supervising her children in the same way her mother supervised her and 12 siblings. She speaks about how northern city living is different than her rural background because urban children learn from "the streets," something she was not accustomed to or prepared to buffer. Deindustrialization and institutional racism, prevalent in the city under study during the time period in which her children were adolescents, definitely contributed to the need for two incomes. Urban decay cut resources formerly available for constructive after-school activities for school-age children.

Grandparents said that another thing that added to self-doubt and that made it difficult to parent *their* children was that forms of discipline considered legitimate in the African-American community were called child abuse by the educational system.

As hard as we try to be good parents, I think at some point, the system says, "You don't know what you're doing because of the way you were brought up. You were abused as a child because your mother spanked you." . . . So I backed down because it is at some point that I said, "Well, maybe I was." . . . I really feel when they said, "OK, when your mother spanks you, you can [call the police]," they gave my child the right to say, "I can do whatever I want to do, and there is nothing you can do about it" (agreement and comments from the other women). . . . So I think the system needs to look at who is teaching our children and where they come up with their ideas of what is abuse, what is discipline, and what each individual child needs because the parents are the only ones who know what their children need.

This grandparent felt that her parenting was compromised because her authority and confidence were undermined by the school system. Grandparents believe that school administrators and teachers do not have grounded knowledge about child development and the cultural exigencies of raising children in urban areas. They also believe that the paradoxical messages given to children about their own agency affects parent-child relationships.

> I felt if I (disciplined her) too much, she would rebel and she would be in the streets. Now I did the best that I knew how. But I think still that (when) the schools teach our children (that they can make their own choices that) for some kids it's good because they have the ability to make choices, but for some it is the wrong thing to teach them (because they are not all mature enough to take on such a responsibility).

Another problem that grandparents identified regarding the schools' approach to African-American parenting is that they did not acknowledge differences in values. The schools were teaching individualism when collectivism is important to many African-American families. According to Patricia Hill Collins, an area in which women of color have struggled for maternal empowerment is fighting the pervasive efforts by the dominant group to control children's minds. An important part of motherwork is challenging mainstream American society's desire to promote individualism (Collins 1994).

> Because the main thing, and I don't know if it started in the 80s or the 70s, is the "me" thing: "I, I, I have rights." And I'm trying to teach my grandchildren, any decisions that anyone makes in this family reflects on the whole family. If I decide not to go grocery shopping, then somebody in that house doesn't eat. If they decide that they don't want to do their chores, then somebody else has got to empty the baskets and take out the trash . . . , and so it's a cooperative thing. . . . Everyone has a responsibility to someone else in the family. You don't teach family anymore; schools don't promote family.

This grandmother said that the contradiction is that even though the schools do not promote family, that they are quick to blame the family when problems arise for children. She implies that the educational system does not acknowledge its own complicity in creating some of the problems the children have. These grandmothers understand that the crucial aspect of motherwork is to challenge the propriety and values of schools that operate primarily to keep subdominant groups in a dislocated social and political space (Collins 1994).

Though grandparents had self-doubts about how well they reared their children, the support group enabled them to let themselves off the hook for their children's behavior because as they shared stories and saw how similar were group members' experiences, they understood that their parenting was only part of what led to their children's choices. One grandparent said:

> I was always in parenting groups, but (never) a grandparent group and eventually someone came up with the idea, you know. . . . And I started from the beginning in the (grandparent support) group because I wanted to talk to some grandparents who were going through the same thing as I was going through.

The the grandparenting group provided the space for self-reflection and the encouragement from others who know the pain of their adult children's poor choices, so that grandparents could stop blaming themselves for their own and their grandchildren's predicament.

> I blamed myself for a long time, but then I stopped blaming myself. (To my children) I said, "I taught you right from wrong. I taught you to take responsibility and to take care of yourself. I taught you how to survive. What you do with that teaching is up to you. But if you think about what you were brought up with and then you still choose to take those drugs, or choose to break in a house, or choose to rob a bank, you have to pay the consequences of that." Because I told them, "You've been taught differently. You know you are doing wrong."

Another grandparent offered:

> You can bring them up to be independent thinking and to choose the right path, but if they choose to get off that path, there ain't nothin' you can do about it. (Agreement from the other women.) Nothing.

Patricia Hill Collins (1994) suggests that women of color have struggled for maternal empowerment by supporting and raising their children regardless of the circumstance that brought them into the world. Such values motivated many grandparents to take on the role of taking care of their grandchildren.

> I was called at work, and they said, "Well, your daughter (has had) a 1-pound baby." . . . So the choice was for us to go ahead and take him. And you (have to) do whatever you can to keep him or . . . he is going to a foster home. . . . And now I have this little one there, and . . . it has changed everything. And the doctors say, "We don't know what kind of medical problems he is going to have." I mean, I am under CPS (Child Protective Services' authority), and I have done nothing (wrong). . . . I have a (caseworker) who comes in every two weeks because of what his mother did. It has nothing to do with me. So because he was born under CPS, I am under CPS. . . . If anything goes wrong with him, I am accountable because of what she did.

The stigmatization of Child Protective Service surveillance did not stop this grandmother from doing all that she could to ensure her grandson's health and happiness.

The constant questions from family members, other acquaintances, health workers, and social service agencies about the whereabouts of the child's mother added to the grandparents' difficulties.

> Grandparent A: I am his legal guardian. And everywhere I go I have to say I am his legal guardian and (I am asked) "Is his mother in the home?" No, she isn't.

> Grandparent B interjects: Right, and that is a constant question.

> Grandparent A: I have all his papers. I have everything. But I can go to the doctor today, and I can go tomorrow and I get the same question, and I have to prove it again.

The greatest difficulty comes when grandparents are unable to get basic resources for their grandchildren, such as medical attention and housing. One grandmother whose daughter was homeless for a while said:

> Everywhere you go (you are constantly asked), "Where is the mother?" Well, now she should be on (Third Avenue) and (Broad Street). Or uh when you go to the hospital, in emergency, "Well we can't do anything without the mother being here. Where is she?" I said well let me walk down the street and see if I can find her and if she is not there, you're going to have to deal with me. You have to get silly with these people. And so finally, you know, I had to say in my mind to walk with authority and carry yourself in authority and speak with authority. That's when you say, "You're going to register this patient, and you're going to stitch this wound up. And we can talk about that other crap later." (Laughter from the other women.) But sometimes you run into stone walls.

The challenges of custody vary depending on the type of custody a grandparent has: an informal custody arrangement worked out between the grandparent and parent (the most common), guardianship, foster care, kinship care, or court-approved full custody. The amount of resources from social services and recognition of parental authority over the child also varies depending upon the type of custody. The best resources are made available to foster care families. This is the most difficult type of custodial arrangement for the grandparents to set up. Many of them do not meet the requirements, essentially because they are not middle-class.

Opportunity structures early in life affect the health and well-being of aging African-Americans. They are three times more likely to be poor; older African-American women are one of the poorest groups in the nation (Jackson, Chatters, and Taylor 1993; Select Committee on Aging 1991). Almost half (44.9 percent) rate their health as fair or poor. African-American men and women are more likely to bear the brunt of the crack phenomenon, whether they are victims of crime and violence (U.S. Department of Justice 1992) or stigmatized as the parents of addicted adult children (Minkler and Roe 1993). While grandparenting remains a valued role within the African-American community, these factors make it a difficult task. Parenting a cocaine-exposed child, with all the attendant risks and problems, is, for many African-American grandparents, an unanticipated but accepted burden (Minkler and Roe 1993; Roe, Minkler, and Barnwell 1994; Joslin and Brouard 1995; Burton 1992).

For a number of years researchers have discussed the deleterious effects of drug abuse and drug trafficking on community and social relations among African-Americans (Brown 1965; Johnson, Williams, Dei, and Sanabria 1990; Wallace, Wallace, and Andrews 1995; Wallace 1990; Wilson 1987). Recent studies have identified increasing social isolation (Fernandez and Harris 1992) and the emotional impact of social stigma for individuals and families of cocaine abusers (Fullilove and Fullilove 1989). Both Burton (1992) and Minkler and Roe (1993) investigated the emotional and social effects of caring for cocaine-exposed grandchildren on people residing in urban areas. The grandparents report the need, for example, to structure their daily routines and their grandchildren's activities to avoid periods of intensified street-level trafficking and the potential for random violence. In addition, they identify changes in their relationships with institutions such as the church. Some of these grandparents report that they no longer find the church environment supportive, because their children's addiction is stigmatized (Minkler and Roe 1993). These studies suggest that the presence of drug abuse and trafficking in the community require parents to negotiate not only physical concepts of community but its social boundaries as well. Jarrett shows that parents buffer deleterious effects of deteriorating urban communities with family protection, child monitoring, resource seeking, and in-home learning strategies (1997). The grandparents we spoke with exercise their agency in similar ways.

Policy and Legal Impediments to Successful Grandparenting of Cocaine-Exposed Children

Families with cocaine involvement in their past or present have a great deal of agency to ensure that children of cocaine-abusing or recovering addicted parents are cared for in as healthy an environment as possible. This has policy relevance because resilient children who live with their grandparents and who are healthy despite intrauterine cocaine exposure are less costly to taxpayers than are children who are abandoned by their families and who end up in foster care. Resilient children, living in a stable and stimulating environment, overcome possible biological, neurological, and physical challenges despite the fact that their mothers used cocaine during pregnancy (Johnson and Rosen 1990). Healthy environments provided by grandparents potentially contribute to the county's revenue in the form of savings that are realized as a result.

Despite the fact that grandparents are doing a great service to their families and communities, they have to contend with various roadblocks. Given the priority of parental rights in American society, grandparents who accept custody of their grandchildren, formally or informally, often find themselves enmeshed in legal and practical barriers that impede their ability to support, nurture, and otherwise care for their grandchildren.

> When I applied for Section 8, I went for my interview, and the lady says, "Oh, I see you're a grandmother taking care of grandchildren." And I said, "Yes, ma'am." And so she says, "Um, do you have your custody papers?" And I said "No. I've applied for my guardianship papers." She says, "Well, . . . Section 8 considers you a single person so maybe you oughta try for a one-bedroom apartment." (Reactions from the other women: "Ooooo!" "Oh no!" etc.) And I almost lost my mind. . . . Because it just didn't make any sense. The social service, the government says, "You are a family unit, and you are the head of household." Another government agency, HUD, says, "Oh, you're a single parent. Put them kids in the garbage."

African-American grandparents raising cocaine-exposed children are at increased risk of being confronted with legal obstacles involving custody as well as the financial and social service support necessary to meet their grandchildren's needs (Mullen 1995).

> Respondent A: It took me almost five years to get the court to give me guardianship papers, and then social service is saying, "Well you didn't get this. You didn't get custody." Well, to get custody papers, and now it's $2,500 to start the paperwork, $2,500 apiece, apiece.

> Respondent B interjects: Each child? I got custody of my grandkids, but I finally got my daughter and the father to sign over custody. . . .

> Respondent A: Well, that's it! . . . The court gives me papers to serve on my grandchildren's parents. (The grandchildren's) momma didn't have an address. So I couldn't serve her the papers. The judge says to my lawyer, "How dare you give her court-ordered papers. That's not her job." (When I tried to find the parents), I got cussed out, I got run off the porch, I got beer bottles thrown at me and all I (was asking for is that they) sign papers so I could get (my grandchildren) in school, get them medical attention when they need it, et cetera.

Existing studies have provided preliminary observations on the differential effects on grandparenting of various types of government assistance such as AFDC, AFDC-Foster Care, kinship care, or having no financial assistance at all (Minkler and Roe 1993; McLean and Thomas 1996; Mullen 1995). Closely related to the type of assistance is a range of custody categories from informal to full legal custody. African-American grandparent caregivers are less likely to have legal custody of their grandchildren (Hegar and Scannapieco 1995; McLean and Thomas 1996; Minkler and Roe 1993). Without legal custody they have difficulties in receiving adequate financial support, enrolling their grandchildren in school, and getting medical care. In the child welfare literature there is evidence to suggest that some types of government assistance and custody categories are associated with lower levels of even routine child health care (Feigelman, Auravin, Dubowitz, Harrington, Starr, and Tepper 1995; Ross 1995; Halfon, Mendonca, and Berkowitz 1995). Even worse, in the absence of social services, some grandparents must negotiate separate systems of agencies and caseworkers to meet the multiple needs of their drug-affected children (McLean and Thomas 1996).

Federal and state laws order a hierarchy of support for children in out-of-home placements. Title IV-E sets the criteria and allocates funds to the states for foster care, the program that provides the most adequate financial and social services support, particularly for children with special needs (Takas 1994). Given the strict licensing standards (including family composition, at least one parent not employed outside of the home, and physical space in the home), however, poor minority families are less likely to qualify (Hegar and Scannapieco 1995; Minkler and Roe 1993) and are relegated to the welfare rolls if they need additional support to care for their grandchildren.

Another impediment for grandparent caregivers of drug-exposed children is that becoming foster parents or adoptive parents requires court proceedings that terminate parental rights. Grandparents, especially those who continue to hope for their adult child's recovery, are often reluctant to participate in a process that involves declaring their child an unfit parent, resulting in disproportionate numbers of drug-exposed children in informal custody (McLean and Thomas 1996; Minkler and Roe 1993).

It was 1979 before the Supreme Court ruled that relatives could not be excluded from eligibility as foster parents for minor family members (Minkler and Roe 1993), but the Court did not specify how relatives were to be included. Since 1979 some states have developed kinship foster care programs. State-level guidelines for kinship foster care vary such that in some states cash and noncash support for relative caregivers is greater than AFDC but less than that for nonrelated foster care families (Takas 1994). In other states with equivalent support for foster care with relatives and nonrelatives, such as New York state, the eligibility criteria are not necessarily uniformly applied. Verbal reports from the Department of Social Services representatives indicate there are counties in New York state where a kinship foster care placement has never been made.

While some states have eliminated or are moving toward eliminating some of the barriers confronting custodial grandparents, the aforementioned legal and practical obstacles result in a system that awards the greatest benefits (cash and noncash) to those who are better off and the smallest benefits to those who are most in need (McLean and Thomas 1996; Minkler and Roe 1993; Mullen 1995). This system not only tends to increase the stressors that grandparents in this situation ordinarily face when they accept responsibility for their grandchildren (Burton 1992; Minkler and Roe 1993; Roe, Minkler, and Barnwell 1994), it can and does also disrupt the process of family preservation it purports to serve.

Most significantly, since the passage of the Personal Responsibility and Work Opportunity Reconciliation Act of 1996, better known as welfare reform, grandparent caregivers who need public assistance to care for their grandchildren are threatened with even fewer resources in the short run and, with a five-year limit on eligibility, no financial assistance in the long run.

Before welfare reform, grandparents could apply for public assistance for a grandchild. With these "child only" grants the grandparents' resources were invisible: social security benefits and other income (within certain limits) were discounted. The legislation of some states disallowed grants for the children only, and all related members of a household are considered a family unit. Disability and other cash benefits previously not counted in a family's resources will now be counted. Consequently, the level of financial assistance available to some grandparent caregivers will, in all likelihood, decrease. The law makes no age distinction for the work requirement, implying that grandparents of any age will be required to seek employment in order to continue to receive benefits. In some states, the Gramm amendment bars their children from ever receiving welfare benefits if they have been convicted of a drug felony (Busch, Cantor, Jellinek, and Sackman 1997; Mullen 1997; Perez-Porter 1996). The impact of the current system and the newly imposed welfare reform provisions suggest that the experience of raising cocaine-exposed grandchildren, which was already difficult at best, has the potential to become even more difficult in the near future.

Policy impediments in the health arena were one of the main themes grandparents discussed. They felt that their grandchildren received substandard medical attention. One grandparent relates this story about her infant grandson.

Respondent A: I called on the phone. And I thought he was having an asthma attack. And the nurse tells me "OK, hold on," then she says, "OK, I'll have the doctor call back." The doctor says, "put him to the phone and let me hear him breathing . . . "

Respondent B: Oh my goodness!

Respondent C: I never heard of that in my life.

Respondent A: He said, "Let me hear him breathing on the phone."

Respondent C: I never heard of that.

Respondent A: He says, "Take him in the bathroom about 20 minutes with the shower on. Get it as hot as you can get it. When you get finished, call me back." (When I called) he said, "Wait till the water runs cold and do this again, all night."

Respondent D: All because they don't want to pay for you to come in!

Sometimes it takes measures that go above and beyond normal protocol and sheer luck to obtain proper medical attention. One of the women told of taking her adolescent granddaughter to the emergency room because she was having a seizure.

When the doctor came in, she wasn't having the seizure anymore, . . . So I said, "What am I going to do?" (The doctor said), "Oh, there is nothing we can do about it.". . . So I said, "I tell you what, every time her eyes roll back, every time she go like this (speaker gestures), she (will be) right here." And we did that about six months. And they got tired. It was like this, "We are going to wear you down."

The woman spoke of long waits at the emergency room with her granddaughter. Then a doctor or nurse would say to them,

"OK, we'll be right back." Then after hours they would come back and ask (my granddaughter), "Oh, how you feeling? How you feeling?" And they go away again. And I am sitting out there. They (in effect were saying to us), "We going to wear you down, Mrs. (X), and you are going to stop coming." And I said, "You know something, if we were at home . . . and her face turned from green to blue or she developed some brain damage or something happened, then you would be saying, 'Why didn't you bring her in?' " And the ambulance kept coming when I called them, and they (always) wanted to know who was here, and what was the deal, and people used to break down what they saw, what stage of the seizure she was in, what her condition was, (tell them) was she conscious, and they used to wait until the seizure was over and talk to her and stuff, write all that down and take her to (the hospital). And finally one time the attendant said, "There is a doctor named so and so," and he said, "When I go out there I'll talk to him." That's the only way we got her in. Because this attendant knew someone else and told them about the case. The attendant said, "How many times have you (come) out here?" So he said, "This is ridiculous that they have you running around here like that." And you know they try to wear you out.

The question is, if this young woman received proper medical attention as an exception, what is the plight of others who find themselves with similar difficulties?

Grandparents' Policy Recommendations

Grandparents' voices make the policy implications of the research quite clear. They say that support for grandparenting groups is crucial. There are three types of groups the American Association of Retired Persons' Grandparent Information Center suggests grandparents might wish to form:

- a discussion group to provide emotional support;
- an educational group that invites teachers, lawyers, and social service workers to talk to members; or
- an advocacy group that works to find solutions to problems.

Many groups decide to have a mix of all three, as was the case with the group we interviewed. One grandparent talked about recruiting new members to the group:

When we get these children, our whole focus is behind that door. And sometimes it takes an act of God or dynamite or somebody just to pull you out of there. And you say, "Now wait a minute. It's not wrong to take two hours for yourself to talk to another adult." Sometimes you have to drag them. And say, "See, it's not going to hurt." It's not just another parent group or "here's another group we want you to meet with" or "come on, give us two hours of your time"; (it's that) there are other things that you have to do to get back on course.

This grandparent suggests that the daily sustenance of grandparents' spirits and the pattern breaking that is necessary to successfully raise grandchildren, as well as the access to information that will ease grandparents' attempts to secure resources, medical care, and other needs for their grandchildren, are facilitated by the emotional support, sharing of experience, and provision of educational programs by the group. Grandparents agreed with the suggestion that a network of grandparent support groups organized by the state would be useful. Such a network might help to make new grandparents aware of support groups in their area, assist brand-new groups, and promote networking among existing groups.

Advocacy is another important goal of the group we interviewed. They visited their congresspersons and other federal and state officials to advocate for better resources for grandparents. Financial aid is sorely needed. One grandmother said of the financial straits that rearing a second family had left her in:

> When grandparents . . . take on . . . raising their grandchildren, I'd like to see them get more financial support. . . . (When) I started raising my grandchildren, . . . I had retired, (and) we had all these plans about what we were going to do. I mean we had (paid off) the house. . . . (Now) we gotta (have) money for (the grandchildren's) clothes. We have to buy all their food. I used to sacrifice for my kids. . . . I am just starting all over again. I just went back to 37 years ago.

Another essential is a special custody status for grandparents. One respondent suggested an option for an "in-limbo" custody arrangement for grandparents awaiting guardianship or other formal custody arrangements and those who temporarily take custody for their grandchildren in hopes that their adult children will someday take back their responsibility. The special custody status could ease tensions that arise when grandparents confront the educational system, attempt to secure health care for their grandchildren, and request public housing and other services.

One of the projects the group currently seeks to pursue is respite care "because," one woman said, "even in wartime there is R&R."

> When I first started out, . . . my other children (were more willing to help out by taking the grandchildren) for the weekend. But this is (several) years later, and my other children don't want to hear it. (When I ask now, they have a ready excuse.) So my respite has been cut down to "I'm going to walk to the store, and take the *long* way around." If someone says . . . "I want to send you to the mountains for a week" I wouldn't have anybody to watch these kids.

Sending children down south (or elsewhere) to stay with grandparents for a few weeks in the summer has been a traditional form of respite for African-American parents who may or may not be able to gain access to quality camps or other summer programs. This option is obviously not open to custodial grandparents.

While the grandparents definitely need a break, they discussed their desire to have a "working" respite.

> But you do need respite, a serious amount of respite. Not just somewhere laying down but maybe even a respite workshop, a weekend of workshops teaching

grandparent skills (such as): How do you tell those children no? . . . How do you (find time to) take a (leisurely) bath (once in a while)? (Laughter and agreement from the other women.)

This grandmother also gave the example that she did not know how to teach her maturing granddaughter about the new feminine products available, and that a respite workshop would help her and others with this. Many grandparents in the room agreed with her.

Another need voiced was more education during a respite workshop or other times about the mental health of grandchildren.

I am finding out that mental health is an . . . issue I have been fighting for two years. Because my grandchildren are in a state of depression. Not because Grandma was depressing them. But there wasn't closure to some issues. We don't have time to think about, well, maybe three years ago I should have said something different. They need to have closure to their parents' taking care of them and us taking care of them, even when they are babies. The baby was (just a few) weeks old when I got him. And he still has closure issues. Some of the decisions I made about seeing your mom or going to see your dad may not have been the right thing. There are . . . issues that they still haven't dealt with. So there are a lot of issues that need to be addressed that we are not aware of.

This woman further suggested that a respite camp for the grandchildren in conjunction with the respite workshops might provide the children an outlet to deal with some of the emotional issues connected to their unusual parental circumstances, while at the same time providing much-needed child care so that grandparents could enjoy their time away from their daily responsibilities.

The final idea voiced by the grandparents was to create special housing for grandparent caretakers, a building or compound in which only grandparents and their grandchildren live that would include its own library, bus stop, health center, community center, and other resources. One grandparent thought that there might be models for such a place in other communities.

Discussion: Limits of Social Agency

Beginning to understand the mechanisms linking successful grandparenting to social context allows us to better understand the multiple factors associated with ways that grandparents adapt to their caretaking roles as well as the ways that their social agency is limited by institutional arrangements. Contextual variables such as legal and policy impediments must be taken into account in order to develop empirically based social theory on race, poverty, and the family.

Viewing mothering from a standpoint that considers how the multiple and connected inequalities of race, class, and gender shape the caretaking context (Collins 1994) is foundational to grandparents' descriptions of their goals for their grandchildren as well as their strategies to achieve those goals. Survival is one of the stated goals, given the embattled social location and family circumstances of some of the grandparents' families. Grandparents state that they use parenting strategies to protect their grandchildren, monitor them, seek resources for grand-children, and ensure their in-home learning (as delineated in Jarrett 1997). While structural forces that created impoverished neighborhoods mold grandparents' goals and strategies, grandparents do not simply accept that their caretaking can-not lead to successful outcomes for their grandchildren. They, as one grandparent stated, "do (their) best" to deliver health care, provide adequate shelter, educate, and otherwise care for the well-being of their grandchildren using every cultural resource at their disposal. Collins describes African-American caretaking as "motherwork" (1994). Grandparents' social agency is evident to the extent that they engage in motherwork, such as their involvement in the grandparents' sup-port group to obtain emotional support as well as to participate in advocacy.

While many grandparents recognized the social forces that influenced their adult children's drug abuse, grandparents were also self-reflective, wanting to in-terrogate their roles in creating their present family circumstances. This balance which considered both the macro- and microlevel influences on their lives and those of their children and grandchildren, is necessary intellectually. The won-derful result of this balance is that it stimulates action: grandparents exercising their social agency.

The frustrating aspect of grandparents' accounts is that even though they are powerful people who work hard at various levels to take care of their grandchil-dren, they are consistently challenged by institutional arrangements and indi-viduals' biases and lack of concern that potentially block their caretaking efforts. One grandmother said that in the course of her multiyear battle to achieve guardianship of her grandchildren, she had great difficulties obtaining Section 8 housing because bureaucrats considered her to be a single adult. An-other spoke of her struggles to obtain proper medical care for her grandchild with seizures. It was finally only luck, an emergency room doctor who decided to intercede on her behalf, that gave her grandchild access to a specialist. It appears that the more one focuses on these African-American, female, poor, and work-ing-class grandparents' social agency, the more one is struck with the structural limitations to that agency. Individual efforts can take grandparents only so far. Collective mobilization leading to social change is the only type of social agency that will achieve long-lasting results.

Hope for the Children

Creating a Community of Care for Foster Children

Community evolves as people develop a sense of being appreciated, of belonging, of deeply caring and being cared for. . . . Community is inspired by collaboration, sharing beliefs in the present and mutual hopes for the future. (Whitney 1995:200)

We are so blessed here at Hope Meadows. Everybody loves each other, and when the children go play outside, there is the attention and caring eyes of Mr. Beiderman, Mr. and Mrs. Saunders, Grandma Vera you know. They care for each other. And you won't be afraid that the children will be out there playing because you know that there are some pairs of eyes watching. And then when I go out just to clean the surroundings, there come the children: "Grandma, Grandma. Can I help you?" It's a family. It's a community. (Rafina, Hope senior)

Hope For The Children (Hope), a nonprofit child welfare agency, created a new intergenerational neighborhood model of care to support foster and adoptive children in Illinois. In this chapter we begin with a brief description of the crisis in foster care, both nationally and in Illinois. Then we describe how Hope provides one solution to this crisis by helping children caught in the system find care and continuity in a supportive community—Hope Meadows. Further, we examine how dimensions of care and community at Hope Meadows stop the discontinuity of people and place by enfolding children into networks of stable, caring intergenerational relationships.

The Foster Care Crisis

> Dwayne was born in May 1983. His mother had a long history with the State's Child Welfare Department dating back to the early 1970s. She had given birth to eight children (the first at age 13), all of whom were in foster care at some point during their lives. Dwayne, her sixth child, was placed in foster care at two years of age because of neglect. After this first stay in foster care he was returned to his mother's home. Shortly thereafter she was reported to the State for beating Dwayne with an extension cord, leaving bruises and welts. He was subsequently removed from her home and again placed in foster care. Dwayne had nine foster placements in seven years prior to coming to stay at Hope in December 1995. (Hope For The Children 1996)

Dwayne's experiences of discontinuity and disruption in foster care are all too typical. Lack of permanency and the resulting absence of care have consistently been major factors in the foster care crisis. The Adoption Assistance Act of 1980 (P.L. 96-272) emphasized the primacy of adoption in its call for permanency planning. According to Cole and Donley (1990:278), "Permanency planning refers to efforts to maintain a child's birthfamily whenever possible, to return a child to his birthfamily as soon as possible, and failing either, to establish for him legally permanent nurturant relationships with caring adults preferably through adoption." Unfortunately, the concept of "permanency planning" as it was established in the 1980s did not work. Neither the foster care system nor adoption placements met the needs of the growing numbers of children needing permanent homes. The National Commission on Family Foster Care explained that the child welfare system was not designed to serve the very troubled population of children that enters the system. It was built on the no-longer-valid premises that children needing care are primarily neglected and can be helped through love alone (cf. Power and Krause Eheart 1995), that sufficient numbers of families have a stay-at-home parent willing and able to care for these children, and that caseworkers have the time and skills to supervise these difficult placements (Child Welfare League of America 1991).

At the end of 1998 an estimated half a million children in the United States were in foster care (GAO Report 1998). Moreover, at least 110,000 children were waiting to be adopted. Typically these children had been abused or neglected, and 63 percent were six or older, with the average age being eight

(North American Council on Adoptable Children 1998). They belonged to a minority or sibling group, and often were medically, developmentally, or behaviorally challenged. These large numbers were the result of the growth of social problems such as poverty and the use of hard drugs (GAO Report 1998; Rosenthal and Groze 1992). In November 1997 the federal Adoption and Safe Families Act was passed by Congress to rectify the weaknesses of the 1980 adoption legislation and to move children more quickly into permanent, safe homes. This new legislation is resulting in more rapid and frequent termination of parental rights, suggesting that even greater numbers of children will be in need of permanent homes in the future (North American Council on Adoptable Children 1998).

The problem in Illinois mirrors the national crisis. According to Janet Key,

> It can take less than 48 hours to place an Illinois child — any child that a DCFS [Department of Children and Family Services] investigator finds at "serious risk of harm" in his or her birth family — into the state's child welfare bureaucracy. The trouble is . . . it can take years to get them out again — and many never make it, trapped in a Kafkaesque netherworld where approximately 33 percent of the children in DCFS foster care are neither adopted nor reunited with their parents." (1994:22)

What happens to these children? The shortage of trained foster parents has resulted in placing more children in each available home, moving children from one home to another, and often separating sibling groups to allow for placement. During fiscal year 1996, 48,964 Illinois children found themselves in substitute or foster care. They typically remained in care for 38.7 months, and during this time these children experienced a median of two placements (Institute for Government and Public Affairs 1996). Clearly, the Illinois child welfare system is not meeting the needs of these vulnerable children.

The low level of progress that has been made in reducing the number of children in foster care and the discontinuity they experience once in the system is not due to a lack of insight and knowledge about the components of effective programs. Experts agree that children need continuity, consistency, and predictability (Krause Eheart and Zimmerman 1998; American Academy of Pediatrics 1993). Every child needs at least one caring adult permanently present in his or her life, a supportive community, and stability and security. The challenge, then, is to apply what we already know — that sustained relationships, created through nurturing families and caring communities, are essential for the healthy development and well-being of children. Hope For The Children was designed to apply these principles to meeting the needs of children trapped in the Illinois child welfare system in the 1990s.

The Hope Model

> If it takes a village to raise a child, Hope Meadows may be just the kind of vil-
> lage it takes to raise a foster child. (Harris 1997)

Hope For The Children provides one solution to the child welfare crisis. A nonprofit child welfare agency, Hope attempts to enhance the well-being of foster
children by providing long-term support to nurturing, permanent families in an
intergenerational community that enfolds children into networks of caring relationships.

The Illinois legislature gave Hope $1 million in 1993 to transform housing on
the former Chanute Air Force Base in Rantoul into a community for foster children in need of permanent homes and specialized care. This community, located
on 22 acres, became known as "Hope Meadows." Thirteen spacious duplexes
were converted into single-family homes for families to raise biological, foster,
and adopted children. Intermingled among these homes are 44 three-bedroom
apartments for senior citizens. Living at Hope Meadows are 13 families, including 54 children of whom 44 are foster or adopted, 64 senior citizens, and key
staff. The parents, most of whom come from working-class backgrounds, are
both single and married, and all have a lifelong commitment to parenting. The seniors are also primarily working-class, both single and married, and have a mean
income of $1,000 a month. In addition, living at Hope Meadows are a therapist
and an administrative assistant. These residents represent diversity of age, race,
education, and social class. Their housing is clustered among expansive lawns,
commons, and a playground with an intergenerational activity center in the
heart of the neighborhood. Right down the street from the activity center is the
agency office. This neighborhood has been described as a

> comfortable and secluded middle-class suburban neighborhood of look-alike,
> bi-level brick homes. Children of all colors parade on bicycles, tricycles, and
> Roller-blades while an equally diverse mix of parents and elderly neighbors sit
> sentry in lawn chairs and on porch steps. (Smith 1999:117)

Core components of Hope's intergenerational neighborhood model include the
provision of child welfare services through a licensed agency, comprehensive assessment and evaluation of the children, adoption by parents within the program,
weekly parent training and ongoing support, on-site therapy and counseling for
all children and families, and a safe, geographically integrated, diverse community. The seniors receive below-market-rate rent in return for six hours a week of
volunteer work with Hope. Examples of volunteer work include tutoring, playing
games, providing child care, guarding school crossings, supervising the playground, and performing numerous other jobs. A principal contribution, how-

ever, lies in the seniors simply becoming a part of the community — their being there, lending an ear, and sharing their wisdom and insight with both the children and the parents. The final component is monetary support for parents. The Hope families receive a large, six- or seven-bedroom home rent free, and $19,000 a year for one of the parents to stay home and be a full-time mom or dad raising up to four children from the foster care system. Through applying these components, Hope developed an intergenerational community where relationships between children and adults have the opportunity to flourish. Given the diversity of residents' backgrounds, this is remarkable. Consider the following examples:

> Stan, a new staff member, had just moved to Hope Meadows. Mark, age seven, came over, looked around, and asked, "You're just moving in, huh?" Stan replied yes and answered several other of Mark's questions. Then Mark asked Stan if he had any children. Stan told him no, but said his wife was going to have a baby in a month. To Stan's amazement Mark then asked, "Are you going to keep it when you have it?"

Clearly this child's experiences were significantly different from Stan's or those of a child who had never known loss, separation, or abandonment. Helen's experiences also illustrate diversity of backgrounds:

> There were no black people where I grew up, absolutely none. I never had much to do with black people till I moved up here to Hope Meadows. I never thought I would love and kiss and hug a black baby, 'cause let's face it, in Basym there's a lot of prejudice people. There's no color difference up here. . . . I never thought we'd be godparents to a little black baby, and now we have Javal. We even went with his family to his adoption.

Ideally, a community is a place "where many races, socio-economic levels and age groups interact and build meaningful relationships [where] everyone in the community is accepted and treated as a valuable, integral member" (Jarman and Land 1995:22). Hope For The Children is working to create such a community at Hope Meadows; it is working to create a community of care.

Care

> I don't think you can put on with children — you can't put on airs at all. There's a saying I read once that applies to children. It says, "People don't care how much you know, until they know how much you care." Children are not interested in what you know, how much you know, but really how much you care. (Jim, Hope senior)

Caring is a relational act (Gilligan 1982, 1988; Brown and Gilligan 1991; Tronto 1993). A caring relationship involves an interaction between two human beings — the caring one or care worker and the cared-for or recipient of care (Noddings 1984, 1992). The care worker really hears, sees, and feels what the cared-for conveys and then becomes involved in thinking, planning, and doing what can be done to help (Noddings 1992). Caring is directed toward the welfare, protection, or enhancement of the cared-for, often with both the cared-for and care worker benefiting from the relationship (Noddings 1984; Gordon, Benner, and Noddings 1996; Gilligan 1988). Noddings argues that we have a deep and natural desire to be in caring relationships and these caring relationships form circles of love and protection within which we are sheltered from harm. "We want to be cared for — loved in the inner circle, recognized and respected in a somewhat larger circle, and at least safe to move about in huge impersonal circles" (1992:117). The social networks at Hope Meadows form circles of care that protect Hope families and provide a safe place where residents can thrive. Within these circles of care, it is not always clear who is the one being cared for and who is the care worker — all benefit. In testimony before the Illinois Appropriations Human Services Committee on March 20, 1998, Jim Saunders illustrated this relationship as he spoke about Hope.

> We have been [at Hope For The Children] for almost four years. . . .We had retired, and we were undecided as to what we wanted to do. You get to a point in your life, you know you feel like, "Well, I am used up. Nothing's left." But then we got involved with Hope. . . . It's so gratifying to see the changes in these children and to feel like we have a part in that. We see the children come in and realize the needs they have. They are so hungry for love and attention. And then we give this to them. And it is so rewarding. I know the primary focus is on the children, but they also make us feel so good because they are concerned about us. I can hardly step outdoors without one of the children asking, "How is Grandma Mary [Saunders's wife] doing? Is she feeling OK?" And they are real concerned. One time we were getting ready to go away for a weekend, and this young man was concerned about where we were going, when we were coming back, and we told him. He said, "I'll watch your house for you." Things like that really make you feel a part of something. I know we use the term *surrogate* grandparents, but I feel like I am more of a member of the family, really. Because these children are closer to me than my own grandchildren or great grandchildren 'cause I see them every day, and I get more involved with them.

As Jim Saunders's testimony illustrates, caring at Hope Meadows is a relational act. Here the old and the young take turns being the care worker and the cared-for with both benefiting from the relationship. The seniors care for the children, and the children care for the seniors.

Caring is also a moral act (Gilligan, Ward, and Taylor 1988; Noddings 1984, 1992; Gordon, Benner, and Noddings 1996; Tronto 1993). Gilligan writes, "The activities of care—being there, listening, the willingness to help, the ability to understand—take on a moral dimension, reflecting the moral injunction to pay attention, and not to turn away from need" (1988:16). Being there requires presence, attentiveness, and responsiveness. Presence is being physically, socially, emotionally, and spiritually available. The care worker must be present before he or she can be attentive or respond. Being attentive recognizes the needs of those around us and demonstrates that others matter (Benner and Wrubel 1989; Tronto 1993). Attention is the act of an active moral agent (Murdoch 1970:34), making care possible. If we do not recognize needs, we cannot address them; we become unresponsive, which signals a failure to care—a moral failure (Gilligan 1988).

A caring commitment is implemented through listening and being listened to and responding and being responded to (Brown and Gilligan 1991); this is the beginning of dialogue. For dialogue to be caring, it also has to involve talk that is "open, honest, spontaneous, easy to do, and frequent" (Tarlow 1996:63–65). It is talk "in which partially formed thoughts and strong feelings can be expressed and heard" (Brown and Gilligan 1991:54). A failure to listen precludes talk and a failure to talk precludes responding to need, making care as a moral act impossible.

Erich Fromm notes that care is interdependent with responsibility, respect, and knowledge (1956:27). Care is furthered by a sense of responsibility or the voluntary response to the needs of another—care is furthered by the willingness to help. This willingness to help is enhanced by respect. Respect is not possible without knowledge that enables one to understand another's unique individuality. "Care and responsibility would be blind if they were not guided by knowledge. Knowledge would be empty if it were not motivated by concern" (Fromm 1956:24). Hope Meadows is a community in which responsibility, respect, and knowledge support the moral injunction to care.

Irene, a Hope senior and former nun, tells the following story of caring as a moral act:

One of the first times Jerome [age 5] came over he asked, "You live alone, don't you?" and I said, "Yes I do." He asked, "Where *is* he?" I said, "Honey, he died." He then asked, "Did you kill him?" and I said, "No." "Did he get real sick?" And I said, "Yes he did." He said, "Do you miss him?" I said, "Yes." "Do you cry?" I said, "Yes." He then said, "I'll be your man." And he went home, called me back, and said, "I'm coming over, and I'm bringing my suitcase. You don't have a man in the house, and you need one." . . . Listening is so important because, if nothing else, down the road, when these children get older, they'll know that there *is* an older person who will listen to them. . . . Sometimes I go to bed, and I think, "Oh Lord, if I could just do more," but you can just do so much. I've done more charity work out here than I ever did in 27 years in my habit. I mean it!

One wonders what this child's prior experiences must have been for him to ask if Irene had killed her husband. The care and concern he showed, nonetheless, were exceptional for such a young child. He saw her need to have a man in the house and responded by offering to come, while she recognized his need to be listened to and responded with open and honest respect. Both demonstrate the moral act of caring.

Community

> To be caring of one another provides witness to the sense of community, and of one's identity as a part of it. Caring demonstrated, is yet one more instance of an acknowledgment of and respect for the meaning of the group. Caring can and does spread throughout the community, perhaps stopping here, but passing on to another there. (Tarlow 1996:81)

A community provides the context in which care is manifested (Benson 1997; McKnight 1995; Noddings 1992). Communities have a shared vision (Benson 1997; Peck 1987), are place-based (Chaskin 1997), and involve a network of social relationships (Paul 1995; Peck 1987). According to John Gardner, a community provides "security, a sense of identity and belonging, a framework of shared assumptions and values, a network of caring individuals, the experience of being needed . . . and responding to need" (cited in Schorr 1997:362). He notes that of all the components of community, shared values are possibly the most important (Gardner 1995). Similarly, Benson writes, "The vision of a healthy community focuses on creating a normative culture in which adults, organizations, and community institutions unite to take action guided by a shared vision" (1997:2). Hope's vision (to enhance foster children's well-being within a caring community) ensures that the children are not seen as "vectors of needs to be properly targeted for services, but as ordinary kids requiring the same embeddedness in family and community that we would want for our own biological children" (Hopping 1998:4). At the core of this vision is John Dewey's mandate, "What the best and wisest parent wants for his own child, that must the community want for all its children" (1902:3). The community of Hope Meadows, guided by this vision, works to embed all of the residents into networks of caring relationships.

> I think the reason people become close here is because of the love for the children and the caring for each other and what each other is trying to do—the seniors caring for the families and what they are trying to do with the children, and the families caring for the seniors because they know we are trying to help them in any way that we can. They know the seniors are here for them, and the seniors know that if we need help, there is a family here for us too. Everyone believes in the Hope program, and that's why we are living here. You have to

love the children and what everybody is trying to do for the children. If you don't have that, you are in the wrong place. (Bill, Hope senior)

Hope's vision is supported by the physical structure of Hope Meadows. The physical proximity of the homes, apartments, and office buildings at Hope encourages interactions between seniors, parents, children, and staff. The meandering sidewalks and commons areas, complete with a neighborhood playground, offer residents the opportunity for chance as well as planned encounters where all members, young and old, come together to talk and listen, to have fun and help, and to just be there together. The density of acquaintances (Chaskin 1997) allows residents to participate in the act of caring. According to Hopping (1998), the physical structure provides the seniors a safe place to live and a purpose for living, the parents the extra help and support they need to provide love and protection for at-risk children, and the children a caring and permanent place to live. In addition, the physical proximity of neighbors at Hope ensures the potential for a rapid caring response to need, especially in times of crisis. Many of us may be able to depend on one or two neighbors, but few can depend on an entire community to care in times of crisis as well as during routine daily encounters.

Last summer my husband was in the hospital for 53 days. When he was in the hospital for so long like that, I was not afraid because everybody watched out for me. I figured if somebody broke in, I could scream loud enough that they'd hear me — if I wasn't too afraid. My neighbors watch after us and when we go on vacation they'll get our mail for us. Just about anybody out here, if I was to call and I needed help, they would be here in a minute, and I would do the same for them. (Helen, Hope senior)

The purposeful integration of the physical dimensions of Hope Meadows provides the context for the social dimensions of a caring community. Gardner describes the social dimension of a "good" community as one where members

deal with one another humanely, respect individual differences and value the integrity of each person. A good community fosters an atmosphere of cooperation and connectedness . . . and an awareness by the members that they need one another. There is a sense of belonging and identity, a spirit of mutual responsibility. (1995:294)

Healthy communities need caring individuals (Benson 1997; McKnight 1995; Schorr 1997). This care cannot be manufactured, bought, or paid for (Benson 1997; McKnight 1995). As McKnight (1995:167) observed, "While a managed system organized as a structure of control can deliver a service, it cannot deliver care. Care is a special relationship characterized by consent rather than control. . . . For those who need care, we must recognize the community as the appropriate social tool." In Hope's community, this special relationship is achieved in large measure by the Hope staff purposefully refraining from micromanaging the lives of the residents. For example, children are not matched to seniors or seniors to families. Hopping writes that this "generally allows copious space for the community to invent itself and unfold in its own way" (1998:5). As this community unfolds and invents itself it continually looks to Hope's vision for guidance and purpose, to the neighborhood for a sense of security, identity, and belonging, and to itself for support through caring relationships.

Conclusion

Hope For The Children, in creating a community of care for foster children, is attempting to give children like Dwayne a childhood—a childhood filled with laughter, a sense of security and of belonging, continuity, and hope, not one filled with hurt, despair, multiple moves, and lack of trust. People as diverse as Father James Harvey, a New York City priest, and Albert J. Solnit, a Yale University child psychiatrist, maintain that all children need good memories of their past. According to Solnit, they need "a useful and self-respecting past, one that gives him or her a sound sense of self-worth and of a future worth anticipating" (cited in Schorr 1988:140–41). Over the past four years, Hope Meadows has been providing troubled children with such a past. Inspired by a vision of enhancing children's well-being by enfolding them into networks of stable, caring, intergenerational relationships, Hope Meadows has evolved into a community of care. Here care is promoted by the physical and social dimensions of the neighborhood, and is demonstrated daily as a relational and moral act. Here, residents, inspired by each other and Hope's vision, share a spirit of mutual responsibility for each other in the present and mutual hopes for the future. Perhaps Effie, a Hope senior, said it best: "There's a type of caring here that these children will remember when their children come along. The sharing, and the giving, and the concern, and the love, the support, and the safety."

To provide a community of care for children in the present, so they will have the memories to create this in their own lives in the future, may be the greatest gift we can give them. For children caught in the foster care crisis, this may be their only hope for developing a sense of self-worth in the present and a future worth anticipating. This is the strongest possible argument for Hope's model of a community of care for foster children.

Part I

Abel, Emily, and Margaret Nelson. 1990. *Circles of Care: Work and Identity in Women's Lives*. Albany: State University of New York Press.
Hooyman, Nancy, and Judith Gonyea. 1995. *Feminist Perspectives on Family Care: Politics for Gender Justice*. Thousand Oaks, CA: Sage.

Chapter 2

Abel, Emily K. In press. *Hearts of Wisdom: American Women Caring for Kin: 1850–1940* Cambridge, MA: Harvard University Press.
Abel, Emily K. 1991. *Who Cares for the Elderly? Public Policy and the Experiences of Adult Daughters*. Philadelphia: Temple University Press.
Arpad, Susan S. (ed.). 1984. *Sam Curd's Diary, The Diary of a True Woman*. Athens, OH: Ohio University Press.
Baker, S. Josephine. 1939. *Fighting for Life*. New York: Macmillan.
Borst, Charlotte G. 1995. *Catching Babies: The Professionalization of Childbirth, 1870–1920*. Cambridge, MA: Harvard University Press.
C.E. 1907. Letter to Lawrence Flick, July 4. Flick Papers. Washington, DC: Catholic University (unpublished).
C.R.S. 1938. Letter to Eleanor Roosevelt, August. Records of the Children's Bureau, record group 102, file 4–9–1–1. Washington, DC: National Archives (unpublished).
Cheney, Ednah D. (ed.). 1892. *Louisa May Alcott: Her Life, Letters, and Journals*. Boston: Roberts Brothers.
Community Service Society. 1888–1918. Case files. New York: Rare Book and Manuscript, Butler Library, Columbia University (unpublished).
Dickson, A. J. 1916. "Social Service in Relation to Contagious Disease Hospitals," *Monthly Bulletin of the Department of Health*, 6:19–20.
Erion, Luella M. 1921. "Francesco of Arizona," *Public Health Nurse*, 13(4):177.
Fraser, Gertrude Jacinta. 1998. *African American Midwifery in the South: Dialogues of Birth, Race, and Memory*. Cambridge, MA: Harvard University Press.
Glenn, Evelyn Nakano. 1986. *Issei, Nisei, War Bride: Three Generations of Japanese American Women in Domestic Service*. Philadephia: Temple University Press.
Glenn, Evelyn Nakano. 1992. "From Servitude to Service Work: Historical Continuities in the Racial Division of Paid Reproductive Labor," *Signs: Journal of Women in Culture and Society*, 18:1–43.
Hedrick, Joan D. 1994. *Harriet Beecher Stowe, A Life*. New York: Oxford University Press.

Hunter, Tera W. 1997. *To 'Joy My Freedom: Southern Black Women's Lives and Labors after the Civil War*. Cambridge, MA: Harvard University Press.

Johnson, Charles Beneulyn. 1926. *Sixty Years in Medical Harness or The Story of a Long Medical Life, 1865–1925*. New York: Medical Life Press.

Marks, Nadine F. 1996. "Caregiving Across the Lifespan: National Prevalence and Predictors," *Family Relations*, 45(1):27.

Massachusetts General Hospital. 1918. "Report of the Social Service Department," *Annual Report*. Boston.

Meckel, Richard A. 1990. *Save the Babies: American Public Health Reform and the Prevention of Infant Mortality*. Baltimore, MD: Johns Hopkins University Press.

New York Society for the Relief of the Ruptured and Crippled. 1918. "Report of the Social Service Out-Patient Department of New York," *Annual Report*. New York: New York Academy of Medicine.

Palmer, Phyllis. 1989. *Domesticity and Dirt: Housewives and Domestic Servants in the United States, 1920–1945*. Philadelphia: Temple University Press.

Peter Brent Brigham Hospital. 1931. "Report of the Social Service Department," *Seventh Annual Report for the Year 1930*. Boston.

Rawick, George P. 1972. *The American Slave: A Composite Autobiography. North Carolina Narratives*, 15. Westport, CT: Greenwood Press.

Reverby, Susan M. 1987. *Ordered to Care: The Dilemma of American Nursing 1850–1945*. New York: Cambridge University Press.

Rosner, David. 1982. *A Once Charitable Enterprise: Hospitals and Health Care in Brooklyn and New York, 1885–1915*. Princeton, NJ: Princeton University Press.

Rothstein, William G. 1985. *American Physicians in the Nineteenth Century: From Sects to Science*. Baltimore, MD: Johns Hopkins University Press.

Rosenberg, Charles E. 1985. "The Therapeutic Revolution: Medicine, Meaning, and Social Change in Nineteenth-Century America." In Judith Walzer Leavitt and Ronald L. Numbers (eds.), *Sickness and Health in America: Readings in the History of Medicine and Public Health*. Madison: University of Wisconsin Press, pp. 39–52.

Rosenberg, Charles E. 1987. *The Care of Strangers: The Rise of America's Hospital System*. New York: Basic Books.

Savitt, Todd. 1978. *Medicine and Slavery: The Diseases and Health Care of Blacks in Antebellum Virginia*. Urbana: University of Illinois Press.

Starr, Paul. 1982. *The Social Transformation of American Medicine: The Rise of a Sovereign Profession and the Making of a Vast Industry*. New York: Basic Books.

Webber, Eliza. 1863. Letter to "Parents," July 22. Parker Family Letters, in the possession of Marianne Parker Brown, Los Angeles (unpublished).

Chapter 3

Support for this research was provided by the Academic Senate of the University of California, Riverside, the UCR Center for Social and Behavioral Science Research, and the UCR Center for Family Studies. We thank Ross Parke and Michele Adams for collaborative work on related fatherhood projects; Madonna Harrington Meyer and Pam Herd for helpful comments on earlier chapter drafts; and Francesca Cancian, Demie Kurz, Sonya Michel, and Madonna Harrington Meyer for organizing the conference.

Abel, Emily K., and Margaret K. Nelson (eds.). 1990. *Circles of Care: Work and Identity in Women's Lives*. Albany, NY: State University of New York Press.

Ariès, Philippe. 1962. *Centuries of Childhood*. New York: Random House.

Barnett, Rosalind C., and Yu C. Shen. 1997. "Gender, High- and Low-Schedule Control Housework Tasks, and Psychological Distress: A Study of Dual-Earner Couples," *Journal of Family Issues*, 18:403–28.

Bernard, Jessie. 1981. "The Good-Provider Role: Its Rise and Fall," *American Psychologist*, 36:1–12.

Bird, Chloe, and Catherine Ross. 1993. "Houseworkers and Paid Workers: Qualities of the Work and Effects on Personal Control," *Journal of Marriage and the Family*, 55:913–25.

Blair, Sampson L., and Daniel T. Lichter. 1991. "Measuring the Division of Household Labor: Gender Segregation of Housework among American Couples," *Journal of Family Issues*, 12:91–113.

Blankenhorn, David. 1995. *Fatherless America: Confronting Our Most Urgent Social Problem*. New York: Basic Books.

Cancian, Francesca M. 1987. *Love in America: Gender and Self-Development*. New York: Cambridge University Press.

Cancian, Francesca M., and Stacey J. Oliker. 1999. *Caring and Gender*. Newbury Park, CA: Pine Forge Press.

Coltrane, Scott. 1988. "Father-child Relationships and the Status of Women." *American Journal of Sociology*, 93:1060–95.

Coltrane, Scott. 1989. "Household Labor and the Routine Production of Gender," *Social Problems*, 36:473–90.

Coltrane, Scott. 1996. *Family Man: Fatherhood, Housework, and Gender Equity*. New York: Oxford University Press.

Coltrane, Scott. 1998. *Gender and Families*. Newbury Park, CA: Pine Forge Press.

Coltrane, Scott. 2000. "Research on Household Labor: Modeling and Measuring the Social Embeddedness of Routine Family Work," *Journal of Marriage and the Family* 62 (4).

Coltrane, Scott, and Michele Adams. In press. "What Should We Expect From Fathers? Gender, Child Centered Parenting, and the Division of Family Work." In Rosanna Hertz and Nancy Marshall (eds.), *Work and Family: Today's Realities and Tomorrow's Visions*. Berkeley, CA: University of California Press.

Coltrane, Scott, and Kenneth Allan. 1994. " 'New' Fathers and Old Stereotypes: Representations of Masculinity in 1980s Television Advertising," *Masculinities*, 2:43–66.

Coltrane, Scott, and Neal Hickman. 1992. "The Rhetoric of Rights and Needs: Moral Discourse in the Reform of Child Custody and Child Support Laws," *Social Problems*, 39:400–420.

Coltrane, Scott, and Ross D. Parke. 1998. "Reinventing Fatherhood: Toward an Historical Understanding of Continuity and Change in Men's Family Lives," Working Paper #98–12A. Philadelphia, PA: National Center on Fathers and Families.

Connell, Robert W. 1987. *Gender and Power: Society, the Person, and Sexual Politics*. Stanford, CA: Stanford University Press.

Coolsen, Peter. 1993. "Half Full or Half Empty?" *Families in Society: The Journal of Contemporary Human Services*, 74:3.

Coontz, Stephanie. 1992. *The Way We Never Were*. New York: Basic Books.

Cowan, Carolyn P., and Phillip A. Cowan. 1992. *When Partners Become Parents*. New York: Basic Books.

Davidoff, Lenore, and Catherine Hall. 1987. *Family Fortunes: Men and Women of the English Middle Class, 1780–1850*. Chicago: University of Chicago Press.

Day, Randal D., and Wade C. Mackey. 1986. "The Role Image of the American Father: An Examination of a Media Myth," *Journal of Comparative Family Studies*, 17:371–88.

Degler, Carl N. 1980. *At Odds: Women and the Family in America from the Revolution to the Present*. New York: Oxford University Press.

Demo, David H., and Alan C. Acock. 1993. "Family Diversity and the Division of Domestic Labor: How Much Have Things Really Changed?" *Family Relations*, 42:323–31.

Demos, John. 1982. "The Changing Faces of Fatherhood." In Stanley Cath, Alan Gurwitt, and John Ross (eds.), *Father and Child: Developmental and Clinical Perspectives*. Boston: Little, Brown.

Demos, John. 1986. *Past, Present, and Personal: The Family and the Life Course in American History*. New York: Oxford University Press.

Dill, Bonnie T. 1994. *Across the Boundaries of Race and Class*. New York: Garland.

Doherty, William J. 1991. "Beyond Reactivity and the Deficit Model of Manhood," *Journal of Marital and Family Therapy*, 17:29–32.

Doherty, William J. 1997. "The Best of Times and the Worst of Times: Fathering as a Contested Arena of Academic Discourse." In Alan J. Hawkins and David C. Dollahite (eds.), *Generative Fathering: Beyond Deficit Perspectives*. Thousand Oaks, CA: Sage, pp. 217–27.

Doherty, William J., Edward F. Kouneski, and Martha F. Erickson. 1998. "Responsible Fathering: An Overview and Conceptual Framework," *Journal of Marriage and the Family*, 60:277–92.

Ehrensaft, Diane. 1987. *Parenting Together*. New York: Free Press.

Federal Interagency Forum on Child and Family Statistics. 1998. Nurturing Fatherhood: Improving Data and Research on Male Fertility, Family Formation and Fatherhood. Washington, DC: Government Printing Office.

Fein, Robert A. 1978. "Research on Fathering: Social Policy and an Emergent Perspective," *Journal of Social Issues*, 34:122–35.

Ferree, Myra M. 1990. "Beyond Separate Spheres: Feminism and Family Research," *Journal of Marriage and the Family*, 52:866–84.

Finch, Janet, and Dulcie Groves (eds.). 1983. *A Labour of Love: Women, Work, and Caring*. London: Routledge and Kegan Paul.

Glenn, Evelyn N. 1992. "From Servitude to Service Work: Historical Continuities in the Racial Division of Paid Reproductive Labor," *Signs*, 18:1–43.

Glenn, Norval. 1997. *Closed Hearts, Closed Minds: The Textbook Story of Marriage*. New York: Institute for American Values.

Goode, William J. 1992. "Why Men Resist." In Barrie Thorne with Marilyn Yalom (eds.), *Rethinking the Family*. Boston: Northeastern University Press, pp. 287–310.

Greenstein, Theodore N. 1996. "Gender Ideology and Perceptions of the Fairness of the Division of Household Labor: Effects on Marital Quality," *Social Forces*, 74:1029–42.

Griswold, Robert L. 1993. *Fatherhood in America: A History*. New York: Basic Books.

Griswold, Robert L. 1997. "Generative Fathering: A Historical Perspective." In Alan J. Hawkins and David C. Dollahite (eds.), *Generative Fathering: Beyond Deficit Perspectives*. Thousand Oaks, CA: Sage, pp. 71–86.

Hareven, Tamara K. 1991. "The Home and the Family in Historical Perspective," *Social Research*, 58:253–85.

Hawkins, Alan J., and David C. Dollahite. 1997. "Beyond the Role-Inadequacy Perspective of Fathering." In Alan J. Hawkins and David C. Dollahite (eds.), *Generative Fathering: Beyond Deficit Perspectives*. Thousand Oaks, CA: Sage, pp. 3–16.

Herdt, Gilbert H. 1981. *Guardians of the Flutes: Idioms of Masculinity*. New York: McGraw-Hill.

Hersch, Joni, and Leslie S. Stratton. 1994. "Housework, Wages, and the Division of Housework Time for Employed Spouses," *American Economic Review*, 84:120–25.

Hochschild, Arlie, with Anne Machung. 1989. *The Second Shift*. New York: Viking.

Hood, Jane C. 1986. "The Provider Role: Its Meaning and Measurement," *Journal of Marriage and the Family*, 48:349–59.

Jackson, Stevi. 1992. "Towards a Historical Sociology of Housework: A Materialist Feminist Analysis," *Women's Studies International Forum*, 15:153–72.

Johnson, Elizabeth M., and Ted L. Huston. 1998. "The Perils of Love, or Why Wives Adapt to Husbands during the Transition to Parenthood," *Journal of Marriage and the Family*, 60:195–204.

Johnson, Miriam M. 1988. *Strong Mothers, Weak Wives: The Search for Gender Equality*. Berkeley, CA: University of California Press.

Kimmel, Michael. 1996. *Manhood in America: A Cultural History*. New York: Free Press.

Lamb, Michael E. 1976. *The Role of the Father in Child Development*. New York: Wiley.

Laquer, Thomas. 1992. "The Facts of Fatherhood." In Barrie Thorne and Marilyn Yalom (eds.), *Rethinking the Family*. Boston: Northeastern University Press.

LaRossa, Ralph. 1988. "Fatherhood and Social Change," *Family Relations*, 37:451–57.

LaRossa, Ralph. 1996. *The Modernization of Fatherhood: A Social and Political History*. Chicago: University of Chicago Press.

LaRossa, Ralph, and Maureen M. LaRossa. 1981. *Transition to Parenthood: How Infants Change Families*. Beverly Hills, CA: Sage.

Lasch, Christopher. 1977. *Haven in a Heartless World*. New York: Basic Books.

Laslett, Barbara, and Johanna Brenner. 1989. "Gender and Social Reproduction: Historical Perspectives," *Annual Review of Sociology*, 15: 381–404.

Levine, James A., and Todd L. Pittinsky. 1997. *Working Fathers: New Strategies for Balancing Work and Family*. New York: Harcourt Brace.

Lorber, Judith. 1994. *Paradoxes of Gender*. New Haven, CT: Yale University Press.

MacDermid, Shelley M., Ted L. Huston, and Susan M. McHale. 1990. "Changes in Marriage Associated with the Transition to Parenthood: Individual Differences as a Function of Sex-Role Attitudes and Changes in the Division of Household Labor," *Journal of Marriage and the Family*, 52:475–86.

Marsh, Margaret. 1988. "Suburban Men and Masculine Domesticity, 1870–1915," *American Quarterly*, 40:165–86.

McBride, Brent A. 1990. "The Effects of a Parent Education/Play Group Program on Father Involvement on Child Rearing," *Family Relations*, 39:250–56.

McDaniel, Antonio. 1994. "Historical Racial Differences in Living Arrangements of Children," *Journal of Family History*, 19:57–77.

Mead, Margaret. 1949. *Male and Female*. New York: Morrow.

Mintz, Steven. 1998. "From Patriarchy to Androgyny and Other Myths: Placing Men's Family Roles in Historical Perspective." In Alan Booth and Ann C. Crouter (eds.), *Men in Families*. Mahwah, NJ: Erlbaum, pp. 3–30.

Muir, Frank, and Simon Brett. 1980. *On Children*. London: Heinemann.

Nock, Steven L. 1998. *Marriage in Men's Lives*. New York: Oxford University Press.

O'Connell, Martin. 1994. *Where's Papa: Fathers' Role in Child Care*. Washington, DC: Population Reference Bureau.

Palkovitz, Rob. 1997. "Reconstructing 'Involvement': Expanding Conceptualizations of Men's Caring in Contemporary Families." In Alan J. Hawkins and David C. Dollahite (eds.), *Generative Fathering: Beyond Deficit Perspectives*. Thousand Oaks, CA: Sage, pp. 200–216.

Palm, Glen. 1997. "Promoting Generative Fathering through Parent and Family Education." In Alan J. Hawkins and David C. Dollahite (eds.), *Generative Fathering: Beyond Deficit Perspectives*. Thousand Oaks, CA: Sage, pp. 167–82.

Parke, Ross D. 1981. *Fathers*. Cambridge, MA: Harvard University Press.

Parke, Ross D. 1995. "Fathers and Families." In Marc H. Bornstein (ed.), *Handbook of Parenting*, vol. 3. Hillsdale, NJ: Erlbaum, pp. 27–63.

Parke, Ross D. 1996. *Fatherhood*. Cambridge, MA: Harvard University Press.

Parke, Ross D. 1999. "Father Involvement: A Developmental Psychological Perspective," *Marriage and Family Review*.

Parke, Ross D., and Peter N. Stearns. 1993. "Fathers and Child Rearing." In Glen H. Elder, John Modell, and Ross D. Parke, *Children in Time and Place: Developmental and Historical Insights*. New York: Cambridge University Press, pp. 147–70.

Pleck, Joseph H. 1983. "Husbands' Paid Work and Family Roles: Current Research Issues." In Helena Z. Lopata and Joseph H. Pleck (eds.), *Research in the Interweave of Social Roles, Vol. 3: Families and Jobs*. Greenwich, CT: JAI, pp. 251–333.

Pleck, Joseph H. 1987. "American Fathering in Historical Perspective." In Michael Kimmel (ed.), *Changing Men*. Newbury Park, CA: Sage, pp. 83–97.

Pleck, Joseph H. 1997. "Paternal Involvement: Levels, Sources, and Consequences." In Michael E. Lamb (ed.), *The Role of the Father in Child Development*. 3rd edition. New York: John Wiley & Sons.

Pollock, Linda A. 1983. *Forgotten Children: Parent-Child Relations from 1500–1900*. Cambridge, MA: Cambridge University Press.

Pollock, Linda A. 1987. *A Lasting Relationship: Parents and Children Over Three Centuries*. London: Fourth Estate.

Popenoe, David. 1996. *Life Without Father: Compelling New Evidence That Fatherhood and Marriage are Indispensable for the Good of Children and Society*. New York: Martin Kessler/Free Press.

Presser, Harriet B. 1994. "Employment Schedules among Dual-Earner Spouses and the Division of Household Labor by Gender," *American Sociological Review*, 59:348–64.

Pruett, Kyle D. 1987. *The Nurturing Father*. New York: Warner Books.

Pruett, Kyle D. 1993. "The Paternal Presence," *Families in Society*, 74:46–50.

Radin, Norma. 1994. "Primary-Caregiving Fathers in Intact Families." In Adele Gottfried and Allen W. Gottfried (eds.), *Redefining Families: Implications for Children's Development*. New York: Plenum Press, pp. 55–97.

Reskin, Barbara F., and Irene Padavic. 1994. *Women and Men at Work*. Thousand Oaks, CA: Pine Forge Press.

Risman, Barbara J., and Danette Johnson-Sumerford. 1998. "Doing It Fairly: A Study of Postgender Marriages," *Journal of Marriage and the Family*, 60:23–40.

Robinson, John P., and Geoffrey Godbey. 1997. *Time for Life: The Surprising Ways That Americans Use Time*. University Park, PA: Pennsylvania State University Press.

Rollins, Judith. 1985. *Between Women: Domestics and Their Employers*. Philadelphia: Temple University Press.

Romero, Mary. 1992. *Maid in the USA*. New York: Routledge.

Rosaldo, Michelle Z. 1980. "The Use and Abuse of Anthropology," *Signs*, 5:389–417.

Rothman, Barbara Katz. 1989. *Recreating Motherhood: Ideology and Technology in a Patriarchal Society*. New York: Norton.

Rotundo, Anthony E. 1993. *American Manhood*. New York: Basic Books.

Rubin, Lillian B. 1976. *Worlds of Pain: Life in the Working Class Family*. New York: Basic Books.

Russell, Graeme. 1983. *The Changing Role of Fathers*. St. Lucia, Queensland: University of Queensland Press.

Ryan, Mary P. 1981. *The Cradle of the Middle Class*. Cambridge, UK: Cambridge University Press.

Sanchez, Laura, and Elizabeth Thomson. 1997. "Becoming Mothers and Fathers: Parenthood, Gender, and the Division of Labor," *Gender and Society*, 11:747–72.

Sanday, Peggy R. 1981. *Female Power and Male Dominance: On the Origins of Sexual Inequality*. Cambridge, UK: Cambridge University Press.

Sattel, Jack W. 1998. "The Inexpressive Male." In *Men's Lives*. Boston: Allyn and Bacon, pp. 423–30.

Schor, Juliet. 1991. *The Overworked American*. New York: Basic Books.

Shelton, Beth A. 1992. *Women, Men, Time*. New York: Greenwood.

Shelton, Beth A., and Daphne John. 1996. "The Division of Household Labor," *Annual Review of Sociology, 22: 299–322*.

Shorter, Edward. 1975. *The Making of the Modern Family*. New York: Basic Books.

Skolnick, Arlene. 1991. *Embattled Paradise: The American Family in an Age of Uncertainty*. New York: Basic Books.

Smith, Dorothy E. 1993. "The Standard North American Family: SNAF as an Ideological Code," *Journal of Family Issues*, 14:50–65.

Spain, Daphne. 1992. *Gendered Spaces*. Chapel Hill, NC: University of North Carolina Press.

Stacey, Judith. 1996. *In the Name of the Family: Rethinking Family Values in the Postmodern Age*. Boston: Beacon.

Straus, Murray A. 1994. *Beating the Devil Out of Them: Corporal Punishment in American Families*. San Francisco: Jossey-Bass.

Suitor, J. Jill. 1981. "Husbands' Participation in Childbirth: A Nineteenth Century Phenomenon," *Journal of Family History*, 6:278–93.

Synnott, Anthony. 1983. "Little Angels, Little Devils: A Sociology of Children," *Canadian Review of Sociology and Anthropology*, 20:79–95.

Thompson, Linda. 1993. "Conceptualizing Gender in Marriage: The Case of Marital Care," *Journal of Marriage and the Family*, 5:557–69.

Thompson, Linda, and Alexis J. Walker. 1989. "Gender in Families: Women and Men in Marriage, Work, and Parenthood," *Journal of Marriage and the Family*, 51:845–71.

Tiffany, Sharon W. 1982. *Women, Work, and Motherhood*. Englewood Cliffs, NJ: Prentice Hall.

Tocqueville, Alexis de. 1969. [1832]. *Democracy in America*. New York: Anchor.

United States Bureau of the Census. 1999. Current Population Reports, Series P–20. Washington, DC: Government Printing Office.

Warren, Carol A. B. 1987. *Madwives: Schizophrenic Women at Mid-Century*. New Brunswick, NJ: Rutgers University Press.

Whitehead, Barbara D. 1993. "Dan Quayle was Right," *Atlantic Monthly* (April).

Whyte, Martin K. 1978. *The Status of Women in Preindustrial Societies*. Princeton, NJ: Princeton University Press.

Chapter 4

1. Lobbying organizations ranged from the Welfare Warriors, a group made up of Aid to Families with Dependent Children (AFDC) recipients, to the Women's Committee of 100, an ad hoc group of academics and social service professionals who opposed the dismantling of AFDC. For discussions of the shift from AFDC to PRWOA, see Goodwin 1997; Michel 1998; Mink 1998.

2. One of the most famous is the National Congress of Mothers. Founded in 1890, it eventually became the Parent-Teacher Association (PTA), boasting millions of members (Ladd-Taylor 1994; Weiner 1999).

3. Sociologist Sharon Hays (1996) argues that women *are* expected both to mother—indeed, to mother intensively—as well as to participate in paid employment; indeed, these conflicting expectations constitute what she calls the "cultural contradictions of motherhood" (chap. 1).

4. In a certain sense, the World Wide Web levels the playing field, giving groups such as Hearts at Home as much exposure as it does the Family Research Council. But a closer look at their Web sites reveals the tremendous resources of the Council, compared to the limited local range of Hearts at Home.

5. How else should we interpret the National Congress of Mothers, the first national organization of this type? See Ladd-Taylor (1994), chap. 2.

6. Such a decision was, of course, more feasible in 1976 than it would be in today's world of managed care and health maintenance organizations.

7. Here the links between Web sites can be particularly informative: the MAH Web page is linked to that of the Center for a New American Dream, a group dedicated to reducing materialism.

8. I found only a few Web sites for stay-at-home fathers, and most of these had been put up by individuals, not organizations (see Sites Relating to House Fathers [n.d.] and Full-Time Dad [n.d.]). The rhetoric of these sites differs markedly from that of at-home mothers. Many are concerned with protecting fathers' rights in divorce.

9. It is not surprising that most of these organizations were founded in the 1980s, at the height of the "Reagan revolution."

Apple, Rima D., and Janet Golden (eds.). 1997. *Mothers and Motherhood: Readings in American History*. Columbus: Ohio State University Press.

At-Home Mothers. n.d. athomemothers.com

Boris, Eileen. 1993. "The Power of Motherhood: Black and White Women Activists Redefine the Political." In Seth Koven and Sonya Michel (eds.), *Mothers of a New World: Maternalist Politics and the Origins of Welfare States*. New York: Routledge.

Burton, Linda, Janet Dittmer, and Cheri Loveless. 1992. *What's a Smart Woman Like You Doing at Home?* Revised edition. Vienna, VA: Mothers At Home.

Cardozo, Arlene Rossen. 1976. *Women at Home*. New York: Doubleday.

Connole, Pauline Arnold. 1998. "Debating the Care of America's Children —Report from a Congressional Symposium," *Welcome Home*, May. mah.org/pub_may98.htm

Family Research Council. n.d. www.frc.org

FEMALE n.d. FEMALEhome.org/advocacy/htm/FEMALE's Mission

Feminist Mothers at Home. n.d. lollygag.com/fmah

Full-Time Dad. n.d. fathersworld.com/fulltimedad

Goodwin, Joanne. 1997. " 'Employable Mothers' and 'Suitable Work': A Reevaluation of Welfare and Wage Earning for Women in Twentieth-Century United States." In Rima D. Apple and Janet Golden (eds.), *Mothers and Motherhood: Readings in American History*. Columbus, OH: Ohio State University Press.

Gordon, Linda. 1991. "Black and White Visions of Welfare: Women's Welfare Activism, 1980–1945," *Journal of American History*, 78:559–90.

Hays, Sharon. 1996. *The Cultural Contradictions of Motherhood*. New Haven, CT: Yale University Press.

Hearts at Home. n.d. hearts-at-home.org

hipMama. n.d. hipmama.com

Koven, Seth, and Sonya Michel (eds.). 1993. *Mothers of a New World: Maternalist Politics and the Origins of Welfare States*. New York: Routledge.

Ladd-Taylor, Molly. 1994. *Mother-Work: Women, Child Welfare, and the State, 1890–1930*. Urbana, IL: University of Illinois Press.

Margolis, Maxine L. 1984. *Mothers and Such: Views of American Women and Why They Changed*. Berkeley, CA: University of California Press.

Michel, Sonya. 1998. "Child Care and Welfare (In)justice," *Feminist Studies*, 24(1) (Spring):1–11.

Mink, Gwendolyn. 1998. *Welfare's End*. Ithaca, NY: Cornell University Press.

Mother Rock Star . . . a Network. n.d. hipmama.com/mrs.html

Mothers at Home. n.d. mah.org

Mothers at Home. n.d. "Mothers at Home, Mission and Values of Our Organization," mah.org/org_ values.html

Mothers at Home. 1996. "Problems and Solutions: Husband Not Supportive of Wife's Decision to Stay at Home," *Welcome Home*, July. mah.org/ps_nonsupportive.htm

Myers, Catherine H. 1997. "MAH Represented at Harvard Conference," *Welcome Home*, August. mah.org/pub_aug97PPU.htm

Otto, Donna. 1991. *The Stay at Home Mom*. Eugene, OR: Harvest House Publishers.

Parlapiano, Ellen H., and Patricia Cobe. 1996. *Mompreneurs: A Mother's Practical Step-by-Step Guide to Work-at-Home Success*. New York: Perigee.

Sefton, Barbara Wylan. 1998. "Art of Mothering," *Mothering Magazine*, January-February. naturodoc.com/artchildcare.html

Sites Relating to House Fathers. n.d. fathersworld.com/fulltimedad/links/housefathers.html

Tillmon, Johnnie. 1972. "Welfare Is a Women's Issue," *Liberation News Service*, No. 415, February 26.

U.S. Congress. 1968. *Income Maintenance Programs*. Joint Economic Committee, Subcommittee on Fiscal Policy. Washington, DC: Government Printing Office.

Villani, Sue Lanci, and Jane E. Ryan. 1997. *Motherhood at the Crossroads: Meeting the Challenge of a Changing Role*. New York: Plenum Press/Insight Books.

Wagner, Barbara, and Roberta Grant. 1984. "The New One-Paycheck Family," *Ladies' Home Journal*, 101:9 (September):87ff.

Weiner, Lynn. 1999. "The PTA and Constructions of Motherhood in the Twentieth Century." Paper presented at the 11th Berkshire Conference on the History of Women, University of Rochester.

Yoest, Charmaine Crouse. 1998. "Parents at Home: Still the Silent Majority," *Family Policy*, 11(1). frc.org/fampol/fp98cc.html

Zimney, Connie Fourré. 1984. *In Praise of Homemaking: Affirming the Choice to Be a Mother-at-Home*. Notre Dame, IN: Ave Maria Press.

Chapter 5

Blumberg, Rhoda Lois. 1990. "Women in the Civil Rights Movement," *Dialectical Anthropology*, 15:133–39.

Brown, Phil, and Faith Ferguson. 1995. "'Making a Big Stink,'" *Gender & Society*, 9(2): 145–72.

Brown, Phil, and Edwin Mikkelsen. 1990. *No Safe Place*. Berkeley, CA: University of California Press.

Cable, Sherry. 1992. "Women's Social Movement Involvement," *Sociological Quarterly*, 33:34–50.

Cable, Sherry, and Charles Cable. 1995. *Environmental Problems, Grassroots Solutions*. New York: St. Martin's Press.

Calhoun, Craig. 1987. "Social Theory and the Politics of Identity." In Craig Calhoun (ed.), *Social Theory and the Politics of Identity*. Cambridge, MA: Blackwell.

Della Porta, Donatella, and Mario Diani. 1999. *Social Movements*. Oxford, UK: Blackwell.

Edelstein, Michael. 1988. *Contaminated Communities*. Boulder, CO: Westview.

Evans, Sara. 1979. *Personal Politics*. New York: Random House.

Farenthold, Frances. 1988. Foreword to *Women Activists*, by Anne Witte Garland. New York: Feminist Press.

Freudenberg, Nicholas. 1984. *Not in Our Backyards!* New York: Monthly Review Press.

Giddens, Anthony. 1991. *Modernity and Self-Identity*. Stanford, CA: Stanford University Press.

Ginsburg, Faye, and Anna Lowenhaupt Tsing (eds.). 1990. *Uncertain Terms*. Boston: Beacon Press.

Hamilton, Cynthia. 1990. "Women, Home and Community." In Irene Diamond and Gloria Feman Orenstein (eds.), *Reweaving the World*. San Francisco: Sierra Club Books, pp. 215–22.

Herda-Rapp, Ann. 1998. *Women's Activism in the Toxic Waste Movement: The Dialectics of Gender and Activism*. Unpublished dissertation, University of Illinois at Urbana-Champaign.

Howard, Judith, and Jocelyn Hollander. 1997. *Gendered Situations, Gendered Selves*. Thousand Oaks, CA: Sage.

Krauss, Celene. 1993a. "Women and Toxic Waste Protests," *Qualitative Sociology*, 16(3):247–62.

Krauss, Celene. 1993b. "Blue-Collar Women and Toxic-Waste Protests." In Richard Hofrichter (ed.), *Toxic Struggles*. Philadelphia: New Society Publishers, pp. 107–17.

Levine, Adeline. 1982. *Love Canal*. Lexington, MA: Lexington Books.

McAdam, Doug. 1988. *Freedom Summer*. New York: Oxford University Press.

McAdam, Doug. 1992. "Gender as a Mediator of the Activist Experience," *American Journal of Sociology*, 97:1211–40.

McMahon, Martha. 1995. *Engendering Motherhood*. New York: Guilford Press.

Miller, Stuart. 1997. "Women's Work," *E Magazine*, January/February:28–35.

Morris, Aldon. 1984. *The Origins of the Civil Rights Movement*. New York: Free Press.

Snow, David, and Leon Anderson. 1987. "Identity Work Among the Homeless," *American Journal of Sociology*, 92:1336–71.

Snow, David, and Richard Machalek. 1984. "The Sociology of Conversion," *Annual Review of Sociology*, 10:167–90.

Szasz, Andrew. 1994. *EcoPopulism*. Minneapolis, MN: University of Minnesota Press.

Thorne, Barrie. 1975. "Women in the Draft Resistance Movement," *Sex Roles*, 1:179–95.

West, Candace, and Don Zimmerman. 1987. "Doing Gender," *Gender & Society*, 1(2):125–51.

Zeff, Robin Lee, Marsha Love, and Karen Stuits. 1989. *Empowering Ourselves*. Arlington, VA: Citizens Clearinghouse for Hazardous Waste.

Part II

Diamond, Timothy. 1992. *Making Gray Gold*. Chicago, IL: University of Chicago Press.

Chapter 6

Baldock, John, and Clare Ungerson. 1991. " 'What d'ya Want if You Don't Want Money?' A Feminist Critique of Paid Volunteering." In Mavis Maclean and Dulcie Groves (eds.), *Women's Issues in Social Policy*. London: Routledge.

Baldock, John, and Clare Ungerson. 1994. *Becoming Consumers of Community Care*. York, UK: Joseph Rowntree Foundation.

Blacksell, Sarah, and David R. Phillips. 1994. *Paid to Volunteer: The Extent of Paying Volunteers in the 1990s*. London, UK: Volunteer Centre.

Challis, David, and Bleddyn Davies. 1986. *Case Management in Community Care*. Aldershot, UK: Gower.

Cheal, David. 1988. *The Gift Economy*. London, UK: Routledge.

Daly, Mary. 1997. "Welfare States Under Pressure: Cash Benefits in European Welfare States Over the Last Ten Years," *Journal of European Social Policy*, 7(2):129–46.

Department of Health. 1996. *Community Care (Direct Payments) Bill: Consultation Paper*. London, UK: Department of Health, the Scottish Office, Welsh Office, Northern Ireland Office.

Eustis, Nancy, and Lucy Fischer. 1991. "Relationships between Home Care Clients and their Workers: Implications for the Quality of Care," *Gerontologist*, 31(4):447–56.

Evers, Adelbert, Marja Pijl, and Clare Ungerson (eds.). 1994. *Payments for Care: A Comparative Overview*. Aldershot, UK: Avebury.

Finch, Janet. 1989. *Family Obligations and Social Change*. Oxford, UK: Polity Press.

Finch, Janet, and Dulcie Groves (eds.). 1983. *A Labour of Love: Women, Work and Caring*. London, UK: Routledge and Kegan Paul.

Finch, Janet, and Jennifer Mason. 1992. *Negotiating Family Responsibilities*. London, UK: Tavistock/Routledge.

Gerard, Jessica. 1994. *Country House Life: Family and Servants, 1815–1914*. Oxford, UK: Blackwell.

Glendinning, Caroline, and Eithne McLaughlin. 1993. *Paying for Care: Lessons from Europe*, Social Security Advisory Committee Research Paper 5. London, UK: HMSO.

Graham, Hilary. 1991. "The Concept of Caring in Feminist Research—The Case of Domestic Service," *Sociology*, 25(1):61–78.

Griffiths, Roy. 1988. *Community Care: Agenda for Action*. London, UK: HMSO.

Hendey, Nicola, and Gillian Pascall. 1998. "Independent Living: Gender, Violence and the Threat of Violence," *Disability and Society*, 13 (3):415–27.

Himmelweit, Susan. 1995. "The Discovery of 'Unpaid Work': The Social Consequences of the Expansion of 'Work'," *Feminist Economics*, 1(2):1–19.

Hochschild, Arlie R. 1995. "The Culture of Politics: Traditional, Postmodern, Cold-Modern, and Warm-Modern Ideals of Care," *Social Politics* (Fall):331–45.

Johansson, Lennarth, and Gerdt Sundström. 1994. "Sweden." In A. Evers, M. Pijl, and C. Ungerson (eds.), *Payments for Care: A Comparative Overview*. Aldershot, UK: Avebury.

Joshi, Heather. 1992. "The Cost of Caring." In Caroline Glendinning and Jane Millar (eds.), *Women and Poverty in Britain: The 1990s*. Hemel Hempstead, UK: Harvester Wheatsheaf.

Keigher, Sharon, and Robyn Stone. 1994. "United States of America." In Adelbert Evers, Marja Pijl, and Clare Ungerson (eds.), *Payments for Care: A Comparative Overview*. Aldershot, UK: Avebury.

Keigher, Sharon M., and Clare Luz. 1997. *A Pilot Study of Milwaukee's Gray Market in Independent Care: Common Stakes in Homecare of the Elderly*. Milwaukee School of Social Welfare, University of Wisconsin-Milwaukee.

Kestenbaum, Ann. 1996. *Independent Living: A Review*. York, UK: York Publishing Services for Joseph Rowntree Foundation.

Kestenbaum, Ann. 1992. *Cash for Care: A Report on the Experience of Independent Living Fund Clients*. Nottingham, UK: Independent Living Fund.

Lakey, Jane. 1994. *Caring About Independence: Disabled People and the Independent Living Fund*. London, UK: Policy Studies Institute.

Leat, Diana. 1990. *For Love and Money: The Role of Payment in Encouraging the Provision of Care*. York, UK: Joseph Rowntree Foundation.

Leat, Diana, with Clare Ungerson. 1993. *Creating Care at the Boundaries Issues in the Supply and Management of Domiciliary Care*. Canterbury, UK: Department of Social Policy, University of Kent.

Lingsom, Susan. 1994. *The Development and Impact of Payments for Care*, INAS-NOTAT 1994:4. Oslo, Norway: Instituut for sosialforskning.

Linsk, N., S. Keigher, L. Simon-Rusinowitz, and S. Osterbusch. 1992. *Wages for Caring: Compensating Family Care of the Elderly*. New York: Praeger.

McLaughlin, Eithne. 1991. *Social Security and Community Care: the Case of the Invalid Care Allowance*, Department of Social Security Research Report no. 4. London, UK: HMSO.

McLaughlin, Eithne. 1994. "Ireland." In Adelbert Evers, Marja Pijl, and Clare Ungerson (eds.), *Payments for Care: A Comparative Overview*. Aldershot, UK: Avebury.

Morris, Jenny. 1993. *Independent Lives? Community Care and Disabled People*. London, UK: Macmillan.

Oakley, Ann. 1974. *The Sociology of Housework*. London, UK: Robertson.

Oliver, Michael. 1990. *The Politics of Disablement*. London, UK: Macmillan.

Qureshi, Hazel, and Alan Walker. 1989. *The Caring Relationship*. London, UK: Macmillan.

Qureshi, Hazel, David Challis, and Bleddyn Davies. 1989. *Helpers in Case Managed Community Care*. Aldershot, UK: Gower.

Seccombe, Wally. 1980. "Domestic Labour and the Working Class Household." In Bonnie Fox (ed.), *Hidden in the Household: Women's Domestic Labour Under Capitalism.* Toronto, Canada: Women's Press.

Thomas, Carol. 1993. "De-Constructing Concepts of Care," *Sociology*, 27(3):649–69.

Twigg, Julia, and Karl Atkin. 1994. *Carers Perceived: Policy and Practice in Informal Care.* Buckingham, UK: Open University Press.

Ungerson, Clare. 1987. *Policy Is Personal: Sex, Gender and Informal Care.* London, UK: Tavistock.

Ungerson, Clare. 1990. "The Language of Care: Crossing the Boundaries." In Clare Ungerson (ed.), *Gender and Caring: Work and Welfare in Britain and Scandinavia.* Hemel Hempstead, UK: Harvester Wheatsheaf.

Ungerson, Clare. 1994. "Payment for Caring: Mapping a Territory." In Nicholas Deakin and Robert Page (eds.), *The Costs of Welfare.* Aldershot, UK: Avebury.

Ungerson, Clare. 1995. "Gender, Cash and Informal Care: European Perspectives and Dilemmas," *Journal of Social Policy*, 24(1):31–52.

Ungerson, Clare. 1997a. "Social Politics and the Commodification of Care," *Social Politics*, 4(3) (Fall):362–81.

Ungerson, Clare. 1997b. "Give Them the Money: Is Cash a Route to Empowerment?" *Social Policy and Administration*, 31(1):45–53.

Chapter 7

The author gratefully acknowledges support for this research from the Open Society Institute Individual Project Fellowship Program, Children's Studies at Harvard, and the Radcliffe Public Policy Institute, where the author was the Matina S. Horner Distinguished Visiting Professor during 1997–1999. Thanks to Jean Galbraith, Sandy Chung, and Araz Zarikian for outstanding research assistance. Thanks also to a wonderful group of caring critics who substantially improved this essay: Emily Abel, Françoise Carre, Lisa Dodson, Susan Eaton, Sholom Glouberman, Suzanne Gordon, Mona Harrington, Rob Hudson, Marty Wyngaarden Kraus, Robert Kuttner, Julie Nelson, Pamela Stone, and Lucie White. Last, but not least, thanks to the home care providers who taught me about extraordinary generosity of spirit in ordinary people.

1. Gender watchers may be surprised to find out that this aide is a male. At another point in the interview, he says he wishes he had been able to become an accountant instead (a stereotypical male profession if ever there was one), but he had to go to work because he was the oldest of 12 kids. He also says he thinks this a good job for a summer, "to get some experience in life," but "not as a life job, at least I wouldn't want my little girl to do it" (Glouberman 1990:36–37).
2. Some "companion" programs are an exception—their avowed goal is to provide companionship. The Senior Companion Program in New Hampshire pairs active, younger seniors with low-income frail elderly people, and pays the former to socialize with the latter. Rebecca Mohoney, "Program Benefits Seniors, Companions," *The Boston Globe*, Sunday, July 12, 1998, NH Weekly Section, p. 1.

Abel, Emily K. 1991. *Who Cares for the Elderly? Public Policy and the Experiences of Adult Daughters.* Philadelphia: Temple University Press.

Abel, Emily K., and Margaret K. Nelson. 1990. "Circles of Care: An Introductory Essay." In Emily K. Abel and Margaret K. Nelson (eds.), *Circles of Care: Work and Identity in Women's Lives.* Albany, NY: State University of New York Press, pp. 4–34.

Cohen, Marion Deutsch. 1996. *Dirty Details: The Days and Nights of a Well Spouse.* Philadelphia: Temple University Press.

Conover, Ted. 1997. "The Last Best Friends Money Can Buy," *New York Times Magazine,* November 30:124–32.

DeVault, Marjorie L. 1991. *Feeding the Family: The Social Organization of Caring as Gendered Work.* Chicago: University of Chicago Press.

Diamond, Timothy. 1990. "Nursing Homes as Trouble." In Emily K. Abel and Margaret K. Nelson (eds.), *Circles of Care: Work and Identity in Women's Lives.* Albany, NY: State University of New York Press, pp. 173–87.

Eaton, Susan. 1995. *Work Organization, Productivity, and Technology in Nursing Homes and Home Health: Beyond 'Unloving Care' and Lousy Jobs.* Washington, DC: U.S. Office of Technology Assessment, Final Contractor Report, Contract M3–0491, June 30.

England, Paula, and Nancy Folbre. 1999. "The Cost of Caring," *Annals of the American Academy of Political and Social Science,* 561(January):39–51.

Evers, Adalbert, Marja Pijl, and Clare Ungerson. 1994. *Payments for Care.* Brookfield, VT: Ashgate Press.

Folbre, Nancy, and Thomas Weisskopf. 1998. "Did Father Know Best? Families, Markets, and the Supply of Caring Labor." In Avner Ben-Ner and Louis Putterman (eds.), *Economics, Values and Organization.* New York: Cambridge University Press, pp. 171–205.

Glasser, Ruth, and Jeremy Brecher. 1997. " 'We Are the Roots': The Culture of Home Health Aides," *New England Journal of Public Policy,* Fall/Winter (special issue):113–34.

Glouberman, Sholom. 1990. *Keepers: Inside Stories from Total Institutions.* London: King's Fund.

Gordon, Suzanne. 1997. *Life Support: Three Nurses on the Front Lines.* Boston: Little, Brown.

Harrington, Mona. 1999. *Care and Equality: Inventing a New Family Politics.* New York: Knopf.

Harris, Phyllis Braudy. 1998. "Listening to Caregiving Sons: Misunderstood Realities," *Gerontologist,* 38(3):342–52.

Himmelweit, Susan. 1999. "Caring Labor," *Annals of the American Academy of Political and Social Science,* 561(January):27–38.

Hochschild, Arlie. 1983. *The Managed Heart.* Berkeley, CA: University of California Press.

Hochschild, Arlie. 1990. *The Second Shift.* New York: Avon Books.

Karner, Tracy X. 1998. "Professional Caring: Homecare Workers as Fictive Kin," *Journal of Aging Studies,* 12(1):69–82.

Kronholz, June. 1998. "Chary Schools Tell Teachers, 'Don't Touch, Don't Hug,' " *Wall Street Journal,* May 28, p. B1.

Leavitt, Robin. 1995. "The Emotional Culture of Infant-Toddler Day Care." In J. Amos Hatch (ed.), *Qualitative Research in Early Childhood Settings.* Westport, CT: Praeger, pp. 3–21.

Lewin, Tamar. 1998. "Struggling for Personal Attention in Day Care," *New York Times,* April 27, p. A1.

Nelson, Margaret K. 1995. "Family Day Care as Mothering." In J. Amos Hatch (ed.), *Qualitative Research in Early Childhood Settings.* Westport, CT: Praeger, pp. 23–42.

O'Sullivan, John. 1999. "Compassion Play," *National Review,* 51:3 (February 22):22–24.

Picker Institute. 1995. "Focus Group with Home Health Aides." Boston: October 26. (Unpublished transcript, used with permission).

Polanyi, Karl. 1944. *The Great Transformation*. Boston: Beacon Press.

Radin, Margaret. 1996. *Contested Commodities*. Cambridge, MA: Harvard University Press.

Ruddick, Sara. 1984. "Maternal Thinking." In Joyce Trebilcot (ed.), *Mothering: Essays in Feminist Theory*. Totowa, NJ: Rowman & Littlefield.

Schwartz, David B. 1997. *Who Cares? Rediscovering Community*. New York: Westview.

Smith, Dorothy. 1974. "The Social Construction of Documentary Reality," *Sociological Inquiry*, 44(4):257–68.

Steinberg, Ronnie J. 1999. "Emotional Labor in Job Evaluation: Redesigning Compensation Practices," *Annals of the American Academy of Political and Social Sciences*, 561(January):143–56.

Steinberg, Ronnie J., and Lawrence Walter. 1992. "Making Women's Work Visible—The Case of Nursing." In *Exploring the Quincentennial: The Policy Challenges of Gender, Diversity, and International Exchange*. Washington, DC: Institute for Women's Policy Research.

Stone, Deborah. 1999. "Care and Trembling," *American Prospect*, 43:61–67.

Strober, Myra, and Suzanne Gerlach-Downie. 1995. "Child Care Centers as Workplaces," *Feminist Economics*, 1(1):93–119.

Waerness, Kari. 1996. "The Rationality of Caring." In Suzanne Gordon, Patricia Benner, and Nel Noddings (eds.), *Caregiving*. Philadelphia: University of Pennsylvania Press, pp. 231–55.

Waring, Marilyn. 1988. *If Women Counted: A New Feminist Economics*. San Francisco: Harper & Row.

Chapter 8

I wish to thank the family day-care workers who participated in this study, Francesca Cancian for her invitation to participate in the Gender, Citizenship and the Work of Caring Conference in November 1997, and Deborah Stone for her support for an earlier version of this work.

1. I use the term "race ethnicity" in order to emphasize the historical and cultural experiences that shape group identity, rather than the term *race,* which defines groups on the basis of purported biological characteristics. While race is a fundamental organizing principle of social relationships, it is the social definition and construction of race that have historically shaped the cultural identities and experiences of groups.

2. The analysis of conflicts within family child-care work presented in this chapter is part of a larger research project, the findings of which are published elsewhere (Tuominen 1997, 1998).

3. Karen refers to the child-care needs of parents enrolled in state-funded job training, job search, or educational programs. Karen was interviewed prior to the 1996 congressional repeal of AFDC (Aid to Families with Dependent Children), when such government programs, while not widespread, were more readily available than under Temporary Assistance to Needy Families.

4. Family child-care workers in middle-class neighborhoods frequently report an unwillingness to care for children through state-subsidized programs. This is due to the state's policy of paying less than market rates for child care (see Tuominen 1997).

Abel, Emily K., and Margaret K. Nelson (eds.). 1990. "Circles of Care: An Introductory Essay." In *Circles of Care: Work and Identity in Women's Lives.* Albany, NY: State University of New York Press.

Abramovitz, Mimi. [1988] 1996. *Regulating the Lives of Women: Social Welfare Policy from Colonial Times to the Present.* Revised edition. Boston: South End Press.

Amott, Teresa, and Julie Matthaei. 1991. *Race, Gender, and Work: A Multicultural Economic History of Women in the United States.* Boston: South End Press.

Buroway, Michael, Alice Burton, Ann Arnett Ferguson, Kathryn J. Fox, Joshua Gamson, Nadine Gartrell, Leslie Hurst, Charles Kurzman, Leslie Salzinger, Josepha Schiffman, and Shiori Ui. 1992. *Ethnography Unbound: Power and Resistance in the Modern Metropolis.* Berkeley, CA: University of California Press.

Center for the Child Care Workforce. 1999. *Current Data on Child Care Salaries and Benefits in the United States.* Washington, DC: Center for the Child Care Workforce, March.

Dill, Bonnie Thorton. 1988. "Making Your Job Good Yourself: Domestic Service and the Construction of Personal Dignity." In Ann Bookman and Sandra Morgen (eds.), *Women and the Politics of Empowerment.* Philadelphia: Temple University Press.

Gilligan, Carol. 1993. *In a Different Voice: Psychological Theory and Women's Development.* Cambridge, MA: Harvard University Press.

Gordon, Linda (ed.). 1990. "The New Feminist Scholarship on the Welfare State." In *Women, the State and Welfare.* Madison, WI: University of Wisconsin Press.

Hill Collins, Patricia. 1992. "Black Women and Motherhood." In Barrie Thorne and Marilyn Yalom (eds.), *Rethinking the Family: Some Feminist Questions.* Boston: Northeastern University Press.

Hill Collins, Patricia. 1993. "Toward an Afrocentric Feminist Epistemology." In Alison M. Jaggar and Paula S. Rothenberg (eds.), *Feminist Frameworks: Alternative Theoretical Accounts of the Relations Between Women and Men.* New York: McGraw-Hill.

Hochschild, Arlie. 1983. *The Managed Heart: Commercialization of Human Feeling.* Berkeley: University of California Press.

Jones, Jacqueline. 1986. *Labor of Love, Labor of Sorrow: Black Women and the Family, from Slavery to Present.* New York: Random House.

Kappner, Augusta Souza. 1984. "Factors Affecting the Visibility of Family Day Care Providers in New York City." Doctoral dissertation, School of Social Work, Columbia University.

Kerber, Linda. 1993. "Some Cautionary Words for Historians." In Mary Jeanne Larrabee (ed.), *An Ethic of Care: Feminist and Interdisciplinary Perspectives.* New York: Routledge.

King, Deborah K. 1992. "Review Symposium: Patricia Hill Collins, Black Feminist Thought: Knowledge, Consciousness, and the Politics of Empowerment," *Gender and Society,* 6(3):512–15.

Macpherson, C. B. 1990. *The Life and Times of Liberal Democracy.* New York: Oxford University Press.

Mazur, Rosaleen. 1981. "The Relationship Between the Life Cycle Status of Caregivers and Caregivers Affiliation with Strategies for Regulating, Training and Support of Family Day Care in New York City." Unpublished doctoral dissertation, Teachers College, Columbia University.

Nakano Glenn, Evelyn. 1986. *Issei, Nisei, War Bride: Three Generations of Japanese American Women in Domestic Service.* Philadelphia: Temple University Press.

Nakano Glenn, Evelyn. 1994. "Social Constructions of Mothering: A Thematic Overview." In Evelyn Nakano Glenn, Grace Chang, and Linda Rennie Forcey (eds.), *Mothering: Ideology, Experience, and Agency.* New York: Routledge, pp. 181–209.

Nelson, Barbara J. 1990. "The Origins of the Two-Channel Welfare State: Workmen's Compensation and Mothers' Aid." In Linda Gordon (ed.), *Women, the State, and Welfare.* Madison, WI: University of Wisconsin Press.

Nelson, Margaret. 1988. "Providing Family Day Care: An Analysis of Home-Based Work," *Social Problems,* 35(1):79–94.

Nelson, Margaret. 1990. *Negotiated Care: The Experience of Family Day Care Providers.* Philadelphia: Temple University Press.

Nelson, Margaret. 1994. "Family Day Care Providers: Dilemmas of Daily Practice." In Evelyn Nakano Glenn, Grace Chang, and Linda Rennie Forcey (eds.), *Mothering: Ideology, Experience, and Agency.* New York: Routledge, pp. 181–209.

Pateman, Carole. 1988. "The Patriarchal Welfare State." In Amy Gutman (ed.), *Democracy and the Welfare State.* Princeton, NJ: Princeton University Press.

Pollitt, Katha. 1992. "Marooned on Gilligan's Island: Are Women Morally Superior to Men?" *The Nation* (December):799–807.

Puka, Bill. 1993. "The Liberation of Caring: A Different Voice for Gilligan's 'Different Voice'." In Mary Jeanne Larrabee (ed.), *An Ethic of Care: Feminist and Interdisciplinary Perspectives.* New York: Routledge, pp. 215–39.

Rollins, Judith. 1985. *Between Women: Domestics and Their Employers.* Philadelphia: Temple University Press.

Romero, Mary. 1992. *Maid in the U.S.A.* New York: Routledge.

Saraceno, Chiara. 1984. "Shifts in Public and Private Boundaries: Women as Mothers and Service Workers in Italian Daycare," *Feminist Studies,* 10(1):7–29.

Sassoon, Anne Showstack. 1987. "Women's New Social Role: Contradictions of the Welfare State." In Anne Showstack Sassoon (ed.), *Women and the State: Shifting Boundaries of Public and Private.* London: Hutchinson.

Segura, Denise. 1994. "Working at Motherhood: Chicana and Mexican Immigrant Mothers and Employment." In Evelyn Nakano Glenn, Grace Chang, and Linda Rennie Forcey (eds.), *Mothering: Ideology, Experience, and Agency.* New York: Routledge, pp. 211–33.

Smith, Dorothy. 1987. *The Everyday World as Problematic: A Feminist Sociology.* Boston: Northeastern University Press.

Stone, Deborah A. 1991. "Caring Work in a Liberal Polity," *Journal of Health Politics, Policy and Law,* 16(9):547–52.

Thorne, Barrie. 1992. "Review Symposium: Patricia Hill Collins, Black Feminist Thought: Knowledge, Consciousness, and the Politics of Empowerment," *Gender and Society,* 6(3):515–17.

Tom, Allison. 1992. "The Messy Work of Child Care; Addressing Feminists' Neglect of Child Care Workers," *Atlantis,* 18(1&2): 70–81.

Tronto, Joan C. 1993. "Beyond Gender Difference to a Theory of Care." In Mary Jeanne Larrabee (ed.), *An Ethic of Care: Feminist and Interdisciplinary Perspectives.* New York: Routledge, pp. 240–57.

Tuominen, Mary. 1994. "The Hidden Organization of Labor: Gender, Race/Ethnicity and Child Care Work in the Formal and Informal Economy," *Sociological Perspectives,* 37(2):229–45.

Tuominen, Mary. 1997. "Exploitation or Opportunity? The Contradictions of Child-Care Policy in the Contemporary United States," *Women and Politics,* 18(2):53–80.

Tuominen, Mary. 1998. "Motherhood and The Market: Mothering and Employment Opportunities among Mexicana, African-American and Euro-American Family Day Care Workers," *Sociological Focus,* 31(1):61–79.

U.S. Department of Commerce, Bureau of the Census. 1982. *Trends of Child Care Arrangements of Working Mothers.* Current Population Reports, Series P–23, No. 117. Washington, DC: Government Printing Office, June.

U.S. Department of Commerce, Bureau of the Census. 1997. *Who's Minding Our Preschoolers? Fall 1994* (Update) (PPL–81) (detailed tables and documentation for P70–62, Issued November 1997). www.census.gov/population/socdemo/child/p70–62/tab01.txt. Table 1: Number of Preschoolers of Employed Mothers in Primary Child Care Arrangements by Selected Characteristics: Fall 1994.

U.S. Department of Health and Human Services. 1981. *Family Day Care in the United States: Summary of Findings*, 1. (Principal author: Steven Fosburg). Washington, DC: Government Printing Office.

U.S. Department of Labor, Bureau of Labor Statistics. 1998. Labor Force Statistics from the Current Population Survey. www/bls/gov.release/famee.to4.htm. Employment Characteristics of Families Summary.

U.S. Department of Labor, Women's Bureau. 1997. Facts on Working Women. No. 98–01, November 1997. www.dol.gov/dol/wb/public/wb_pubs/childc.htm.

Uttal, Lynet. 1996. "Custodial Care, Surrogate Care, and Coordinated Care: Employed Mothers and the Meaning of Child Care," *Gender and Society*, 10(3): 291–311.

Vogel, Lise. 1993. *Mothers on the Job: Maternity Policy in the U.S. Workplace.* New Brunswick, NJ: Rutgers University Press.

Chapter 9

The author is indebted to Stacey Oliker for numerous helpful discussions on this issue, and to Frank Cancian, Sam Gilmore, and Judy Stepan-Norris for valuable comments on earlier drafts of the paper. An earlier version of this paper was presented at the Conference on Gender, Citizenship and the Work of Caring, University of Illinois, Urbana-Champaign, November 14–16, 1997.

Abel, Emily K., and Margaret K. Nelson. 1990. *Circles of Care: Work and Identity in Women's Lives.* Albany, NY: State University of New York Press.

Browner, C. H., Kelly Ann Ellis, Theresa Ford, Joscelyn Silsby, Joanne Tampoya, and Cathy Yee. 1987. "Stress, Social Support, and Health of Psychiatric Technicians in a State Facility," *Mental Retardation*, 25:31–38.

Brownstein, Ronald. 1997. "Firms on Economy's Cutting Edge Show Government How It Can Excell" *Los Angeles Times*, June 30, A5.

Degler, Carl N. 1980. *At Odds: Women and the Family in America from the Revolution to the Present.* New York: Oxford University Press.

Diamond, Timothy. 1992. *Making Gray Gold: Narratives of Nursing Home Care.* Chicago: University of Chicago Press.

England, Paula. 1992. *Comparable Worth: Theories and Evidence.* New York: Aldine De Gruyter.

Feree, Myra Marx. 1990. "Beyond Separate Spheres: Feminism and Family Research," *Journal of Marriage and the Family*, 52:866–84.

Finch, Janet, and Dulcie Groves. 1983. *A Labour of Love: Women, Work and Caring.* London,UK: Routledge and Kegan Paul.

Foner, Nancy. 1994. *The Caregiving Dilemma: Work in the American Nursing Home.* Berkeley, CA: University of California Press.

Gelles, Richard J., and Claire Pedrich Cornell. 1985. *Intimate Violence in Families.* Beverly Hills, CA: Sage Publications.

Glazer, Nona. 1993. *Women's Paid and Unpaid Labor: The Work Transfer in Health Care and Retailing.* Philadelphia: Temple University Press.

Hooyman, Nancy R., and Judith Gonyea. 1995. *Feminist Perspectives on Family Care.* Thousand Oaks, CA: Sage Publications.

Jenkins, David. 1973. *Job Power: Blue and White Collar Democracy.* Garden City, NY: Doubleday.

Lundgren, Rebecka Inga, and Carole H. Browner. 1990. "Caring for the Institutionalized Mentally Retarded: Work Culture and Work-Based Social Support." In Emily Abel and Margaret Nelson (eds.), *Circles of Care.* Albany, NY: State University of New York Press, pp. 150–72.

Newman, Katherine S. 1988. *Falling from Grace: The Experience of Downward Mobility in the American Middle Classes.* New York: Free Press.

Ouchi, William, and Jerry B. Johnson. 1978. "Types of Organizational Control and Their Relation to Emotional Well-Being," *Administrative Science Quarterly,* 23:293–317.

Parsons, Talcott, and Robert Bales. 1955. *Family Socialization and Interaction Process.* Glencoe, IL: Free Press

Popenoe, David. 1993. "American Family Decline, 1960–1990: A Review and Appraisal," *Journal of Marriage and the Family,* 55:527–55.

Rothschild, Joyce, and J. Allen Whitt. 1986. *The Cooperative Workplace: Potentials and Dilemmas of Organizational Democracy and Participation.* Cambridge, UK: Cambridge University Press.

Ryan, Mary. 1979. *Womanhood in America (From Colonial Times to the Present).* New York: New Viewpoints.

Sacks, Karen. 1988. *Caring by the Hour: Women, Work, and Organizing at Duke Medical Center.* Urbana, IL: University of Illinois Press.

Scott, W. Richard. 1992. *Organizations: Rational, Natural and Open Systems.* Englewood NJ: Prentice Hall.

Weber, Max. 1947. *The Theory of Economic and Social Organization.* Translated by A. M. Parsons and T. Parsons. New York: Free Press.

Wesorick, Bonnie. 1991. "Creating an Environment in the Hospital Setting That Supports Caring via a Clinical Practice Model (CPM)." In Delores A. Gaut and Madeleine M. Leininger (eds.), *Caring: The Compassionate Healer.* New York: National League for Nursing Press, pp. 135–49.

Chapter 10

Bakan, Abigail B., and Daiva Stasiulis. 1997. "Foreign Domestic Worker Policy in Canada and the Social Boundaries of Modern Citizenship." In Abigail B. Bakan and Daiva Stasiulis (eds.), *Not One of the Family: Foreign Domestic Workers in Canada.* Toronto: University of Toronto Press, pp. 29–52.

Baker, Susan Gonzalez, Frank D. Bean, Augustin Escobar Latapi, and Sidney Weintraub. 1998. "Immigration Policies and Trends: The Growing Importance of Migration from Mexico." In Marcelo Suarez-Orozco (ed.), *Crossings: Mexican Immigration in Interdisciplinary Perspectives.* Cambridge, MA: Harvard University Press, pp. 81–109.

Burawoy, Michael. 1976. "The Functions and Reproduction of Migrant Labor: Comparative Material from Southern Africa and the United States," *American Journal of Sociology*, 81:1050–87.

Chan, Sucheng. 1990. "European and Asian Immigration into the United States in Comparative Perspective, 1820s to 1920." In Virginia Yans-McLaughlin (ed.), *Immigration Reconsidered: History, Sociology, and Politics*. New York: Oxford University Press, pp. 37–75.

Chavez, Leo. 1990. *Shadowed Lives: Mexican Undocumented Immigrants*. Case Studies in Cultural Anthropology Series. Fort Worth, TX: Harcourt Brace Jovanovich.

Constable, Nicole. 1997. *Maid to Order in Hong Kong: Stories of Filipina Workers*. Ithaca, NY, and London: Cornell University Press.

Cornelius, Wayne. 1998. "The Structural Embeddedness of Demand for Mexican Immigrant Labor: New Evidence from California." In Marcelo M. Suarez-Orozco (ed.), *Crossings: Mexican Immigration in Interdisciplinary Perspectives*. Cambridge, MA: Harvard University Press, pp. 113–44.

Dill, Bonnie Thornton. 1988. "Our Mothers' Grief: Racial-Ethnic Women and the Maintenance of Families," *Journal of Family History*, 13:415–31.

Dill, Bonnie Thornton. 1994. "Fictive Kin, Paper Sons, and Compadrazgo: Women of Color and the Struggle for Family Survival." In Maxine Baca Zinn and Bonnie Thornton Dill (eds.), *Women of Color in U.S. Society*. Philadelphia: Temple University Press.

Garcia y Griego, Manuel. 1983. "The Importance of Mexican Contract Laborers to the United States, 1942–1964." In Peter G. Brown and Henry Shue (eds.), *The Border That Joins: Mexican Immigrants and U.S. Responsibility*. Totowa, NJ: Rowman and Littlefield, pp. 49–98.

Glenn, Evelyn Nakano. 1986. *Issei, Nisei, War Bride: Three Generations of Japanese American Women in Domestic Service*. Philadelphia: Temple University Press.

Glenn, Evelyn Nakano. 1992. "From Servitude to Service Work: Historical Continuities in the Racial Division of Women's Work," *Signs*, 18(1):1–43.

Hondagneu-Sotelo, Pierrette. 1994. *Gendered Transitions: Mexican Experiences of Immigration*. Berkeley, CA: University of California Press.

Hondagneu-Sotelo, Pierrette. 1995. "Women and Children First: New Directions in Anti-Immigration Politics," *Socialist Review*, 25:169–90.

Hondagneu-Sotelo, Pierrette, and Ernestine Avila. 1997. "'I'm Here, But I'm There': The Meanings of Latina Transnational Motherhood," *Gender & Society*, 11:548–71.

Laslett, Barbara, and Johanna Brenner. 1989. "Gender and Social Reproduction: Historical Perspectives," *Annual Review of Sociology*, 15:381–404.

Mahler, Sarah J. 1999. "Engendering Transnational Migration: A Case Study of Salvadorans," *American Behavioral Scientist*, 42(4):69–719.

Palerm, Juan-Vincente. 1994. *Immigrant and Migrant Farmworkers in the Santa Maria Valley of California*. Santa Barbara, CA: Report for the Center for Survey Methods Research.

Parrenas, Rhacel Salazar. 1998. "The Global Servants: (Im)Migrant Filipina Domestic Workers in Rome and Los Angeles." Doctoral dissertation, Berkeley, CA: University of California Press.

Richmond, Anthony. 1994. *Global Apartheid: Refugees, Racism, and the New World Order*. Toronto: Oxford University Press.

Rollins, Judith. 1985. *Between Women: Domestics and Their Employers*. Philadelphia: Temple University Press.

Romero, Mary. 1992. *Maid in the U.S.A.* New York: Routledge.

Romo, Ricardo. 1983. *East Los Angeles: History of a Barrio.* Austin, TX: University of Texas Press.

Taylor, Paul. 1983. "Mexicans North of the Rio Grande." In Paul Taylor (ed.), *On the Ground in the Thirties.* Salt Lake City, UT: Peregrine Smith.

Yeoh, Brenda S. A., Shirlena Huang, and Joaquin Gonzalez, III. 1999. "Migrant Female Domestic Workers: Debating the Economic, Social and Political Impacts in Singapore," *International Migration Review,* 33:114–36.

Part III

Korpi, Walter, and Joakim Palme. 1998. "The Paradox of Redistribution and Strategies of Equality: Welfare State Institutions, Inequality and Poverty in Western Countries," *American Sociological Review* 63(October):661–87.

Mink, Gwendolyn. 1998. *Welfare's End.* Ithaca, NY: Cornell University Press.

Quadagno, Jill. 1994. *The Color of Welfare.* New York: Oxford University Press.

Quadagno, Jill. 1999. "Creating a Capital Investment Welfare State," *American Sociological Review,* 64 (February):1–10.

Chapter 11

1. Historian E. P. Thompson used the term "moral economy" to connote the cultural embeddedness of patterns of collective action in the marketplace (1971). I apply his term to individual action on the part of single mothers, to show how work and family strategies are embedded in communal norms and commitments.
2. Numerous writers have emphasized continuing class differences in norms of maternal care (Glenn, Chang, and Forcey 1994). Nonetheless, the similarities among contemporary mothers seem greater when we compare any contemporary group's norms with those that were pervasive before the rise of "sentimental" motherhood and "precious" childhood (Ryan 1979; Ulrich 1982; Zelizer 1985).

Anderson, Elijah. 1990. *Streetwise: Race, Class, and Change in an Urban Community.* Chicago: University of Chicago Press.

Bielby, Denise D. 1992. "Commitment to Work and Family," *Annual Review of Sociology,* 18:281–302.

Blank, Rebecca M. 1997. *It Takes a Nation.* New York: Russell Sage Foundation. Princeton, NJ: Princeton University Press.

Burtless, Gary. 1998. "Can the Labor Market Absorb Three Million Welfare Recipients?" *Focus,* 19(3):1–6.

Cancian, Francesca M., and Stacey J. Oliker. 2000. *Caring and Gender.* Thousand Oaks, CA: Pine Forge Press.

Collins, Patricia Hill. 1990. *Black Feminist Thought.* New York: Unwin/Hyman/Routledge.

Derus, Michele. 1998. "W-2 Families Squeeze in Together," *Milwaukee Journal-Sentinel,* January 18, p. F1.

Edin, Kathryn, and Laura Lein. 1997. *Making Ends Meet.* New York: Russell Sage Foundation.

Feld, Scott L. 1981. "The Focused Organization of Social Ties." *American Journal of Sociology,* 86:1015–35.

Fischer, Claude S., Robert M. Jackson, Ann Steuve, Katherine Gerson, and Lynn M. Jones. 1977. *Networks and Places*. New York: Free Press.

Furstenberg, Frank F. 1993. "How Families Manage Risk and Opportunity in Dangerous Neighborhoods." In William J. Wilson (ed.), *Sociology and the Public Agenda*. Newbury Park, CA: Sage.

Garfinkel, Irwin, Sara McLanahan, Daniel Meyer, and Judith Seltzer. 1998. "Fathers Under Fire: The Revolution in Child Support Enforcement," *Focus*, 19(3):24–28.

Gerson, Kathleen. 1985. *Hard Choices: How Women Decide about Work, Career, and Motherhood*. Berkeley, CA: University of California Press.

Glenn, Evelyn Nakano, Grace Chang, and Linda Rennie Forcey (eds.). 1994. *Mothering: Ideology, Experience, and Agency*. New York: Routledge.

Goldberg, Carey. 1999. "Most Get Work After Welfare, Studies Suggest," *New York Times*, April 17, A1.

Hao, Lingxin, and Mary Brinton. 1997. "Productive Activities and Support Systems of Single Mothers," *American Journal of Sociology*, 102(5):1305–44.

Hochschild, Arlie. 1989. *The Second Shift*. New York: Viking Penguin.

Hodgkinson, Virginia A. 1995. "Key Factors Influencing Caring, Involvement, and Community." In Paul G. Schervish et al. (eds.), *Care and Community in Modern Society*. San Francisco: Jossey-Bass, pp. 21–50.

Hofferth, Sandra L. 1984. "Kin Networks, Race, and Family Structure," *Journal of Marriage and the Family*, 46:791–806.

Hogan, Dennis P., David J. Eggebeen, and Clifford Clogg. 1993. "The Structure of Intergenerational Exchange in American Families," *American Journal of Sociology*, 98(6): 1428–58.

Hogan, Dennis P., Ling-Xin Hao, and William Parish. 1990. "Race, Kin Networks, and Assistance to Mother-Headed Families," *Social Forces*, 68:797–812.

Huston, Margo. 1998. "More Women in Shelters," *Milwaukee Journal-Sentinel*, December 12, p. B1.

Janofsky, Michael. 1999. "West Virginia Pares Welfare, but Poor Remain," *New York Times*, March 7, p. A12.

Kaplan, Elaine Bell. 1997. *Not Our Kind of Girl*. Berkeley, CA: University of California Press.

Kaus, Mickey. 1992. *The End of Equality*. New York: Basic Books.

Kleppner, Paul, and Nicholas Theodore. 1997. "Work After Welfare." DeKalb, IL: Office for Social Research, Northern Illinois University.

Kotlowitz, Alex. 1991. *There Are No Children Here*. New York: Anchor Books.

Mahler, Sarah J. 1995. *American Dreaming*. Princeton, NJ: Princeton University Press.

Martin, Elmer P., and Joanne Mitchell Martin. 1978. *The Black Extended Family*. Chicago: University of Chicago Press.

McAdoo, Hariette Pipes. 1986. "Strategies Used by Black Single Mothers against Stress." In Margaret C. Simms and Julianne Malveaux (eds.), *Slipping through the Cracks*. New Brunswick, NJ: Transaction Books.

Mead, Lawrence M. 1992. *The New Politics of Poverty*. New York: Basic Books.

Minkler, Meredith, and Kathleen M. Roe. 1993. *Grandmothers as Caregivers*. Newbury Park, CA: Sage.

Oliker, Stacey J. 1995a. "The Proximate Contexts of Workfare and Work," *Sociological Quarterly*, 36(2):251–72.

Oliker, Stacey J. 1995b. "Work Commitment and Constraint Among Mothers on Work-fare," *Journal of Contemporary Ethnography*, 24(2):165–94.

Pawasarat, John. 1997. "The Employer Perspective: Jobs Held by the Milwaukee County AFDC Single Parent Population (January 1996–March 1997)." Milwaukee, WI: University of Wisconsin-Milwaukee Employment and Training Institute.

Rochefort, David A. 1998. *From Poorhouses to Homelessness: Policy Analysis and Mental Health Care*. Westport, CT: Auburn House.

Rochelle, Anne R. 1997. *No More Kin: Exploring Race, Class, and Gender in Family Networks*. Thousand Oaks, CA: Sage.

Rosier, Katherine Brown, and William A. Corsaro. 1993. "Competent Parents, Complex Lives: Managing Parenthood in Poverty," *Journal of Contemporary Ethnography*, 22: 171–204.

Ruggles, Steven. 1994. "The Origins of African American Family Structure," *American Sociological Review*, 59:136–51.

Ryan, Mary P. 1979. *Womanhood in America from Colonial Times to the Present*. New York: Franklin Watts.

Schweizer, Thomas, and Douglas R. White (eds.) 1998. *Kinship, Networks, and Exchange*. Cambridge, UK: Cambridge University Press.

Stack, Carol B. 1974. *All Our Kin*. New York: Harper & Row.

Stack, Carol, and Linda M. Burton. 1994. "Kinships: Reflections on Family, Generation, and Culture." In Evelyn Nakano Glenn, Grace Chang, and Linda Rennie Forcey, (eds.), *Mothering*. New York: Routledge, pp. 45–66.

Thompson, E. J. 1971. "The Moral Economy of the English Crowd in the Eighteenth Century," *Past and Present*, 50:76–136.

Torrey, E. Fuller. 1997. *Out of the Shadows*. New York: John Wiley.

Uehara, Edwina. 1990. "Dual Exchange Theory, Social Networks, and Informal Support," *American Journal of Sociology*, 96:1305–44.

Ulrich, Laurel Thatcher. 1982. *Good Wives*. New York: Knopf.

U.S. General Accounting Office. 1999. "Welfare Reform: Information on Former Recipients' Status." Washington, DC: GAO/HEHS.

Voydanoff, Patricia (ed.). 1987. *Work and Family Life*. Newbury Park, CA: Sage.

Wellman, Barry, and S. D. Berkowitz (eds.) 1988. *Social Structures: A Network Approach*. Cambridge, UK: Cambridge University Press.

Wellman, Barry, Peter Carrington, and Alan Hall. 1988. "Networks as Personal Communities." In *Social Structures*, ed. Barry Wellman and S. D. Berkowitz, pp. 130–89. Cambridge, UK: Cambridge University Press.

Wellman, Barry, and Scott Wortley. 1990. "Different Strokes for Different Folks: Community Ties and Social Support," *American Journal of Sociology*, 96(3):558–88.

Wilson, William Julius. 1987. *The Truly Disadvantaged*. Chicago: University of Chicago Press.

Zelizer, Viviana. 1985. *Pricing the Priceless Child*. New York: Basic Books.

Chapter 12

1. While divorced mothers receive child support at a higher rate than single mothers do, many of them also do not receive child support. In 1989, of the 58 percent of divorced women nationwide who had a child support order, 51 percent received full support, 24 percent received partial support, and 25 received no child support (U.S. Bureau of the Census 1991). Since many of those 28 percent of divorced women who have no child

support order receive no child support, the actual number of divorced women receiving no child support is much higher than 25 percent.
2. The women were interviewed in 1987 and 1988. Most women lived within the limits of the city of Philadelphia, which is contiguous with the County of Philadelphia and has a population of approximately 1.6 million. A small minority lived in the suburbs. The women in this sample shared many characteristics with women in a national sample of divorced women (Maccoby and Mnookin 1992:62). The racial distribution of the sample approximates that of the city, with 61 percent white women, 35 percent black women, and 3 percent Hispanic women (Philadelphia Health Management Corp. 1988). Forty-eight percent of those contacted agreed to be interviewed—a good response rate for divorced mothers, who can be difficult to locate because they move more frequently than married mothers (Weitzman 1985:408). A detailed description of the data analysis and the sample is reported elsewhere (Kurz 1995).

Arendell, Terry. 1995. *Fathers & Divorce*. Newbury Park, CA: Sage.

Bergmann, Barbara, and Sherry Wetchler. 1994. "Child Support Awards: State Guidelines versus Public Opinion," unpublished paper, department of economics, University of Maryland.

Daniels, Arlene K. 1987. "Invisible Work," *Social Problems*, 34(5):403–15.

Dao, James. 1993. "Divorce Lawyers Assailed in Study by Albany Panel," *New York Times*, Wednesday, May 5, p. A1.

Ellis, Desmond, and Walter DeKeseredy. 1996. *The Wrong Stuff: An Introduction to the Sociological Study of Deviance*. 2nd edition. Toronto: Allyn & Bacon.

Ellis, Desmond, and Noreen Stuckless. 1992. "Preseparation, Marital Conflict Mediation, and Post-Separation Abuse," *Mediation Quarterly*, 9:205–25.

Garfinkel, Irwin. 1992. *Assuring Child Support: An Extension of Social Security*. New York: Russell Sage.

Garfinkel, Irwin, Marygold S. Melli, and John G. Robertson. 1994. "Child Support Orders: A Perspective on Reform," *The Future of the Family: Children and Divorce*, 4:1 (Spring):84–100.

Goldfarb, Sally. 1987. "What Every Lawyer Should Know about Child Support Guidelines," *Family Law Reporter*, 13:3036–37.

Johnson, Holly, and Vincent Sacco. 1995. "Researching Violence Against Women: Statistics Canada National Survey," *Canadian Journal of Criminology*, 37(3):281–304.

Kamerman, Sheila B., and Alfred J. Kahn. 1988. *Mothers Alone: Strategies for a Time of Change*. Newbury Park, CA: Sage.

Katz, Sanford. 1994. "Historical Perspective and Current Trends in the Legal Process of Divorce," *The Future of the Family: Children and Divorce*, 4:1(Spring):44–62.

Kurz, Demie. 1995. *For Richer, For Poorer: Mothers Confront Divorce*. New York: Routledge.

Maccoby, Eleanor E., and Robert H. Mnookin. 1992. *Dividing the Child: Social and Legal Dilemmas of Custody*. Cambridge, MA: Harvard University Press.

Mahoney, Martha. 1991. "Legal Images of Battered Women: Redefining the Issue of Separation," *Michigan Law Review*, 90(1):1–94.

National Resource Center on Domestic Violence. 1997. "The Violence Against Women Act Analysis Series." Prepared by and for the National Resource Center on Domestic Violence and the Battered Women's Justice Project.

Nichols-Caseboldt, Ann. 1992. "The Economic Impact of Child Support Reform on the Poverty Status of Custodial and Noncustodial Families." In Irwin Garfinkel, Sara McLanahan, and Philip Robins (eds.), *Child Support Assurance*. Washington, DC: Urban Institute Press, pp. 189–202.

Philadelphia Health Management Corporation. 1988. *Philadelphia Health Management Household Management Survey 1987*. Philadelphia: Philadelphia Health Management Corporation.

Rhode, Deborah. 1989. *Justice and Gender*. Cambridge, MA: Harvard University Press.

Roberts, Paula G. 1994. *Ending Poverty as We Know It: The Case for Child Support Enforcement and Assurance*. Washington, DC: Center for Law and Social Policy.

Rotella, Elyce. 1995. "Women and the American Economy." In Sheila Ruth (ed.), *Issues in Feminism*. Mountain View, CA: Mayfield Publishing Co., pp. 320–33.

Sawhill, Isabel V. 1977. "Developing Normative Standards for Child Support and Alimony Payments," working paper (September):992–1004. Washington, DC: Urban Institute.

Seltzer, Judith. 1991. "Legal Custody Arrangements and Children's Economic Welfare," *American Journal of Sociology*, 96:895–929.

Seltzer, Judith, and Irwin Garfinkel. 1991. "Inequality of Divorce Settlements: An Investigation of Property Settlements and Child Support Awards," *Social Science Research*, 19:82–91.

Sidel, Ruth. 1996. *Keeping Women and Children Last*. New York: Penguin Books.

Thoennes, Nancy, Patricia Tjaden, and Jessica Pearson. 1991. "The Impact of Child Support Guidelines on Award Adequacy, Award Variability, and Case Processing Efficiency," *Family Law Quarterly*, 25(Fall):325–45.

U.S. Bureau of the Census. 1991. *Child Support and Alimony*. Current Population Reports, Series P–60, No. 173. Washington, DC: Government Printing Office.

U.S. Department of Health and Human Services (DHHS). 1993. *Sixteenth Annual Report to Congress*. DHHS Administration of Children and Families, Office of Child Support Enforcement. Washington, DC: Department of Health and Human Resources.

U.S. General Accounting Office. 1994. "Child Support Enforcement: Credit Bureau Reporting Shows Promise." Letter Report HEHS–94–175 (June 3). Washington, DC: General Accounting Office.

Weitzman, Lenore J. 1985. *The Divorce Revolution*. New York: Free Press.

Chapter 13

The author acknowledges funding from the National Institute on Aging.

Burton, Lynda, Judith Kasper, Andrew Shore, Kathleen Cagney, Thomas LaVeist, Catherine Cubbin, and Pearl German. 1995. "The Structure of Informal Care: Are there Differences by Race?" *Gerontologist*, 35(6): 744–52.

Cantor, Marjorie H. 1989. "Social Care: Family and Community Support Systems," *Annals of the American Academy of Politics and Social Science*, 503(May):94–112.

Coronel, Susan and M. Kitchman. 1997. *Long Term Care Insurance in 1995*. Washington, DC: Health Insurance Association of America.

Doty, Pamela, Mary E. Jackson, and William Crown. 1998. "The Impact of Female Caregivers' Employment Status on Patterns of Formal and Informal Eldercare," *Gerontologist*, 38(3):331–41.

Ettner, Susan L. 1995. "The Impact of 'Parent Care' on Female Labor Supply," *Demography*, 32(1): 63–80.

Falcone, David, and Robert Broyles. 1994. "Access to Long Term Care: Race as a Barrier," *Journal of Health Politics, Policy and Law*, 19(3):583–95.

Gallagher, Dolores, Jonathan Rose, Patricia Rivera, Steven Lovett, and Larry W. Thompson. 1989. "Prevalence of Depression in Family Caregivers," *Gerontologist*, 29(4): 449–56.

George, Linda K., and Lisa P. Gwyther. 1986. "Caregiver Well-Being: A Multidimensional Examination of Family Caregivers of Demented Adults," *Gerontologist*, 26(2):253–60.

Harrow, Brooke S., Sharon L. Tennstedt, and John B. McKinlay. 1995. "How Costly Is It to Care for Disabled Elders in a Community Setting?" *Gerontologist*, 35(6):803–13.

Health Care Financing Administration. 1998. *HCFA-2982 Report*. Center for Medicaid and State Operations. Baltimore, MD.

Health Care Financing Administration. 1999a. *National Health Expenditures Tables*. Office of the Actuary, National Health Statistics Group. Baltimore, MD.

Health Care Financing Administration. 1999b. *HFCA Statistics*. Available on HCFA Web site: www.hcfa.gov/stats/hstats96/blustats.html.

Henretta, John C., Martha S. Hill, Wei Li, Beth J. Soldo, and Douglas A. Wolf. 1997. "Selection of Children to Provide Care: The Effect of Earlier Parental Transfers," *Journals of Gerontology: Social Sciences*, 52B (Special Issue):110–19.

Institute of Medicine. 1986. *Improving the Quality of Care in Nursing Homes*. Washington, DC: National Academy Press.

Kuttner, Robert. 1999. "One More Hoax," *The Washington Post*, January 8, 1999, p. A21.

Life Plans, Inc. 1992. *Who Buys Long Term Care Insurance?: Policy and Research Findings*. Washington, DC: Health Insurance Association of America.

Life Plans, Inc. 1995. *Who Buys Long Term Care Insurance?: 1994–95 Profiles and Innovations in a Dynamic Market*. Washington, DC: Health Insurance Association of America.

Max, Wendy, Pamela Webber, and Patrick Fox. 1995. "Alzheimer's Disease: The Unpaid Burden of Caring," *Journal of Aging and Health*, 7:179–99.

Mellor, Jennifer M. 1999a. "Private Long Term Care Insurance and the Asset Protection Motive," mimeo, Department of Economics. Williamsburg, VA: College of William and Mary.

Mellor, Jennifer M. 1999b. "Long Term Care and Nursing Home Coverage: Are Adult Children Substitutes for Insurance?" mimeo, Department of Economics. Williamsburg, VA: College of William and Mary.

National Alliance for Caregiving and the American Association for Retired Persons (AARP). 1997. *Family Caregiving in the U.S.: Findings from a National Survey*. June. Washington, DC: American Association for Retired Persons.

Quadagno, Jill. 1999. "Creating a New Capital Investment Welfare State: The New American Exceptionalism," *American Sociological Review*, 64(1):1–11.

Pavalko, Eliza K., and Julie E. Artis. 1997. "Women's Caregiving and Paid Work: Causal Relationships in Late Midlife," *Journal of Gerontology: Social Sciences*, 52B(4):S170–79.

Rice, Thomas, Marcia L. Graham, and Peter D. Fox. 1997. "The Impact of Policy Standardization on the Medigap Market," *Inquiry*, 34 (Summer):106–16.

Robinson, Julie, Phyllis Moen, and Donna Dempster-McClain. 1995. "Women's Caregiving: Changing Profiles and Pathways," *Journal of Gerontology: Social Sciences*, 50B(6): S362–373.

Robinson, Katherine Morton. 1997. "Family Caregiving: Who Provides the Care, and At What Cost?" *Nursing Economics*, 15(5):243–47.

Schulte, Bernd. 1996. "Social Protection for Dependence in Old-Age: The Case of Germany." In Roland Eisen and Frank Sloan (eds.), *Long Term Care: Economic Issues and Policy Solutions*. Boston: Kluwer Academic Publishers, pp. 149–70.

Spitze, Glenna, and John Logan. 1990. "Sons, Daughters, and Intergenerational Support," *Journal of Marriage and the Family*, 52(2):420–30.

Stephens, Susan A., and Jon B. Christianson. 1986. *Informal Care of the Elderly*. Lexington, MA: Lexington Books.

Stoller, Eleanor Palo. 1983. "Parental Caregiving by Adult Children," *Journal of Marriage and the Family*, 45(4):851–58.

Stone, Robyn, Gail Lee Cafferata, and Judith Sangl. 1987. "Caregivers of the Frail Elderly: A National Profile," *Gerontologist*, 27(5):616–26.

U.S. Bureau of the Census. 1997. *Statistical Abstract of the United States. 117th Edition*. Washington, DC: Government Printing Office.

U.S. General Accounting Office. 1995. *Long Term Care: Current Issues and Future Directions*. Washington, DC: Government Printing Office, April.

Ward, Debbie. 1990. "Gender, Time and Money in Caregiving," *Scholarly Inquiry for Nursing Practice: An International Journal*, 4(3):223–39.

Wiener, Joshua M. 1998. Prepared statement before the United States Senate Special Committee on Aging. "Can Private Insurance Solve the Long Term Care Problems of the Baby Boom Generation?" Washington, DC: Federal Information Systems Corporation, March 9.

Wiener, Joshua M., and Raymond J. Hanley. 1992. "The Connecticut Model for Financing Long Term Care: A Limited Partnership?" *Journal of the American Geriatric Society*, 40(10):1069–72.

Wiener, Joshua M., Laurel Hixon Illston, and Raymond J. Hanley. 1994. *Sharing the Burden: Strategies for Public and Private Long Term Care Insurance*. Washington, DC: The Brookings Institution.

Wolf, Douglas A., Vicki Freedman, and Beth J. Soldo. 1997. "The Division of Family Labor: Care for Elderly Parents," *Journals of Gerontology: Social Sciences*, 52B (Special Issue):102–9 .

Wolf, Douglas A., and Beth J. Soldo. 1994. "Married Women's Allocation of Time to Employment and Care of Elderly Parents," *Journal of Human Resources*, 29(4):1259–76.

Zweifel, Peter, and Wolfram Strüwe. 1998. "Long Term Care Insurance in a Two-Generation Model," *Journal of Risk and Insurance*, 65(1):13–32.

Chapter 14

For their suggestions and comments on earlier drafts, the authors thank Pam Herd, Deborah Stone, Jill Quadagno, Marjorie DeVault, members of the 1997 "International Conference on Gender, Citizenship, and the Work of Caring," Champaign, Illinois, and members of the Center for Demography and Economics of Aging Seminar, Center for Policy Research, Syracuse University.

Brody, Elaine. 1981. "Women in the Middle and Family Help to Older People," *Gerontologist*, 21(5):471–80.

Cantor, Marjorie. 1983. "Strain Among Caregivers: A Study of Experience in the United States," *Gerontologist,* 23:597–604.

Commonwealth Fund. 1987. *Medicare's Poor.* Washington, DC: Commission on Elderly People Living Alone.

Esping-Andersen, Gosta. 1989. "The Three Political Economies of the Welfare State," *Canadian Review of Sociology and Anthropology,* 26:10–36.

Estes, Caroll. 1989. "Aging, Health, and Social Policy: Crisis and Crossroads," *Journal of Aging and Social Policy,* 1(1–2):17–32.

Estes, Caroll, and J. Swan and Associates. 1993. *The Long Term Care Crisis.* Newbury Park, CA: Sage.

Ettner, Susan. 1993. "Do Elderly Medicaid Patients Experience Reduced Access to Nursing Home Care?" *Journal of Health Economics,* 11:259–80.

Ferguson, Tim. 1992. "Nursing Home Operator Fights to Stop Old Shell Game," *Wall Street Journal,* April 7, p. 17.

Georges, Christopher. 1995. "Republican Plans to Curb Medicaid Spending May Hit Purse Strings of Middle-Class Families," *Wall Street Journal,* September 13, p.14.

Glazer, Nona. 1990. "The Home as Workshop: Women as Amateur Nurses and Medical Care Providers," *Gender & Society,* 4:479–99.

Harrington Meyer, Madonna. 1994a. "Institutional Bias and Medicaid Use in Nursing Homes," *Journal of Aging Studies,* 8(2):179–93.

Harrington Meyer, Madonna. 1994b. "Gender, Race, and the Distribution of Social Assistance: Medicaid Use Among the Frail Elderly," *Gender & Society,* 8(1):8–28.

Hendricks, Joe, and L. R. Hatch. 1993. "Federal Policy and Family Life of Older Americans." In Joe Hendricks and C. Rosenthal (eds.), *The Remainder of These Days: Domestic Policy and Older Families in the United States and Canada.* New York: Garland, pp. 49–74.

Hilkevitch, J. 1993. "State Medicaid Officials Defend Program Against Abuse Charges," *Chicago Tribune,* December 17, p. 4.

Hooyman, Nancy, and Judith Gonyea. 1995. *Feminist Perspectives on Family Care.* Thousand Oaks, CA: Sage.

Kane, Rosalie, and Robert Kane. 1985. "The Feasibility of Universal Long Term Care Benefits: Ideas from Canada," *The New England Journal of Medicine,* 312:1357–64.

Katz, Michael. 1986. *In the Shadow of the Poorhouse: A Social History of Welfare in America.* New York: Basic Books.

Katz Olson, Laura. 1994. "Public Policy and Privatization: Long Term Care in the United States." In L. Katz Olson (ed.), *The Graying of the World.* New York: Haworth, pp. 25–49.

Lavin, Cheryl. 1993. "The Medicaid Game," *Chicago Tribune,* January 31, p. 1.

Margolis, Richard. 1990. *Risking Old Age in America.* Boulder, CO: Westview.

Minnesota Departments of Health and Human Services. 1996. *Profile of Minnesota Nursing Homes and Long-Term Care Alternatives.* St. Paul, MN: Minnesota Departments of Health and Human Services

Moses, Stephen. 1990. "The Fallacy of Impoverishment," *Gerontologist,* 30(1):21–25.

Myles, John. 1988. "Decline or Impasse? The Current State of the Welfare State," *Studies in Political Economy,* 26:73–107.

Neuschler, Edward. 1987. *Medicaid Eligibility for the Elderly in Need of Long Term Care.* Congressional Research Service Contract No. 86–26. Washington, DC: National Governors Association.

Rivlin, Alice, and Joshua Wiener. 1988. *Caring for the Disabled Elderly: Who Will Pay?* Washington, DC: Brookings Institution.

Siegel, Jacob. 1993. *A Generation of Change*. New York: Russell Sage.

Stone, Robyn, Gail Lee Cafferta, and Judith Sangl. 1987. "Caregivers of the Frail Elderly: A National Profile," *Gerontologist*, 27:616–26.

U.S. General Accounting Office. 1990. *Nursing Homes: Admission Problems for Medicaid Recipients and Attempts to Solve Them*. GAO/HRD–90–135. Washington, DC: Government Printing Office.

U.S. House of Representatives. 1998. *Green Book*. Committee of Ways and Means. Washington, DC: Government Printing Office.

U.S. House of Representatives. 1994. *Green Book*. Committee on Ways and Means. Washington, DC: Government Printing Office.

U.S. House of Representatives. 1993. *Medicaid Source Book*. Committee on Energy and Commerce, Subcommittee on Health and the Environment. Washington, DC: Government Printing Office.

Wessel, David. 1991. "Medicaid Is Beginning to Look More Like Part of the Problem with the Health Care System," *Wall Street Journal*, August 8, p. 14.

Wiener, Joshua, and L. Illston. 1994. "Health Care Reform in the 1990s: Where Does Long Term Care Fit In?" *Gerontologist:* 34(3):402–408.

Part IV

Hooyman, Nancy and Judith Gonyea. 1995. *Feminist Perspectives on Family Care: Politics for Gender Justice*.

Chapter 15

Alber, Jens. 1995. "A Framework for the Comparative Study of Social Services," *Journal of European Social Policy*, 5(2):131–49.

Balbo, Laura. 1987. "Crazy Quilts: Rethinking the Welfare State Debate from a Woman's Point of View." In Ann Showstack Sassoon (ed.), *Women and the State. The Shifting Boundaries of Public and Private*. London: Hutchinson, pp. 45–71.

Baldock, John. 1993. "Patterns of Change in the Delivery of Welfare in Europe." In Peter Taylor-Gooby and Robin Lawson (eds.), *Markets and Managers: New Issues on the Delivery of Welfare*. Buckingham, UK: Open University Press, pp. 24–37.

Boeije, Hennie R., A. W. L. Dungen, A. van den Pool, M. H. F. Grijpdonk, and P. A. H. van Lieshout. 1997. "Een Verzorgde Toekomst." Toekomstscenario's voor Verpleging en Verzorging. Utrecht: Vakgroep Verpleging/NIZW.

Boot, J. M., and M. H. J. M. Knapen. 1993. *DeNederlandse Gezondheidszorg*. Utrecht: Het Spectrum.

Clarke, John, and Elizabeth Newman. 1997. *The Managerial State*. London: Sage.

Commissie Structuur en Financiering Gezondheidszorg. 1987. *Bereidheid tot Verandering*. Rijswijk.

Daly, Mary, and Jane Lewis. 1998. "Introduction: Conceptualizing Social Care in the Context of Welfare State Restructuring." In Jane Lewis (ed.), *Gender, Social Care, and Welfare State Restructuring in Europe*. Aldershot, UK: Ashgate, pp. 1–24.

de Boer, A. H., J. C. Hessing-Wagner, M. Mootz, and I. S. Schoemaker-Salkinoja. 1994. *Informele Zorg: Een Verkenning van Huidige en Toekomstige Ontwikkelingen*. Rijswijk/Den Haag: Sociaal en Cultureel Planbureau/VUGA.

Finch, Janet. 1989. *Family Obligations and Social Change.* Cambridge: Polity Press.

Finch, Janet, and Dulcie Groves. 1983. *A Labour of Love: Women, Work, and Caring.* London: Routledge and Kegan Paul.

Fraser, Nancy. 1990. "Struggle over Needs: Outline of a Socialist-Feminist Critical Theory of Late-Capitalist Political Culture." In Linda Gordon (ed.), *Women, the State and Welfare.* Madison: University of Wisconsin Press, pp. 199–225.

Habermas, Jurgen. 1981. *Theorie des Kommunikativen Handelns.* Frankfurt am Main: Suhrkamp Verlag.

Hattinga-Verschure, J. C. M. 1981. *Het Verschijnsel Zorg.* Lochem: De Tijdstroom.

Henshel, R. H. 1990. *Thinking about Social Problems.* San Diego, CA: Harcourt Brace Jovanovich.

Hernes, Helga. 1987. *Welfare State and Women's Power: Essays in State Feminism.* Oslo: Norwegian University Press.

Hoggett, P. 1994. "The Politics of the Modernisation of the UK Welfare State." In R. Burrow and B. Loader (eds.), *Towards a Post-Fordist Welfare State?* London: Routledge.

Jamieson, A. 1991. *Home Care for Older People in Europe. A Comparison of Policies and Practices.* Oxford: Oxford University Press.

Knijn, Trudie C. M. 1998. "Social Care in The Netherlands." In Jane Lewis (ed.), *Gender, Social Care and Welfare State Restructuring in Europe.* Aldershot: Ashgate, pp. 85–110.

Leira, Arnlaug. 1990. "Coping with Care. Mothers in a Welfare State." In Clare Ungerson (ed.), *Gender and Caring: Work and Welfare in Britain and Scandinavia.* Hemel Hempstead, UK: Harvester Wheatsheaf, pp. 133–59.

Lewis, Jane. 1998. *Gender, Social Care and Welfare State Restructuring in Europe.* Aldershot: Ashgate.

Los, Tessa. 1997. "Bureaucratisering, Managementisme en de Ondergang van het Beroep Gezinsverzorgster," *Amsterdams Sociologisch Tijdschrift,* 23:709–32.

Maessen, P. J. J. 1989. *Bezuinigingen op de Gezinsverzorging; Besluitvorming in de Verzorgingsstaat.* Amersfoort/Leuven: Acco.

Ministerie van Cultuur Recreatie en Maatschappelijk Werk. 1973. *Schaalvergroting in de gezinsverzorging en het algemeen maatschappelijk werk.* Rijswijk.

Nationale Raad voor de Volksgezondheid (National Council for Public Health). 1992. "Advies kwalitie, organisatie en financiering thuiszorg," Publikatie 33/90. Zoetermeer.

Niej, R. 1989. *De Organisatie van het Maatschappelijk Werk.* Zutphen: De Walburg Pers.

Ostner, Ilona. 1998. "The Politics of Care Policies in Germany." In Jane Lewis (ed.), *Gender, Social Care and Welfare State Restructuring in Europe.* Aldershot, UK: Ashgate, pp. 111–38.

Simonen, Leila, and Anne Kovalainen. 1998. "Paradoxes of Social Care Restructuring: The Finnish Case." In Jane Lewis (ed.), *Gender, Social Care and Welfare State Restructuring in Europe.* Aldershot, UK: Ashgate, pp. 229–56.

Sociaal en Culureel Planbureau. 1996. *Sociaal en Cultureel Rapport 1996.* Rijswijk: Sociaal en Cultureel Planbureau.

Szebehely, Marta. 1998. "Changing Divisions of Carework: Caring for Children and Frail Elderly People in Sweden." In Jane Lewis (ed.), *Gender, Social Care and Welfare State Restructuring in Europe.* Aldershot, UK: Ashgate, pp. 256–83.

Ungerson, Clare. 1997. "Social Politics and the Commodification of Care." In Trudie Knijn and Clare Ungerson (guest eds.), *Social Politics,* special issue: *Gender and Care Work in Welfare States,* 4(3):362–81.

van Doorn, J. A. A., and C. J. M. Schuijt. 1978. *De Stagnerrende Verzorgingsstaat.* Amsterdam/Meppel: Boom.

Vulto, Marij, and Marjolein Moree. 1996. *Thuisverzorging als Professie. Een Combinatie van Hoofd, Hart en Hand*. Utrecht: De Tijdstroom.
Waerness, Kari. 1984. "Caring as Women's Work in the Welfare State." In H. Holter (ed.), *Patriarchy in a Welfare Society*. Oslo: Universitetsforlaget, pp. 67–87.
Weber, Max. 1964. *The Theory of Social and Economic Organization*. New York and London: Free Press.
Wilson, Elizabeth. 1977. *Women and the Welfare State*. London: Tavistock.

Chapter 16

Preparation of this chapter was supported in part by the U.S. Department of Education, Office of Special Education and Rehabilitative Services, National Institute on Disability and Rehabilitation Research under Cooperative Agreements no. H133B0003–90 and H133B80048 awarded to the Center on Human Policy, Syracuse University. The opinions expressed herein are those of the author, and no endorsement by the U.S. Department of Education should be inferred. Support was also provided by the Icelandic Research Council. The author would like to thank Steven Taylor, Marjorie DeVault, Robert Bogdan, Bonnie Shoultz, Zana Lutfiyya, Barbara Ayres, and Pam Walker for their contributions to this chapter.

Abel, E. K. 1991. *Who Cares for the Elderly? Public Policy and the Experience of Adult Daughters*. Philadelphia: Temple University Press.
Abel, E. K. and M. K. Nelson (eds.). 1990a. *Circles of Care: Work and Identity in Women's Lives*. Albany, NY: State University of New York Press.
Abel, E. K. and M. K. Nelson. 1990b. "Circles of Care: An Introductory Essay." In E. K. Abel and M. K. Nelson (eds.), *Circles of Care: Work and Identity in Women's Lives*. Albany, NY: State University of New York Press, pp. 4–34.
Amado, A. N. (ed.) 1993. *Friendships and Community Connections between People with and without Disabilities*. Baltimore: Paul H. Brookes.
Baldwin, S., and C. Glendinning. 1983. "Employment, Women and their Disabled Children." In J. Finch and D. Groves (eds.), *A Labour of Love: Women, Work and Caring*. London: Routledge and Kegan Paul, pp. 53–71.
Berg, B. J. 1986. *The Crisis of the Working Mother: Resolving the Conflict between Family and Work*. New York: Summit Books.
Bogdan, R. and S. K. Biklen. 1998. *Qualitative Research for Education: An Introduction to Theory and Methods*, 3rd edition. Boston: Allyn and Bacon.
Bogdan, R., and S. J. Taylor. 1987a. "Conclusion: The Next Wave." In S.J. Taylor, D. Biklen, and J. Knoll (eds.), *Community Integration for People with Severe Disabilities*. New York: Teachers College Press, pp. 209–13.
Bogdan, R., and S. J. Taylor. 1987b. "Toward a Sociology of Acceptance: The Other Side of the Study of Deviance," *Social Policy*, 18(2):34–39.
Braddock, D. and R. Hemp. 1997. "Toward Family and Community: Mental Retardation Services in Massachusetts, New England, and the United States," *Mental Retardation*, 34 (4):241–56.
Bradley, V. J. 1988. *The Medicaid Family and Community Service Act: How Does It Address Research Findings, Quality Assurance, and Family Support?* A statement prepared for the U.S. Senate Finance Committee, United States Senate, Washington, DC.

Brown, C., and J. A. Pechman (eds.). 1987. *Gender in the Workplace*. Washington, DC: Brookings Institution.

Bulmer, M. 1987. *The Social Basis of Community Care*. London: Allen and Unwin.

Chodorow, N. 1978. *The Reproduction of Mothering: Psychoanalysis and the Sociology of Gender*. Berkeley, CA: University of California Press.

Coltrane, S. 1989. "Household Labor and the Routine Production of Gender," *Social Problems*, 36(5):473–90.

Daniels, A. K. 1987. "Invisible Work," *Social Problems*, 34(5):403–15.

Daniels, A. 1988. *Invisible Careers: Women's Civic Leaders from the Volunteer World*. Chicago: University of Chicago Press.

DeVault, M. L. 1991. *Feeding the Family: The Social Organization of Caring as Gendered Work*. Chicago: University of Chicago Press.

Dornbusch, S. M. and M. H. Strober (eds.). 1988. *Feminism, Children and the New Families*. New York: Guilford.

Farber, B. 1986. "Historical Contexts of Research on Families with Mentally Retarded Members." In J.J. Gallagher and P. M. Vietze (eds.), *Families of Handicapped Persons: Research, Programs, and Policy Issues*. Baltimore: Paul H. Brookes, pp. 3–23.

Fisher, B. 1990. "Alice in the Human Services: A Feminist Analysis of Women in the Caring Professions." In E.K. Abel and M. K. Nelson (eds.), *Circles of Care: Work and Identity in Women's Lives*. Albany, NY: State University of New York Press, pp. 108–31.

Fisher, B., and J. Tronto. 1990. "Toward a Feminist Theory of Caring." In E. K. Abel and M.K. Nelson (eds.), *Circles of Care: Work and Identity in Women's Lives*. Albany, NY: State University of New York Press, pp. 35–62.

Forest, M. 1989. *It's About Relationships*. Toronto, Ontario: Frontier College Press.

Gardener, J., and M. S. Chapman. 1992. *Developing Staff Competencies for Supporting People with Developmental Disabilities: An Orientation Handbook*. Baltimore: Paul H. Brookes.

Gallagher, J. J., and P .M. Vietze (eds.). 1986. *Families of Handicapped Persons: Research, Programs, and Policy Issues*. Baltimore: Paul H. Brookes, pp. 3–23.

Gerson, J. H., and K. Peiss. 1985. "Boundaries, Negotiation, Consciousness: Reconceptualizating Gender Relations," *Social Problems*, 32(4):317–31.

Gilligan, C. 1982. *In a Different Voice: Psychological Theory and Women's Development*. Cambridge, MA: Harvard University Press.

Graham, H. 1983. "Caring: A Labour of Love." In J. Finch and D. Groves (eds.), *A Labour of Love: Women, Work and Caring*. London: Routledge and Kegan Paul, pp. 13–30.

Hagner, D., P. Rogan, and S. Murphy. 1992. "Facilitating Natural Supports in the Workplace: Strategies for Support Consultants," *Journal of Rehabilitation*, 58(1):29–34.

Hicks, C. 1988. *Who Cares: Looking After People at Home*. London: Virago Press.

Hutchison, P. 1990. *Making Friends: Developing Relationships between People with a Disability and Other Members of the Community*. Toronto: G. Allan Roeher Institute.

Kaiser, A. P. and C. M. McWhorter (eds.). 1990. *Preparing Personnel to Work with Persons with Severe Disabilities*. Baltimore: Paul H. Brookes.

Knoll, J. and A. Ford. 1987. "Beyond Caregiving: A Reconceptualization of the Role of the Residential Service Provider." In S.J. Taylor, D. Biklen, and J. Knoll (eds.), *Community Integration For People With Severe Disabilities*. New York: Teachers College Press, pp. 129–46.

Krauss, M. W., M. M. Seltzer, and S.J. Goodman. 1992. "Social Support Networks of Adults with Mental Retardation Who Live At Home," *American Journal on Mental Retardation*, 96(4):423–41.

Lewis, J., and B. Meredith. 1988. *Daughters Who Care: Daughters Caring for Mothers At Home*. London: Routledge.

Lundgren, R. I. and C. H. Browner. 1990. "Caring For the Institutionalized Mentally Retarded: Work Culture and Work-Based Social Support." In E. K. Abel and M. K. Nelson (eds.), *Circles of Care: Work and Identity in Women's Lives*. Albany, NY: State University of New York Press, pp. 150–172.

Lutfiyya, Z. M. 1991. " 'A Feeling of Being Connected': Friendships between People With and Without Learning Difficulties," *Disability, Handicap and Society*, 6(3):233–45.

McKnight, J. 1987. "Regenerating Community," *Social Policy*, 17(3):54–58.

McKnight, J. 1995. *The Careless Society: Community and Its Counterfeits*. New York: Basic Books.

Nisbet, J., and M. Callahan. 1987. "Achieving Success in Integrated Workplaces: Critical Elements in Assisting Persons With Severe Disabilities." In S. J. Taylor, D. Biklen, and J. Knoll (eds.), *Community Integration for People With Severe Disabilities*. New York: Teachers College Press, pp. 184–201.

Noddings, N. 1984. *Caring: A Feminine Approach to Ethics and Moral Education*. Berkeley: University of California Press.

Norris, J. 1988. *Daughters of the Elderly: Building Partnerships in Caregiving*. Bloomington: Indiana University Press.

O'Brien, J., and C. L. O'Brien. 1996. *Members of Each Other: Building Communities in Company with People with Developmental Disabilities*. Toronto, Ontario: Inclusion Press.

O'Connor, S. 1995. "More Than They Bargained For: The Meaning of Support to Families." In S. J. Taylor, R. Bogdan, and S. M. Lutfiyya (eds.), *The Variety of Community Experience: Qualitative Studies of Family and Community Life*. Baltimore: Paul H. Brookes, pp. 193–210.

Oliver, J. 1983. "The Caring Wife." In J. Finch and D. Groves (eds.), *A Labour of Love: Women, Work and Caring*. London: Routledge and Kegan Paul, pp. 72–88.

Perske, R. 1988. *Circles of Friends*. Nashville, TN: Abingdon Press.

Racino, J. A. 1990. "Preparing Personnel to Work in Community Support Service." In A. P. Kaiser and C. M. McWhorter (eds.), *Preparing Personnel to Work with Persons with Severe Disabilities*. Baltimore: Paul H. Brookes, pp. 203–226.

Rich, A. 1986. *Of Woman Born: Motherhood As Experience and Institution*, 10th anniversary edition New York: W. W. Norton.

Ruddick, S. 1989. *Maternal Thinking: Toward a Politics of Peace*. Boston: Beacon Press.

Sherman, B. R. 1988. "Predictors of the Decision to Place Developmentally Disabled Family Members in Residential Care," *American Journal on Mental Retardation*, 92(4):344–51.

Singer, G. H. S., and L. K. Irvin (eds.). 1989. *Support for Caregiving Families: Enabling Positive Adaptation to Disability*. Baltimore: Paul H. Brookes.

Smith, D.E. 1987. *The Everyday World As Problematic: A Feminist Sociology*. Boston: Northeastern University Press.

Smull, M. W. and G. T. Bellamy. 1991. "Community Services for Adults with Disabilities: Policy Challenges in the Emerging Support Paradigm." In L. Meyer, C. Peck, and L. Brown (eds.), *Critical Issues in the Lives of People with Severe Disabilities*. Baltimore: Paul H. Brookes, pp. 527–36.

Schwartz, D. 1992. *Crossing the River: Creating a Conceptual Revolution in Community and Disability*. Boston: Brookline.

Taylor, S. J., and R. Bogdan. 1998. *Introduction to Qualitative Research Methods: A Guidebook and Resource*, 3rd edition. New York: John Wiley and Sons.

Taylor, S. J., and R. Bogdan. 1989. "On Accepting Relationship between People with Mental Retardation and Nondisabled People: Towards an Understanding of Acceptance," *Disability, Handicap and Society*, 4(1):21–36.

Taylor, S. J., R. Bogdan, and J. A. Racino (eds.). 1991. *Life in the Community: Case Studies of Organizations Supporting People with Disabilities*. Baltimore: Paul H. Brookes.

Taylor, S. J., J. A. Racino, J. A. Knoll, and Z. Lutfiyya. 1987. *The Nonrestrictive Environment: On Community Integration for People with the Most Severe Disabilities*. Syracuse, NY: Human Policy Press.

Taylor, S. J., R. Bogdan, and Z. M. Lutfiyya (eds.). 1995. *The Variety of Community Experience: Qualitative Studies of Family and Community Life*. Baltimore: Paul H. Brookes.

Thorne, B., and M. Yalom (eds.). 1982. *Rethinking the Family: Some Feminist Questions*. New York: Longman.

Traustadóttir, R. 1987. *Idaho Personal Care Home Providers* [Unpublished field notes]. Syracuse, NY: Center on Human Policy, Syracuse University.

Traustadóttir, R. 1991. "Mothers Who Care: Gender, Disability, and Family Life," *Journal of Family Issues*, 12(2): 211–228.

Traustadóttir, R. 1992. *Disability Reform and the Role of Women: Community Inclusion and Caring Work*, unpublished Ph.D. dissertation. Syracuse, NY: Syracuse University.

Traustadóttir, R. 1993. "The Gendered Context of Friendship." In A. N. Amado (ed.), *Friendships and Community Connections between People with and without Disabilities*. Baltimore: Paul H. Brookes, pp. 109–27.

Traustadóttir, R. 1995. "A Mother's Work is Never Done: Constructing a "Normal" Family Life." In S.J. Taylor, R. Bogdan, and S. M. Lutfiyya (eds.), *The Variety of Community Experience: Qualitative Studies of Family and Community Life*. Baltimore: Paul H. Brookes, pp. 47–65.

Traustadóttir, R., and S. J. Taylor. 1998. "Invisible Women, Invisible Work: Women's Caring Work in Developmental Disability Services." In S. J. Taylor and R. Bogdan (eds.), *Introduction to Qualitative Research Methods: A Guidebook and Resource*, third edition. New York: John Wiley and Sons, pp. 205–20.

Trebilcot, J. (ed.). 1984. *Mothering: Essays in Feminist Theory*. Totowa, NJ: Rowman and Allanheld.

Ungerson, C. 1983. "Why Do Women Care?" In J. Finch and D. Groves (eds.), *A Labour of Love: Women, Work and Caring*. London: Routledge and Kegan Paul, pp. 31–50.

Waring, M. 1988. *If Women Counted: A New Feminist Economics*. New York: Harper Collins.

Wearing, B. 1984. *The Ideology of Motherhood: A Study of Sydney Suburban Mothers*. Sydney, Australia: George Allen and Unwin.

West, C., and D. H. Zimmerman. 1987. "Doing Gender," *Gender and Society*, 1(2):125–51.

Wolfensberger, W. 1987. "Values in the Funding of Social Services," *American Journal of Mental Deficiency*, 92(2):141–43.

Chapter 17

This work was funded by a National Institute on Aging grant from Syracuse University's Aging Center. I want to thank Rae Banks, my co-investigator, for her labor on the project and comments on this paper. I want to also recognize useful comments from Marti Rawlings, Monisha Das Gupta, and Fanon Che Wilkins, as well as administrative support provided by the Center for Policy Research.

Bandstra, Emmalee S. 1992. "Assessing Acute and Long-Term Physical Effects of In Utero Drug Exposure on the Perinate, Infant and Child," *NIDA Research Monograph Series,* 117. Washington, DC: National Institute on Drug Abuse.

Barton, Sharon, Rosanne Harrigan, and Alice M. Tse. 1995. "Prenatal Cocaine Exposure: Implication for Practice, Policy and Development, and Needs for Future Research," *Journal of Perinatology,* 15(1):10–22.

Brown, Claude. 1965. *Manchild in the Promised Land.* New York: Signet Books.

Bryson, Ken, and Lynne M. Casper. 1999. Coresident Grandparents and Grandchildren. Bureau of the Census. Current Population Reports Special Issue. May 1999.

Burton, Linda. 1992. "Black Grandparents Rearing Children of Drug-Addicted Parents: Stressors, Outcomes, and Social Service Needs," *The Gerontologist,* 32(6):744–51.

Busch, Allison, Marjorie Cantor, Igal Jellinek, and Bobbie Sackman. 1997. "The Impact of Welfare Reform on the Elderly of New York City," mimeo. New York: Council of Senior Centers and Services of New York City.

Casper, Lynne M., and Kenneth R. Bryson. 1998. Coresident Grandparents and Their Grandchildren: Grandparent Maintained Families. Bureau of the Census. Population Division Working Paper Number 26. March 1998.

Collins, Patricia Hill. 1994. "Shifting the Center: Race, Class and Feminist Theorizing About Motherhood." In Evelyn Nakano Glenn, Grace Chang, and Linda Renne Forc (eds.), *Mothering: Ideology, Experience, Agency.* New York: Routledge.

Dicker, Marvin, and Eldin A. Leighton. 1994. "Trends in the US Prevalence of Drug-Using Parturient Women and Drug Affected Newborns 1979 through 1990," *American Journal of Public Health,* 84(9):1433–38.

Feigelman, Susan, Susan Auravin, Howard Dubowitz, Donna Harrington, Raymond Starr, and Vicki Tepper. 1995. "Sources of Health Care and Health Needs among Children in Kinship Care," *Archives of Pediatrics and Adolescent Medicine,* 149(8):882–86.

Fernandez, R., and D. Harris. 1992. "Social Isolation and the Underclass." In A. V. Harrell and G. E. Peterson (eds.), *Drugs, Crime, and Social Isolation: Barriers to Urban Opportunity.* Washington, DC: Urban Institute.

Franklin, Donna L. 1997. *Ensuring Inequality: The Structural Transformation of the African-American Family.* New York: Oxford University Press.

Fullilove, M. T., and R. E. Fullilove. 1989. "Intersecting Epidemics: Black Teen Crack Use and Sexually Transmitted Disease," *JAMWA,* 44(5):146–53.

Giele, Janet. 1997. "Introduction: Windows on New Family Forms: Insights from Feminist and Familist Perspectives," *Qualitative Sociology,* 20(2):143–52.

Halfon, Neal, Ana Mendonca, and Gale Berkowitz. 1995. "Health Status of Children in Foster Care: The Experience of the Center for the Vulnerable Child," *Archives of Pediatrics and Adolescent Medicine* 149(4):386–92.

Hegar, Rebecca, and Maria Scannapieco. 1995. "From Family Duty to Family Policy: The Evolution of Kinship 'Care'," *Child Welfare,* 74(1):200–216.

Jackson, James, Linda Chatters, and Robert Taylor. 1993. *Aging in Black America.* Newbury Park, CA: Sage.

Jarrett, Robin L. 1993. "Focus Group Interviewing with Low Income Minority Populations: A Research Experience." In David Morgan (ed.), *Successful Focus Groups: Advancing the State of Art.* Newbury Park, CA: Sage.

Jarrett, Robin L. 1994. "Living Poor: Family Life Among Single Parent, African-American Women," *Social Problems,* 56:101–16.

Jarrett, Robin L. 1997. "African-American Family and Parenting Strategies in Impoverished Neighborhoods," *Qualitative Sociology*, 20(2):275–88.

Jendrek, Margaret. 1994. "Grandparents Who Parent Their Grandchildren: Circumstances and Decisions," *Gerontologist*, 34(2):206–16.

Johnson, Bruce, Terry Williams, Kojo Dei, and Harry Sanabria. 1990. "Drug Abuse in the Inner City: Impact on Hard-Drug Users and the Community." In Michael Tonry and James Q. Wilson (eds.), *Drugs and Crime*. Chicago: University of Chicago Press.

Johnson, H., and T. S. Rosen. 1990. "Mother-Infant Interaction in a Multirisk Population," *American Journal of Orthopsychiatry*, 60(2):281–88.

Johnson, H., M. B. Glassman, K. B. Fiks, and T. Rosen. 1988. "Resilient Children: Individual Differences in Developmental Outcome of Children Born to Drug Abusers," *Journal of Genetic Psychology*, 151(4):523–39.

Joslin, Daphne, and Anne Brouard. 1995. "The Prevalence of Grandmothers as Primary Caregivers in a Poor Pediatric Population," *Journal of Community Health*, 20(5):383–401.

Kivett, Vira. 1993. "Racial Comparisons of the Grandmother Role," *Family Relations*, 42:165–72.

McLean, Beth, and Rebecca Thomas. 1996. "Informal and Formal Kinship Care Populations: A Study in Contrasts," *Child Welfare*, 75(5):489–505.

Minkler, Meredith, and Kathleen Roe. 1993. *Grandmothers as Caregivers: Raising Children of the Crack Cocaine Epidemic*. Newbury Park, CA: Sage.

Mullen, Faith. 1995. *A Tangled Web: Public Benefits, Grandparents, and Grandchildren*. Washington, DC: Public Policy Institute American Association of Retired Persons (AARP).

Mullen, Faith. 1997. "Grandparents and the Welfare Reform Act," *Parenting Grandchildren: A Voice for Grandparents*. American Association of Retired Persons (AARP), 3(1):4–7.

Perez-Porter, Melinda. 1996. "The Effect of Welfare Reform on Grandparents Who Are the Primary Caregivers of Their Grandchildren." Testimony given at a public hearing of the New York City Council Committee on Aging. New York: Council Committee on Aging.

Roe, Kathleen, Meredith Minkler, and Rama-Selassie Barnwell. 1994. "The Assumption of Caregiving: Grandmothers Raising the Children of the Crack Cocaine Epidemic," *Qualitative Health Research*, 4(3):281–303.

Ross, Jane. 1995. *Foster Care—Health Needs of Many Young Children Are Unknown and Unmet*. Washington, DC: Government Accounting Office.

Rovner, Sandy. 1995. "Families Calling Granny 'Mom'—People Raising Their Children's Children," *Washington Post*, April 24, p. D5.

Select Committee on Aging and the Congressional Black Caucus. 1991. *The Challenging Health Care Issues Affecting Older African-Americans*. House of Representatives, 102nd Congress, First Session.

Takas, Marianne. 1994. *Kinship Care and Family Preservation: Options for States in Legal and Policy Development*. Final revised edition. Washington, DC: American Bar Association Center on Children and the Law.

U.S. Department of Justice, Office of Justice Programs. 1992. *Criminal Victimization in the United States, 1991*. Washington, DC: Bureau of Justice Statistics.

Vega, William, Bohdan Kolody, Jimmy Hwang, and Amanda Noble. 1993. "Prevalence and Magnitude of Perinatal Substance Exposure in California," *New England Journal of Medicine*, 329(12):850–54.

Wallace, R. 1990. "Urban Desertification, Public Health and Public Order: 'Planned Shrinkage,' Violent Death, Substance Abuse and AIDS in the Bronx," *Social Science and Medicine*, 31(7):801–13.

Wallace, R, D. Wallace, and H. Andrews. 1995. "AIDS, Tuberculosis, Violent Crime and Low Birthweight in Eight U.S. Metropolitan Areas: Public Policy and the Regional Diffusion of Inner City Markers," *Environment and Planning A 1997*, 29:1–13.

Wilson, William J. 1987. *The Truly Disadvantaged: The Inner City, the Underclass and Public Policy*. Chicago: University of Chicago Press.

Chapter 18

This paper was funded in part through a grant from Ronald McDonald House Charities. We thank the residents of Hope Meadows, who so willingly shared their stories and insights with us.

American Academy of Pediatrics, Committee on Early Childhood Pediatrics. 1993. "Adoption and Dependent Care," *Pediatrics*, May: 1007–9.

Benner, Patricia, and Judith Wrubel. 1989. *The Primacy of Caring: Stress and Coping in Health and Illness*. Menlo Park, CA: Addison-Wesley.

Benson, Peter L. 1997. *All Kids Are Our Kids*. San Francisco: Jossey-Bass.

Brown, Lyn Mikel, and Carol Gilligan. 1991. "Listening for Voice in Narratives of Relationship." In Mark B. Tappan and Martin J. Packer (eds.), *Narrative and Storytelling: Implications for Understanding Moral Development*. San Francisco: Jossey-Bass, pp. 43–62.

Chaskin, Robert J. 1997. "Perspectives on Neighborhood and Community: A Review of the Literature," *Social Service Review*, December: 521–47.

Child Welfare League of America. 1991. *Children at the Front: A Different View of the War on Alcohol and Drugs*. North American Commission on Chemical Dependency and Child Welfare Final Report and Recommendations. Washington, DC: Child Welfare League of America.

Cole, Elizabeth S., and Kay S. Donley. 1990. "History, Values, and Placement Decisions in Adoption." In David M. Brodzinsky and Martin D. Schechter (eds.), *The Psychology of Adoption*. New York: Oxford University Press.

Dewey, John. 1902. *The School and Society*. Chicago: University of Chicago Press.

Fromm, Erich. 1956. *The Art of Loving*. New York: Harper & Row.

GAO Report. 1998. *Agencies Face Challenges Securing Stable Homes for Children of Substance Abusers*. Washington, DC: General Accounting Office. September 30.

Gardner, John W. 1995. "The New Leadership Agenda." In Gozdz Kazimierz (ed.), *Community Building: Renewing Spirit & Learning in Business*. San Francisco: Sterling & Stone, pp. 283–303.

Gilligan, Carol. 1982. *In a Different Voice*. Cambridge, MA: Harvard University Press.

Gilligan, Carol. 1988. "Remapping the Moral Domain: New Images of Self in Relationship." In Carol Gilligan, Janie Victoria Ward, and Jill McLean Taylor (eds.), *Mapping the Moral Domain*. Cambridge, MA: Harvard University Press, pp. 3–19.

Gilligan, Carol, Janie Victoria Ward, and Jill McLean Taylor. 1988. *Mapping the Moral Domain*. Cambridge, MA: Harvard University Press.

Gordon, Suzanne, Patricia Benner, and Nel Noddings. 1996. *Caregiving: Readings in Knowledge, Practice, Ethics, and Politics*. Philadelphia: University of Pennsylvania Press.

Harris, Mark. 1997. "It Takes This Village." *Hope Magazine*, February:32–39.

Hope For The Children. 1996. *Progress Report.* January 1 – June 30. Rantoul, IL.

Hopping, David. 1998. *Community as intervention: Creating an intergenerational network of care and human service.* Unpublished manuscript.

Institute for Government and Public Affairs. 1996. *Current Data on Foster Care and Adoption in Illinois.* Urbana: University of Illinois Press.

Jarman, Beth and George Land. 1995. "Beyond Breakpoint: Possibilities for New Community." In Gozdz Kazimierz (ed.), *Community Building: Renewing Spirit & Learning in Business.* San Francisco: Sterling & Stone, pp. 21–33.

Key, Janet. 1994. "Saving Our Children: DCFS Struggles to Get It Right," *Chicago Enterprise,* September/October:18–23.

Krause Eheart, Brenda, and Martha B. Power. 1988. "An Interpretive Study of Adoption: The Interplay of History, Power, Knowledge, and Emotion," *Contemporary Ethnography,* 17:326–47.

Krause Eheart, Brenda, and Martha. B. Power. 1995. "Understanding the Past, Present, and Future Through Stories," *Sociological Quarterly,* 36(1):197–213.

Krause Eheart, Brenda, and Christopher T. Zimmerman. 1998. "Hope For The Children: Ending Discontinuity in Foster Care," *Zero to Three,* 18(6):21–26.

McKnight, John. 1995. *The Careless Society: Community and Its Counterfeits.* New York: Basic Books.

Murdoch, Iris. 1970. *The Sovereignty of Good.* Great Britain: Cox & Wyman. Reading.

Noddings, Nel. 1984. *Caring: A Feminine Approach to Ethics & Moral Education.* Berkeley: University of California Press.

Noddings, Nel. 1992. *The Challenge to Care in Schools: An Alternative Approach to Education.* New York: Teachers College Press.

North American Council on Adoptable Children. 1998. "More Children Need Families," *Adoptalk,* Fall:1.

Paul, Jordon. 1995. "The Personal Elements of Effective Community." In Gozdz Kazimierz (ed.), *Community Building: Renewing Spirit & Learning in Business.* San Francisco: Sterling & Stone, pp. 202–19.

Peck, Scott M. 1987. *The Different Drum: Community Making and Peace.* New York: Simon & Schuster.

Power, Martha Bauman, and Brenda Krause Eheart. 1995. "Adoption, Myth, and Emotion Work: Paths to Disillusionment," *Social Perspectives on Emotions,* 3:97–120.

Rosenthal, J. A., and V. K. Groze. 1992. *Special-Needs Adoption: A Study of Intact Families.* New York: Praeger.

Schorr, Lisbeth B. 1988. *Within Our Reach: Breaking the Cycle of Disadvantage.* New York: Anchor.

Schorr, Lisbeth B. 1997. *Common Purpose: Strengthening Families and Neighborhoods to Rebuild America.* New York: Doubleday.

Smith, Wes. 1999. "Hope Meadows: A Town Where Abused Children Reclaim Their Childhood," *Biography,* January:87–89, 117.

Tappan, Mark B., and Martin J. Packer. 1991. *Narrative and Storytelling: Implications for Understanding Moral Development.* San Francisco: Jossey-Bass.

Tarlow, Barbara. 1996. "Caring: A Negotiated Process That Varies." In Suzanne Gordon, Patricia Benner, and Nel Noddings (eds.), *Caregiving.* Philadelphia: University of Pennsylvania Press, pp. 56–82.

Tronto, Joan C. 1993. *Moral Boundaries: A Political Argument for an Ethic of Care.* New York: Routledge.

Whitney, Rondayln Varney. 1995. "Caring: An Essential Element." In Gozdz Kazimierz (ed.), *Community Building.* San Francisco: Sterling & Stone, pp. 199–206.

EMILY K. ABEL is professor of health services and women's studies at UCLA. She is co-editor (with Margaret K. Nelson) of *Circles of Care: Work and Identity in Women's Lives,* and author of *Who Cares for the Elderly? Public Policy and the Experiences of Adult Daughters* and *Hearts of Wisdom: American Women Caring for Kin, 1850–1940.*

MARTHA BAUMAN POWER is an associate professor of child development and family relations at Illinois State University. She has published in the areas of foster care/adoption and early childhood socialization.

FRANCESCA M. CANCIAN is a professor of sociology at the University of California at Irvine. She is author of *Caring and Gender* (with Stacey Oliker) and is currently working on standards for child care within the family and in day care.

SCOTT COLTRANE is a professor of sociology at the University of California, Riverside, and associate director of the Center for Family Studies. He is the author of *Sociology of Marriage and the Family* (with Randall Collins), *Gender & Families,* and *Family Man: Fatherhood, Housework, and Gender Equity.* His current research interests include cultural images of gender, fatherhood movements, and the effects of economic stress on family functioning and child development.

JUSTIN GALT is a student in the sociology doctoral program at the University of California, Riverside. His research interests include adolescent development, social psychology, and sociolegal studies.

MADONNA HARRINGTON MEYER is an associate professor of sociology and senior research associate for the Center for Policy Research at Syracuse University. She is the author of a series of articles on economic and health security in old age, appearing in such journals as the *Journal of Health and Social Behavior, Gender & Society, The American Sociological Review,* and *The Gerontologist.*

PAM HERD is working on her Ph.D. in sociology at Syracuse University. Her research areas include the welfare state, care work, and aging. She is a 1999–2000 recipient of an AARP Andrus Foundation Scholarship.

ANN HERDA-RAPP is an assistant professor in the department of anthropology and sociology at the University of Wisconsin, Marathon. Her areas of research interest include gender, environmental sociology, social movements, and social problems.

PIERRETTE HONDAGNEU-SOTELO is the author of *Gendered Transitions: Mexican Experiences of Immigration,* co-editor of *Challenging Fronteras: Structuring Latina and Latino Lives in the U.S.,* and co-editor of *Through the Prism of Difference: Readings on Sex and Gender.* She teaches in the department of sociology and in the American studies and ethnicity program at the University of Southern California.

TRUDIE KNIJN is an associate professor of social sciences at the University of Utrecht. She is the coordinator of the European Network on Women, Welfare State and Citizenship. Her current research is on transformations in social care and care relationships from a comparative perspective.

BRENDA KRAUSE EHEART is a research associate with the sociology department and the director of the Hope For The Children Research and Policy Program in the Institute of Government and Public Affairs at the University of Illinois, Urbana-Champaign. She has published books and articles in the areas of child care and adoption.

DEMIE KURZ, who teaches women's studies and sociology at the University of Pennsylvania, studies family and gender issues. She is the author of *For Richer, For Poorer: Mothers Confront Divorce.* Her current research concerns the work of parenting, in particular the care work that parents do with their teenage children.

JENNIFER M. MELLOR is an assistant professor of economics at the College of William and Mary in Williamsburg, Virginia. Her research focuses on aging and long term care and the relationship between health and income inequality.

SONYA MICHEL is the author of *Children's Interests/Mothers Rights: The Shaping of America's Child Care Policy* and founding co-editor of the journal *Social Politics: International Studies in Gender, State, and Society*. Michel teaches the history of women, men, and gender at the University of Illinois at Urbana-Champaign, where she is also director of the Women's Studies Program.

STACEY J. OLIKER is associate professor of sociology and urban studies at the University of Wisconsin-Milwaukee. She is the author of *Caring and Gender* (with Francesca Cancian) and *Best Friends and Marriage: Exchange among Women*. Currently, she is studying networks of support and caregiving at welfare's end.

DEBORAH STONE, formerly professor of politics and social policy at Brandeis University, is an independent scholar. She is the author of three books, most recently *Policy Paradox: The Art of Political Decision Making* and numerous articles on health and social policy.

MICHELLE KESTERKE STORBAKKEN is employed by the Human Resource Department, The Village at Manor Park, a large retirement community in Milwaukee. The Village at Manor Park is a life-care community consisting of a skilled nursing facility, assisted living facility, and an independent senior apartment complex.

RANNVEIG TRAUSTADÓTTIR is associate professor and chair of the department of education, faculty of social science, University of Iceland, where she teaches disability studies, women's studies, multiculturalism, and qualitative research methods. Her current research project focuses on three groups of minority women in Iceland: women with disabilities, lesbians, and immigrant women.

MARY TUOMINEN is an associate professor of sociology/anthropology at Denison University. She is the author of several articles on child care and her current research project is an ethnographic analysis of political mobilization among childcare workers of diverse racial ethnic and cultural identities.

CLARE UNGERSON is professor of social policy in the department of sociology and social policy at the University of Southampton in the United Kingdom. She has worked for many years on the relationship between women and social policy in general, and more particularly on informal care. She is currently looking at forms of commodification of informal care and recently completed a small qualitative study of personal assistants employed by disabled employers.

ASSATA ZERAI is an assistant professor of sociology and a senior research associate for the Center for Policy Research at Syracuse University. Her research focuses on the ways that antidrug laws and policy limit choices for women who have a cocaine-involved past and on adaptive strategies for such women and their families, including grandparenting.

Parenting; *see also* Companionate marriage ideal;
  Motherhood
  activity-based approach, 34
  gender-neutral, 19–20
  gender-segregated; *see* Fatherhood/conserva-
    tive
  impact of separate spheres ideal, 24–25, 33
Parsons, Talcott, 138
Personal assistants; *see* Caregiver
Personal Responsibility and Work Opportunity
  Act of 1996, 37, 164
  child support component, 187
  grandparent caretakers, 287
Personal services; *see* Reproductive labor

Quayle, Dan, attack on Murphy Brown, 20

Race
  alternative sources of power and, 272
  care work and, 6, 116
  contract labor and, 153
  elder care and, 207
    impact of discrimination against Medicaid,
      227–28
  "racial safety" and child-care work, 129
  reproductive labor, 156
  struggle to care for intimates, 9
  value systems, 281
Reproductive labor, 16, 156
  cultural tastes and, 156–57
  gendered, 157–58

Scandinavian countries
  home care in, 239
  philosophy of care, 2
  shifts to privatization, 233
  systems of care, 69–70, 73–75
Sharing the Burden, 209–10
Social activism
  care work issues, 45, 50–51, 54
  environmental issues and women, 50–51
  "identity work", 47
Social activism consequences for individuals
  gender identity
    for at-home mothers, 45, 64
    identity stretching, 55–63
    negotiation process, 61
    politics reshaping and, 57
  literature review, 46–49
  negative consequences, 46, 58–59

previous activism, 51–54
research, 49
  methods, 49–50
  results, 55–63
  world view transformation, 46
Social insurance; *see* Germany
Social reproduction; *see* Reproductive labor
Symbolic interactionism, and identity of activists, 46–47

Toxic waste movement
  leadership opportunities for women, 62
  as women's issue, 50–51

United States, and family as care center model, 2

Welfare end, 168–69; *see also* Personal Responsi-
    bility and Work Opportunity Act of 1996
  caregiving and, 172–73, 175, 185
    family networks, 170, 178, 181–83
    repeal of discretion, 176–77
    social network analysis methodology,
      167–70, 173–74
  impact on fathers, 180–81
  maternal stress and, 184–85
Welfare states' care solutions, 1–2, 164; *see also*
    Britain; Germany; The Netherlands; Scan-
    dinavian countries
  bureaucratic/professional/familial systems bal-
    ance, 234
    bureaucratic administrative system, 234–35
    familial care system, 236–37
    professional system, 236
  corporist principle, 240
  costs, 238
  logics of care struggle, 234–36, 246–47
  payment for care, 69
  politicization, 233
  shift toward privatization, 230, 232, 237–39,
    246–48
Women's movement; *see also* Motherhood organi-
    zations
  hostility to motherhood, 38
Work; *see also* Reproductive labor
  realm of rationality and, 99, 110–11
  unpaid (domestic)
    second-wave feminism and, 68, 70, 90
    vs. paid, 38, 42, 66, 138
    valuation and gender, 140
    vs. paid, literature, 68–69